Photo taken at War Memorial Stadium in Laramie, Wyoming, by Art Shay, Oct. 25, 1969. Shay was on assignment from Chicago for *Sports Illustrated*. Eleven of the Black 14 are shown. L-R front row: Earl Lee of Chattanooga, Mel Hamilton of No. Car. and Boys Town, Guillermo Hysaw of Bakersfield, Lionel Grimes of Alliance, Ohio, John Griffin of San Fernando, Calif., Ivie Moore of Pine Bluff, Ark. and Don Meadows of Denver. Second row: Tri-captain Joe Williams of Lufkin, Texas, Jerome Berry of Tulsa, Anthony McGee of Battle Creek, Mich., and Ron Hill of Bessemer, Ala. and Denver. Not pictured: Tony Gibson of Pittsfield, Mass., Ted Williams of Port Hueneme, Calif., and James Isaac of Hanna, Wyo. The last photo in this book shows six of the players in Orlando in 2017. Photo courtesy of Art Shay Archive Chicago and curator Erica DeGlopper.

Vietnam Moratorium marchers on October 15, 1969 at Ivinson & 9th St. in Laramie, two days before the Black 14 were dismissed from the football team. The tall clergyman on the left is Laramie Methodist minister David Steffenson, a leading peace activist who founded a draft information center during the Vietnam War. Steffenson had previously participated in voter registration demonstrations in Hattiesburg, MS in 1964. After Laramie he spent most of his clerical career in Wisconsin, emphasizing environmental ethics. He was a Founding Director of the Wisconsin Interfaith Climate and Energy Campaign. Steffenson died in Wisconsin in 2016. The man looking toward the "Give Peace A Chance" sign in front of Steffenson is University of Wyoming English Professor Ken Craven, whose peace efforts are described in this book. To his left is his wife, and their three children are in front of them. Four days later Craven put his academic career at risk by pledging to resign if the Black 14 football players were not reinstated. He did resign at the end of his contract and never again held a tenure-track position at a university. (Don Rich photo from UW Branding Iron, October 17, 1969).

WYOMING IN MID-CENTURY

Prejudice, Protest and The Black 14

2023 Revision

By Phil White Jr.

Originally published 2019
©2022 Philip White Jr.
philwyoming@yahoo.com

Cover Photo: From September 11-14, 2019, eight of the Black 14 players – and the son of a deceased player – returned to the University of Wyoming campus to participate in a 50th Anniversary Commemoration of their dismissal from the team. They visited classes, participated in panel discussions and unveiled a plaque placed by UW in their honor on the east side of Memorial Stadium. UW Athletic Director Tom Burman read a letter of apology to the Fourteen, signed by him and UW President Laurie Nichols, which said in part: "To have your collegiate careers derailed as both students and athletes is a tragedy. ... Please accept this sincere apology for the unfair way you were treated and for the hardships that treatment created for you." The group was honored with loud applause at halftime of the UW football game on the 14th. For most of them it was the first time they had stepped onto the field in 50 years. Earlier that day they posed for this photo. They are, in front, Mel Hamilton of S.C., and in back L-R John Griffin of Colo., Tony Gibson of Mass., Lionel "Dowdy" Grimes of Ohio, Anthony McGee of Ga., Ted Williams of Ill., Guillermo Hysaw of Calif., Ron Hill of Ala.. and Brian Lee, son of Earl Lee, of Md. Photo by Cayla Nimmo of the Casper Star-Tribune used with permission.

TABLE OF CONTENTS

OVERVIEW..1
    1947: Casper "Baby Contest"..1
    1954-57: Incident at Plains Hotel leads to legislation..................4
    1954: World-famous singer Marian Anderson at the University of Wyoming.........4
    1947: Bonnie Mae Fermon: First African American UWyo Graduate?..........6
    1956: Theodore Jefferson: First African American UWyo Law Graduate...........6
    1961: Casper NAACP fund-raising campaign.................................7
    1958-62: Selective equality in the "Equality State".....................8
    1969: "Black 14" purged from UW football team..........................10

1897-1964: AFRICAN AMERICANS AT UW AND NORTHWEST COLLEGE.......18
    1903: Carrie R. Burton (later Carrie Burton Overton)...................18
    Early 1930s: Multi-sport athlete Taft Harris of Casper.................21
    1960-1963: Curt Jimerson, Ron Bostick & Flynn Robinson.................26
    1964: African American athletes at Northwest College..................30

1958: APPEAL TO CHEYENNE - THE ATLAS MISSILE PROTESTS.............31
    Cheyenne greets protesters with hostility..............................32
    Protest moves to the missile site.....................................33
    1959: Calkins takes protest to Omaha..................................38
    WAFB: "Peace Is Our Profession".......................................40

1958: ERNIE RUDOLPH AND ART RENNEISEN OF CHEYENNE..............42

1960: DAWNING OF A NEW DECADE....................................43

1960-1963: JFK AND WYOMING.......................................44
    1960: Vinich and Wyoming put JFK over the top.........................44
    1963: JFK visits the U.S. Naval Academy...............................45
    1963: August: Kathi Hill at Girls' Nation.............................46
    1963: September: JFK visits UW..47
    Presto: A press pass..51
    JFK's first visit to Grand Teton......................................52
    Other news on September 25..53
    Appointment with tragedy..53

1961: TED GOSTAS - THE FUTURE LOOKED BRIGHT.....................54
    1961-1967: Ted's long U.S. Army road leads to Vietnam.................55
    1973: From the Hanoi Hilton to the White House........................57

1962: MISSILES BRING RICHARD BRUCE CHENEY BACK TO WYOMING......58

1957-1969: THE PATH TO THE BLACK 14.............................58

1957: Coach Devaney moves West with Eaton in tow. 58
1958-1962: Devaney thrills the Cowboy faithful.. 59
1962: Devaney bolts, Lloyd Eaton hired. 59
1962: Dave Marion - Super Soph from Bakersfield. 61
1963: Tragedy after Eaton's first season -- Dave Marion paralyzed. 62
1963-1965: Eaton - Building a program. 66
1966-68: Cowboys win three straight WAC championships.. 66
1966: Sun Bowl. 67
1967: Sugar Bowl Season -- The Cowboys go marching in. 68
1968: WAC champs get no bowl bid. 70

1964-68: RONNIE GRAY, FREEDOM SUMMER, INTERRACIAL DATING. 72
1964: White students -- and the "Wyo Days" group -- catch "Beatlemania". 72
1964: Civil Rights, the "Green Book" and War Drums.. 73
1964: Two Wyoming Women Go South for "Freedom Summer". 74
1968: "Guess Who's Coming to Dinner" at UW-Interracial dating. 76

1965: THE LIGHT WITHIN - JAMES REEB OF CASPER. 76
1947: Into the Ministry. 77
1965: Bloody Sunday brings Reeb to Selma. 79
1965: Reeb's murder pushes passage of the Voting Rights Act. 82

1869-1965: MIXED RACE MARRIAGE LAWS - LIMITS ON LOVING LIFTED. 85
1882: Repeal and William Jefferson Hardin. 86
1913: Interracial marriage becomes a felony again in Wyoming.. 86
1965: Finally, repealed again in Wyoming. 87

1964-66: REVOLVING DOOR AT OLD MAIN BRINGS WILLIAM D. CARLSON. . . . 88
1964: Duke Humphrey retires and Fey says 'Hi'. 88
1965: UW Civil rights group takes on racial and gender discrimination.. 89
1966: Fey says "bye-bye". 90
1966: John E. King crowned as President of UW. 90
1967: Protest over "Loco" parentis rules at UW. 91
1967: Presto - King dethroned. 92
1967: Reaction of State Media.. 96
1967: Dr. William D. Carlson of Fort Collins, Colorado moves north. 96

1967-70: AUTHORITIES ATTACK THE LONG HAIR EVIL. 97
Hair and dress codes in the schools. 97
Sheriff Ogburn of Rawlins, Wyoming. 101

1967: MUSIC AND RADICAL SPEAKERS AT U DUB. 103
1965-1967: Two trios and The Rhythm Method. 103
1967: Loren Watson and Corky Gonzales come to UW. 104

1967-1971: BETRAYAL IN CHEYENNE.. 105

1968: COACH EATON AND THE GREAT APRIL SNOWSTORM. 106

1968: MARTIN LUTHER KING KILLED IN MEMPHIS - RESPONSE IN WYOMING
. . . . 107

1968: REACTIONS FROM WYOMING'S BLACK COMMUNITY. 110

1963-1973: VIETNAM AND WYOMING.. 113
   1963: Into the quagmire. 114
   Laramie's Sanchez brothers. 115
   1958-77: UW Prof. Gale McGee and the 1947 Textbook Inquiry.. 115
   1966: Charlie Simpson of Cheyenne. 119
   1967: English Professor Ken Craven. 120
   1966-67: Peace Corps, Marines and protesters in the Union. 122
   1967: University of Wyoming Vietnam Memorial. 123
   1963-1971: From Cheyenne to Vietnam - Jim Steadman. 125
   1943-1967: The Tragedies of Two Wars: Curtis Tadashi Ando. 127
   1963-1969: From Cheyenne to Vietnam: John William Kobelin II. 129
   1968: Tragedy comes even to tiny Hanna. 130
   1968: Dow Chemical-Napalm-Agent Orange. 132
   1968: Jackson Hole and My Lai: Stanley Rogers Resor. 132
   1969: Vietnam Moratorium in Wyoming. 135
   1969: The November Moratorium. 136
   1968-69: War opposition not healthy for Wyoming clergy. 137
   1970-Elver Barker of the Fellowship of Reconciliation in Wyoming. 137
   1963-73: Propaganda on progress in Vietnam. 138

1964-1973: THE DRAFT - EVERY WAKING MOMENT. 139
   1967: Gen. Hershey and Cheyenne East's James Oestereich. 140
   1968: Oestereich goes to the U.S. Supreme Court.. 142
   1968: Gen. Hershey and Kevin McKinney. 143
   1962-1967: The Draft and Dick Cheney. 146
   2016: Liz Cheney follows her father's path to Congress. 146
   1969: Draft Lottery. 147
   1970: Randy Kehler and Daniel Ellsberg.. 147
   1947: Heart Mountain draft resisters pardoned. 150
   1944: U.S. District Judge T. Blake Kennedy.. 152
   1944: Prosecution of Heart Mountain's Fair Play Committee. 153
   1970: Randy Kehler Trial. 154
   Prosecutor Toshiro Suyematsu from Casper, Wyo.. 159

1967: THE BLACK 14'S JAMES L. ISAAC OF HANNA. 161
   The other Isaac siblings. 164

1969-70: Tragedies strike the Isaac family. 165
1944-1965: Marquette Frye: From Hanna to the Watts Riots. 166

1967: THE WORLD OUTSIDE OF HANNA. 168
1966-67: Assembling the Black 14 cast - Hathaway becomes governor. 170
1968-69: Black Students Alliance formed at UWyo. 170

1969-70: ATTEMPTING TO LOWER THE VOTING AGE. 171
"Old enough to kill [and be killed], but not for votin'". 171
1969: Wyoming stuck in Myers' embarrassing mire. 172
1970: Wyoming Supreme Court: "Take a walk". 173
1970: Congress acts to lower voting age. 175

1969: SPRING LECTURE SERIES ON AFRO-AMERICAN LIFE AND CULTURE. . . 175

100TH YEAR FOR COLLEGE FOOTBALL - 100TH WIN FOR UW'S COACH. 177
1969: Great expectations. 178
Wyoming 23, Arizona 7. 179
UW 27, Air Force Academy 25 at Falcon Stadium. 180
UW 39, CSU 3. 181
UW 37, UTEP 9. 181
Protest comes to Laramie. 183
Appointment with destiny. 186
Same day: Clifton Wharton Jr. named president of Michigan State U. 195

1936-1979: TREAGLE STAG FOOTBALL TRAIN. 196
1979: Men only ... or no Treagle at all. 198

BLACK 14 REACTION ON THE GRIDIRON AND BEYOND. 200
First newspaper reports. 200
"Cowboys don't need those blacks". 201
Demonstration rule quickly amended, but no reinstatement of the players. 204
Irene Schubert's Letter to UW Personnel Director. 209
Homecoming routine unaffected-Memorial to Eaton proposed. 210
Wyoming editors: The Black 14 were the ones violating people's rights. 215

A VOICE OF REASON IN RIVERTON: STEVE MURDOCK. 220
Culture shock in Riverton. 220
Steve Murdock's Journey to Riverton. 222
Murdock's remarkable *The Nation* article. 223
Suzanne Hawley Hunsucker's Riverton High "Love Festival". 224

1969-70 - ENGLISH PROFESSOR KENTON CRAVEN EXITS UW. 225
Craven risks his academic career. 225
Casper football zealots renege on moving expenses pledge. 226

1970: End of tenure track for Craven.. 227

IRENE KETTUNEN AND FRANK SCHUBERT. 227
    Other letters and opinions. 229

1869: RELIGIOUS RIGHTS 100 YEARS EARLIER: POLYGAMY. 230

1969-70: DESCENT INTO OBLIVION. 232
    NCAA NEWS December 1969.. 235
    1970: End of the Eaton era.. 238
    1970: The post-season fallout. 240
    1970: Eaton "retires". 241
    1971: Years of frustration follow.. 242
    The players Move On.. 242
    Mel Hamilton and his Boys Town Friend Kenn Gilchrist.. 245

ANTHONY MCGEE'S FATHER, HERMAN MCGEE. 248

MORE TRAGEDIES FOR THE FOURTEEN. 250
    1970: Ron Hill's brother Roosevelt.. 250
        1976: Don Meadows' brother Melvin. 250

WHITE PLAYERS AFFECTED ALSO. 251
    Forrest "Frosty" Franklin of Powell.. 251
    Larry "Bo" Nels of North Syracuse, N.Y.. 252
    Ramifications at BYU and LDS.. 252
    The Denver Post's 1982 Retrospective. 253
    U.S. District Judge turns a blind eye. 253
    Sophistry in the federal courts. 258

1955-1992: JUDGE KERR AND THE U.S. DISTRICT COURT OF WYOMING. 262

EARLY 1970S: CIVIL RIGHTS SPEAKERS AT UW. 264

1973: NUKES BELOW PINEDALE. 266

CHEYENNE CENTRAL 1972: COMFORTS AND ADVANTAGES. 267
    Hair and dress codes. 268
    1962: NAACP Youth Council. 269
    1972: Brisson and Urbigkit vs. the Constitution in Cheyenne.. 270
    NAACP seeks "sensitivity training" for Brisson. 272
    More suspensions and expulsions in 1973.. 272

THE SPIRIT OF LIBERTY: SYDNEY SPIEGEL. 274
    Even WWII veterans had better toe the line. 274

Parade Magazine profiles Spiegel. 275
1972: Another teacher challenges the power structure and pays the price. 276
1974: Spiegel calls for recognition of Hispanic culture. 277
1974: Judge Kenneth Hamm affirmed by Wyoming Supreme Court. 278
Brisson and Lutjeharms move to Nebraska. 280

1970: ANOTHER RULE, ANOTHER DEBACLE. 281

END OF VIETNAM, NIXON PRESIDENCY AND THE DRAFT. 282
1970: Let Freedom Ring. 282
1971: "Wyoming Green". 283
Milestones for the war, the draft and Nixon. 285

1990-POSTSCRIPT: POLITICS ON THE FOOTBALL FIELD. 285
1990: Sen. Harriet Elizabeth Byrd's MLK Holiday. 286
1990: Copper Bowl. 288

2015-2018: DEJA VU AT OL' MIZZOU. 289

OVERVIEW

We have gone through a remarkable couple of weeks lately. We have heard hundreds of people affirm, unendingly, the need for rules and discipline, while ignoring the very rules upon which the whole nation was founded.

--Undergraduate student Owen Peterson's column about the "Black 14" in the University of Wyoming's student newspaper, the *Branding Iron*, October 31, 1969.

"And the College throws its portals/Open wide to all men free
... Shrine of many joys and tears ..."
UW's Alma Mater

Between the end of World War II and the end of the Vietnam War, a review of events in Wyoming provides a poignant depiction -- in microcosm -- of the dominant themes, protests and struggles affecting the nation as a whole: nuclear weapons, Vietnam War, the draft and draft resistance, racial inequality and civil rights. As to the latter, events at either end of that spectrum illustrated that much remained to be done: a "Baby Contest" in Casper in 1947 and the "Black 14 incident" at the University of Wyoming in October, 1969, which is still being discussed and analyzed 50 years later and is the central focus of this book.

In the middle of that period, a 1945 Natrona High graduate in Casper named James Reeb was murdered in Selma, Ala., when he joined other Unitarian ministers in support of Rev. Martin Luther King's voting rights action there.

1947: Casper "Baby Contest"

Just as African American soldiers returning from World War I had to endure horrible racial violence in 1918, evidence that the slaughter and triumphs of World War II had not erased prejudice and discrimination against the minorities who had helped win the war was not long in arising. During the war, Harry Gray, an African American tech sergeant stationed at the Casper Army Air Base, had met and married Effie Mae Davis, a black native of Casper, and they soon brought son Ronnie into the world. On November 1, 1947, articles in newspapers in Casper and across America described how Mrs. Gray had first been invited to enter her 3-year-old boy in a baby contest sponsored by the Moose Lodge Auxiliary, and then had been informed she had to withdraw her child because he was black.

Mrs. Gray had her son with her when she registered him for the contest with the Moose Auxiliary women, and at the same time Mrs. Roscoe Howard, another African American mother from a long-time Casper family, had also registered her child. Mrs. Gray had then sold many raffle tickets, making her son a leader in the contest.

All was going well, she later said, until the men of the Moose saw the required photograph of Ronald -- wearing boxing gloves and a big smile -- and directed that the black babies be removed from the contest. After informing her she had to withdraw, the Auxiliary returned the money she had deposited from her ticket sales, which she then returned to her contributors.

But this incident was reported in the Rocky Mountain News and became national news. Baby Ronnie's photo was printed on the front page of the Casper Tribune-Herald on Oct. 31 and then appeared in numerous newspapers across the country. An AP article in the Des Moines

Register and elsewhere on Nov. 1st reported
that one of the Moose Auxiliary women said the
men's organization had brought pressure on the
women to remove the black children. She said
this was because no member of a non-Caucasian
race could join in any Moose activity. The same
article said the governor of the Casper Moose
chapter claimed, without amplification, that the
Moose Lodge did not sponsor the baby contest,
but was investigating. A couple of white
mothers whose children were entered demanded
that the black children be reinstated and said
they were banding their votes together for
Ronnie.

     Black war veterans including M. E.
Sanders, Commander of the Benjamin Carter
American Legion post in Casper "and well-
known leader of Casper's colored community
numbering an estimated 400 Negroes"[1],
condemned "the act of racial discrimination"
and "also the spirit of poor sportsmanship
shown".

     A white attorney from Denver, Samuel
D. Menin, flew to Casper in a chartered airplane
to investigate the case. (Menin was involved
earlier as an attorney in two other incidents
described elsewhere in this book: the defense of
Japanese-American draft resisters in 1944 in
federal court in Cheyenne and the assaults upon
the persons and property of Jehovah's
Witnesses in Rawlins in June, 1940. See p.
152).

Ronnie Gray in 2011 in Yakima.

     The Casper Tribune-Herald on Nov. 2nd led its report by saying "The nation today waited
to see what action, if any, the Moose lodge of Casper will take in the case."

---

[1] Casper Tribune-Herald 11/2/1947.

On Nov. 7th, the Lodge and the Auxiliary released a joint statement saying the precepts of the organization demanded "tolerance, brotherhood and individual and community service."[2] The statement blamed the action on an "out-of-state contractor" and expressed regret. However, the contest manager in Des Moines was contacted and denied the charge. Her attorney said she had been instructed by Moose members to have the babies removed and called the Moose's statement "clearly an attempt to shift blame."

Despite the uproar, the Moose proceeded with its contest without reinstating the black children and named five white children as King, Queen, Miss Casper (two shared the honor) and Master Casper.

The Tribune-Herald's Nov. 2nd article referred to an incident in Ahoskie, N.C., five months earlier, in which Harvey Jones, a 24-year-old black Navy veteran and tenant farmer, was awakened at 1:30 a.m. by the county sheriff and two lawyers and was told that, although his ticket had been drawn in a Kiwanis Club raffle for a new Cadillac, he was not eligible to win because he was black and therefore could not attend the dance during which the drawing occurred. They refunded the dollar he had paid for the ticket (which said "you do not have to be present to win") and returned to the dance for another drawing. A retired physician who already owned a Cadillac was the winner. Club officials said members had been instructed to sell chances only to white persons.

This incident provoked an immediate outcry from everywhere and within a day the national Kiwanis organization directed the local group to obtain another Cadillac and award it to Jones. Eventually, Jones received a check for $3,200 in lieu of the car, and he used the money to build a new six-room house "just like the one I dreamed about when I was in the Navy".[3]

Editor Ernest Linford of the Laramie Republican-Boomerang, while acknowledging that the Moose Lodge in Laramie did many good works, condemned the exclusion of Ronnie Gray. "The Casper incident goes to uphold what this column has long contended. Here in Wyoming our highly-touted spirit of equality and enlightenment doesn't hold up when tested. 'Jim Crow' is one of our influential citizens. We are going to have to have the active cooperation of lodges and benevolent associations if we [are to] remove this influence." In another editorial, Linford said the Casper lodge's attempt to "pass the buck" to its agent "appeared to be saying that it was a mistake to admit the Negro babies in the first place."[4]

---

[2] UP report in San Bernardino (Calif.) Sun, 11/9/1947. One has to wonder what sort of "tolerance" and "brotherhood" the Lodge embraced. Even as late as 1968, the Constitution of the Supreme Lodge of the World, Loyal Order of Moose, provided that "the membership of the lodges shall be composed of male persons of the Caucasian or White race ... and not married to someone of other than the Caucasian or White race, who are of good moral character, physically and mentally normal, who shall profess a belief in a Supreme Being." This provision is quoted in *Irvis v. Scott*, 318 F.Supp. 1246 (1970), a case where a Moose Lodge in Pennsylvania refused to serve a member's black guest. The Lodge appealed a district court ruling in the black guest's favor but the U.S. Supreme Court in 1972 reversed the lower court, ruling that the state's regulation of liquor licenses for private clubs was insufficient to allow a conclusion that the lodge's rule could be considered "state action" facilitating racial discrimination in violation of the 14th Amendment. 407 U.S. 163. See also this book's chapter on an incident at the Laramie Moose Lodge in 1970 at p. 281.

[3] Minneapolis Star-Tribune 11/5/1947; UP dispatch in Lead (S.D.) Call, 7/15/1947; AP report in Decatur (Ill.) Review, 7/16/1947; Acme telephoto in Waukesha (Wisc.) Freeman, 7/28/1947.

[4] Laramie Republican-Boomerang 11/3 and 11/10/1947.

1954-57: Incident at Plains Hotel leads to legislation

Another unfortunate act of discrimination involving an African American serviceman occurred in Cheyenne's historic Plains Hotel in 1954, according to Cheyenne lawyer and future congressman Teno Roncalio and Dr. Francis Barrett of Cheyenne.[5] They observed the man and his wife being escorted out of the café by the manager because of their race. Their complaint to the owners went unanswered. This incident began a push by those observers that eventually led to a change in Wyoming law.

In early 1957, Gov. Milward Simpson urged the Legislature to pass a law banning discrimination in public accommodations on the basis of race, religion, color or national origin. He reminded them that Wyoming was one of only six states outside the South without such a law. When a bill appeared to die because of procedural manipulations, state chairman of the Democratic party and future Wyoming Congressman Roncalio wrote a letter to the editor urging reconsideration. A law was eventually passed. However, enforcement was left to local county attorneys and the maximum fine was small.

In 1964, however, the federal government banned discrimination under its interstate powers act and this "largely rendered meaningless the relatively anemic" Wyoming statute.[6]

Racially-discriminatory provisions in property deeds was another form of Jim Crow that found its way into Wyoming. In 1926, the U.S. Supreme Court ruled that such restrictions in deeds were enforceable. As a result, such restrictions were imposed in deeds in upscale developments in Wyoming even into the 1960s.

For example, an abstract of title to a property in "The Avenues" in Cheyenne in 1951 showed that the deeds carried a clause reading as follows: "No persons of any race other than the Caucasian race shall use or occupy any building or any lot, except that this covenant shall not prevent occupancy by domestic servants of a different race domiciled with an owner or tenant."[7]

The Supreme Court reversed itself in 1948 and such covenants were banned by the federal Fair Housing Act of 1968. But even as late as 2002 some home sellers believed they were legally, or at least morally, bound by such covenants.[8]

1954: World-famous singer Marian Anderson at the University of Wyoming

In early February, 1954 both the Laramie Boomerang and the UW student newspaper The Branding Iron carried articles announcing a February 8 concert by African American contralto Marian Anderson at UW. "A voice like yours is heard once in a hundred years," the great conductor Toscanini had once told her after a concert in Austria.[9]

---

[5] Kim Ibach and William Howard Moore, "The Emerging Civil Rights Movement: 1957 Wyoming Public Accommodations Statute", 73 *Annals of Wyoming* (Winter 2001). Despite Gov. Simpson's support for the statute at the state level, as a U.S. Senator Simpson opposed civil rights laws, saying he opposed "the misguided efforts of some militant civil rights groups and the efforts of the communist and Nazi parties in this country." This article includes a brief biography of Roncalio in a footnote.

[6] *Id.*

[7] Lot 20 and the South 10 feet of Lot 21, Block 1009 in Replat of Capital Heights Addition.

[8] "Restrictive Covenants Stubbornly Stay on the Books," New York Times, 4/21/2005.

[9] UW Branding Iron, 2/5/1954; Laramie Boomerang 2/8/1954 (including a photo of her in front of Knight Hall). Both papers also ran reviews of the concert afterwards.

Ms. Anderson had been thrust into a lifetime involvement in the civil rights struggle of her people when, in 1939, the Daughters of the American Revolution refused to allow her to appear before an integrated audience at Constitutional Hall in Washington. First Lady Eleanor Roosevelt and the President then helped arrange an open-air concert on April 9, 1939, on the steps of the Lincoln Memorial. She attracted a crowd of 75,000 and the performance was broadcast to millions. Twenty-four years later she sang at the 1963 March on Washington during which Martin Luther King Jr. gave his "I have a dream" speech.

Dean of Education Eugene Cottle and his high school-age daughter Stephanie were thrilled to hear Anderson's 1954 performance at the UW "Liberal Arts Building" (built by workers hired by President Franklin Roosevelt's Public Works Administration program in 1936 and later dubbed Arts and Sciences Building). "I really was impressed with her stature as a human being, as well as her fantastic voice quality, and her presence as a person of high regard," Mrs. Cottle-Gordon recalled in 2016. The resounding applause produced four encores, concluding with "Ave Maria", the Branding Iron reported on February 12.

But shortly thereafter, Stephanie learned from her Presbyterian minister of troubling allegations that UW arranged for Ms. Anderson to stay overnight at the Knight Hall dormitory on campus because the Connor Hotel, Laramie's finest accommodation at the time, would not accept her.[10]

In its February 12 edition, the BI carried an article challenging this claim. Headlined "Anderson Rumors Proved Not True," the article said UW President G. D. Humphrey had invited her to stay at Knight Hall in December. "When no reply was received, the president inquired of the Connor Hotel if they would allow her to stay there, should she prefer not to stay on campus. The hotel replied emphatically in the affirmative. Then Miss Anderson accepted the invitation" to stay at Knight Hall, the article reported. Law professor John O. Rames and his wife, the article said, had met her at the railroad depot the day before the concert and "the trio took a Sunday afternoon automobile ride to Happy Jack." Rames was quoted as saying that "she was most enthusiastic about the University and her reception here. There never was anyone more appreciative of what has been done for her."

Whether UW's story is true or not, Mrs. Gordon recalled that "the young women who lived in the dorm had a ball helping her get dressed for the concert, etc." After two days in Laramie, Ms. Anderson again boarded the Union Pacific's City of St. Louis streamliner, continuing a tour that would eventually take her to the Far East.[11]

The UW President's story seems suspect in light of an article and editorial in the Branding Iron on April 20, 1956, more than two years after Ms. Anderson's visit. The student newspaper reported that a law student had sent a letter to the BI saying that African American law student Theodore Jefferson had been denied service at the Connor on April 12th. According to an editorial in the same edition of the BI, the Connor's manager, Marguerite Deti, told the editor that the incident was "highly regrettable" and that she personally had no objection to serving Blacks. She said that the owner's husband, who lived in Florida and was visiting in

---

[10] E-mails to the author from Stephanie Cottle Gordon, December 2016.

[11] In 1937, Anderson was denied accommodation at the Nassau Inn in Princeton, N.J. before her appearance at Princeton Univ. She was then invited by physicist Albert Einstein to stay at his home, according to Wikipedia, citing *Einstein: His Life and Universe*, Simon & Schuster 2007 p. 445. Apparently she stayed with the Einsteins on several occasions between 1937 and the professor's death in 1955. See also Jerome and Taylor, *Einstein on Race and Racism*.

Laramie at the time, "ordered the bar waitress not to serve Jefferson, who entered the lounge with a group of Potter Law Club members." This prompted the Club to move its spring banquet from the Connor to another venue.

The BI then did a survey of businesses and found that almost a third of the 30 restaurants and bars contacted "[said] flatly that they did not serve Negro patrons". The survey also reported that four downtown barber shops "told the BI this week that they do not provide service for Negro patrons." Jefferson told the BI that he had been rejected by many Laramie landlords when he was attempting to rent an apartment for him and his wife the previous year.

1947: Bonnie Mae Fermon: First African American UWyo Graduate?

The August, 1996, edition of the Journal of Blacks in Higher Education carried the results of a survey of the 50 states' flagship public universities attempting to identify and describe each school's first Black graduate. For Wyoming, the article reports: "The University of Wyoming has not been able to identify its first black graduate."

The stories of Carrie Burton, a black student in 1904, and Taft Harris, a student-athlete in the early 30s, are set forth below. But neither of them graduated from UW, according to UW records. Other black students shown in yearbooks before 1945 may have been foreign students.

Bonnie Fermon, one of many children of a Rock Springs coal miner and his wife, may be UW's first African American graduate. Ms. Fermon came to UW in the mid-40s. She is pictured several times in the WYO yearbooks of that time, the only African American in each of them: as a member of Alpha Epsilon Delta Pre-med Honor Society in 1947 and with Quill Club (creative writers) in 1946 and 1947. She graduated with a degree in science in 1947 and then went to the University of Wisconsin at Madison, where she was a graduate teaching assistant in 1951-52, and where she met and married Lendell Alston, who graduated with a master's in zoology.

In July of 1952, she sent a postcard asking about an opening to do lab work in the fall for Prof. Joshua Lederberg. She said "[I] would like a job which requires no homework so I can spend more time on my research and my own course work. I'm coloured. Seemingly, this has made me ineligible for many jobs I have sought thus far this summer." Assoc. Prof. of Genetics Lederberg responded with a letter five days later saying that job had been filled. But he told her, "We do not practice discrimination in this laboratory." He suggested she should consult the faculty committee on Human Rights if she wished to pursue her charge.[12]

The Univ. of Wisc. Archives found no further entries for the couple. Bonnie died at age 52 in 1977 and is buried in Madison.

1956: Theodore Jefferson: First African American UWyo Law Graduate

Theodore Jefferson, a 1956 law grad from Memphis, was also an early graduate.

Jefferson was quite active during his law school years. He was involved with the Methodist youth group, a cancer research fund-raising drive and the Omicron Delta Kappa men's leadership honorary on campus. He also was the primary speaker at a panel on race relations described in the Feb. 12, 1954 Laramie Republican Boomerang. He graduated and was admitted

---

[12] Joshua Lederberg Papers at the National Library of Medicine, National Institute of Health, #101584906X2405. In 1958, 33-year-old Lederberg shared the Nobel Prize in Physiology or Medicine with two others.

to the Wyoming Bar in 1956. The following photo from the WYO yearbook shows him among the Potter Law Club members, including George W. Hopper and Carl Williams. Many years later, Williams was one of the major donors for a law library addition, and he directed that the addition be named in honor of his classmate Hopper.

THOMAS C. BOGUS
SENIOR
DEAN W. BORTHWICK
SENIOR
CARL L. BURLEY
SENIOR

STERLING CASE
SENIOR
JERALD E. DUKES
SENIOR
GEORGE W. HOPPER
SENIOR
MYRON C. HOWARD
SENIOR

TED JEFFERSON
SENIOR
DONALD L. JENSEN
SENIOR
NORMAN V. JOHNSON
SENIOR
RALPH M. KIRSCH
SENIOR

RICHARD VAN THOMAS
SENIOR
RICHARD A. TOBIN
SENIOR
CARL WILLIAMS
SENIOR

1961: Casper NAACP fund-raising campaign

The Casper Morning Star of May 16, 1961, included a photo from Anniston, Ala., of a burning Greyhound bus which had been carrying "Freedom Riders", both black and white, who were testing the application of federal laws prohibiting racial discrimination on interstate carriers. They had left Washington D.C. 11 days earlier. Freedom riders had also been attacked in Birmingham, Ala. That state's Gov. John Patterson said he could not be responsible for the safety "of a group of renegades who are here for the avowed purpose of stirring up trouble."

Alongside the photo and article was a small story telling readers that the NAACP Casper branch had established a "Freedom Fund" and would conduct a fund-raising campaign out of its office at 114 E. First to support a job training program, culminating with "Freedom Day" on May 17. Fund chairman Mrs. Mable S. Gray, who had lived in Casper for 11 years, said there had been no trouble between the races in Casper and that relations had been very good.

A week later, the Casper Tribune Herald reported that a "huge rock" had been thrown through the front window of the Casper offices of the NAACP. The article said the incident was "obviously the work of juvenile vandals" because school notebook paper was used for the "childishly-scribbled inscription: 'Casper Chapter, K. K. K., Montgomery, Ala.'"

1958-62: Selective equality in the "Equality State"

On August 8, 1958, the Casper Morning Star carried a UPI report with this lead: "Wyoming coaches will not hesitate to recruit any top Negro athlete in the state but has no plans to go far afield just to establish them on the campus, athletic director Glenn (Red) Jacoby said Thursday."

Jacoby was responding to an August 5 column by Riverton Ranger sports writer Hugh Ellis, a UW journalism student and BI writer interning for the summer at the Ranger, which said that university students had been informed "this spring" by an athletics official that head football coach Bob Devaney "had been and still is considering recruiting Negro athletes to play football."

The Ellis column said "unfavorable social conditions" in the community could prevent black players from attending:

> In the past there has been but one barber shop in Laramie which would give a haircut to a colored person and that was the student union barber shop. Similarly, many of the city's restaurants and bars will not serve colored trade.
>
> The University's Potter Law Club still will not patronize the Connor Hotel because the management of that establishment refused to serve a colored law student[13]. And, of course, a colored student would be denied the social activities of membership in a social fraternity, because most of the Wyoming fraternities have strict white clauses.

Nonetheless, Ellis predicted that the athletic department "should have no trouble in gaining the support of the University students and Wyoming citizens to take the steps necessary to bring the first Negro athletes to the campus. We believe that most Wyoming people do, after all, believe that Wyoming should be the Equality State, not only in name alone. There is only one regret: that this whole thing wasn't done years ago." By 1958, apparently, few Wyoming folks remembered that Taft Harris of Casper had played for Wyoming in the early 30s. See p. 21

In the UPI article, Jacoby was quoted as saying: "Actually, our feeling is that we could get some real fine colored athletes in the Midwest or farther away, but we don't want to go that far just to get a colored athlete." Jacoby acknowledged that a black player would have "an awfully difficult time" in Laramie because of the very small black population in the town.

In November, 1959, the Wyoming Advisory Committee to the U.S. Commission on Civil Rights held its first open meeting and heard from two African American women residing in Cheyenne who alleged racial discrimination in housing and employment. Mrs. Jettie Giles told the committee she needed a bigger house in a better neighborhood farther from the railroad tracks and she had the resources necessary to purchase one. She said she had called real estate dealers and found they "were happy to do business over the phone, but when I walked into the offices they looked like a snake rolled in. They won't even quote a price. They say 'in 6 months, in 6 months'.... It has been this way three years." Committee Chairman Rev. John McConnell, a Presbyterian minister from Laramie, pointed out that restrictive covenants in housing documents which ban resale of homes to non-whites were illegal.

---

[13] That student was Ted Jefferson who was admitted to the Wyoming State Bar in July, 1956. In the Branding Iron's news story, Jefferson said that the previous year he had been rejected "at least 70 times" when he appeared at apartments advertised as available.

Mrs. Robert Rhone (mother of future legislator Elizabeth Byrd) said she had to send her three children out of state to get a college education. Her daughter, she said, and other black teachers had been denied jobs in Cheyenne public schools. Mrs. Rhone said her son, who became a basketball star at Denver University, was discouraged from attending the University of Wyoming in 1951.[14] In response, UW Athletic Director Glenn "Red" Jacoby said UW coach Ev Shelton had tried to recruit Rhone. Jacoby repeated his concern that a black athlete would face a tough problem with social activities at Laramie because of the small black population in the area.[15]

Taft Harris, an African American from Casper who played both football and basketball for UW in the early 30s, was contacted by a reporter to respond to Rhone's allegations. "Things have changed considerably in the last 26 years if there is discrimination against Negroes" at UW, he said. "No one tried to discourage me from entering the University. In fact, they tried everything possible to encourage me. The Casper Rotary Club even offered me money to attend."[16] Harris said he saw no discrimination "in classes, athletics or anywhere else. We traveled together on football and basketball trips and there was no such thing as discrimination."

In March, 1961, the UW *Branding Iron* reported that Cody attorney Melvin Fillerup, Vice-chair of the Committee on Civil Rights, had said in Cody that athletes of "Indian and Negro background" were not welcome at UW. Fillerup said, according to the BI report, that "'the practical policy' seems to be one of discouragement." UW President Duke Humphrey dismissed the accusation, saying "I have no idea what the committee is talking about. It's kind of like a gestapo."[17]

In his column appearing March 24, 1961, BI sports editor Dave Bonner also challenged Fillerup's assessment. Bonner acknowledged, however, that "Wyoming athletics did come in for racial criticism" in the 1950s under football coaches Bowden Wyatt and Phil Dickens, who both came to UW from Tennessee.[18]

Six months later, the Advisory Committee reported to its Commission in Washington that while "conditions are improving" in several Wyoming cities, "a restaurant that is opened to all

---

[14] Laramie Boomerang, 11/11/1959, p. 1; Casper Star, 11/12/1959. Mrs. Rhone's daughter was Elizabeth Byrd, who finally was able to obtain a teaching position in the public schools and served for many years in the Legislature. See the Martin Luther King Holiday chapter at p. 286. Mrs. Rhone's son Tom, with 10 points, was the leading scorer for Denver U. in a 73-46 loss to Wyoming at Laramie on 1/4/1953. Ron Rivers scored 20 for Wyoming. Rhone had a brief run with the New York Knicks in fall 1954. In January, 1955, UPI reported that Rhone had returned home and joined former UW All-Conference star John Pilch, another UW alum Dr. Leonard Larson and Pete Cook on a pro basketball team in Cheyenne. Casper Star 1/7/1955.

[15] Casper Tribune-Herald, 11/11/1959, p. 1.

[16] Laramie Boomerang, 11/11/1959. See the Taft Harris chapter at 21.

[17] UW Branding Iron student newspaper, 3/24/1961 p. 1.

[18] On Dec. 13, 1957, the Montgomery, Ala., Advertiser carried an AP report saying that Colorado State College in Greeley (now University of Northern Colorado) had decided to cancel its three-game trip to Louisiana after learning of that state's law "that prohibits athletic contests in which Negro and white players participate together." CSC had one black player, guard Ollie Bell of Colorado Springs. Democrat Gov. Steve McNichols had directed the CSC president to "either take the whole team as it is or we don't play." Thomas Girault of Denver, president of the CSC trustees, agreed with McNichols. "The money we would forfeit would be peanuts compared with the principle here involved," he said.

diners is the exception rather than the rule throughout the state." The principal complaints from minority citizens to the Committee, the report said, "are that they feel they are more subject to arrest and are subjected to more severe treatment after arrest in cases of petty crimes ... than the whites. The committee heard reports of police brutality in two cities." In Laramie, the report said, "union policy discriminates against Negroes in barbershops."

The committee concluded that, in the "Equality State", the "equality is largely limited to Caucasian citizens."

Other members of the Committee were Mrs. P. E. Daley of Rawlins, Mrs. Nellie Scott of Fort Washakie and William Wexall of Casper.

They reported that housing for Native Americans was sub-standard on the Wind River Reservation and "those who wish to live in Lander and Riverton were unable to obtain rental other than in limited areas."[19]

At a meeting in Casper in late 1962, the Advisory Committee heard from several black residents who reported resistance from owners, real estate agents, "trust officers" or neighbors when they attempted to purchase houses in white neighborhoods.[20]

1969: "Black 14" purged from UW football team

In the fall of 1969, James Tyler, one of the children in a large African American family in Cheyenne, came to the University of Wyoming as a freshman. Years earlier, at the behest of the head of the Cheyenne NAACP chapter, James had become one of the first African Americans to integrate Goins Elementary School in south Cheyenne. Unfortunately, Tyler's introduction to college life soon was shattered by an awful injustice done to 14 of his fellow black students. Within two months, he was protesting the dismissal of the Black 14 from UW's undefeated football team. Forty-five years later, during a panel discussion at the UW College of Law, Tyler explained why the Black Student Alliance had called for a protest of a tenet of the LDS Church before the October 18, 1969, game at UW's War Memorial Stadium against the Brigham Young University Cougars. At that time, young black men could not become lay ministers in the LDS Church as white young men were expected to do. (This tenet was expunged by church leaders after a revelation in 1978). At the panel discussion, Tyler remembered that the protest also involved the university's interactions with BYU:

> When someone has a belief about you that you are deficient in some way
> before the Creator, you know they see you as an inferior being. We felt that
> student monies, university monies, should not be used in any sort of activity with
> an institution that holds those sorts of beliefs about black people and we wanted to
> register our protest about it. What we wanted to do was eminently reasonable, but
> we were met with an unreasonable response. No one saw that the athletes here
> would be called upon to pay the price for a freedom which most of us thought
> should be understood. A conversation. The freedom to express. Most of us were
> the first members of our families to attend colleges. There was a lot at stake for
> us. We were very young. We were called upon to make a stand at that time. I

[19] AP report from Washington in Casper Star 9/11/1961.

[20] Casper Star 12/1/1962, p. 2.

salute these brothers, the Black 14, who paid the price for academic freedom for instructors, athletes, students here in this state and around the country.

The Black 14 incident at UW was a crushing blow to many of us who had come to college at Wyoming in the early and mid-60s. While major protests against the Vietnam War and the companies manufacturing Agent Orange and napalm had occurred on most college campuses around the country beginning as early as 1964, the state and university leaders were proud that the Cowboy State had not yet had any disquieting incidents (prior to October, 1969). Many of the histories that have been written about the 1960s include no reference to Wyoming.[21] In the following chapters, this book will set forth in much more detail the stories of the people and events which led to the Black 14 incident and the consequent unraveling of the UW football program afterwards.

Around the country in the decade of the 2010s, graduates of high schools in the early and mid-60s were celebrating their 50th reunions, including those of us who entered Cheyenne Central High School as sophomores in the fall of 1960, the first sophomore class for Central following the split-up of Cheyenne High School. These reunions have provoked many to look back at that tumultuous decade which brought nuclear weapons, the Vietnam War, the draft and the tragedies and some triumphs of the civil rights movement.

For many of us, the Sixties was a decade that had opened on a very high note with the election and inauguration of President John F. Kennedy in November, 1960 and January, 1961[22]. The picture of 87-year-old poet Robert Frost attempting to read his new poem "Dedication" in the bright sunlight and cold became etched on everyone's memory of the inauguration, along with JFK's "ask not" statement in his inaugural address.[23]

---

[21] For example, the word "Wyoming" does not appear in the index of *The Sixties Chronicle*, a 450-page large-format book published in 2004. However, on p. 9 of the book, in a Preface by one of the leading voices against the Vietnam War in the 1960s, is a reference to then (in 2004) Vice-President Dick Cheney's wife Lynne, who grew up in Casper, Wyo. In his Preface, Tom Hayden referred to Lynne Cheney's column "The End of History" published in the Wall Street Journal on October 20, 1994, blasting the national history standards which were about to be released after years of work by many experts in the field. In her op-ed, Mrs. Cheney, Chair of the National Endowment for the Humanities from 1986-1993, blamed "political correctness" for placing too much emphasis on subjects important to African American and Native American organizations -- such as the Ku Klux Klan's terror and Harriet Tubman, the former slave who rescued many slaves through the Underground Railroad during the Civil War -- than on the traditional white male icons of American history. UCLA history professor Gary B. Nash, one of many on the committees that developed the standards, in 2004 wrote a review of Lynne Cheney's actions regarding the standards 10 years earlier. Nash wrote that Mrs. Cheney wanted "guidelines that would exalt traditional heroes, put a happy face on the American past, and broadcast the triumph of western civilization." Hayden, elected to the California Legislature for 18 years, died in October, 2016. He drafted the famous Port Huron Statement of the Students for a Democratic Society in 1962, one of the first manifestations of the younger generation's turn away from the regimentation of the Fifties.

[22] Just over two weeks prior to JFK's inauguration, three military personnel were killed in a steam explosion and meltdown at the Army's experimental nuclear power reactor located west of Idaho Falls, Idaho, not far from the Wyoming border.

[23] Robert Frost traveled from his home in South Shaftsbury, Vt., to participate in the dedication of the Robert Frost Poetry Library in Hoyt Hall at the University of Wyoming April 17-18, 1939, according to an article in the Christian Science Monitor, April 18, 1939. He was delighted by a reading of his poem "The Birches" by the UW "Verse Speaking Choir" during the dedication. He said he had never heard one of his poems read in that manner before. Frost contributed numerous signed first editions of his work to the library.

As the decade opened, few Americans had more than the vaguest notion of what and where Vietnam was, and most young men thought the military draft was only a meaningless anachronism, what with nuclear weapons proliferating. Early in 1962 the U.S. Army announced it was slashing the draft rate by more than half what it was during the Berlin crisis the previous year. The call would be only 6,000 in March. The Army's announcement did not mention Vietnam. But even in fall, 1962, trouble was already brewing in that country. On Nov. 6th, the Cheyenne Eagle carried a UPI report of two American fliers killed when their plane crashed "while bombing and strafing Communist guerilla positions south of Saigon," bringing the American death count in Vietnam to 37.

On April 3, 1963 CBS broadcast a report on Rachel Carson's *Silent Spring*, which warned Americans of the dangers of pesticides from persistent poisons such as DDT, including the thinning of the eggshells of the nation's symbol, the Bald Eagle. DDT was sprayed everywhere in some towns in Wyoming to kill flies. According to Mark Ritchie of Laramie, the propaganda about the healthful benefits of DDT had been so persuasive that he and his friends rode their bicycles down the street behind the truck spraying the poison.

At the end of summer, 1963, several high school graduates left Cheyenne headed for the service academies. Central High's Jim Steadman went south to the Air Force Academy and 10 years later was added to the Vietnam MIA list. (See Steadman chapter *infra*). Another Central grad, Steve Toelle, reported to West Point with 845 other appointees. A 2012 documentary titled "Into Harm's Way" focused on that class, describing the sobering transformation of the future that the 583 graduates had experienced during their four years on the Hudson. The documentary's web page sets the stage this way:

> The West Point Class of 1967 arrived at the United States Military Academy during the heady days of the early 1960s when it appeared that America was destined for a century of unrivaled success. Four years later, when the members of that class were graduated and commissioned as officers in the United States Army, the country was embroiled in a strange and unpopular war in Southeast Asia. The Class of 1967 paid a high price in that war, yet most stayed strong, bonding as brothers and as soldiers in a way that has endured through to the present.[24]

Yes, by the middle of the decade, Vietnam was on the front page of every newspaper in the country almost every day, and became the location of death of thousands of young men and women in the obituaries printed in those newspapers.

Although it is correct to say that the University of Wyoming never saw the occupations of buildings, property destruction and huge demonstrations that occurred at many other campuses during the 1960s, the state actually experienced protests by pacifists before the 1960s even began. Two years before our class entered high school, an Atlas nuclear missile construction site under the command of Cheyenne's Warren Air Force Base had experienced a civil disobedience

---

[24] The documentary can be purchased at Amazon. See two trailers at thedocumentarygroup.com. In one of the trailers, a 1967 graduate relates that immediately after graduation ceremonies the new Army officers climbed onto buses at a West Point barracks quadrangle, then aboard two airplanes, and the next thing they knew they were at Da Nang, Vietnam. As a band played and roll call was being taken at the quadrangle, one new officer climbed to the roof of a dormitory and yelled "I'm not going. I can't do this" before jumping to his death. Thirty of the '67 West Point class were killed in action in Vietnam.

protest during which one protester suffered a broken pelvis when he was struck by a 12-ton gravel truck. (See the Atlas Missile chapter).

WAFB was the nation's first ICBM base. Its missiles were put on "red alert" during the Cuban Missile Crisis in October, 1962. The red light at a nearby Atlas silo alarmed Albin-area rancher Mae Kirkbride (who 20 years later would become a leader of an unsuccessful movement to stop the MX missile from coming to the Cheyenne area).[25] The Cuban crisis delivered a shock to our confidence in the future, but JFK called the Soviets' bluff and they backed down, removing their missiles from Cuba and avoiding a catastrophe.

On March 16, 1963, the Central High Indians won their third straight state basketball tournament with a 61-56 win over Riverton. Central's Paul Rayko, Blaine Price, Dick Gish, Dennis Scheer and Jerry Kleager led a comeback from seven points down near the game's end, taking advantage of the fifth foul by Wolverines' star Jack Petsch. Ev Befus kept Riverton close, but according to the Laramie Boomerang's report by Gene Bryan, "Billy Davis, a scrappy little player who seems to be everywhere at once", stole a pass and scored a layup to seal the win.[26]

As we graduated in May of 1963, our joy and hope were tempered by television news footage from Birmingham, Ala., showing Commissioner Bull Connor's police using fire hoses and attack dogs on demonstrators challenging segregation, many of them children. On June 12, 1963, African American civil rights activist Medgar Evers, a veteran of World War II, was shot in the back and killed in front of his Mississippi home. Three participants in Freedom Summer were also killed that summer.[27]

For those of us in the Class of '63 who entered the University of Wyoming in the fall, a remarkable thing happened only ten days into our freshman year: President Kennedy came to our campus in Laramie, Wyoming. JFK spoke at the packed Memorial Fieldhouse after riding with Sen. Gale McGee (D-Wyo.) on a quick tour around "Prexy's Pasture" in an open convertible on a glorious fall day.

During the next few years the students at the University of Wyoming had many opportunities to hear former UW history professor McGee, a marvelous orator who became one of the leading "hawks" for LBJ and his Vietnam War.

Of course our joy at seeing the youthful, ebullient Kennedy on our campus became, only two months later, a dreadful sorrow when we learned from the television in the Hill Hall lobby at about noon on Nov. 22 that our president had been killed in Dallas.

That was the beginning of a downward spiral that dominated the rest of the '60s and well into the 70s. That spiral included two more horrific assassinations in 1968, awful violence to those working to extend voting rights and equality of education and opportunity to African Americans in the South, and the seemingly endless horror that was the Vietnam War.

During the late-60s, a junior high boy in Casper joined many others around the country who were dismissed from school for violating rules prohibiting long hair or beards. "Long hair

---

[25] In 2001, when the Air Force announced plans to retire the MX as a cost-saving measure, Mae Kirkbride was quoted in a New York Times report as saying "we've been fighting these things tooth and nail. I'm very happy they're going. I never thought they were the sort of thing that kept us safe from any oppressor or invader anyway. We'd fire ours, then they'd fire theirs. So what's left?"

[26] Billy Davis died in 2014 in Arizona.

[27] See p. <u>74</u> for the story of two UW alumni who went to Mississippi to teach as part of the Freedom Summer program.

isn't safe or healthy, it leads to disruption," the school boards proclaimed. At the same time, the school board members saw nothing ironic about the prospect that those same boys they had saved from the dangers of long hair could soon be sent off to dodge bullets in Vietnam.

At the University of Wyoming, most of the 1960s passed quietly[28] and traditionally. A regular student newspaper column called "Who's Whose" told, for the most part, which sorority woman had become "pinned" or "lavaliered" or engaged or married to which fraternity man. Most in the older generation continued to believe that the reason for women to be in college was only to obtain their "MRS. degrees."

But the '60s in Wyoming came to a particularly disgraceful, callous and unbelievable conclusion when, in a fit of rage on the morning of Friday October 17, 1969, UW's highly-successful head football coach, without consulting with his assistant coaches or even with the athletic director, dismissed all 14 of the African American players from his undefeated and 12th-ranked team. Considering how important black players had been to UW's success on the football field in the '60s, and considering how important UW football was to the people of Wyoming, the complete lack of understanding shown by the coach and state officials of the long, bloody struggle of African Americans for basic rights remains a mystery nearly 50 years later. After all, only one of the 14 players grew up in Wyoming. The remainder came from 10 other states, many from urban areas. Jerome "Jay" Berry was from Tulsa where one of the worst race riots in American history occurred in 1921. Three hundred people, both black and white, were killed and 10,000 black people were left homeless.[29]

The Black 14's attorney, William Waterman of Pontiac, Mich., discerned the situation perfectly. He said Eaton had made an error in judgment which was compounded by the praise heaped upon the coach by residents of the state. "Wyoming can't have black athletes and be unmindful of their rights and dignity," he said, predicting that the state's reputation – and UW's ability to recruit black athletes – would suffer.[30]

The Cowboys were to take the home field against Brigham Young University on October 18. The Black Students Alliance, formed earlier in 1969, had called for a protest symbolized by black armbands to show objection to a since-revoked tenet of the Latter Day Saints church, which owned BYU. The tenet prohibited African American men from becoming priests[31]. In

---

[28] Except for a 1961 "panty raid." See p. <u>54</u>.

[29] Even the articles in Wyoming newspapers quoting Wyoming residents before October, 1969, if taken to heart, should have educated the coach and state officials of that struggle. For example, the Rawlins Daily Times and most other state papers on Feb. 27, 1968, carried a long UPI article quoting Johnnie McKinney, the president of the Cheyenne NAACP branch, who spoke of the anger, desperation and hopelessness of the poor and the lack of concern by Congress and local leaders. "Unemployment in the ghettoes is of depression proportions, and the housing is unworthy of a wealthy nation--and surely an insult to the black veterans of our wars," McKinney said. In a Casper Star article on Feb. 29, 1968, Fred Devereaux, president of the Casper NAACP, said some 700-1,000 African Americans lived in the north Casper area which he called "a ghetto." He said Casper was more concerned with planning for a civic center than with improving housing conditions. He said he and other NAACP leaders had recently met with Gov. Stan Hathaway and asked for more representation of blacks, Hispanics and Native Americans on draft boards and on the Fair Employment Practices Commission.

[30] UPI report in Ogden Standard-Examiner October 28, 1969.

[31] To this day LDS women, like Roman Catholic women, cannot be ordained as priests. According to mormon.org, the LDS web site, Gordon B. Hinckley, former President of the LDS Church has offered this explanation: "Women do not hold the priesthood because the Lord has put it that way. It is part of His program."

solidarity with their fellows in the BSA, the players had donned black arm bands and walked to coach Lloyd Eaton's office in that same Fieldhouse where Kennedy had spoken six years earlier, to talk to him about what involvement they might have in the BSA's call for protest.

Upon seeing them wearing black arm bands, Eaton directed them to sit in the upper bleachers of the Fieldhouse, told them they were all off the team and then insulted them in a racially-charged tirade that immediately polarized the situation beyond repair, given that no one higher in authority at UW or the state had the backbone to challenge the coach. In the ensuing days and months, the state attorney general, the governor, the university president, the trustees and the university's legal counsel, all turned blind eyes to the coach's disregard of those students' constitutional right to wear those armbands that morning (one of the players, Mel Hamilton, was a veteran of the U.S. Army). None of those leaders ever expressed any concern publicly about the coach's angry denunciation of the 14 young men.

Most of the people of Wyoming supported the coach and never gave a thought to the shattering of the dreams of the Fourteen, the majority of whom were minors under the laws in effect at that time. The fact that the coach's unwritten rule was unconstitutional – and that the punishment far exceeded the "crime" – seemed to be irrelevant. The fact that the coach had denigrated them was ignored. "Winning football requires discipline. These ungrateful players didn't follow the rule against participating in demonstrations. End of discussion" -- was the prevailing attitude.

Ironically, just two days before the Black 14 were dismissed, UW President William Carlson spoke to the Casper Chamber of Commerce and bragged about UW having remained an exception to the angry campus demonstrations that had occurred at hundreds of campuses across the country during the previous five years. "University of Wyoming students do not advocate violence or vicious confrontation," Carlson said. "They come to us to talk things over." The Black 14 never had a chance to do that with Eaton.

In a starkly contrasting incident two days earlier in arch-conservative Powell in northwest Wyoming, no action was taken against some high school students who wore black armbands to school in a Vietnam protest. "We don't interfere with personal expression of protest – like the black armbands – as long as it doesn't disrupt school," assistant principal Ken Mullan explained.[32]

When the depleted Cowboys lost the last four games in 1969 and won only one game in 1970, the swaggering Eaton supporters of 1969 -- falling all over themselves to applaud Eaton's standing up to the blacks -- were nowhere to be found, and Eaton suddenly "retired" from coaching after a special Board of Trustees meeting.

On May 4, 1970, six months after the Black 14 disaster, the Ohio National Guard fired 67 shots at unarmed Vietnam War protesters at Kent State University in Ohio, killing four and permanently paralyzing another. A group of about 300 UW students headed by Joe Romero of Torrington and Donn McCall, both future lawyers, went to Old Main to ask that the flag in Prexy's Pasture be lowered to half mast. They were informed by UW officials that only the president could order the lowering of the American flag.

Student Senator Corbin Fowler and others then asked Gov. Hathaway to lower the state flag. He refused. "What Hathaway wants is to become the Reagan of Wyoming," Lex Wadsworth, son of a western Wyoming rancher, charged, referring to California Gov. Ronald

---

[32] Powell Tribune, 10/17/1969.

Reagan. "He realizes, as does Vice-President Agnew, that you get political mileage out of putting students down."[33]

As tensions rose, "they [UW administrators] made Old Main a fortress," an unidentified faculty member was quoted as saying three years later. "All the students were doing was sitting around in a semi-circle. All they wanted to do was to lower the flag as a gesture to people killed at Kent State."[34] Governor Hathaway sent Highway Patrol troopers to the pasture, armed with shotguns. Were they under orders to prevent -- by force if necessary -- the lowering of the flag? We'll never know. Because of the intervention of three University Common Ministry clergy and some faculty members -- all of them opposed to the war -- violence was averted during the all-night vigil. Some observers felt that the real danger in that situation came from the "law and order" Nixon supporters who were driving around Prexy's with rifles in their gun racks, shouting epithets at the peace protesters.

---

[33] Article by UW student Jerry Mahoney in the Casper Star-Tribune 5/7/1969. Across the front page from these articles was a notice that Agnew was expected to be in Cody the next day to address the Republican State Convention.

[34] McAuley, Phil, "UW fires are banked temporarily," Casper Star-Tribune, May 22, 1973, p. 1. The same faculty member said the Black 14's visit to the coach "could have been handled tactfully in about 15 minutes" by a strong president, but instead the ratification of the coach's action was continuing to have "wrenching consequences" for the university and the state four years later.

Vietnam War and Kent State protesters, including the author, show the "V for peace" sign on May 14, 1970 at UW.

Ten days after the Kent State tragedy, a large number of peace marchers filled the "Knothole Section" at UW's Memorial Stadium during the ROTC Governor's Day ceremonies.

At Cheyenne Central in 1972, the principal and the school board let 120 high school students know that the authorities would find a way to punish any students who showed insufficient patriotism, no matter what the U.S. Supreme Court might have ruled many years earlier about the right to refuse to salute the flag and recite the pledge of allegiance. After that, the Cheyenne school board dismissed a long-term and innovative history teacher who, on his own time, had opposed the war and supported the Black 14.

This book tells these and other stories of prejudice and protest in Wyoming, intertwined with the major issues of the times characterized by the "generation gap" between the "older" generation -- scarred by the Depression and World War II -- and their children who, as the 1960s opened, could not have imagined that the future of bright dreams they envisioned would metamorphose so tragically into a decade that brought conflict and bloodshed and sadness to so many lives. These stories are presented in a semi-chronological fashion, moving forward between civil rights, nuclear missiles and protest, Wyomingites serving in the Vietnam War, the draft and draft resistance and, in large measure, the personalities and events leading up to and following the "Black 14" incident at UW.

1897-1964: AFRICAN AMERICANS AT UW AND NORTHWEST COLLEGE

> The university shall be equally open to students of both sexes, irrespective
> of race or color ....
> Wyoming Constitution Article 7 Sec. 16 (1890)

To put into perspective what happened to the 14 African American football players on the Wyoming Cowboys' varsity roster in 1969, a look back at the history of people of that race at UW is most interesting.

An 1897 photo of the UW "Cadet Corps" clearly shows one black man lined up with 27 white males on a treeless and structure-less plain with the snowy Laramie Mountains in the background.

At p. 179 of UW professor Deborah Hardy's centennial history, *Wyoming University - The First 100 Years 1886-1986*, is a photograph of seven basketball players with their coach. The caption on the photo says, "Men's basketball team c. 1900", but 1919-20 is probably more accurate. These players are wearing jerseys which say "PREPS" on the front, and one of the players is an African American. This team appears to be a university high school team and the black player may be Robert Rhone.

1903: Carrie R. Burton (later Carrie Burton Overton)
The first African American UW student was most likely a young woman named Carrie Burton who took classes at UW beginning at age 15 (which was not uncommon in those days, before secondary schooling was extended to 12 years).

In 1960, Carrie Burton Overton returned to Laramie for a reunion of her UW classmates and wrote "The Lady in the Ivinson Mansion", a reminiscence about her interactions with Mrs. Edward Ivinson.[35] Jane and Edward were among Laramie's very first residents in 1868 and became the city's most notable and generous citizens ever.

In her reminiscence, Carrie remembered picking vegetables for Mrs. Ivinson and later serving as her secretary of sorts, writing letters for her. She remembered being paid with a $5 gold piece on one occasion. Carrie's memoir said that Mrs. Ivinson had sponsored a 1908 piano recital to raise funds for Carrie's move to D.C.

Carrie Burton began taking classes at UW in 1903, soon becoming well-known about town as a pianist and musician. Her name appears numerous times in the Laramie newspapers between 1895 and 1912, most of them regarding her piano recitals.

She appeared in the Boomerang as early as June 18, 1896, when she played or sang "Only a Little Child" for children's day at the Methodist Church.

Ms. Burton is pictured with other members of "The School of Music in 1904" on p. 135 of the *Chronicles of the Alumni of the University of Wyoming* (1911) published in conjunction with UW's 25th anniversary.

---

[35] Quoted in article by Alice Stevens, Laramie Boomerang, 3/1/1972. Her life is also described in a Laramie Bulletin article on 12/5/1942.

THE SCHOOL OF MUSIC IN 1904.
Mrs. Frank Bross, Shirley Lewis, Ollie McDermott, Ethel Rauner, Luella Case, Helen Clark, Mrs. H. E. McCollum, Mrs. Clark, Hattie Tilton, Elizabeth De Forest, Carrie Burton, Mrs. Frank Spafford, Nellie Skinner, Rena Elias.

A Laramie Republican article on the celebration of Arbor Day at UW on April 21, 1905, noted that local attorney N.E. Corthell spoke on "The Symbolism of Tree Planting as Applied to Education, with Miss Carrie Burton, a student of the university, following with a piano solo, 'The Rustle of Spring.'" In October, 1905, the Boomerang reported simply that "Miss Carrie Burton has again entered school" and in March, 1907, in a review of a recital at the university, the newspaper exclaimed that "Miss Carrie Burton also did splendidly and will undoubtedly develop into a pianist of more than ordinary renown."

Then came the following remarkable article on the front page of the Laramie Boomerang on August 29, 1908:

Headline: Miss Carrie Burton to Give Recital

Most people in Laramie know Miss Carrie Burton but we undertake to say that not many appreciate what she has done for herself or the conditions under which she has worked. Born in Laramie July 20, 1888, she is now just past 20 years of age, a colored girl who has had to face the prejudice against her race, yet so careful to avoid being in any way offensive to others, so kind and considerate of others' rights, so attentive to her own duties, ... she has been universally recognized as deserving of the most respectable consideration.

In 1903 she entered the commercial department of the University of Wyoming and two years later completed the stenography course, keeping up her music work through the assistance of her mother, who took in washing to get the necessary funds. Then her mother got the rheumatism and Carrie did the washing.

19

Since 1905 and until this last June she has been in attendance at the University, taking bookkeeping and music and doing stenographic work for the different departments beside doing considerable stenographic work for people about the city. She is a good stenographer and every one for whom she has worked speaks well of her.

She has repeatedly appeared at students' musical recitals and has invariably been in favor.

Her recital at the university auditorium next Tuesday evening is likely to be the last which she will give in Laramie for some time, she having already arranged for admission to the musical department of Howard University at Washington, D.C. ... She counts on being entered there as a junior and to complete the musical course of that school in two years. ... She will be largely dependent upon her earnings as stenographer to carry her through Howard University, but will surely appreciate any help she may get through the sale of tickets to the Tuesday evening recital, and surely anyone disposed to help an ambitious and deserving student could not find a better opportunity than this occasion affords.

The Boomerang published a letter from Ms. Burton to a friend in Laramie on March 26, 1909, under the headline "A Laramie girl in Washington". Written from Miner Hall, she reported that at first she "did not find things as I had expected them. I was permitted to work for my board only and did not know how the other expenses would be paid. I wanted to return home but could not. I therefore worried myself sick and was under the doctor's care for three weeks." But then Ms. Burton became secretary to a professor, which allowed her to buy "a new typewriter at teachers' rates ($75) and paying $5 a month for it." She was also working as assistant operator at the switchboard. She continued:

I see and hear so many things here that I could not enjoy at home. On Lincoln's birthday a number of great men spoke to the students of Howard University. Among them were Senator Dolliver of Iowa, Hon. Mr. Cannon, speaker of the House of Representatives, and Secretary of the Interior Garfield. Last Sunday I heard Mr. Edward Everett Hale, the man who wrote 'A Man Without a Country.' I heard Paderewski and the great Boston Symphony Orchestra. ... I called on Mr. Mondell, our [Wyoming's] representative, who gave me a hearty welcome and signed a civil service voucher for me. ...

I find great pleasure in studying our race. Our Prof. Kelly Miller is one of the three greatest Negroes in the United States. He has just gotten out a book, "Race Adjustment."

On May 27, 1912, the Boomerang said that Miss Burton had become the private secretary to the president of Howard University. The book *Howard University: The First Hundred Years*, states that in 1913 she was one of the first two graduates of the Howard Conservatory of Music.

According to a short biography accompanying her collection of papers at Wayne State University in Detroit, she married George W. B. Overton, principal of the African American schools in Cumberland, Md., in 1913 and in 1923 the couple moved to New York City where she studied music at the Juilliard School and English literature at Columbia. At various times she was employed as a secretary by the Vanguard Press, the Community Church of New York, the

NAACP (from 1924-28), the National Urban League and the Eastern Division of Colored Voters of the Democratic party.[36]

In a 1942 Laramie Bulletin article Carrie credited one of UW's founding professors who became an authority in Rocky Mountain plant taxonomy and served as UW president from 1918-22. "My life has been little less than phenomenal and I owe most of it to Dr. Aven Nelson who set me straight when he was superintendent of the Sunday school."[37]

An article about Mrs. Overton and Jane Ivinson by Alice Hardie Stevens appeared in the Boomerang on March 1, 1972, noting that Carrie had participated in fund-raising efforts on behalf of the Laramie Plains Museum, which eventually was able to purchase the Ivinson Mansion where the Museum is located to present day.

Carrie Burton Overton and her husband George at UW 1960 Reunion

Carrie died in New York City in 1975. In that 1942 article she was quoted as saying, "In all these things I have tried to repay the good people of Laramie for the faith they had in me."[38]

Early 1930s: Multi-sport athlete Taft Harris of Casper

In his column published November 8, 1961, long-time Salt Lake Tribune sports editor John Mooney included a correction of a previous article he had written in which he apparently stated that Mike Walker, a running back on the 1961 UW roster, was the first black football player at the University of Wyoming. (See the Marion chapter at p. 61). Mooney said this statement had provoked "Readers Joe Sandoval and James Johnson to send us a correction," Mooney wrote. "Both readers point out that Taft Harris of Casper, Wyo., played football and basketball for Wyoming in the 1930s, under Dutch Witte."

Laramie Boomerang sports editor Bob Hammond, a Class of '63 star athlete for Laramie High School, had the same experience in 2005. In a wonderful feature story on Curt Jimerson published Feb. 19, Hammond suggested that Jimerson may have been UW's first African American basketball player.

---

[36] On Oct. 29, 1969, Whitney M. Young Jr., executive director of the NUL, sent a telegram to UW President Carlson saying "The National Urban League views with deep concern [the dismissal of the Black 14] because they desired to symbolically protest the existence of racism...." The NAACP was involved in obtaining legal representation for the players.

[37] The Aven Nelson Building on the UW campus houses the Rocky Mountain Herbarium which Nelson started in 1893. Nelson was the university's first librarian and also taught a wide range of subjects including zoology, physical geography and calisthenics. Today the Herbarium holds 1.3 million specimens from around the world.

[38] Viner, Kim, "First African-American Female Student at UW", wyohistory.org; "Carrie Burton Overton," Annals of Wyoming, 89:4 (Autumn 2017).

Taft Harris and mates in Half Acre 1932

Like Mooney more than 40 years earlier, Hammond received calls from old-timers who told him about Taft Harris of Casper.

Taft was born in 1911 in El Dorado, Ark. When he was nine his mother sent him to live with her sister Alabama Hart and her husband William in Casper, Wyo. The Casper City Directory for 1924 shows William as a "hostler" for the CB&Q Railroad, living with Alabama at 105 N. Melrose. The 1937 directory shows him as a "pumper" for the railroad, living at 241 N. Grant.

In 1928 and 1929, Harris was an All-state football player for the Natrona County High School Mustangs. He was also a star in basketball and track and played in the band. He appears on the Natrona High Hall of Fame as an All-Stater by himself in 1928 and along with Lloyd Dowler and Glen Richey in 1929. In May, 1927, Harris tied the state record in the 120-yard high hurdles and placed second in the discus. In 1929 he set a new state record in the 120 hurdles.

On April 2, 1928, the Casper Daily Tribune society column reported that the high school basketball squad were entertained with a turkey dinner by Mr. and Mrs. C. A. Hughes and Mr. and Mrs. Dan Sullivan. "Those present were favored with a number of saxophone solos by Taft Harris, which were enjoyed by all," the article said. Among the guests were Harris, Lloyd Dowler and his brother Walter Dowler, father of future NFL star Boyd Dowler of the Green Bay Packers. A couple years later the Dowlers were teammates of Harris at UW.

On March 24, 1929 the Casper Tribune reported that the tournament sports staff of the Laramie Republican-Boomerang had selected Harris to its All-State first team, along with Richey of Casper, Rugg of Wheatland, Byrne of Laramie and Sarvey of Glenrock. Just below that article was one headlined "Veiled Threat Sent Casper Cage Player at State Tournament." Natrona coach Frank Scott told the paper that Harris had received "[a] threatening letter" about 15 minutes before the first game of the tournament in Laramie. The article said "The big Negro guard ... was considerably upset, and the threat tended to affect his playing. University authorities launched an investigation to determine the author, Scott said. The report said Harris had been named all-state

22

in both football and basketball in 1928 and 1929. "He is popular with his fellow students and associates on athletic teams."

Harris was one of three African American classmates who attended the Casper 2nd Baptist Church, and in the fall of 1929 Harris was joined by both of them, Arthur Henry and Alfred Bell, on a trip to Iowa City to enroll at the University of Iowa. Harris' play on the football field soon attracted the attention of the campus newspaper, calling him a "stickler" for the freshmen playing the varsity. On December 3, 1929, the Casper Herald reported that Harris had been praised in two different articles in the U.I. student newspaper, the Daily Iowan, for stopping the varsity halfbacks by "wrapping his abnormally long arms" around them and "dashing them to the ground like one hurling a piece of crockery against a concrete floor." After the season, Harris and Henry were awarded freshman team "numerals".

But Harris transferred to UW the next year, and from 1930-33 played on both the basketball and football teams. He also was a hurdler for the UW track team.[39]

Lane Demas, author of a book titled *Integrating the Gridiron*, relates that the appearance of an African American on a college team in the 1930s was probably rare for the Mountain West, but was far from a first nationally. "I'd estimate that there had probably been at least 30-40 African American footballers at various major schools by the late 1920s," Demas reported in a 2013 e-mail. "That would include Brice Taylor at USC, Paul Robeson at Rutgers, Fritz Pollard at Brown, and -- even going back to the 1890s -- William Lewis at Harvard and George Flippin at Nebraska." But in *College Football* by John Sayle Watterson at 309-10, the author explained that simply having a black player on the roster was not the end of the story. "When a team with black players scheduled a southern opponent, the southerners almost always demanded that the black player be held out of the game, and, as a matter of courtesy, the northern team almost always complied. In 1934 Michigan agreed not to play its African American star Willis Ward against

Taft Harris with UW football team 1930 or '31

Georgia Tech," even though it was a home game for Michigan in Ann Arbor.

An article in the December 4, 1930 Branding Iron (the UW student newspaper) described the basketball team's prospects for the season and declared that "Harris is a fine defensive player and will be a large asset to the team."

Sports writers in the region seemed to be intrigued by Harris' presence on those teams. On September 6, 1931, the Salt Lake Tribune carried an Associated Press preview of the Wyoming football team coached by "John (Choppy) Rhodes". The article said that "Mucho, Rugg, Schwartz and Wells, last year's wingmen, will fight to win positions along with Taft Harris, husky Casper negro star...." The Bridger Valley Enterprise on Nov. 24, 1932 called him "the rangy Negro guard."

[39], The Casper Tribune-Herald reported on April 17, 1932, that Harris had placed in two hurdles events in a meet that day against "Colorado Teachers". See also Harris' obituary in the Casper Tribune Herald, March 29, 1961.

The article presented UW coach Rhodes' assessment of the forthcoming football season. "I think we'll win four games," he said, "and with any kind of luck we will win more than four."

The article says Rhodes thought his team would be able to beat Ott Romney's Brigham Young Cougars, along with Colorado Teachers of Greeley, the University of New Mexico and "the Chadron, Nebraska Teachers, who open the season in Laramie." Wyoming was to play nine games, including contests with Creighton and Santa Clara (a game to be played in Cheyenne). Only two of the games were scheduled for Laramie.

The article mentions William Engstrom, a Rawlins high school star, Herbert Gage of Cheyenne, Walter Dowler of Casper and Ed Ross of Cheyenne. In 1933 Harris played with future Laramie High School coaching legend John Deti.

The sports writer for the Tribune-Republican in Greeley, Colo., took the rhetoric about the Harris phenomenon to an extreme. On October 8, 1931, that newspaper printed action shots of Wyoming's quarterback and receiver in front of UW's Half Acre Gym, with this cutline: "Ed Ross (left) to Taft Harris may become all too familiar at Jackson Field when Wyoming meets Colorado Teachers. Ross, son of the late Governor Ross, throws a football fast and accurate, while Harris, gangling panther striding negro, hooks 'em out of the air."[40]

A Casper Daily Tribune review of UW basketball on Jan. 26, 1931, said freshman Taft Harris was starting most games, calling him "the giant Negro star from Casper". The Bridger Valley Enterprise on Christmas Day 1930 said Joe Schwartz and Harris, former Casper stars, "played heads-up ball all the time on both offense and defense" during Wyoming's basketball games in Utah. The Feb. 11, 1932 Jackson's Hole Courier reported that Ed McGinty, Wheatland, and Taft Harris, Casper, had been "turning in fine performances" for the UW basketball team.

Some of Taft's other basketball teammates during those years were Kenneth Rugg, Willard West, Arthur Hamon, Jack McNiff (future Laramie dentist), Schwartz, John Kimball, Leslie Witte, Lloyd Dowler, Wilfred Byrne, Claude Thomas, Blake Fanning, Hilton and Sanford Dearinger and Jack Bugas.[41]

Taft is pictured in the 1931 yearbook along with his basketball teammates. The team went 11-1 that season, winning the eastern division title, and then lost to Utah in Salt Lake in the championship. He is also pictured in the yearbook with Co. A of R.O.T.C. first year basic.

After spending three years in Laramie, Taft returned to Casper and worked in maintenance at the courthouse. During that time he met and married Eloise Walker who had come to Casper with her grandmother from Palo Pinto, Texas. They had two children, Taft Harris Jr. and Sally Harris Findley. In 2015, Taft Jr. was living in New Jersey and Sally was retired in Denver.

---

[40] Colorado Teachers today is the University of Northern Colorado. The article appears to be incorrect about Ed being the son of "the late Governor Ross". Gov. William Bradford Ross died in 1924 and his widow, Nellie Tayloe Ross, was elected to replace him, becoming the nation's first woman governor. They did have a son who could have been of the right age to play football at Wyoming in 1929-31, but his name was William Bradford Ross II and he was called "Brad", according to an article by Tom Rea at wyohistory.org.)

[41] John S. Bugas was from Wamsutter and Casper who earned a law degree at UW in 1934 and then became an FBI agent, becoming special agent in charge in Detroit. In 1941 it was reported FBI agent Bugas was "given credit for 'cracking' the Ford Motor theft case" which was costing the company large losses. (Casper Tribune 12/8/1941 p. 4. Pearl Harbor news dominated p. 1) On March 5, 1957, the Casper Star reported that Bugas, by then vice-president of the Ford Motor Co., had visited in Casper with attorney Barry Mahoney. Bugas made some large scholarship endowments to UW, one of which was a vital help to the author's law school attendance. The Dearinger brothers became fire-fighters in Cheyenne.

In July, 1934, Taft Sr. was elected vice-president of the Colored Men's Progressive Club at the A. M. E. church hall in Casper.

In March of 1935, Harris was playing for the Casper Merchants AAU team. A Tribune-Herald report on the state AAU basketball tournament on March 7th described Harris as "the tall Negro who helped make athletic history at Wyoming in the last five years."

On Oct. 10, 1935, the Tribune-Herald noted on its sports page that the "Globe Trotters of Des Moines, Ia., famous colored traveling basketball club" had sent a letter to the Casper Chamber of Commerce asking to put them in touch with Harris. But on Feb. 28, 1936, the paper previewed an upcoming appearance in Casper of "The Harlemites". This "circus in action" team, including Casper's hometown star Taft Harris, were to play the "Terrible Swedes."

Six years later, on Feb. 6, 1941, Harris was on the Casper Elks team that played against the Harlem Globe Trotters in Casper.

During WWII, Taft Sr. was a production manager in California for North American Aviation, building P-51 fighter aircraft . He returned to Wyoming and worked for a time at the Noble Hotel in Lander before finishing his career with Ohio Oil Co. in Casper. In February, 1953, he was listed in a legal notice as one of the trustees of the Second Baptist Church, along with his aunt's husband William Hart.

Pallbearers for his Casper funeral in 1961 were Jim Winfrey, Gaurdie Bannister, Roscoe Howard, George Smith, Ernie Davis and Chester Roseburr, with honorary pallbearers Charles and Howard Speese, Doc Gray, Robert Moore and Charles Wilson.[42]

Taft was a friend of Dan and Mike Sedar of Casper who played football at UW in the mid-30s. Their younger brother Dick Sedar, a former legislator, has tended Taft Harris' grave at Casper's Highland Cemetery for many years.

Taft's son Taft Harris Jr. was the only African American in his graduating class from Natrona County High School. He joined the Air Force and was a flight engineer stationed in Vietnam during the war there. He flew out of Phan Rang and Da Nang air bases, among others. When he was home on leave in 1961 he met future UW great Flynn Robinson who was playing basketball for the Casper College Thunderbirds. Taft Jr. retired after 20 years in the Air Force and then worked as a civilian consultant for the Defense Department. In 2014 he was 79 and living in New Jersey.

In February 2021, the National Football Foundation and the Chick-fil-A College Football Hall of Fame listed Taft Harris and The Black 14 for Wyoming in their list of African American players and coaches at many universities who "used their exceptional skills to help integrate the game."

---

[42] The Speeses may well have been involved with, or relatives of, the African American families who in 1908 sold their lands and equipment in Nebraska and traveled by wagon or railroad to homestead new lands along the Wyoming-Nebraska border north of Torrington. Their agrarian community was called Empire, Wyo., but they encountered some "racist, hostile neighbors", according to Todd Guenther's article titled "The Empire Builders, An African American Odyssey in Nebraska and Wyoming," *Nebraska History* 89 (2008), 176-200. An Empire resident named Baseman Taylor died in Torrington after three days of torture by the sheriff, his deputies and another prisoner, according to Guenther's article. Following WWI, economic and social conditions forced many homestead families to leave their land, including those struggling to make a living at Empire. Almost no sign of Empire can be seen today, according to Guenther's article. He interviewed a Margaret Speece in Casper in 1991 (spelled with a "c" in his footnotes; all others of that name in the article are spelled "Speese").

1960-1963: Curt Jimerson, Ron Bostick & Flynn Robinson

More than a quarter-century passed before another African American athlete played for the Cowboys. In the fall of 1960, two junior college transfer basketball players joined football player Mike Walker in the UW athletic dorm. Jimerson, an El Paso native, had come to UW in the fall of 1960 after being selected as a junior college All-American while playing at Pueblo, Colo., and had quickly become a star with the Cowboys.

When Jimerson visited UW and other colleges in the spring of 1960, the cold, snowy weather in Laramie contributed to his decision to take his talents to the University of Colorado. But shortly thereafter he happened to see a letter from the CU coach to Jimerson's junior college coach in the latter's office. The CU coach said he could not promise to start Jimerson because he already had two African American starters and some boosters wouldn't be comfortable with three. This letter changed Jimerson's mind about which university's "weather" was colder.

On Jan. 4, 1962, the Billings Gazette carried an AP article saying that four Laramie High School players on their "previously glassless" team had obtained spectacles after Jimerson wore glasses in a game for the first time two weeks earlier and scored 34 points.

He and Flynn Robinson were among the main attractions at the 100th Anniversary of Cowboy basketball celebration in 2005, which is where Bob Hammond learned that after graduating from UW in 1963 Jimerson had become one of the first black FBI agents. He was involved in high-profile investigations such as the Patty Hearst case and the Black Panthers during his 30-year career. After retiring from the FBI he was chief of security for the NBA's San Francisco Warriors. In October, 2013, Jimerson returned to UW for the 50th reunion of his class. One of his classmates who also attended was Cliff Osborne, a former UW baseball player who became UW's director of housing.

Jimerson said the only instance of racial prejudice to him personally occurred at Raleigh, N.C. in late-December, 1960. "We were playing in the Dixie Classic and decided to go to a movie one night. We were told that I would not be admitted, so all my teammates walked away with me."

When he arrived on the UW campus, Jimerson learned he had been assigned a roommate who was another African American junior college transfer to the UW basketball team, Ron Bostick from Saratoga Springs, New York. "He [Jimerson] was intelligent, amicable, cheerful and unpretentious," Bostick wrote in his autobiography many years later. Bostick was a starter and finished among the top scorers and rebounders on the team in what was to be his only year at UW.

In his memoir, Bostick said he had met a coed from Iowa and they had become friends. But after the basketball season, according to his memoir, he was called into the coach's office and was informed "that it was not acceptable for me to date a white girl and that I was forbidden to see her again if I wanted to keep my scholarship." He said his girlfriend later informed him that at the same time she was called to the Dean of Women's office and was given the same message. So at the end of the school year Bostick went to California, into the Air Force and then into a law enforcement career. He eventually became an executive with the International Association of Chiefs of Police. He died in 2009 in Pennsylvania, and in October, 2016, his wife was in attendance at Saratoga Springs as Bostick was inducted into his high school's hall of fame. His daughter Robyne was the leading scorer and rebounder for Saint Joseph's University in her senior year in college and was head coach of Northern Arizona's women's team in 2016-17.[43]

Hammond's article in the Boomerang on Feb. 19, 2005, described how Jimerson was among the first African Americans to integrate El Paso's all-white Austin High School in 1955.

Before Flynn Robinson began his amazing career on UW's Memorial Fieldhouse floor in the fall of 1962, the Elgin, Ill. product played at Casper College during the 1960-61 season and then sat out a year. His first mention in the Casper Star was in December, 1960, when a sports columnist noted that "some of coach Swede Erickson's newcomers, Flynn Robinson in particular, proved quite adept in the game of roundballs" during the team's first game two days earlier. George Clark, who played with Flynn at Elgin High, was a teammate at Casper also and was the leading rebounder (he later played three years for the Harlem Globetrotters). In CC's first three conference games in early 1961, Flynn averaged 35 points per game, including a 38-point game against McCook Nebr. College in Casper on Feb. 4. One has to wonder whether the thought occurred to any of the fans at McCook two weeks later when he scored 27 points, or at any of the other small towns where he played, that they might be looking at a future NBA all-star.

---

[43] Ron had told his wife Narvia during their marriage that while in Wyoming he had lost his Saratoga Springs High School graduation ring. More than fifty years later, four years after Ron's death, Narvia received a call from a woman at Saratoga Springs High School saying that Mary George, a secretary at the Hanna, Wyo., schools, had e-mailed to say the Hanna schools' "lost and found" box included a 1958 Saratoga Springs High class ring with the initials "RJB" etched inside. The only graduate with those initials was determined to be Ron Bostick, leading to the return of the ring to the family. Narvia was the daughter of Wilson Riles, the first African American elected to a statewide office in California and the first in the nation of his race to be elected as a state superintendent of schools. He upset far right incumbent Max Rafferty in 1970 and served in that position for three terms.

CURT JIMMERSON
"W" Club; Basketball letterman

The 1964 WYO yearbook's Who's Who on American Colleges page includes Curt Jimerson.

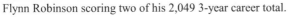

Flynn Robinson scoring two of his 2,049 3-year career total.

In May, 1961, the Star reported that Flynn was running in the sprints, the quarter mile and relays for the Casper College track team.

Flynn Robinson, #30, first attracted national attention at the end of 1962 when his shooting powered UW past Creighton (Flynn scored 27) and Oklahoma City to reach the finals of the All-College Tournament in Oklahoma City played on December 29. Wyoming, called the "cinderella club" of the tournament, was down only two points against the undefeated and highly-ranked Loyola of Chicago near the end, but the Ramblers pulled away and won the tournament title. Flynn was voted the most valuable player in the tournament.[44]

Flynn was the first of several African American stars from the Chicago-area to play for UW in the '60s, along with Randy Richardson of New York City. Flynn's scoring average per game for each of his three seasons still rank 1-2-3 in the UW record book, including a 27 ppg average in 1963-64. His highest-scoring night was 48 points at Arizona State in February, 1964.

Flynn played with four teams in the NBA and was selected to play in the NBA All-Star game in 1970. He was the sixth man for the 1972 Los Angeles Lakers championship team that won 33 games in a row during the regular season. Flynn gave Chick Hearn, the famous Lakers' radio voice, many opportunities to say, "He stops and pops from way out."

After he retired in LA, he sponsored fishing excursions for low-income kids. He and

Flynn Robinson, center, pictured in the Bay Area, Calif., on New Year's Eve 2006 with Curtis Jimerson and Curt's son Craig, left.

---

[44] Three months later, in March of 1963, Loyola was involved in a history-making game in the NCAA tournament at East Lansing, Mich., where the Ramblers were to play Southeast Conference champion Mississippi State. At the last moment, the President of Mississippi State announced that the school's (21 wins 5 losses) basketball team would compete in the NCAA tournament despite the state's "unwritten law" prohibiting state-supported schools from competing at events in which they possibly would meet integrated teams. That rule had prevented the Maroons, as they were known at the time, from competing in the tournament in 1959, '61 and '62. In reaction to the MSU president's statement, some members of the legislature threatened to cut off the state's appropriation to the school and an injunction was issued. The Bulldogs essentially snuck out of town and traveled to East Lansing, Mich., where they lost by 61-51 to the eventual national champion Loyola Ramblers, with four African American starters. Documentaries titled "One Night in March" and "Game of Change" have been made about this event. On December 15, 2012, nearly 50 years later, the two teams had their first rematch, this time in Chicago. Loyola prevailed again, 59-51, over the Bulldogs coached by Rick Ray, MSU's first black basketball coach. In December, 2013, Loyola made its first appearance in Mississippi and this time MSU prevailed by one point in overtime. The full story of Loyola's 62-63 season is told here: https://www.youtube.com/watch?v=nQhiMNKIFM0

Jimerson renewed their friendship and became close. Flynn died in May, 2013 at the age of 72.

Following him to UW were three top players from Thornton High in Harvey, Ill: Leon Clark (although only 6-6 he was twice the WAC's leading rebounder and still holds UW's career rebounds per game record), Reuben Poindexter and Harry Hall.

Leon Clark dribbling down
Sorority Row. 1966 WYO
Yearbook

1964: African American athletes at Northwest College

By 1964, even the small 2-year college in Powell, Northwest Junior College, was bringing in talented black basketball players. But this was a very difficult transition for them right from the beginning. On October 30, 1964, the young Powell Tribune editor, Dave Bonner, published an editorial reporting that two of these athletes were going home because of the racism they had encountered, including that "two barbershops in town won't cut Negroes' hair until after hours with the shades drawn for fear what it will do to their clientele." The athletes were returning to Indianapolis, according to Trappers' coach Hank Cabre, after being subjected to "dirty behind-the-hands comments wherever they appeared in public," the editorial said. "The Negro boys have no trouble on campus. These weren't unknowing juveniles who caused the trouble. These were ADULTS."

The editorial continued:

It's an unpleasant task to write what comes so hard, what shouldn't need to be written--an indictment of our own community. But there are things that must be told, things of which people should be made aware. ... Until the incensed of the community stand up and say, 'Hold on, we don't want to wear a black eye,' the stigma of hate and discrimination attached to the city will stick.

On Nov. 6th, the Powell paper reported that one of the players, freshman guard John Dowdell, had decided to return to NWCC "after encouragement from his high school coach and his parents." Cabre said Dowdell indicated he was appreciative of the scholarship offer and wanted to do the best he could to repay the school for it.

In that same issue a letter from Powell residents Harold and Bertha Newton appeared. They said they were "heartsick" at the treatment of these "really nice kids. ... They are not out burning haystacks that someone labored all summer to produce or in Shoshone Canyon tearing apart a picnic ground that we all enjoy. They are simply young men who are doing and giving their best to be better citizens."

On Nov. 10th, a page one editorial in the Tribune reported that the Powell Ministerial Association had conducted an investigation and determined that, although discrimination did exist among town businesses, it was "only in isolated, individual instances." Most businesses, they found, "embrace equality as a real philosophy."

On January 5, 1965, the Casper Tribune's sports columnist, Stan Bowker, reported that NWCC was leading the Mountain Plains Conference and that Dowdell was among the conference leaders in rebounding and free throw shooting.

Discrimination against black athletes in Wyoming colleges in the '60s was probably not too unusual, but the courage to condemn it in a highly public fashion, as the Powell editor did, was rare indeed.[45]

1958: APPEAL TO CHEYENNE - THE ATLAS MISSILE PROTESTS

Documentaries and books about the late 1950s inevitably portray the nuclear war fears that affected most Americans at that time. The films show children practicing getting under their desks after an air raid warning (as if that really offered any protection). Many citizens built and stocked fallout shelters in their houses or backyards.

But those living in southeast Wyoming at the end of the 1950s experienced the Cold War and the nuclear fears in a visible and personal way because, in late-1957, Cheyenne's Warren Air Force Base was chosen to become the nation's first operational Intercontinental Ballistic Missile (ICBM) base. This was an economic godsend to the city because the base was facing an impending shutdown. Fort D. A. Russell, the old cavalry post of the 1860s had previously been reborn as Fort Francis E. Warren in 1930 and then as an Army Quartermaster Corps training center, beginning in early 1941. The Cheyenne newspapers included numerous articles about the "cantonment", frequently mentioning the "colored troops" coming to Cheyenne. Separate facilities were built for the black troops, including a training center, chapel, guest house and service club. On May 20, 1941, the Wyoming State Tribune reported that "two dances have been held already. One dance was for the 1st and 2nd regiments of white selectees with girls being transported by the Army from the recreational center in the City. The other dance was presented for the 4th regiment of colored selectees. Their dates were brought to the club from Greeley and Denver, Colo."[46]

---

[45] In 1966-67, an African American player named John "J. J." Johnson of Milwaukee set scoring and rebounding records for Northwest Junior College in Powell and went on to do the same for Iowa, before becoming an All-Star player in the NBA for the Cleveland Cavs and Seattle Supersonics. In 1978-79 his Sonics team won the NBA championship. See the Powell Tribune 3/15/1968.

[46] Newspaper excerpts compiled in Robert Fred Gish's *Cheyenne, Wyoming 1940-1955*, published by the author, 2016. Fred Gish was the first of three brothers to star in basketball for Cheyenne High (Fred) and Central High (Ron and Dick). Fred then played for Bill Strannigan's Cowboys in Laramie. On Feb. 2, 1962, while lining up against the great Bill "The Hill" McGill of Utah, Gish set a school record with 22 rebounds. Hill led the NCAA in scoring that year with a 38.8 points per game average.

Soldiers who came through Cheyenne during WWII included Sammy Davis Jr. and thousands of other black soldiers, up to 2,400 at one time.[47]

The post became the nation's first U.S. Air Force Base in 1947, but, without an air field, its importance to the nation's defense was becoming questionable by the mid-50s. Then the base founded to "protect" railroad workers from Native Americans came to the forefront of the Cold War nuclear arms race with the U.S.S.R.

On June 7, 1958, Gen. Nathan Twining, chairman of the joint chiefs of staff, and other military brass joined Gov. Milward Simpson and U.S. Sen. Frank Barrett (R-Wyo.), for ground-breaking ceremonies at WAFB. "Why are we building this monster here?" Twining asked. "We want to protect our way of life and to help other people to live the way they want to." [48] The military, political and industrial group then moved to the Frontier Park Pavilion to answer questions for Cheyenne residents. The State Tribune reported that "a lone Cheyenne housewife, Mrs. Robert [Margaret] Laybourn, the mother of six children, picketed the Pavilion with a cardboard sandwich sign protesting the theory of nuclear and missile defense. 'There's no possible defense from it,' she said. 'I had to do something today to draw the attention of someone to the fact that we have to have peace.'" According to a 2015 interview with Mrs. Laybourn, the dignitaries entered through the side door because of her protest at the main door.

Construction on four widely-separated Atlas missile sites quickly got underway. The sites, each with six Atlas missile launching pads, were located amid private agricultural lands at a radius of about 20 miles from WAFB itself.

1958: Cheyenne greets protesters with hostility

Articles about the much-protested decision to locate the MX missile at Cheyenne in the early 1980s often stated that the Atlas missile sites had been constructed and triggered 20 years earlier without any opposition. This is not true.

In 1958, a 23-year-old University of Chicago history graduate student named Kenneth Calkins was among a small group of peace activists who came to Cheyenne, he said in a 2016 phone interview, "as an experiment on whether we could build a meaningful local movement against nuclear weapons at a place like Cheyenne." Calkins remembered that it didn't take long for their presence in town to provoke a response:

> We had permission to camp in a city park. During the night, some young guys
> came and started threatening us. These people were telling us "get out of here.
> What are you guys doing?" So we were confronted with an issue of non-violent
> resistance immediately in the middle of the night. I stood up in my underwear and

---

[47] According to his book *Yes I Can*, Davis suffered horrible experiences at the hands of white soldiers from the South during his time at the Cheyenne base. Davis Jr., billed as "The World's Greatest Entertainer", brought his musical show to UW's Fieldhouse on April 19, 1967. He must have mentioned his time with the Army in Cheyenne 25 years earlier. In a lively report by Henry Pacheco on April 21st, the Branding Iron quoted him as saying: "'Cheyenne ... How's the old swinging town? Wasn't much in 1944.... wasn't but two colored ladies in town'. He slaps on a slouchy cowboy hat and gun holster. He twirls." At the top of that BI page was a report about three UW students and a recent graduate being arrested for possession of marijuana and facing 2-5 years in prison. The headline read: "Cops pull narcotics raid."

[48] Wyoming State Tribune 6/9/1958, p. 1.

started talking to them, explaining what we were doing. Our conversation was impressive enough that they lost their interest in assaulting us and went away.

Ken Calkins talking to Air Force MP 1958

Calkins and his group organized a "meeting of meditation" attended by 10 opponents at an Atlas launch site northwest of WAFB. Calkins then released a statement to the press expressing his intention to walk on to the site and pass out leaflets asking workers to stop construction. He also said he would "stand in the road of the construction equipment" to prevent its operation and to draw attention to what he called the hopelessness of an armament race. The commander of the 706th Missile Wing stated that Calkins had been told he would not be admitted to the base again "since he has clearly indicated that his proposed visit would be contrary to the best interests of the U.S. government."

The protesters rented an apartment and for six weeks took their message to the city about nuclear weapons.

Protest moves to the missile site

The Wyoming State Tribune reported on August 11th that a group of 13 protesters had again gathered near the missile site for meditation on Aug. 9, the 13th anniversary of the atomic bomb drop on Nagasaki, Japan. They were disappointed that only one of the thirteen Cheyenne ministers had accepted their request to say something from the pulpit about the nuclear arms race. Their poll of 411 Cheyenne households showed only 15 percent were opposed to building the missile sites and none of the 15 percent was willing to join their "Appeal to Cheyenne".

In Cheyenne, "as in the South, most of the 'good people' kept quiet," two of the protesters wrote later in a report.

The group was led by Arthur Springer of Brooklyn, N.Y., a former member of the American Friends Service Committee (Quaker), and Theodore Olson, a Baptist minister from

Fallsington, Pa. The group included Calkins from Chicago, a typist from Philadelphia, a secretary and a school teacher from Illinois, an Iowa dairy farmer and others who were not named.

Kenneth Calkins' father had been a Methodist minister in Detroit and became the head of that church's ministers' pension fund in Chicago. His mother was regional secretary of the Fellowship of Reconciliation, a peace group founded in 1914. His 22-year-old wife Ellanor, a Swarthmore graduate, was a laboratory technician at the University of Chicago Medical School.

In the 2016 interview, Calkins said that the group's leaders had met with the Air Force officer in charge of the missile site, gave him the American Friends Service Committee pamphlet titled "Speak Truth to Power" to explain their motivations and expected that the Air Force would arrest them when they trespassed, resulting in a jail term. But the Air Force officers simply escorted them out of the site and then stood at the boundary to prevent them from re-entering.[49] So the protesters decided that a more direct non-violent action was necessary: blocking the road into the site. The Air Force, however, left the task of removing them from the road to the construction company drivers.

> There were a tense few hours when the drivers would drag me over to the side and then drive through. Some were rather rough about it. The next day Ted joined me. We started sitting down in the road. Ted had been preaching at the Air Force police. The tension mounted. One of the drivers kept coming closer and closer with a gigantic truck and he couldn't actually see down to the wheels where I was sitting. Instead of stopping as the others did, he slowly came up against me and started to crush my hip and I yelled out and my wife yelled out and the driver stopped. Otherwise I would have been killed. My injury resulted in widespread publicity about our protest which would not have happened otherwise.

Calkins was taken to a Cheyenne hospital by the Doolittle Construction Co. ambulance and was hospitalized for 10 days. Upon his release he was arrested and taken to the Laramie County Jail, where the effects of his injury became more pronounced. But he believes he suffered no permanent effects from the incident.

News articles at the time reported Calkins had suffered a "crushed pelvis". Calkins was quoted as saying he and Ellanor were "just doing this as our duty to our consciences." He hoped their non-violent resistance would invite others to oppose "weapons that kill millions of people."

The Tribune on Aug. 19th reported that Justice of the Peace Tosh Suyematsu (a decorated WWII hero. See the Tosh Suyematsu chapter at pg. 159) had issued a warrant for the arrest of Olson and Kenneth and Ellanor Calkins who had blocked the entrance to the site. B. D. Ward, project manager for Doolittle Construction Co. of Wichita, was the complainant. Sheriff N. E. Tuck said he would arrest the three as soon as possible and they would be booked and jailed on trespass charges. Ward told the Tribune that Calkins "tried to hold my car back and hung onto the fender for a little ways." Ward expressed fear one of the drivers for his firm might fail to halt his vehicle for the three pacifists, despite orders not to harm them.

On August 21st, newspapers across the West carried an AP article quoting Deputy County Attorney Lou Mankus as saying during the hearing: "We shall arrest them again and

---

[49] An AP wirephoto in the Casper Star on 8/19/1958 shows Kenneth and Ellanor talking to an Air Force policeman alongside an article about their ejection from the site.

again and again. ... My pity for your perverted ideas is exceeded only by my duty to enforce the law."[50]

An AP article published August 29, 1958, said the protesters had been ridiculed and heckled by Cheyenne residents. Kenneth Calkins said the protest was patterned after the non-violent resistance program of Mohandas Gandhi in India.

A *Wyoming Eagle* editorial on Sept. 10th praised the citizenry for not subjecting the protesters to violence. "Cheyenne and air force law enforcement officials ... have been patient beyond all reasonable expectation; that all concerned have met the unreasonable requests of this misguided group with calm words rather than violent action is a fine display of self-control."

According to a 1986 article in "The Progressive" by Samuel H. Day Jr., based on interviews with Calkins and several others who participated in the Appeal to Cheyenne, the construction superintendents became frustrated having to pull the protesters out of the way and yelled "'come on ahead-they're just bluffing'. One driver stepped on the gas and then slammed on the brakes, his front bumper coming to a stop just inches from Olson's nose. The two pacifists did not move."[51]

Ellanor said she believed it was a Western Concrete of Denver truck which struck her husband. The Progressive article says that the driver had twice stopped short of Calkins but was commanded to move forward again. "A cry of pain was followed by stunned silence. The truck's right front wheel had come to rest against Calkins' hip, crushing his left pelvis. 'Can't you see you've run over him!', cried Ellanor Calkins."

The ambulance that took Kenneth and Ellanor to the Cheyenne hospital passed Sheriff Tuck headed toward the site, where he arrested Olson and Springer. When Ellanor appeared at the hearing the next day, she was arrested.

On August 20, 1958, Olson, 26, and Ellanor Calkins pleaded guilty to trespassing and were fined $100 each and court costs by Justice of the Peace Suyematsu. The judge also fined Olson $20 and sentenced him to two days in jail for contempt of court when he said he would continue his resistance action. Arthur Springer pleaded not guilty and a bond of $350 was set.

The Rev. Dr. Charles Calkins, secretary of the board of pensions of the Methodist Church in Chicago, appeared at the hearing on behalf of Ellanor. "My son and daughter-in-law are on a mission of conscience," he said. "They have developed a desire to resist what they believe to be a great wrong. They do not want to avoid any penalty. They were willing to undertake the consequences. It was a deliberate choice of religious belief."

---

[50] Arizona Daily Star, August 21, 1958. In 1982-3, Mankus was a vocal supporter of bringing the MX missile to Cheyenne. Sister Frances Russell, who founded and operated a shelter for homeless women in Cheyenne and was a leader of the MX opposition, was named "Social Worker of the Year" by the National Association of Social Workers in 1983. Mankus and State Tribune Editor James Flinchum attacked her and the award. See Washington Post, 11/27/1983 (available on-line) and Casper Star-Tribune 5/29 and 11/3/1985 (which has a photo of Russell).

[51] *The Progressive*, 1986/08 -"Showdown at Cheyenne", ppg. 19-20. Samuel H. Day was editor of the Boise-based *Intermountain Observer* from 1964-74 and later edited *The Progressive*, a peace and social justice magazine in Madison, Wisc. In 1980 he joined an American Friends Service Committee organization opposing nuclear weapons. In 1988 he was convicted of trespassing on missile silos in Missouri and served six months in federal prison. He died in 2001.

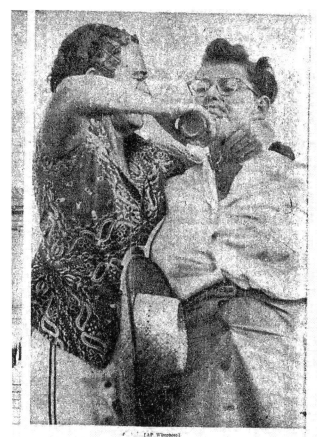

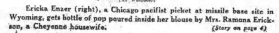

Ericka Enzer (right), a Chicago pacifist picket at missile base site in Wyoming, gets bottle of pop poured inside her blouse by Mrs. Ramona Erickson, a Cheyenne housewife.　(Story on page 4).

2017-Ken Calkins at age 84

On Aug. 22nd, the Tribune reported that an Omaha company's bid of $2.151 million was apparently the low bid for providing six power generators for the first of the four Atlas sites. (An amount equal to nearly $18 million in buying power in 2016 when adjusted by the CPI).

On that same day, several protesters carrying signs marched at the county jail where Elleanor Calkins and Olson were being held in lieu of paying their $100+ fines. One of the signs said the protesters were not communists or fanatics. "They believe the missile race must be stopped to save mankind. They believe we are losing the struggle with totalitarianism because we have been dominated by faith in violence." Kenneth was still in Laramie County Memorial Hospital. When the picketing started, the jail was placed on lock-down, which meant that no visitors were allowed for any of the prisoners. So the protesters moved their demonstration away from the courthouse block.

Two other demonstrators – Erica Enzer and John White – were arrested later after repeatedly attempting to enter Site A. On August 30th, a Denver Post photo that appeared in newspapers around the country showed a confrontation at the missile site. The cutline said: "Mrs. Ramona Erickson, a Cheyenne housewife, angry at pacifist demonstrator Erica Enzer, 32, ... angrily pours soda pop down the blouse of Miss Enzer. Mrs. Erickson first berated her, then tried to force her to drink pop. When the Chicago woman refused, the Cheyenne housewife held her and poured it down her blouse."[52] According to an article in the Cheyenne Eagle by Chuck Graves, who 11 years later as a Cheyenne attorney would represent the Black 14 in their lawsuit, Erickson told Enzer "you ought to be sent to Russia where you belong." This incident prompted County Attorney Walter Phelan to issue a statement cautioning the public that "it was unnecessary" for them to interfere with the demonstrations at the site and that any such action constituting a breach of the peace by either the protesters or those objecting to the protest would be prosecuted. But Erickson apparently was not charged.

On Aug. 29 Calkins also was fined $100 after a guilty plea to trespassing. The Associated Press report appeared in newspapers across the country on Aug. 30. The Spokane newspaper's headline read: "Tongue Lashing Given Pacifist", and quoted Suyematsu as telling Calkins: "You are attempting to force the rest of the nation to accept your infantile views through exhibitionistic blackmail. Your act was done knowingly and with deliberate planning--without consideration for others." During his jail time, Calkins received, in absentia, a master's degree in history from the University of Chicago. He was in the county jail until Sept. 18th when he paid the remaining amount of his fine. Olson continued serving out his fine at $1/day.

Calkins, who had a bachelor's degree from Haverford College --founded by the Quakers in 1833 near Philadelphia -- received less welcome news while in the jail. The Evanston, Ill., draft board had previously approved his application for conscientious objector status. But when they read of his protest at Cheyenne, the draft board sent him a notice saying he had been re-classified as 1-A, Calkins recalled in a 2016 interview with the author. "I appealed that, and the officer who heard the appeal agreed that it was nonsensical to say that someone injured and jailed in a demonstration against nuclear weapons was not serious about his conscientious objections."

By September 4th, the jailed protesters had been replaced by a Quaker housewife from Palo Alto and four men from San Francisco who engaged in "a silent moral protest" at the missile site 20 miles northwest of Cheyenne but did not trespass onto private land.[53]

As Randall Kehler would do 11 years later (See Kehler chapter at pg. 147 where Haverford College is also mentioned), the missile protesters became jail reform advocates. Calkins recalled the events this way:

> It was a big shock when we learned we were not permitted to read anything in the jail. We weren't allowed to have any reading material, even a Bible. We had supporters outside and they got some of the Cheyenne ministers to take up the Bible issue and eventually the sheriff relented as to Bibles, to begin with, and then other materials. We also helped some people who had never been charged with anything to get out of jail because we were able to hire an attorney for them.

---

[52] E.g., AP report and photo on Page 1 of the Huntsville (Ala.) Times, August 29, 1958. In 1958, Wyoming Statute 6-68 said: "Whoever, in a rude, insolent or angry manner, unlawfully touches another, is guilty of an assault and battery" punishable by up to six months in jail. But there is no evidence Mrs. Erickson was arrested. Ms. Enzer, however, was arrested and jailed for trespassing. She also participated in the Omaha missile protests a year later. Thirty years later, Ms. Enzer was still concerned about war. The Ukiah (Calif.) Journal on New Year's Eve in 1989 carried a photo of Enzer within a compilation of local citizens' new year resolutions. "I want to do more for peace," Ms. Enzer was quoted as saying. "I'm going to try to resist taxes for war as much as I can, even though the IRS is now garnisheeing my wages for nonpayment of taxes, leaving only $325 per month to live on, which isn't enough."

[53] Casper Star, 9/5/1958 p. 22.

On September 11, 1958, Lawrence Scott, coordinator for the Committee of Non Violent Action Against Nuclear Weapons, announced that Atlas demonstrations were being discontinued. A UPI article in the Casper Star the next morning said six protesters, including Erica Enzer, had been arrested since the protest began in June.

"The Appeal to Cheyenne was one of the earliest attempts in this country to confront the budding nuclear arms buildup with nonviolent direct action at the scene," the *Progressive* article says.[54]

On Memorial Day 1960, at least 10 "peace marchers" walked from Greeley, Colo., to an Atlas site west of that town carrying signs saying "Help UN disarm all" and "No Memorial After Missiles." The group included Jim Murphy, Cheyenne High swim coach and a Methodist Sunday School teacher, along with the "Peace Pilgrim", Mildred Lisette Norman, who walked around the U.S. for 28 years bringing her peace message to groups, media interviews and one-on-one. She never had much money on her person and depended upon peace advocates like Mignon Hill and Matilda Hansen in Laramie and Margaret Laybourn in Cheyenne to give her food and a place to sleep when she came through Wyoming. She died in 1981 in Indiana while on her seventh cross-country pilgrimage at the age of 72.[55]

1959: Calkins takes protest to Omaha

In 1959, Calkins continued his peace work. In a Lincoln (Nebr.) Journal article published June 23rd, Calkins was identified as one of the marchers on their way to a protest at a missile site at Mead, near Omaha. "I was there when the long-time peace activist, A. J. Muste [74 years old at the time], climbed over the fence at the missile site and was arrested, along with the Catholic Worker's Karl Meyer," Calkins recalled.[56] Muste, Meyer and others were fined $500 and placed on one-year probation by a federal court judge.

---

[54] In 1983, Mrs. Laybourn also protested the proposed "dense pack" (eventually called "dunce pack") MX missile siting plan based at Cheyenne. At a scoping hearing in Cheyenne on Feb. 5th she told the Air Force, "With the super hardening of the silos, wouldn't it be wonderful if we could super harden Cheyenne." AP article in Rapid City Journal 2/6/1983, p. 8. The Air Force's choice of the person to make the announcement that Cheyenne had been selected had a name full of irony: Col. Tom Holycross. On August 12, 1984, Margaret joined a protest march to a silo south of Scottsbluff. An AP article in the Lincoln Star the next day said she described the horrors seen by her husband, Robert Laybourn Sr., one of the first Marines to enter Nagasaki after the atomic bomb devastated that city. In March 1985, Mrs. Laybourn was among protesters at the Capitol Building in Cheyenne challenging a proposal in Congress to fund 21 more MX missiles. "It is not patriotic to have a weapons system that puts the people in danger," she said. Rapid City Journal, 3/17/1985 p. 2. In 2001, when the Air Force announced plans to retire the missile as a cost-saving measure, 78-year-old Mrs. Laybourn said she was "happy to get them out. Living in Bulls-eye Wyoming is no fun." New York Times report in Indianapolis Star 7/22/2001 p. 13. At one of these protests she carried a sign saying: "Mankind must put an end to war before war puts an end to mankind," a phrase used by JFK in a U.N. address 9/25/1961.

[55] Documentaries about the Peace Pilgrim can be accessed through peacepilgrim.org/free-offerings

[56] Meyer's father William Meyer was, at the time, Vermont's sole representative in Congress. In 1958, Meyer had become the first Democrat to have been successful in a Vermont statewide election since the Republican party had been founded more than 100 years earlier. Rep. Meyer was sympathetic to his son's actions. A syndicated column appearing in the Freeport, Ill., newspaper in July, 1959, said that "at times [Rep. Meyer] is overcome by something like despair as he confronts what he fears is an inevitable drift toward nuclear war." Meyer was unseated in his bid for re-election in 1960.

Calkins also helped to organize a Student Peace Union headquartered at Chicago which eventually spread to many campuses. Sen. Bernie Sanders, who ran against Hillary Clinton in the 2016 Democratic presidential primaries and spoke at the UW Arts & Sciences auditorium, joined the Student Peace Union when he studied at the University of Chicago.

Some years later Calkins returned to the Univ. of Chicago for a Ph.D., and shortly after becoming a professor at Kent State in 1967 he participated in his first protest against the Vietnam war. He published a book on Hugo Haase, a German socialist politician and pacifist in the years before WWI.

After President Nixon sent American troops into Cambodia on April 30, 1970, provoking protests on campuses nationwide, Calkins and other Kent State faculty issued a statement objecting to the sending of National Guard troops to their campus and to statements made May 2nd at a Kent press conference by Ohio Gov. James Rhodes about the anti-war protesters. Rhodes said: "They're worse than the Brownshirts and the Communist elements and also the Night Riders and Vigilantes. They're the worst type of people we harbor in America."

The faculty members' statement, Calkins recalled in a memoir 10 years later, "appeared to have no effect at all except to provide yet another excuse for the exponents of 'law and order' to castigate the subversive element among the professoriate."[57]

Calkins was present wearing a blue arm band as a faculty marshal on May 4th when the Ohio National Guard opened fire, killing four students (one of them an ROTC student just walking to class), and injuring nine, including Dean Kahler who was paralyzed for life. Only two of the four students killed were actively participating in the anti-war rally. A stunned Calkins walked among students facing-off opposite the troops and "did my best to persuade the students to get up and leave in fear that the Guard would unleash still another deadly volley."

Later that day, Calkins placed a sign in his yard saying "Don't send a murderer to the Senate," a reference to Gov. Rhodes who was running for the U.S. Senate. Two days after the killings Rhodes lost in the Republican primary to U.S. Rep. Robert Taft Jr.

In a memo, FBI Director J. Edgar Hoover wrote that "the students invited and got what they deserved." Vietnam veteran Robert Gabriel, a Guard helicopter pilot over KSU that day, said in an interview: "I suppose I thought that the shootings were a good thing, because they stopped everything right there. .. That took the hot air right out of the radical stuff in the nation."[58] A Gallup poll showed 58% of the American people placed the blame for the killings on the demonstrating students.

But the President's Commission on Campus Unrest concluded that "the indiscriminate firing of rifles into a crowd of students [was] unnecessary, unwarranted and inexcusable." In his book *The Ends of Power*, H. R. Haldeman, one of Nixon's inner circle at the White House, said the Kent State shootings initiated the slide into Watergate, eventually destroying the Nixon administration.[59]

Calkins and two other faculty members submitted "An Analysis of the Ohio Special Grand Jury Report" to the Faculty Senate in January, 1971, questioning many of the grand jury's

---

[57] Bills, Scott L. (Ed.), *Kent State/May 4: Echoes Through a Decade*, Kent State Press 1982, p. 104.

[58] *Id.* at 24.

[59] Lewis, Jerry M. and Thomas R. Hensley, "The May 4 shootings at Kent State: The Search for Historical Accuracy," Ohio Council for Social Studies Review, Vol. 34, No. 1 (Summer 1998), pp. 9-21 (http://www.kent.edu/may-4-historical-accuracy).

statements and alleging the grand jury ignored "the right of peaceful dissent and the nature of protest assemblies" and didn't even mention the governor's inflammatory remarks.[60]

Ten days after the KSU shootings, two black students were killed by police gunfire at Jackson State in Mississippi. At Kent State, the killings at both schools are always remembered jointly.[61]

WAFB: "Peace Is Our Profession"

As the 50s came to a close and the '60s began, attention shifted to the civil rights movement in the South and eventually to the Vietnam War. A long UPI article in the Cheyenne Eagle on July 10, 1959, datelined San Francisco, said some in the younger generation were seeking satori -- "a cataclysmic flash of inner truth" -- through Zen Buddhism. The article quoted poet Gary Snyder, 28, as saying "the Beat Generation was part of a nationwide need, even thirst, of some people to get away from arbitrary, self-centered thinking where the emphasis is on material things and prestige. The interest in Zen also is a symptom of getting away from such unproductive and even destructive attitudes." He said Zen was catching on in San Francisco because "there is a strong pacifist and anarchistic intelligentsia here."

Meanwhile, a welcoming attitude by Cheyenne and state leaders during the quarter-century after Calkins' protest was rewarded by Washington with three generations of ICBMs, each more deadly than the predecessor. As the Atlas missile sites were being built, the Army announced on Sept. 6, 1958, it was considering placing the Nike surface-to-air missile at Cheyenne. That did not come to fruition. But almost as soon as the Atlas sites were completed they were already considered too vulnerable and the Air Force moved to the Minuteman program in which 200 missiles were placed in silos in Nebraska, Colorado and Wyoming. This complex "will have a destructive capability exceeding the total of all high-explosive bombs touched off by all participants in World War II" and "will eventually have the potential of destroying a good part of the world," a March 13, 1963 Associated Press report said.[62]

---

[60] On-line from the Kent State Library's special collections.

[61] Bills, *Kent State / May 4, supra* at 25.

[62] Riverton Ranger, 3/13/1963.

1958-Air Force hosted junior high student leaders on a tour of WAFB. Future UW basketball star Dick Sherman is 4th from left. The author is 5th from left. Karen Ready, on the left, graduated from the University of Wyoming with a master's degree in sociology. Under her married name of Karen Reinertson, she served Colorado governors Romer and Owens in cabinet-level positions and in 2005 became President of Front Range Community College in Denver.

The first 10-warhead MX missile became operational not far from Atlas Site A in 1986. The MXes were placed at Cheyenne largely because of political rather than logistical reasons. Wyoming's Republican congressional delegation and Democratic governor supported it. "The political climate has been very friendly out here," the Air Force's "Peacekeeper" liaison in Cheyenne said.[63] In 1982-83 Lou Mankus, the prosecutor of the 1958 protesters in Cheyenne, and Tribune editor James Flinchum blasted the people opposing the MX. In an editorial Nov. 19, 1982, for example, Flinchum proclaimed that MX opposition by the Wyoming Episcopal and Catholic bishops "threatens to perform good works for the devil."

Each independently-targetable warhead was a 300-kiloton bomb, 20 times stronger than the Hiroshima bomb. The MX missiles were "retired" in 2005, but WAFB remains the headquarters for 150 Minuteman missiles still deployed in the farmlands of the tri-state area.

During the MX missile debate, one Cheyenne resident explained his lack of concern about living in what could be called the nuclear weapons capital of the free world this way: "If it happens, I'd rather be at ground zero."

---

[63] Hartford Courant article carried in Billings Gazette 7/8/1984.

Kenneth Calkins returned to Cheyenne in 2015, but his visit was not connected to the events of 1958. His older brother Charles, a Duke forestry graduate, had worked in the West for the U.S. Forest Service and other agencies. He retired in Cheyenne, where he died in September, 2015.

In around 2000, trichloroethylene, a chemical used to clean missile launchers at the old Atlas sites, was found in alarming concentrations in the groundwater near a site 20 miles east of Cheyenne. Through an extensive drilling operation, the Army Corps of Engineers found plumes of TCE extending up to 10 miles from the Atlas site. In 2016, groundwater samples from below the site found concentrations of 240,000 parts per billion (up to five ppb is considered safe for human consumption). Remediation efforts could cost tens of millions of dollars and take more than 100 years to complete, the Corps reported.

1958: ERNIE RUDOLPH AND ART RENNEISEN OF CHEYENNE

Only a few days after the events at the Atlas missile site in 1958, Cheyenne dedicated its new high school football field down the hill from where the new East High School was being built. It was called "Memorial Stadium" until the early 70s when it was renamed "Okie Blanchard Stadium" in honor of the long-time Cheyenne High football and basketball coach and athletic director (he also was head football coach at UW for one year).

In the first game played in the $190,000 stadium, on Friday night September 12, 1958, Cheyenne High defeated Craig, Colo., 27-6. Ernie Rudolph, an African American halfback for the Indians, scored the first touchdown in the stadium. Future UW basketball player Fred Gish, and Gene Bryan, future Laramie Boomerang editor and director of the Wyoming Travel Commission, played for CHS before a crowd of 5,000, the largest throng ever to watch a high school football game in Cheyenne.

The newspaper carried a multi-page special article about the new stadium's dedication and local football teams. One of the players shown in a photo of the McCormick Junior High football team was Art Renneisen. After graduation, Renneisen studied pre-med at Wyoming until deciding to enlist and fulfill a duty he felt to serve his country. He enlisted just as the Vietnam War was ramping up and eventually served three tours as a medic for the Army's 1st Infantry Division (the "Big Red One") in that war. Art died in Cheyenne at 48 years of age on April 7, 1992, from Non-Hodgkins lymphoma arising from severe exposure to Agent Orange. Two days later, Vietnam War supporter, former Sen. Gale McGee (D-Wyo.), died in Bethesda, Md., at the age of 77.

During the days leading up to the Cheyenne High game, civil rights battles were being described almost every day in Cheyenne's *Wyoming Eagle*. In Alexandria, Va., on Sept. 2nd the county school board claimed before a federal judge that the application of 30 black students to attend white schools had been rejected for reasons other than race.[64] (Not a credible claim. Some public school districts in Virginia eventually closed their public schools altogether rather than permit any black students to attend. The white students then went to all-white private schools).

---

[64] This is four years after the U.S. Supreme Court's landmark decision in *Brown v. Board of Education of Topeka*, 347 U.S. 483 (1954) in which the court rejected its 1896 ruling that segregated schools which were separate but equal did not violate the Constitution. In the unanimous *Brown* decision, the court said racially separate schools were inherently unequal.

On Sept. 5, a UPI report said the U.S. Justice Department was seeking an injunction against the Terrell County, Georgia, voting registrars to bar them from preventing qualified African Americans from voting. One of the blacks turned away had bachelor's and master's degrees from NYU. He and several other teachers had been refused registration because of alleged inability to write correctly and legibly.

The bold headline on page one of the Sept. 13th edition of the Eagle read: "GOV. FAUBUS CLOSES LITTLE ROCK SCHOOLS." Faubus shut all of the high schools in the city in defiance of a U.S. Supreme Court ruling that Little Rock's Central High was to be opened that Monday with black students admitted.

1960: DAWNING OF A NEW DECADE

January 1960	Sen. John F. Kennedy announces candidacy for presidency. American population is 179 million. (324 million as of Jan. 1 2017)
February 1960	African American students stage first lunch counter sit-in at Woolworth's in Greensboro, N.C.
March 1960	Elvis Presley's two-year Army hitch ends
May 1960	Russia shoots down Francis Gary Powers' U-2 spy plane over Sverdlovsk, ending what seemed to be a warming of relations between the two countries spawned by Chairman Nikita Khrushchev's two-week tour of the U.S. in Sept. 1959 (even though he was upset a planned visit to Disneyland was canceled for alleged security reasons) Pulitzer prize awarded to Allen Drury's *Advise and Consent*, based on the suicide of Wyoming governor and U.S. Senator Lester C. Hunt in 1954
September 1960	Denver University students "kidnap" UW's Shetland pony mascot Cowboy Joe prior to the football game between the schools. The governors of Wyoming and Colorado exchanged telegrams about the situation. The pinto pony was the first in a series of five Cowboy Joes which have been donated to UW by the Farthing Ranch northwest of Cheyenne, beginning in fall 1950.
October 1960	Soviet Premier Khrushchev banged his fists and perhaps a shoe on his desk at the United Nations in protest of a speech by a Philippine delegate.
January 1961	Ham the Astrochimp, essentially a baby at age 3 ½, was rocketed into space from Cape Canaveral and traveled through 6 ½ minutes of weightlessness before splashing down 130 miles from the target. He was rescued after several hours and lived for 22 years at American zoos.

1960-1963: JFK AND WYOMING

I hope that all of you who are students here will recognize the great opportunity that lies before you in this decade, and in the decades to come, to be of service to our country. The Greeks once defined happiness as full use of your powers along lines of excellence, and I can assure you that there is no area of life where you will have an opportunity to use whatever powers you have, and to use them along more excellent lines, bringing ultimately, I think, happiness to you and those whom you serve.
President John F. Kennedy, University of Wyoming, September 25, 1963.

1960: Vinich and Wyoming put JFK over the top

As he made his stops in Wyoming on his western tour in 1963, one has to wonder whether President Kennedy was recalling Wyoming's decisive role in his selection as the Democratic nominee for president in 1960. According to an article by Phil Roberts in *Buffalo Bones*, Kennedy's hopes for defeating Sen. Lyndon Johnson of Texas for the nomination would have been seriously harmed if he failed to win enough votes on the first ballot. Only 10 ½ of the Wyoming delegation's 15 votes were pledged to JFK, but he needed 14 votes to capture the nomination when Wyoming's name was called.

One of JFK's Wyoming delegates was Hudson's Mike Vinich. On November 2, 1943, Marine Platoon Sgt. Vinich and 40 other Marines were ambushed on Choiseul Island in the South Pacific. They were vastly outnumbered by Japanese forces. Vinich climbed aboard Navy PT-59 which had been sent to rescue the men. That vessel was commanded by Lt. John F. Kennedy. (His PT-109 had been cut in half by a Japanese destroyer two months earlier). Vinich was later injured in combat on Iwo Jima.[65]

At the 1960 state Democratic convention in Thermopolis, Vinich told an AP reporter: "I owe the guy my life. Certainly I'm morally obligated to vote for him." On May 19, 1962, Vinich was a guest at a celebration of JFK's upcoming 45th birthday held at the third Madison Square Garden in New York. Marilyn Monroe sang "Happy Birthday Mr. President." She died two months later.

Phil Roberts has described the action at the convention this way:

Tracy McCracken, Cheyenne newspaperman and UW trustee, was state Democratic chairman and leader of the Wyoming delegation. Ted Kennedy, the nominee's youngest brother (and, later, long-time U. S. Senator from Massachusetts), was standing in the Wyoming delegation. The convention chairman called out, "Wyoming....15 votes." Without polling the delegation, McCraken shouted into the microphone, "Wyoming casts all 15 of its votes for the next President of the United States...." Johnson partisans tried to grab the mike,

---

[65] See Christine Peterson's article, Casper Star-Tribune, July 6, 2010 (available on-line). In November, 2013, Vinich appeared with Kathy Karpan of Cheyenne and Dan Nelson of Laramie on a Wyoming PBS program recalling JFK on the 50th anniversary of his death. Vinich died just over two years later at the age of 91. Casper Star 11/20/2015.

but it was too late. The balloons were falling, the bands were playing, and the Democrats had their 1960 nominee.

Mike Vinich with Kathy Karpan at the Wyoming PBS studios in Riverton in 2013. They were panelists on a memoir of JFK's visit to Wyoming in 1963. Photo by author.

During the campaign, Sen. John F. Kennedy spoke at Frontier Park in Cheyenne on Sept. 23, 1960, and recognized Wyoming's contribution to his nomination:

> I know that Wyoming is a small state, relatively, but it is a fact that Wyoming, which was not talked about as a key state in the days before the convention, when they were talking about what California and what Pennsylvania and what New York and Illinois would do at the convention, not very many people talked about what Wyoming would do, and yet, as you know, Wyoming did it.

1963: JFK visits the U.S. Naval Academy

On Aug. 1, 1963, President Kennedy paid a brief visit to the Naval Academy at Annapolis and greeted the freshman class who were in the midst of "Plebe Summer", prior to the arrival of the upper classes. Three of those midshipmen were from Cheyenne: Don Hefkin of Central High, Gary Wasson of East (Class of '62) and Bob Hanscum of St. Mary's (who transferred to the University of Wyoming at some point and was elected president of the student body). No one

45

present could have imagined that one statement Kennedy made toward the end of his remarks would become manifested tragically all too soon: "So I express our very best wishes to you and tell you that though you will be serving in the Navy in days when most of those who hold public office have long gone from it ...."

Although he didn't mention it in his remarks, Kennedy's visit to the USNA must have been in recognition of the 20th anniversary of the harrowing ordeal visited upon him and his crew when a Japanese destroyer rammed JFK's PT-109 in the Solomon Islands.

At a later date, when asked to explain how he had come to be a war hero, Kennedy replied with his usual wit, "It was easy. They cut my PT boat in half."

1963: August: Kathi Hill at Girls' Nation

On July 26, 1963, two seniors-to-be at Wyoming high schools left Cheyenne by train for the American Legion's Girls' Nation in Washington D.C. Kathi Hill of Cheyenne Central and Karla Baston of Rock Springs met up with 35 other delegates in Chicago's Union Station. They arrived on Sunday the 28th and took up residence for the week at a dorm of American University.

Kathi had been elected as Governor at the Girls' State in Wyoming and had her hopes pinned on meeting President Kennedy in D.C. One sure way to make that happen would be to win election as President of Girls' Nation. But Kathi knew that would be a difficult objective for a girl from Wyoming. So she cagily opted to seek the office of press secretary to the Girls' Nation president, which worked out beyond her wildest dream. Winning that post allowed her to meet President Kennedy's press secretary, Pierre Salinger, on Friday, Aug. 2, after all 100 delegates had been greeted as a group by the president in the Rose Garden. Salinger showed Hill around the White House and then took her to the president's office where she met JFK's secretary, Evelyn Lincoln. Salinger told her to wait there and she might have a surprise in store.

At that time, First Lady Jackie Kennedy was vacationing at Hyannis Port, Mass., and was in the latter stages of a pregnancy. The Kennedy clan gathered that afternoon at the president's office and Kathi Hill not only shook hands with JFK but also met his brothers Bob and Ted Kennedy and his brothers-in-law Peter Lawford and Sergeant Shriver. She saw the group leave the White House in two helicopters enroute to Cape Cod.

Five days later, Jackie gave birth by caesarean section to Patrick Bouvier Kennedy. He was five and one-half weeks premature and weighed only four pounds 10 ounces. Although doctors at first pronounced him to be in good condition, the infant died 39 hours later of a respiratory problem. Salinger announced that "the struggle of the baby to keep breathing was too much for his heart."

Kathi Hill became involved as a volunteer in Teno Roncalio's successful run for U.S. Representative in the fall of 1964 and then joined his staff in D.C. When Teno ran for the Senate two years later and lost, Hill stayed in Washington and worked for the government security contractor Booz, Allen & Hamilton (which later employed classified documents leaker Edward Snowden for a short time). Through her work there and some classes on computer programming (she was the only woman) at a community college, Kathi developed computer literacy very early and landed a United Nations job in Geneva, Switzerland. She worked for 30 years at the U.N. European Center with the International Labor Office. She retired to a family property at Eaton, Colo.

Kathi Hill is standing behind U.S. Rep. Teno Roncalio in this 1966 staff photo taken in Washington D.C. On Teno's left is Kathy Karpan, future Wyoming Secretary of State, and on his right is Cathryn Chambers Rikard from Lander. From left in the back row is future Wyoming district judge Dan Spangler of Cody, Joanie Halderman, Hill, Terri Haddad and Bill Bagley of Afton, later a long-time attorney in Cheyenne. On Oct. 25, 1966, Bagley, Karpan and Rikard were driving to Casper for a Democratic rally featuring Sen. Robert F. Kennedy when the driver of a pickup swerved into their lane and collided with their vehicle, sending all three to the hospital.

1963: September: JFK visits UW

On June 21, 1963, the Casper Star carried a front page Associated Press article in which Republican Superintendent of Public Instruction Dr. Cecil Shaw said President Kennedy's plans to improve educational opportunities for minorities was "frightening" and a direct step to federal control of education. Shaw said he did not think racial discrimination was a problem in Wyoming. Shaw claimed Kennedy was encouraging racial violence by telling people it will come unless civil rights are guaranteed.

Presumably Shaw was not pleased about the news that broke three months later as the Class of 1963's freshmen registered for classes at the University of Wyoming (a record 5,137 students eventually enrolled). The town was abuzz with word that President John F. Kennedy would be making a swing through Western states that would include three stops in Wyoming on September 25-26, including a visit to the campus.

The articles said JFK would fly into Cheyenne on Air Force One, board a smaller airplane to fly over to Laramie for a speech, then on to Billings for another speech and finally back into Wyoming for a night in the shadow of the Grand Tetons.

Soon after the announcement, men who were assumed to be Secret Service advance agents were seen all over the UW campus. Even so, the president's advance team had no compunction about releasing a map of JFK's route from the airport to the UW Fieldhouse and back, which the Laramie newspaper published on page one.

Short articles about Vietnam appeared on the front page of the Laramie Daily Boomerang on both Sept. 15 and 18. The front page on the 18th portended the struggles that would dominate the news for the next 10 years. "Viet Nam Forces Kill 122 As Lodge Visits Delta" was one of the headlines, referring to U.S. Ambassador to Vietnam Henry Cabot Lodge. Who could have predicted that the Mekong Delta would soon become a frequent news location on American front pages?

An article headlined "Bomb Victim 'Heroine'" told of the funeral in Birmingham, Ala. of 14-year-old Carol Robertson, one of four black girls killed in the 16th Street Baptist Church bombing while they attended Sunday School two days earlier. The bombing was most likely in retaliation for President Kennedy's action a few days before by which he federalized Alabama National Guard troops and served Gov. George Wallace with a federal court order enjoining him from interfering with the integration of public schools in Birmingham. That retaliation was undoubtedly stoked when, a week before the bombing, Gov. Wallace was quoted in the New York Times as saying that Alabama needed " a few first-class funerals" to derail integration.[66]

In a UPI article by White House correspondent Merriman Smith, President Kennedy voiced "outrage and grief" over the bombing and expressed hope the tragedy would awaken the entire nation "to a realization of the folly of racial injustice. It is regrettable that public disparagement of law and order has encouraged violence which has fallen on the innocent," Kennedy said, an indirect reference to Wallace.

The Boomerang's top story was about the public accommodations section of Kennedy's civil rights bill being considered in a congressional subcommittee, a provision that would outlaw racial discrimination by hotels, restaurants, theaters, stores and so forth. It would take the killing of Kennedy before the bill was passed by Congress, in 1964.

Kennedy was also dealing with the Cold War that month. A few days before JFK came to UW, he met with a delegation from the Soviet Union, including Foreign Minister Andrei Gromyko. He told them:

I would say to the leaders of the Soviet Union, and to their people, that if either of our countries is to be fully secure, we need a much better weapon than the H-bomb – a weapon better than ballistic missiles or nuclear submarines – and that better weapon is peaceful cooperation.

Kennedy's four-day, 11-state trip was formed around the theme of conservation of natural resources. He first stopped at Milford in northeast Pennsylvania where he attended the dedication of the ancestral home of Gifford Pinchot, first director of the U.S. Forest Service, as a national center for natural resource conservation.

A 1,000-mile flight brought JFK to Duluth, Minnesota and then he visited Ashland, Wis. and the University of North Dakota at Grand Forks.

From there he flew into Cheyenne on the morning of the 25th with Wyoming's Democratic U.S. Senator Gale McGee alongside. Mayor Bill Nation and county Democratic chairman Rod Crowlie, a Cheyenne Central teacher, welcomed them.

---

[66] See McWhorter, Diane, "The Way We Live Now", New York Times Magazine, 7/29/2001.

Wyoming Eagle Editor Bernard Horton's lead story on Sept. 26th told of the excitement generated by JFK's visit. "More than 30,000 persons, one-tenth of Wyoming's total population, turned out yesterday to see, hear and cheer" the president in Cheyenne, Laramie and Jackson. The Cheyenne Police estimated 15,000 to 20,000 people were at the Cheyenne Municipal Airport when the president arrived. Horton declared this gathering to be by far "the largest ever to greet a visiting dignitary" in Cheyenne.

During his brief remarks, the president said that Wyoming personal income had risen 8 percent since 1960, fifth largest increase in the nation. He asked how many people in the crowd were actually born in Wyoming. He also referred to the fact that the late Joseph C. O'Mahoney, who had represented Wyoming in the U.S. Senate, was a native of Kennedy's home state of Massachusetts. Kennedy then descended from the platform and walked the length of a chest-high fence, shaking hands with onlookers, some of whom had waited for more than two hours.

Kennedy was greeted in Laramie by Republican Gov. Cliff Hansen, UW President George "Duke" Humphrey and Laramie Mayor William Steckel, a UW history professor who had replaced Prof. McGee after he was elected to the U.S. Senate. (Steckel drove a Mustang bearing the Wyoming license plate 5-1776). A video of Kennedy's plane arriving in Laramie -- and his interaction with a group of Boy Scouts along the fence -- has been posted on the internet. Kennedy, who had been a Boy Scout himself, purportedly asked them to recite the Scout Oath.

Prior to the 50th anniversary of JFK's visit to Laramie, local historian Dan Nelson purchased an original AP wirephoto which had been transmitted that day in 1963 and showed Kennedy with the Scouts. Nelson recognized and knew how to contact one of the Scouts, then 11-year-old Don Bunn, and Bunn was able to identify Jon Robert Howe, Pat Stevens and Roger Howe.

With Kennedy in Laramie were Democratic National Committeeman William Norris and State Chairman Walter Phelan, both of Cheyenne.

At Memorial Fieldhouse, two UW student folk singers, Marcie Ford and Vern Swain, provided entertainment while a crowd of much more than the 12,500 seating capacity waited, the Eagle article reported. Athletic Director Red Jacoby said it was the biggest crowd since a 1952 basketball game against BYU.

Many more stood along the motorcade in Laramie to catch a glimpse. One of those was the author's future father-in-law, Paul George Dekanek, a U.S. Army veteran who fought in Africa, Italy, France and Germany during WWII. He was twice wounded, the second time resulting in the loss of one eye. Paul snapped two slides of Kennedy and McGee in the back seat of the open limousine as it passed between the Half Acre Gym and the Education College.

A UPI article appearing on Sept. 26th describing the JFK visit noted that some young Republicans carried anti-McGee signs visible from the president's motorcade. One said, "Yankee si, McGee no" and another said, "Keep politics and McGee in D.C." Two of the students were from arch-conservative Cody in northwest Wyoming, Michael McClellan (now deceased), a senior, and Bob Frisby, a sophomore and the son of a future member of the Wyoming Legislature. Another was Bob Stolts, a sophomore from Casper (who became a geophysicist in Oklahoma).

Inside the Fieldhouse, state Young Democrats President Ken Lester carried a sign saying, "Hi Jack." An ROTC student took the sign from him and tore it up. A Secret Service representative later said his agency had no concern about signs. Lester registered an objection to the denial of his First Amendment rights. Lester graduated in business in 1964 and lived in San Francisco in 1991. He is deceased.

Early in his speech Kennedy said, "there is nothing more encouraging than for those of us to leave the rather artificial city of Washington and come and travel across the United States and realize what is here, the beauty, the diversity, the wealth, and the vigor of the people."

Eagle Editor Horton reported that the president initially departed from his prepared remarks to speak to the students directly. "What we are attempting to do is develop talents in a nation which requires education," he said, adding that "knowledge is power" and that it "can be brought to bear to improve our lives." But he said the university is not maintained merely to help graduates enjoy a prosperous life, but to prepare graduates to serve their state and country.

The bulk of his speech was devoted to the use and the conservation of natural resources, during which he mentioned converting oil shale into usable fuels, coal gasification at the mines, liquefaction of coal into gasoline and mining Wyoming's soda ash (which JFK's Boston accent converted to "soder ash"). (These topics are still very much in the news in Wyoming still today).

JFK talked about "very large scale nuclear reactors" being used for desalinization of sea water. He said Sen. McGee "has proposed an energetic study of the technology of electrometallurgy." (JFK's full speech as given – and some handwritten notes for his "knowledge is power" segment – are available on-line at JFK's presidential library).

Among the challenges facing the country, he said, was "what we should do in the Congo or Vietnam, or in Latin America."

Pres. John F. Kennedy speaking at the University of Wyoming Memorial Fieldhouse on Sept. 25, 1963. Photo courtesy of the UW American Heritage Center. (The author of this book is on the extreme left, leaning forward beyond the man in the white T-shirt. Former UW journalism and photography lecturer Bob Warner is down on one knee holding a flash left center. One of the White House press corps accompanying the president at the table beyond is Ben Bradlee of Newsweek who became editor of the Washington Post and guided its coverage of Watergate).

One of the thousands of UW students who heard JFK speak that day in the Fieldhouse was future Wyoming Secretary of State Kathy Karpan who grew up in Rock Springs, graduated from Rawlins High School and is now a retired attorney in Cheyenne. Karpan was editor of the

Branding Iron and shook JFK's hand as he exited. In an article she wrote a year or so later for the book *Those Good Years at Wyoming U*, Karpan set down her impressions of the man who is still the youngest president ever elected to that office[67]:

> In the thousand times I have tried to recall what he looked like, I remember mostly an impression of health, a deep tan, and his young, full head of hair brushed back by the slight wind, and something more that defies description. ... He radiated an intense personality, an exciting vitality .... As Governor Hansen said later, 'If one word might describe the average reaction, it was that here, indeed, was Greatness.'"

One member of the JFK entourage on the tour was Mike Manatos of Rock Springs, a White House aide. Nine years earlier, Manatos was chief of staff to Wyoming's Democratic Sen. Lester C. Hunt. When he reported for work at Sen. Hunt's office on June 19, 1954, he had the misfortune to discover that Hunt had committed suicide.[68]

Also with Kennedy was another Rock Springs native, Teno Roncalio, a Cheyenne attorney who had been appointed by JFK as chairman of the U.S. section of the U.S.-Canada Joint International Commission on water rights. Roncalio had traveled from hearings in Vermont to join Kennedy for the flight from Cheyenne to Laramie. In the Democratic national landslide the next year, Roncalio, a winner of the Silver Star for gallantry with the 1st Infantry Division at Normandy, was elected as Wyoming's sole representative in the U.S. House. After losing a bid for the Senate in 1966, Roncalio was elected to the House again in 1970, 1972, 1974 and 1976. McGee was reelected in 1964 and 1970, but lost in 1976. As of this writing, McGee was the last Democrat to serve Wyoming as a U.S. Senator and Roncalio was the last Democrat from Wyoming in the U.S. House. That 40-years-and-counting one-party hold on a state's Congressional delegation is by far the longest run in any of the states since 1978. Hawaii is second, but that state's one-party run was only for eight years after the 1978 election, when Hawaii voters elected a Republican senator.

No sitting president has ever visited Laramie since Kennedy's plane left the Brees Field runway that day 50 years ago.

Presto: A press pass
The author of this book had gone to the Fieldhouse about an hour before Kennedy was supposed to arrive and ran into a UPI reporter from the Cheyenne bureau located in the Tribune-Eagle Building, where the author had been a part-time sports and news reporter throughout his high school years. Within minutes, the UPI staffer had obtained a press pass for him and gave him the assignment of carrying the equipment bags for UPI's photographer traveling with the president. Thus he was able to watch Kennedy speak from the very front and was only a few feet from him as he exited the building at the northeast door. Another photo in Kathy Karpan's collection shows her in the White House press section west of the dias. Wearing a dark blouse

---

[67] Teddy Roosevelt was slightly younger when he became president, but he assumed the office because of the assassination of President McKinley, not by election.

[68] For the full story on this event, see former State Sen. Rodger McDaniel's book, *Dying for Joe McCarthy's Sins*.

with a name tag, Karpan was unknowingly standing next to Ben Bradlee, then of Newsweek who would become famous as the managing editor of the Washington Post during the Watergate scandal.

It was a heady time. Class of '63 grads like the author were just launched on our college careers and our university had already hosted the president of the United States. They were floating on air.

But just under two months later, of course, those soaring happy emotions suffered a blow that is still, 50+ years later, hard to believe and bear.

Also on the day JFK was in Wyoming, his special fact-finding team in Vietnam heard a report from American military officials that the war against the Communist Viet Cong "is progressing well." Kennedy, the UPI article said, had sent Defense Secretary Robert McNamara and Gen. Maxwell Taylor, joint chiefs chairman, "to find out why it was taking so long to defeat the Communist guerrillas."

The result of the first day of briefings, a spokesman said, showed that "all measurable factors ... continue to be favorable."

But most likely, at least one or two of the students who were being encouraged by Kennedy to pursue their education that September day in Laramie, would eventually have their young lives cut short in a war that continued for another 10 years, during much of which time presidents and cabinet members and senators and military leaders would be telling the American people the war was "progressing well."

JFK's first visit to Grand Teton

From Laramie, Kennedy flew to Billings, gave a speech, and then flew to Jackson Hole Airport where he was cheered by a crowd of 3,000 people, according to the Jackson Hole Guide. He was greeted by Mayor Harry Clissold and county Democratic chairman Phil Baux.

Again he went to the crowd and shook many hands.

At the Lodge he patted the heads of each of the 27 students from the Moran grade school who welcomed him.

An article by Jack Langan and Phil McAuley in the Casper Tribune of Sept. 27 said Kennedy's visit was probably the first visit to Jackson Hole by a president since Chester A. Arthur in the 1880s. JFK reportedly had a refreshing overnight stay during which he viewed a moose through binoculars.

The next morning, as Kennedy prepared to board the DC6B airplane at the Jackson Airport after his night in Grand Teton National Park, he proclaimed to the crowd on hand: "I'm coming back."

From Jackson he flew to Great Falls, Mont. During one of his Montana speeches he called the West "this golden area of the United States. The great writer from my home state, Thoreau, was right: 'eastward I go only by force, westward I go free. I must walk towards Oregon and not towards Europe.'"

Kennedy also stated: "I am confident that history will write that in the 1960s we did our part to maintain our country and make it more beautiful."

From Montana he dedicated an electric generating plant at the Hanford nuclear energy site in Washington. He flew to Salt Lake City for the night and the next morning gave a foreign policy speech in the Mormon Tabernacle and participated in a ceremony recognizing the Flaming Gorge Dam -- then nearing completion -- which stores Wyoming's Green River water. Next he flew to Tacoma and gave a speech at the baseball stadium there, made an aerial inspection of the

Oregon dunes near Coos Bay, Ore., dedicated the Whiskeytown Dam near Redding, Calif., and spoke to a crowd of 7,500 at a new convention center in Las Vegas, where he lamented the fact that 8-9 million children would drop out before graduating from high school.

In California, Kennedy predicted that "as machines take more and more jobs from men, we are going to see the [40-hour] work week reduced," allowing more and more Americans to use the recreational resources of the nation.

From Las Vegas, Kennedy flew to Palm Springs, Calif., for a weekend retreat at singer Bing Crosby's Palm Desert home, where the temperatures were expected to reach 112.

In an editorial in the Cheyenne State Tribune on Sept. 26th, editor James M. Flinchum challenged the White House assertion that the western tour was non-political. "If anyone really believed the fable that this was a non-political tour, he ought to have his head examined," Flinchum wrote. "So things were really swinging for the New Frontier in this part of the Old Frontier yesterday."

Other news on September 25

Articles in the Wyoming Eagle on that September 26th showed that President Kennedy had plenty on his plate as he toured the West and as he anticipated what should have been his re-election campaign in 1964. Racial violence in Birmingham was continuing. A UPI report said that two bombs had exploded in a black neighborhood the day before. The first bomb was a decoy, police said, designed to draw frightened residents streaming into the streets so as to be injured or killed by a second bomb loaded with nails, bolts and shrapnel (much like the Boston Marathon bombers' devices in spring, 2013).

A UPI article datelined White Sands, N.M. reported that the Army had successfully fired two Pershing ballistic missiles from Blanding, Utah, to the White Sands Missile Range. They were the second and third in a five-shot overland test series. The 350-mile flights took about seven minutes. The Pershing missiles were named after Gen. John "Black Jack" Pershing, commander of American forces in WWI who married the daughter of Sen. Francis E. Warren of Wyoming, namesake of the Army's Fort Warren and later Warren Air Force Base in Cheyenne.

On Saturday, Sept. 28, 1963, the NAACP chapter in Casper sponsored a Freedom Fund dinner at the First Methodist Fellowship Hall. Mrs. Gaurdie Bannister sang "Nobody Knows the Trouble I've Seen." The speaker, Irving Andrews, a prominent African American attorney in Denver, was introduced by Judson Phillips. Andrews drew cries of "Amen" and "thunderous applause" when he said, according to the Casper Star report the next day, "the Negro is no longer willing to compromise in the civil rights issue and will never relax his efforts until he can join the ranks of other Americans as first class citizens." Andrews said 1963 would be "our year of discontent."

Appointment with tragedy

Among those who saw Kennedy speak at UW was Central High graduate, Morris Gardner. "I went to the speech and observed the motorcade. It was awesome." A classmate from Cheyenne, Virginia Ottoes Casto, says "I remember all the girls falling in love."

Little did we know that Kennedy would never have a chance to return to the Tetons.

At lunchtime on Friday Nov. 22nd, we walked through Hill Hall's west doors and up the breeze way toward the cafeteria and lunch. Hundreds of students were standing near the dormitory's desk looking at the black and white television affixed to the wall. "President Kennedy has been shot in Dallas," someone told us.

We were in shock. Soon we heard that classes had been canceled. Hundreds crowded into the Newman Center for a hastily-arranged service before we headed home for a long Thanksgiving vacation spent watching the sad, horrible story unfold on television.

The innocence and hopefulness with which the '60s had begun had been shattered and would never return.

Kathy Karpan wrote an eloquent tribute to JFK for the Dec. 6th Branding Iron:

> He lives forever -- not for what he said and not for what he did, but for what he dreamed. President Kennedy ran his appointed distance with the torch of his dreams for a world without hunger, without poverty, without ignorance and without hate. ... He held the torch high as he ran his course.

1961: TED GOSTAS - THE FUTURE LOOKED BRIGHT

> Why do we keep having wars? Because we only live to 75 or 80 and after we die nobody cares what we had to say.
> -Ted Gostas 2013

At the University of Wyoming in the spring of 1961, Theodore W. Gostas of Cheyenne was finishing his bachelor's degree in English literature with minors in history and languages. He was thinking of going into teaching, but he also was considering a military career. Like everyone his age, Ted thought the world had turned the corner from horrors such as those WWII had brought.[69]

Nearly twelve years later, the name Ted Gostas turned up in a UPI article published around the country on September 9, 1972, about the Miss America pageant in Atlantic City. Miss Wisconsin Terry Meeuwsen, 23, of DePere, Wisc., near Green Bay, had won the talent competition on Thursday night and the swimsuit competition

---

[69] In contrast to the massive anti-war disturbances which would occur at colleges around the country a few years later, the only destructive student uprising at the University of Wyoming during the '60s was a "panty raid" in spring, 1961, carried out by around 500 masked male students on the first warm night of the year. They ripped screens and broke windows to enter women's dorms and sororities and made off with 50 pairs of underwear, according to a Branding Iron report on May 12th. A photo shows a campus cop with a nightstick repelling a student while a smoke bomb explodes in the background. Some of the women were frightened to hysteria, the BI editorial in the same issue said. At least two freshmen raiders were charged with breach of the peace.

on Friday: "She wore a blue bathing suit, blue shoes with four-inch heels, and the bracelet she wears everywhere. It bears the name of Army Maj. Theodore Gostas of Wyoming, missing in action in Vietnam since 1968." That night Miss Meeuwsen, who had sung with the New Christy Minstrels for two years, became the first Miss Wisconsin to be crowned Miss America. She went on to a career on the Christian television program 700 Club.[70]

In an AP article two days later, Ted's wife Johanna Gostas, then living in Sheridan, Wyo., was thankful for the attention Miss Meeuwsen had brought to the MIA/POW cause. She said neither the North Vietnamese nor Viet Cong had acknowledged that Gostas was a prisoner and he had never appeared in any films released from North Vietnam.[71]

1961-1967: Ted's long U.S. Army road leads to Vietnam

Gostas, son of a Greek immigrant father, was born in 1938 in Butte, Montana. His parents ran a restaurant there. At age 2, Ted and his parents moved to Bayard, Nebr., for five years. Ted remembers winning five stamps in the Defense Stamp Marble Championships.

When Ted was in first grade they moved to Cheyenne where his parents ran the Albany Delicatessen across from the railroad depot, where the Albany Bar is located now. Ted and his brother had thrown ink at each other on the train enroute to Cheyenne and upon arrival were scrubbed by two cleaning ladies who worked at the Greyhound bus station. The boys helped at the café, shined shoes and also hawked newspapers. Ted remembers a cowboy sitting for a shine of his expensive purple cowboy boots. "I only had brown polish, so I used that and ruined the boots."

---

[70]   Wire service stories about the Pageant at that time actually included the measurements of the named contestants, something that no one would think of doing today. Apparently the measurements were given to the press by the Pageant. The articles even included measurements for Miss Vermont, Kathy Hebert, who had startled Pageant officials and her parents by telling an Associated Press reporter early in the week, "I'm anti-Nixon; I've demonstrated against the war; I supported Jane Fonda, and believe in premarital sex". She also said that her Pageant persona "is not the real me. I'd be here in jeans, T-shirt, no bra and with my hair hanging loose and natural." The Pageant's executive director stood up for her. He said that "I respect her opinions and even more so her right to express them." But needless to say Miss Hebert did not win. Appearing elsewhere in many of the newspapers of September 9, 1972, was a UPI article from Harrisburg, PA, reporting that Jane Fonda had called for a resurgence of the peace movement during an anti-war rally there. "Anyone who is speaking out against this war is speaking out on behalf of the democratic ideals on which this country was founded," she said. Other speakers included a former POW, George Smith, and Chicago Seven defendant Tom Hayden (1939-2016), who had gone to Hanoi with Fonda earlier in 1972, then married her in 1973 and served as a California state senator 1992-2000. At the 1973 Miss America Pageant, Miss New Hampshire Michelle Annette Cote said in an interview she supported the Women's Liberation and Gay Liberation initiatives. "Any liberation movement that's going to give people more dignity." (Nashua N.H. Telegraph, Sept. 5, 1973).

[71] In 1974, Cheryl Johnson of Cheyenne was crowned the first black Miss Wyoming and became only the 4th African American to compete in the Miss America Pageant. After the opening parade, Miss Johnson said the public response to her had been "fantastic." She said a group of teenagers, black and white, rushed to her limousine to shake hands. The only unfortunate incident during the pageant was that Miss Johnson received an envelope during a break in rehearsals which contained a paper saying: "Ticket back to Africa" (AP version) or "Two coon tickets to Africa. We don't want you here." (UPI version). The head of the Pageant called it "lousy, dirty, rotten hate mail" and said he was relieved that the 20-year-old radiology student did not appear too disturbed by the incident. AP article in the Billings Gazette 9-5-1974. Seven years earlier, Patty Martinez of Lingle, a soloist and music education major at UW, was selected as Miss Wyoming. UPI article by Phil White in Laramie Boomerang 9-3-1967.

Eugene Zigmond owned a music business and routinely came to the Gostas establishment to change records in the Wurlitzer juke box. "He often gave me old records," Ted recalls.[72]

When he was 13 Ted won two prizes for paintings he had entered in the Cheyenne Junior Artists Guild show. At 15, he wanted to escape from a tense domestic atmosphere and persuaded his parents to send him to Kemper Academy in Boonville, Mo. "It was a horrible experience. There were a lot of problem cases there, sons of wealthy parents. I was maltreated by some of the students. One guy from Texas had a bullwhip which he would snap at me. Kemper is closed down now."

Returning to Cheyenne, Gostas was an officer in R.O.T.C. at Cheyenne High and then traveled over the hill to Laramie for college.

Gostas met his first wife Johanna at UW. As part of his R.O.T.C. program there, Ted went to basic training at Fort Leonard Wood in Missouri in the summer before his senior year. After graduating from UW, Ted's parents encouraged him to attend law school, but he had two children and another on the way, so he decided to make the military his career. "I figured it was better to go in as an officer, giving me some say in what would happen to me, and better pay," he said during a 2013 interview. "I had a feeling I was doing a patriotic service."

He was sent to language school in Monterrey, Calif., where he became fluent in German. On Nov. 22, 1963, he was in class when news of JFK's assassination came in. "Kennedy was my idol," Ted recalls. "I thought he and his brother were good moral people. I liked his desire, his charisma, wanting to venture into space. He was a hero in my eyes."

Ted was then trained at the U.S. Army Intelligence School at Fort Holabird, Baltimore. He was stationed in Germany for three years.

In 1967 he was transferred to Vietnam for what was supposed to be a one-year tour. Upon his arrival at Cam Ranh Bay he was shocked to see an airplane in the water with seven dead Americans inside.

On Jan. 31, 1968, Gostas was stationed with the 135th Military Intelligence Battalion at Hue (the former imperial capital. Pronounced "WAY"). During the Tet Offensive, his unit came under an intense attack. "A rocket came right into our room and exploded. Shrapnel went everywhere. A sniper shot a soldier who had just received a message he was the father of a baby boy. I had 11 days left before I could return home, but there I was, 29 years old, holding a man in my arms as he bled to death," he says. "I felt so powerless. I felt him die."

Gostas was taken prisoner and spent the next five years, one month and 15 days in captivity in the jungles of South and North Vietnam, perhaps in China also.

Eventually he was sent to the "Hanoi Hilton" where he met Floyd Thompson. "He said to me, 'Ted, if I don't pick you up and make you walk around this room, you're going to die.' I said I didn't care. My abscessed teeth were draining into my stomach and causing my heart to fibrillate. Dr. Floyd Kushner wrapped twine around three of my teeth and he ripped them out without anaesthetic while others held me down."

Ted believes he was the highest-ranking Army Intelligence officer captured during the war. During his captivity, Gostas endured unimaginable torture and deprivation. His immune system was almost destroyed. He had parasites in his intestines and blood leaking in his brain.

---

[72] The author in the early '60s bought numerous used juke box 45 RPMs at Gene and Helen Zigmonds' The Record Shop (everything from "Hey Paula" to "Whole Lotta Shakin' Goin' On"). The Zigmonds later moved into the home adjacent to the Whites' home. We learned that Mrs. Zigmond was a Nazi concentration camp survivor.

1973: From the Hanoi Hilton to the White House

When a cease fire went into effect Jan. 28, 1973, the Communists said they held 585 American prisoners.

In an AP article datelined Saigon on March 13, a Viet Cong spokesman was quoted as saying that Maj. Theodore William Gostas, 34, was suffering from a "nervous illness." His was among the names of 32 more prisoners to be released March 16th.

On March 19th, Gostas flew home from Clark Air Force Base in the Philippines with 25 other freed prisoners, including his Hanoi Hilton compatriot Maj. Floyd Thompson, 39, of New Milford, N.J., the longest-held prisoner of war in U.S. history. Thompson had been held since 1964 and had not seen his family for ten years. Among the other prisoners was Marine Pfc. Ronald Ridgeway of Houston, who had been reported killed near Khe Sahn five years earlier. His mother attended what was thought to be his funeral, but she told UPI that she never believed the remains sent to her and buried were those of her son.

The UPI article said Gostas was carried onto his hospital plane at Clark under "light sedation." Upon arrival in Denver, Gostas walked from the plane to an ambulance and was rushed to Fitzsimons Army Hospital where he was reunited with his wife Johanna and children Demietrius, 11, Laura, 8 and Jason, 5. He credits Army psychiatrist Dr. Clotilde Dent Bowen (1923-2011) with saving his life and rescuing him from the severe post-traumatic stress syndrome from which he was suffering. "They thought I would be going into a military mental health facility for the rest of my life," Gostas remembers. "But she gave me 18 shock treatments, sodium pentathol and atropine." Dr. Bowen was the first African American female to graduate from Ohio State's medical school, as well as the first African American female physician in the U.S. Army. For a time she was chief of psychiatry at the VA Hospital in Cheyenne.

On April 24, 1973, Maj. Gostas saw his entire family for the first time since his release, when he flew from Fitzsimons to Sheridan for the Easter holiday. He returned the next week for continued treatment for internal physical problems.

A month later, the AP reported that Gostas and his wife Johanna escaped serious injury when their small foreign car overturned near the Sheridan airport. They were headed to a White House dinner for ex-prisoners.

"I had an opportunity to meet President Nixon," he recalls. "Everybody was telling me, 'you just say 'how do you do Mr. President' and move on,' but I told them I'm going to talk to him. I said, 'Mr. President, it's such an honor. Your speech was so inspirational. It made all the pain and suffering go away.' He pulled his hand away and stepped back and said, 'On you go.' So I can say I had a conversation with him."

After Ted's release in Vietnam he remained in the military for a couple of years and retired as a major. He had been awarded the Bronze Star, two Purple Hearts and the POW Medal.

Gostas returned to UW for graduate work in English and renewed his friendship with legendary UW English professor, poet and historian Wilson Clough, who became a frequent dinner guest in the Gostas home after Clough's wife died. Ted named his daughter Laura after Clough's wife. He obtained his master's in English, writing a long paper on his Vietnam experience and a commentary on the works of Thomas Wolfe and Emily Dickinson.

He published a book about his experience titled "Prisoner", which included drawings. Five of his paintings were on display in 2006 at the Chicago National Vietnam Veterans Art Gallery.

"I never really survived that war," he said in his interview. "I just live from day to day. I'm thankful I have a wife who has tolerated me for 35 years. I'm thankful to be alive." He then quoted from the character Joe Galloway in the 2002 movie "We Were Soldiers" about the Battle of Ia Drang in November, 1965: "We who have seen war, will never stop seeing it. In the silence of the night, we will always hear the screams. So this is our story, for we were soldiers once, and young."[73]

1962: MISSILES BRING RICHARD BRUCE CHENEY BACK TO WYOMING

Warren Air Force Base's missile projects brought a future Secretary of Defense and Vice-President of the U.S. to Cheyenne in 1962.

Following the Atlas, the Pentagon put in place succeeding generations of nuclear missiles, each more powerful than its predecessors. The Atlas was quickly followed by the announcement on March 27, 1962, that WAFB would control 200 Minuteman missiles to be scattered over a huge area in southeast Wyoming and neighboring Nebraska and Colorado. The project was expected to bring 2,000 construction workers and 500 additional military personnel to the Cheyenne area and cost an estimated $158 million. Some of the individual sites were to be as much as 100 miles from WAFB itself. Wyoming's Democratic senators Gale McGee and J. J. Hickey, and Cheyenne mayor Bill Nation, were ecstatic.

In October, 1962, Dick Cheney, having been dismissed from Yale because of poor grades, was working as a groundman for an electrical contractor installing communications cable between those missile silos near Cheyenne. His after-hours activities resulted in him forfeiting bond on a charge of drunkenness and driving while intoxicated, resulting in a 30-day suspension of his driver's license. According to his autobiography he and his co-employees consumed vast quantities of beer and bourbon at a Cheyenne bar that would carry a tab until payday. He wrote that he brushed off his first DUI, but then in the summer of 1963 in Rock Springs he added another DUI conviction to his record, which forced him to take stock. He thought about how many of his friends had just graduated from Yale and that Lynne Vincent, his Natrona High classmate and future wife, had graduated summa cum laude from Colorado College after spending a semester in Europe. He, on the other hand, thought about how he was sleeping off a hangover in the Rock Springs jail.

Thus, the President and Vice-President of the United States who served between 2001-2009 both had regrettable lines on their resumes. President George W. Bush collected a DUI in Maine in 1976 at the age of 30.

1957-1969: THE PATH TO THE BLACK 14

1957: Coach Devaney moves West with Eaton in tow

The front page of the University of Wyoming Branding Iron's special Homecoming Edition on October 20, 1967, was a salute to Coach Lloyd Eaton. It included a wonderful drawing of the coach by Quita Pownall of Laramie, along with a long profile of the coach by the BI sports editor. The page was printed in brown type (UW's colors are brown and gold).

The article began with a description of a phone call from 10 years earlier:

---

[73] Galloway was a UPI reporter who covered Ia Drang, the first major battle of the war. He received a Bronze Star in 1998 for rescuing a wounded soldier during the battle.

One cold January day in 1957, the phone rang in the office of the head football coach at Northern Michigan University in Marquette, Mich.

After the coach said hello, the caller asked if he'd like to drop over for a cup of coffee. "Sure," the coach replied, "tell me the address and I'll come over."

"It's a drive of only a few hours. I'm down in East Lansing," was the reply.

As far as Wyoming football fortunes go, it was one of the most fortuitous phone calls ever made.

The caller was Bob Devaney, assistant coach at Michigan State who had just been named head coach at Wyoming. The man who answered was Lloyd Eaton, whose Northern Michigan team had finished 7-0-1 in his first year as head coach. [74]

1958-1962: Devaney thrills the Cowboy faithful

Playing in the Skyline Conference under the now-legendary Devaney, the Cowboys went 8-3 in 1958, including a win over Hardin-Simmons in the Sun Bowl. In 1959 they went 9-1 but received no bowl invitation. (Guard Len Kuczewski was the captain and earned an all-conference award. In the fall of 1960, Kuczewski became a teacher at the newly-split-off Cheyenne Central High, and also was named the Indians' wrestling coach, even though he had never coached wrestling previously).

In 1960 the Cowboys went 8-2 but again no bowl invite was forthcoming. In 1961 their record was six wins, two losses and two consecutive 6 to 6 ties, at Kansas and at home against Utah State. The Cowboys won or shared the conference title five years in a row.

1962: Devaney bolts, Lloyd Eaton hired

Devaney had 4 ½ years to run on his contract in January, 1962, when he announced he was being hired as Nebraska's head coach. The resignation provoked much discussion at the university and around the state as to whether UW should release him. His formal appointment to head the Huskers was delayed until he obtained his release.

Devaney was in Laramie early in the week of Jan. 15 to determine the desires of his assistant coaches. Jim Ross and John Melton had definitely stated they would follow their head coach to Lincoln, but three of the other assistants, according to John Mooney's column in the Jan. 10th Salt Lake Tribune, were interested in the UW head coaching position. "They are Mike Corgan, a top recruiter who is backfield coach; Lloyd Eaton, the defensive coach who married a Wyoming girl, and Carl Selmer, former Wyoming high school coach. ... An insider says Jacoby [Athletic Director Red Jacoby] is believed to favor Eaton." Mooney predicted Devaney would be released by the trustees after Jacoby and UW President George "Duke" Humphrey "explain the facts of coaching life to the board."

In another news article, however, Humphrey indicated he would most likely hire a new head coach from outside, although he didn't completely rule out choosing one of Devaney's

---

[74] Two years after that 1967 BI article appeared, the news from East Lansing and Laramie coincided again, but in a stark contrast. On the morning of Friday, October 17, 1969, at the same time Coach Eaton was tragically dismissing all 14 African American players from the team -- and destroying his own coaching career in the bargain -- the Board of Trustees of Michigan State called a news conference to announce that an African American man had been named President of MSU.

assistants. "I won't go that far, but a present coach has to be awfully, awfully good" to be hired, Humphrey said. On Jan. 17, UW Athletic Director Red Jacoby said at least one of the assistants was being considered to succeed Devaney but he was not saying which one.

An AP article printed on Feb. 3rd reported that after a six-hour discussion the board voted 7-5 to release Devaney, who had traveled to Laramie from Lincoln for the meeting but was not called before the board.

Later that day, Eaton, 43, was hired under a three-year "letter of appointment" with a salary rumored to be around $14,000. Jacoby announced that all of Devaney's other assistants would follow him to Nebraska. They did well down there. As the 1969 season began, Devaney was the winningest coach in major college football.

Lloyd Eaton was born March 23, 1918 in Belle Fourche, S.D., son of Thomas W. and Rosa Hall Eaton, and grew up on a ranch on the Belle Fourche River, six miles east of the town of the same name and only 17 miles east of the Wyoming border. In January, 1936, Eaton was one of 15 boys who competed in the ninth annual lamb feeders day for the northern Black Hills. Each of them had 15 lambs for three months.

Also in 1936, the Deadwood S.D. Pioneer-Times reported on Aug. 6th that Eaton was a corporal in a group of "Belle Fourche boys attending the Citizen's Military Camp at Ft. Lincoln, N.D." In 1939 the newspaper reported that Eaton was among the Black Hills Teachers College students selected to take a Civil Aeronautics Authority flight training course. He completed his initial solo flight in April 1940.

Eaton had a leading part in a production of "Our Town" by BHTC students in May, 1939. Eaton, the left tackle, "injured some neck muscles" in a football game in October 1939.

In March, 1940, he was elected president of the student council at that school. The next month Eaton and Jack Zolnoski of Casper (who must be the future guidance counselor at Cheyenne Central in the early '60s) were working toward a private flying license, training in "an all-metal side-by-side Luscombe" at the Black Hills airport.

The Spearfish Queen City Mail newspaper reported on Feb. 22, 1940, that BHTC coeds had elected Eaton, outstanding lineman and captain of the Yellow Jackets football team, as "the most glamorous boy on campus." A newspaper columnist said Eaton shied away from the honor. "Glamour boy? I'm working as a janitor; I've played football four years."

As with most rural areas of Wyoming, it is highly unlikely that Eaton had very many occasions to interact with black people in Butte County where he grew up. The 1940 census showed Butte County, S.D. had 8,004 whites and zero African Americans. In 2010, the population was up to 10,110 but only six-tenths of one percent were African American.

Eaton's demographic surroundings soon changed dramatically, although even the U.S. Army was segregated until after WWII. On July 14, 1942, the newspaper said Eaton was among 30 area men who would be inducted into the Army at Deadwood that day. By April, 1943, Eaton had been promoted to sergeant and was posted at Ft. Benning, Ga. By June he had completed officer training there.

In August, 1943, the Mail announced that El'Louise Dickey of Spearfish, a Colorado University graduate, would be married soon to Lt. Lloyd Eaton of Camp Shelby, Miss. They were married later that month in Hattiesburg, Miss.[75] When Eaton and assistant coaches Paul Roach and Fritz Shurmur traveled to Louisiana in late November, 1967 to sign the Sugar Bowl contract and scout LSU in the Tigers' last game, Eaton recalled he had seen LSU play once nearly a quarter-century before, when he was 65th Division Athletic Officer at Camp Shelby during WWII. "They had Alvin Dark (future MLB player and manager) in the backfield," he said. "That was a long time ago," he said, "but I'm a pretty well-preserved buck for 49, wouldn't you say."[76]

In December, 1944, the Mail said Mrs. Eaton "is living with her parents for the duration while her husband is overseas."

According to an article in the Lincoln Nebr. Star on Feb. 4, 1962, Eaton had served in the Caribbean and in South America during WWII and was discharged in 1946 as a captain. However, in a sports column in the Casper Star on Sept. 5, 1971, sports editor Harold Sohn said Eaton's service during WWII was all in the U.S.[77]

In 1946 and 1947, Eaton coached the Bennett County High School football team at Martin, S.D. In Feb. 1948, the Mail reported that Eaton had left for Ann Arbor, Mich., to enroll at the University of Michigan and that his wife and daughter would follow as soon as he secured an apartment.

In Sept. 1949, the Black Hills Weekly reported the Lloyd Eatons of Spearfish were parents of a daughter born at St. Joseph's Hospital in Deadwood. Eaton coached at Alma College in central Michigan from 1949 through 1955. The Scots won 40, lost 20 and tied two games during his tenure. On Oct. 18, 1950, his father took a bus from Belle Fourche to Rapid City and checked into a hotel to await an early morning flight to visit Lloyd at Alma. Thomas Eaton, 59, was found dead of natural causes when the clerk went to wake him for his flight. His mother Rosa had died in 1946.

Eaton became head coach of Northern Michigan in 1956, taking over a team that had a winless season the year before. Thanks to an ex-Marine walk-on quarterback, Northern rolled to a 7-win 1-tie record,, earning Eaton one newspaper's nomination as "Michigan's Football Miracle Man." The article said during the war Eaton served in the infantry, special services division and was discharged as a captain.[78]

1962: Dave Marion - Super Soph from Bakersfield
In 1951-52, Paul Briggs was head football coach at Natrona County High School in Casper after earning All-America honors as a tackle at the University of Colorado, being

---

[75] Lloyd and El-Louise were the parents of two girls. By May, 1961, El'Louise Eaton was living in San Bernardino, Calif. An article in the Rapid City Journal on Nov. 8, 1969, said Eaton was married to Ann and they had two children, Glen 22 and Christie, 15 (probably Ann's children from a previous marriage). Eaton's obituary in the Black Hills Pioneer on March 19, 2007, said he married Marie McCleskey of Boise, Idaho in 1984 and she survived him. The article said "poor health for Coach Eaton became a way of life" but he enjoyed gardening and traveling.

[76] AP report in Sioux Falls Argus-Leader 11/25/1967.

[77] Sohn was in the service when the Black 14 happened and in this 1971 column at the time Eaton left UW, Sohn said he sensed a change in Eaton when he saw the coach again. Sohn had written a column criticizing the upcoming football schedule which slated six home games each against South Dakota and Idaho State in the 1970s. Eaton was so upset about the column, "which he took as an attack on the Cowboy Joe Club, that he turned and walked away when I tried to discuss it with him. That, I guess, was the end of the friendship," Sohn wrote.

[78] Rapid City Journal 12/2/1956.

awarded a bronze star during WWII and playing for the Detroit Lions for one year. In 1953 he became head coach for the Bakersfield, Calif. High School Drillers and in about 1961 he introduced UW head coach Bob Devaney to one of his players, Dave Marion, a multi-sport star. Devaney was able to convince Marion to take his tremendous football talents to UW.

Sophomore Dave Marion finished the 1962 season at Laramie as the nation's leading punt returner. But Marion was in a class by himself as a football player because he also excelled as a punter, finishing second in the NCAA with an average over 42 yards per punt. He also finished first on the team in yards per carry, rushing 28 times for an average of 6.5 yards per. As of 2022 his name is still in the Cowboy record book for punt and kickoff return yardage/game in a season[79].

Dave's brother Jerry was a star performer for the freshman team in 1962 and the two of them were looking forward to playing together in the backfield the next season.

The team's starting left halfback, Mike Walker from Detroit, also lived in the athletic dorm with the Marions and was excited about his upcoming senior season. In 1961, Walker had scored 32 points, led the team in pass receiving and finished third in rushing. His 27-yard touchdown run at Memorial Stadium prevented CSU from scoring a huge upset over the Cowboys. He was one of only two sophomores to make the all-conference team.[80] In 1962 Walker was second in rushing yardage (behind Rick Desmarais) and in yards per carry (behind Marion). Walker and Marion were the first African Americans to play football for Wyoming since Taft Harris in the 30s.

Dave Marion at UW 1962

rabbits.

1963: Tragedy after Eaton's first season -- Dave Marion paralyzed

Eaton's Cowboys went 5-5 in his first year, defeating Arizona 19-0 in Laramie. But just two months after the season ended, an awful twist of fate prevented the Marions' and Walker's dreams from being fulfilled. The accident occurred in the Athletic Dorm at UW (today McWhinnie Hall between Wyo Hall and Education College) on January 6, 1963, just after students returned from Christmas break. Curt Jimerson was a proctor in the dorm and was finishing up his degree under a fifth-year scholarship the athletic department had awarded him. Also in the dorm was assistant football coach C.W. "Wimp" Hewgley, dorm director.

Late on that Sunday evening, someone came to Jimerson's room and called him to the room shared by 20-year-old Dave Marion and his brother Jerry. The Marions' teammate Walker, also 20, had returned from Christmas vacation with an automatic .22 pistol, and he had been out that day hunting

---

[79] Cowboy sports historian Bill Schrage of Laramie in 2022 alerted the UW Sports Information office that this record was set by Dave Marion in 1962, not by his brother Jerry as the media guide showed.

[80] Laramie Boomerang April 14, 1962. Spring football roundup by Gene Bryan.

On the way back to his room he stopped to visit with the Marions. The next day Mike told Albany County Sheriff Ted Burnstad, "I took the clip out of the gun, and then I turned around to show them that there were no bullets in the gun." But a round remained in the chamber and Mike somehow accidentally fired the round into the left front of Dave Marion's neck. It lodged at the right rear of the neck, just under the skin.

Jimerson said those in the room were furiously trying to help Dave, and became impatient when the ambulance did not arrive. They decided to carry Marion to one of their cars and on to the old Ivinson Hospital near Old Main. Jimerson said in an interview in 2013 that immediately after the shooting Marion was saying he could not feel his legs.

Hewgley was quoted in the Jan. 8th Laramie Boomerang: "I rushed right down there when I heard the noise. Dave was conscious and told me that he couldn't move his arms. The wound didn't look to be serious when I first looked at it, and I thought he was just suffering from shock. I wrapped him in some blankets and rushed him to the hospital. They took x-rays there and informed me then that the bullet had severed the spinal column."

Marion was transported to DePaul Hospital in Cheyenne in critical condition. Mike, who was overcome with grief, was put under sedation. Assistant coach Bill Baker said the two were "very good friends."

Emergency surgery Sunday night removed the slug and relieved the pressure on the spinal cord, according to an article in Cheyenne's Wyoming Eagle on Tuesday January 8th. Marion was removed from the critical list late Monday night. He was conscious and was able to talk some, but the outlook was that he would be almost completely paralyzed.

Coach Eaton was in Los Angeles for the NCAA football coaches' association meeting and was informed of the tragedy by telegram. Eaton told Hewgley that he would go to Bakersfield to see how he could help the family.

An emotional and moving Eagle article by Wyoming Cowboys' broadcaster Larry Birleffi of Cheyenne was published on Thursday morning. Birleffi quoted Dave's 49-year-old father Elbert, who had driven to Cheyenne Monday with his lifetime friend and employer, Joe Fambrough. "We managed a smile out of Dave last night," he said. "We think maybe his spirits are improving."

Birleffi's article continued:

> The father said he had a firm talk with his son about having strength and faith. He said he told Dave he must now "face a new kind of life. He must show more courage than he ever did on a football field."
>
> "I told my younger boy to go back to class at the university and show strength and courage too," Marion said. "I want him to play football at Wyoming.
>
> "I also drove to Laramie for the first time Wednesday. I wanted to talk with Mike. I told him in the words I could find and as sincerely as I could that there was no bitterness. I urged him to return to his classes and that he should continue to play football at Wyoming. I told him he needs his education and the worst thing he could do now would be to give it up."

Birleffi followed with an article in the Wyoming Eagle of January 11th, describing Marion's progress. This article said Dave's mother Cora had remained in Bakersfield in shock and under a doctor's care.

Mr. Marion was reading to Dave all the cards and letters pouring into the hospital from around the state and the nation. He reported that Dave had said, "I believe Jerry can replace me okay. He's pretty fast, you know." Dave was also joking with his father about the light coats his father and friend were wearing in the 12-below-zero weather, Birleffi reported.

Mr. Marion was quoted as saying: "I wish I could let the people here in Cheyenne know how wonderful they have been to us since we have been here. I can understand now why both Dave and Jerry said they wanted to work out here this summer instead of coming back to Bakersfield."

Briggs, the Marions' high school coach, was quoted that week as saying Dave Marion was "the greatest natural football player I've seen in my coaching career."

At the end of January, Marion was flown in a Wyoming Air National Guard plane to Bakersfield, where he was taken to the Kern County General Hospital. A statewide campaign to raise $50,000 for a Dave Marion Trust Fund was undertaken, headed by Gov. Cliff Hansen. Wyoming Supreme Court Chief Justice Glenn Parker and Alan Simpson, a Cody attorney who would become a U.S. Senator, were on the Fund's coordinating committee. Early in March, the UW symphonic band conducted by Charles Seltenrich entertained at a fund-raiser for the David Marion Trust Fund at Crane-Hill Cafeteria. Emcee Gordon Dudley, a member of the band, said he hoped to attract 1,000 people paying 50 cents per person for admission.

Marion was later treated at a Los Angeles hospital and then underwent rehabilitation at the Bakersfield Convalarium, near his home. The trust fund eventually provided for an addition to the Marion home so that Dave could live with his family.

In an article in his local paper two years later, reprinted in the Boomerang on December 8, 1964, the reporter described how Dave could now move an arm to his face and could control a special wheelchair with his head. The article continued:

> But since the shock has worn off, Dave is very cheerful and hopeful that [his progress would continue]. "If it weren't for the wonderful people of Bakersfield and Wyoming, maybe I wouldn't feel this way," Dave said. "But they have all been great and I want to thank them for everything they've done."

On October 10, 1972, Boomerang sports editor Bob Hammond reported that Dave Marion had died. He had recently returned in high spirits from a trip to Lourdes, France, funded by Father Taylor and the Newman Club at U.W. Coach Briggs told Hammond: "He was real elated for three weeks after his return." Then he began to hemorrhage, which required surgery, but doctors found that Dave had deteriorated so badly that nothing could be done. "Dave just finally reached a point where he couldn't go anymore," Briggs said.

Briggs spoke about one day, when he was driving to football practice, he saw Marion sitting in his wheelchair at an abandoned filling station near Dave's home. Briggs was having a tough day. Marion told Briggs: "' Hey big coach, look up. Have you ever seen the sky as blue as it is today?' I had never heard a more humane statement about reality to life. All of a sudden my problems were not that significant. All I could say was, 'Dave Marion, you're one all by yourself.'"

Dave still holds the Cowboys' record for average yards per return in a season (519 yards on 20 kickoff and punt returns in 1962).

U.W. coach Fritz Shurmur was quoted in the Boomerang article as saying: "He was a great back. Dave had it all. There wasn't a thing he couldn't do on the football field. He was the best punter I have ever seen. Not only was he a great football player, he was a fine young man."

Jerry Marion, who managed to continue on to a great career at UW in both football and baseball, was still living in Bakersfield in 2018. Jerry was named to the 1966 All-WAC team at end and played in six games for the Pittsburgh Steelers in 1967. In April, 1964, he was leading the baseball team in nearly every batting category.

But Jerry also had talents other than on the playing field. A Branding Iron article and picture published March 20, 1964, said Marion sang tenor for a quartet called the Chevelles whose performance at the Wyoming Union Talent Show brought "wild applause." The group also cut a record in Denver that week. Besides Marion, the members of the group, all African Americans, were freshmen Charles Thomas of Denver, Al Washington of Flint, Mich., and Ed Rose from Beaver, Pa. Thomas said he hoped the quartet's record would take off. "Now that the uniqueness of the Beatles has worn off, there is a place for something new," he said. "The Chevelles feel they can fill that place." [81]

The Chevelles (L-R) Ed Rose, Al Washington, Charles Thomas and Jerry Marion. BI photo by Bob Warner 3/20/1964.

Jerry Marion married Sharon Robinson, an African American woman from Cheyenne, and their son, Brock, played in the NFL for several years.

Mike, who was of course devastated by the terrible accident at UW, was a very promising player himself. In a Laramie Boomerang article on April 14, 1962, Sports Editor Gene Bryan called the Marions' Detroit friend "the finest halfback in the conference." As a sophomore, he tied quarterback Chuck Lamson in scoring, led the team in pass receiving and finished third in rushing. This performance earned him a first-team All-Skyline-Conference selection. His 17-yard touchdown reception was Wyoming's only score in a 6-6 tie with heavily-favored Kansas at Lawrence in 1961.

But after the shooting in early 1963, his career, like that of Dave Marion, came to a premature close. He left UW within a few months after the incident.

Michael Heywood Walker, 57, died in 2000 in Gilbert, AZ

In October, 1969, another outstanding football player for coach Briggs at Bakersfield saw his career at Wyoming come to an abrupt and unfortunate end. Flanker Guillermo (then called "Willie") Hysaw was one of the Black 14.

---

[81] The UW track teams' records wall in the east Fieldhouse lobby in 2018 showed that a long jump of 25' 1 ½" by Charles Thomas in 1965 still ranked second in the record books.

In 1972, Dave Marion was inducted into the Bob Elias Kern County Sports Hall of Fame in California, but nominations on behalf of the Marion brothers for induction into the UW Athletics HOF have been passed over.[82]

1963-1965: Eaton - Building a program

In 1963, UW was 5-1 through October, including a 26-23 win over Utah in Salt Lake, but then lost conference games at Arizona, New Mexico and Arizona State and finished with a 6-4 record.

African American Earland Ezell of Grand Rapids, Mich., played both ways. He had a 45-yard touchdown reception in the opening win over Montana and played in the defensive secondary in the Arizona game, making three unassisted tackles and seven assists. The Cowboys' last game against Texas Western was delayed for a week because of the assassination of President Kennedy.

In 1964 Ezell was one of 14 players from Michigan on the roster.[83] Wyoming started 5-0 and finished 6-2-2. Following the 1964 loss to Arizona on October 24th, Eaton was quoted in the Tucson Citizen saying: "**... eventually Arizona's speed caught up with us. ... we couldn't contain Arizona's speed or receivers.**" (Eaton balanced the playing field in future years in substantial part by bringing in African American players with speed and other special skills).

Earland Ezell, courtesy
UW Athletics

The late-season difficulties continued the next year when the Cowboys, led by quarterback Tom Wilkinson of Greybull, started 6-1 but finished 6-4, including a devastating 56-6 loss at USC in the last game.

1966-68: Cowboys win three straight WAC championships

The three years leading up to the fateful 1969 season were among the best in Wyoming's football history. These Cowboy teams were composed overwhelmingly of white players, including stars like future Miami Dolphins running-back Jim Kiick, safety-turned-quarterback Paul Toscano, kicker Jerry DePoyster[84], tackle Mike LaHood (1944-2013) and defensemen like Jerry Durling, Mike Dirks, Jim House of Laramie and Larry Nels.

But no one would dispute that the speed and athleticism of several African American players contributed greatly to the 27-5 record posted by the Cowboys during that period. Cornerbacks Vic Washington (1946-2008) and Dick Speights were selected to the all-WAC first team two seasons in a row. Hub Lindsey tied a school record with eight touchdown receptions in 1967. Gene Huey was selected to the All-WAC second team at flanker in 1967 and to the first

---

[82] Photo at http://kcsportshalloffame.org/inductees/dave-marion/

[83] Ezell went on to a career as a teacher and football coach at a Denver-area public school. He died in 2017.

[84] When his 3-year career in the thin air of Wyoming ended, DePoyster, from Omaha, had scored more points by kicking than any other player in college football history. Using the conventional straight-ahead kicking style of the period, Depoyster kicked two 54-yard and a 52-yard field goal against Utah on October 8, 1966, in windy Laramie. His successor, Bob Jacobs of Bozeman, soon set a new record for career field goals, but he never kicked one longer than 48 yards.

team as a defensive back in 1968. (UPI named him to both teams). Joe Williams was All-WAC 2nd team running back in 1968 (and one of the Black 14 the next year).

Gene Huey and Paul Toscano, Laramie, 2017

Due to Wyoming's dominant defense during his years here, and his own world-class ability, Vic Washington of Plainfield, N.J. (1946-2008) as of 2013 still held season and career Cowboy records for numbers of returns, average yards and total yardage from punt returns, and also the record for average yards on kickoff returns in a single game. #33 set an NCAA season record for numbers of kick returns in 1967.[85]

1966: Sun Bowl

In 1966, the Cowboys went 9-1 during the regular season. They beat Utah by 33 points and Arizona by 30. Their average margin of victory in the nine wins was 29 points. At Provo, Utah, they beat BYU 47-14.[86]

Their only loss was a 12-10 heartbreaker against Colorado State at Fort Collins which resulted from the infamous "bounce pass" play (CSU had alerted the officials to this play prior to the game). In the third quarter, CSU quarterback Bob Wolfe bounced a seemingly-incomplete pass to halfback Larry Jackson in the left flat. The UPI report says, "Jackson shrugged his shoulders, retrieved the ball and then tossed it down field to end Tom Pack on the 10 yard line."

---

[85] Vic Washington set these records in only two seasons at UW, and then went on to three years in the Canadian Football League and six in the NFL. He was named MVP of the 1968 CFL Grey Cup game and was selected to the Pro Bowl while with the San Francisco 49ers in the NFL where he was a starting running back and returner as well as playing on defense occasionally. During both the 1972 and 1973 seasons, Washington returned an opening kickoff for a 49ers touchdown. In 1982 he was selected to the Western Athletic Conference's 20-year all-star team. Vic died Dec. 31, 2008 in New Jersey at the age of 62. Blogger Tom Hawthorn described him this way: "Of all the spectacles possible in football, few matched the fury and grace of Vic Washington in an open-field dash." Washington's life-long struggles, including his premature expulsion from UW, are described in the Hawthorn article. His daughter in a 2018 interview said Vic got into trouble at UW "because of being called inappropriate names." Vic waged a long battle against the NFL seeking a reasonable disability pension.

[86] Sports Illustrated on Nov. 28, 1966 carried a long article about the Cowboys' win at Provo and their kicker Jerry Depoyster. The article (which can be read on-line at the SI Vault) reported that BYU coach Hudspeth had shored up his 1966 team with six Marines he recruited from the Marine base at San Diego.

He walked in for the Rams' only touchdown. The officials ruled the bounce pass was a lateral, not a forward pass, giving 10th-ranked Wyoming its only loss.

In 1966, Wyoming's offense ranked 3rd nationally in points/game, and the defense was 1st in rushing defense and 5th in total defense.

African American player Jerry Marion (See the Dave Marion chapter at pg. 61) and nine other Cowboys were named to the All-WAC first team. A Tucson Citizen sportswriter reported on Dec. 12th that Eaton was a "very strong" candidate to become head coach at Kansas State. The columnist noted that K-State was "not the most appealing situation," being the doormat of the Big Eight, but added that "neither is Wyoming's 'Moon Country' the easiest place to recruit and Eaton has been on thin ice each year at Laramie with the exception of this one big one."

On Christmas Eve, the Cowboys beat Florida State in the Sun Bowl 28-20, after trailing 14-7 at halftime. In his last game for UW, Marion was on the receiving end of a 39-yard touchdown pass. The defense held the Seminoles to a minus 21 yards rushing.

Vic Washington in action on the road against San Jose State Nov. 4, 1967. Following this game Wyoming was ranked 7th in the UPI coaches' poll, ahead of Notre Dame, Oklahoma and Alabama.

In 1992, Victor Washington ran unsuccessfully for Maricopa County Supervisor in Phoenix. He said he wanted to revitalize central and south Phoenix, "an area where there has been less economic opportunity for people of color," he said.

1967: Sugar Bowl Season -- The Cowboys go marching in

Wyoming plowed through the 1967 regular season schedule without a loss, winning by 28 at Utah and by 36 at New Mexico, but they also survived three squeakers: at home against CSU (13-10) and at ASU (15-13) and UTEP (21-19). Gene Huey caught three touchdown passes in a 37-10 win over Air Force in Laramie. AFA coach Ben Martin said "Huey may be the best receiver in college football."[87] Sophomore Joe Williams was the leading rusher, ahead of Kiick, in the Cowboys' 26-10 win over BYU in Laramie. When BYU returned two years later, Joe was one of the 14 black players watching from the stands.

The Arizona Republic sports page on October 29, 1967, featured a photo of #24 Gene Huey shedding an ASU defender on a 63-yard touchdown pass on Wyoming's first play from scrimmage. Washington and Speights each had an interception for the 8th-ranked Cowboys. Their black teammate, Hub Lindsey, caught five passes for 57 yards and had a 28-yard kickoff return. The 42,344 fans on hand was the largest crowd ever to see a football game in Arizona.

After that ASU win the Cowboys were rated 7th by UPI, ahead of Texas, Alabama, Oklahoma, Notre Dame and Michigan State.

---

[87] Uniontown (Pa.) Herald, 11/7/1968

Huey also had a 64-yard reception at El Paso to set up one of the Cowboys' two touchdowns.

When the regular season ended, the 1967 team had set or tied 47 school, conference or NCAA records.

Two days later, the sixth-ranked Cowboys were invited to play LSU in the Sugar Bowl. They were the only undefeated team in major college football and their 14 game win streak was the longest. But it had taken an amazing set of circumstances on the previous Saturday to change Wyoming's chances to play in one of the big-four bowls from extremely remote to actual. (See the history section at sugarbowl.com. Most of the Sugar Bowl game is viewable on the internet).

On a gloomy, wet New Year's Day, Wyoming took a 13-0 lead into halftime, but succumbed to the Tigers' greater depth in the second half to lose 20-13. As time ran out, Huey caught a pass and struggled forward but was taken down at the LSU five yard line. LSU had no black players or coaches.

The next week, a UPI article reported that the NFL's 49ers were interested in luring Eaton to San Francisco.

Half a world away, at 3:30 a.m. Jan. 2, 1968, Army Sgt. Dave Hammond of Laramie was attempting to listen to the Sugar Bowl game on a transistor radio while riding out a Viet Cong mortar attack, according to a Boomerang article by Pete Fetsco which appeared May 16th when Hammond was home on leave. The former all-state football player now had a Purple Heart and a Combat Infantryman's Badge to add to his mementoes. Dave, the son of Oscar Hammond, a former Laramie mayor and legislator, and the brother of Bob Hammond future Boomerang sports editor, met his nine-month-old daughter for the first time during his leave.

"It got to the point where you just had to watch where you were going – every step, every moment," Hammond told Fetsco. "My senses improved quite a bit. It made me appreciate the little things in life." He said he had fought both Viet Cong and North Vietnamese. The latter, he said, "were real good fighters but with all our firepower they just couldn't match us."

Although he had some close calls in Vietnam, Dave went on to a successful career as a manager for Western Electric and Lucas Aerospace. He died of a heart attack at age 60. "Boomerang Bob" Hammond, who started as an apprentice printer in 1964 and became sports editor in 1968, served in that role for more than 40 years.

During 1968, 16,899 Americans were killed in Vietnam, an average of 46 per day. The Big Horn Basin lost two of its sons during one week in early November: Marine Pfc Lawrence Green, 20, of Cody and Pfc Elton Anderson, 19, of Lovell.

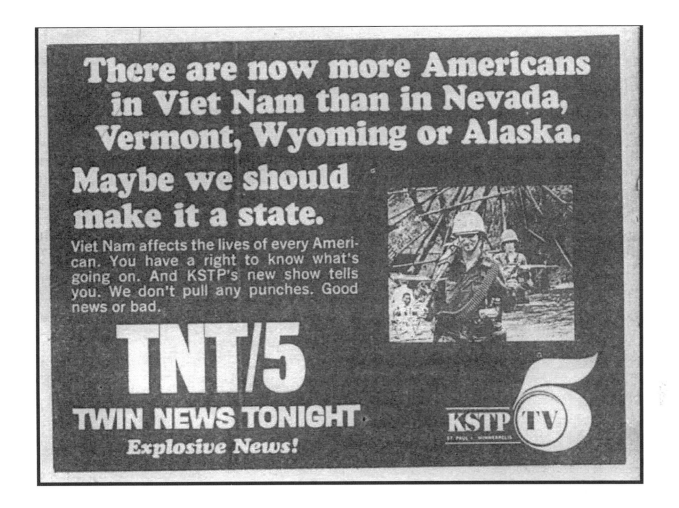
1968: WAC champs get no bowl bid

In an interview published Sept. 18, 1968, after Nebraska's 13-10 win over the Cowboys in Lincoln -- thanks to a 51-yard field goal with 21 seconds to go -- Nebraska coach Bob Devaney said of Wyoming's #24: "That Gene Huey is the finest defensive back we've seen." In that game, Dave Hampton, another superb African American player who would go on to star in the NFL, had 73 yards rushing on 17 carries and Joe Williams, one of the Black 14 the next year, collected 51 yards, also on 17 carries.

In a 48-3 win over Utah State at Laramie Sept. 28, 1968, four African American players figured prominently. Huey racked up 86 yards receiving, including two receptions for touchdowns, Hampton ran for another, defensive end Anthony McGee recovered a fumble to set up a touchdown and cornerback Laverne Dickinson took an interception 28 yards for a TD.[88]

At Provo, Utah on October 12, 1968, Wyoming quarterback Skip Jacobson, who had 283 yards passing on the day, engineered three scoring drives in the fourth quarter to overcome BYU 20-17 on a field goal by Bob Jacobs with six seconds left.[89] Gene Huey caught 12 passes for 156

---

[88] The next day, Marlin Briscoe, an African American quarterback from Omaha, took over in the fourth quarter for the AFL's Denver Broncos and led them, passing and running, on an 80-yard touchdown drive. The next week he became the first black quarterback to start in the AFL.

[89] In '68 and '69 Jacobs led the nation in field goals made with 14 and 18 respectively.

yards and scored both of Wyoming's touchdowns, which brought his season total to 82 receptions for 1,262 yards and 11 touchdowns. Huey had broken the season receptions and yards records set 18 years earlier by All-American Dewey McConnell.

The next season, some of the Black 14 stated that one of the reasons they went to the Fieldhouse to talk to Coach Eaton on the day before the BYU game was because they had seen or heard that BYU officials had turned on the sprinklers while the Cowboys were on the field celebrating their last-minute victory and/or that BYU players had uttered racial slurs or taken dangerous cheap shots at black players. Eaton did not give them an opportunity to ask about these matters.

In 1965, a BYU student named Allan Weinstock stated in a letter to the Daily Universe, the campus newspaper, published Feb. 16th:

> When I first heard a heckler earlier this fall at a BYU football game call a Negro member of an opposing team a derogatory term I was shocked, not so much by the particular individual's comment but by the number of students who actually laughed and mocked in unison. ... [I]t has happened every time I have witnessed an athletic event where Negroes have participated at BYU.

Weinstock pointed out that not too many years earlier "a group of people called Mormons were heckled and jeered in much the same manner."[90]

Four days after Wyoming's win at BYU, an iconic moment occurred at the XIX Olympiad in Mexico City. The 200-meter dash gold-medal winner Tommie Smith and his teammate and bronze medalist John Carlos, African Americans from San Jose State, stood on the medal platform each holding a black-gloved fist aloft and looking down as the flag was raised and the national anthem was played. Smith had just broken his own world record despite injuring a muscle in the semifinal earlier that day.

The U.S. Olympic Committee apologized the next day for the display on the medal stand but said that no sanctions would be made against the two athletes. Nevertheless, under pressure from the international committee, the athletes were dismissed from the team two days later. Smith said the gesture was "to show blacks are united. We're glad we did it."[91] The runners' black glove protest occurred almost exactly one year before the Black 14 were to be dismissed in Laramie. Soon after the Olympics salute, a black football player at Eastern Washington showed the closed fist during the national anthem, resulting in his dismissal. In early 1969, the athletic department adopted a rule banning the clenched fist salute by athletes. Athletic Director Brent Wooten said the ban was in recognition that a team is an "autocratic society" under the sole

---

[90] Referenced in Bergera, Gary and Ronald Priddis, *Brigham Young University: A House of Faith*, Signature Books, 1985, at p. 297. This book's chapter titled "THE PROTEST YEARS" contains a detailed discussion of the furor over BYU's racial tenets by black athletes, including some major protests at several campuses following the Black 14 incident. Both authors graduated from BYU. The authors wrongly stated at p. 300, as many others have done, that Wyoming's "fourteen black players decided not to participate in the [BYU game] and were therefore dismissed from the team." In fact, they were dismissed by Coach Eaton for wearing armbands on their civilian clothes the day before the game.

[91] UPI report in Pittsburgh Press and numerous other papers 10/17/1968.

authority of the coach. The faculty senate and the Black Students Union criticized the ban as a violation of free speech rights and when the BSU threatened suit the ban was withdrawn.[92]

Back on Wyoming's 1968 football trail, Hampton caught a 21-yard pass and followed that with a 24-yard run on one touchdown drive -- and Huey intercepted a pass -- in the win over Utah at Laramie October 19th.

In a 35-6 win over New Mexico on October 26, 1968, Hampton had three touchdowns and 144 yards on 13 carries, including a 51-yard touchdown run. Joe Williams had 107 yards on 17 carries. Hampton scored another three touchdowns in a 46-14 win over CSU at Fort Collins. Joe Williams had a 26-yard touchdown run and Huey had a 63-yard touchdown reception.

On Nov. 16th, coordinators Paul Roach and Fritz Shurmur coached the team to a 26-19 win at Texas El-Paso. According to an article in the Tucson Citizen three days later, Eaton was unable to make that trip and was being treated at Ivinson Hospital in Laramie because of "an undiagnosed virus which has caused him to lose 16 pounds."

The Cowboys finished 7-3, but no bowl came calling.

1964-68: RONNIE GRAY, FREEDOM SUMMER, INTERRACIAL DATING

1964: White students -- and the "Wyo Days" group -- catch "Beatlemania"

The University of Wyoming Branding Iron of February 21st carried a full-page article about the 24 students who had been selected to make the week-long "Wyo Days" tour of nine Wyoming high schools with their singing, dancing and comedy program.

Master of ceremonies for UW's "good will tour" was Steve Carlson, a junior from Cheyenne, who played guitar and sang. He went on to a long career as an actor and writer in Hollywood, including an extended collaboration with Dick Clark of Bandstand fame. Carlson was a regular on General Hospital and The Young and the Restless and appeared in many other TV roles, such as Captain Maddox in the final episode of Seinfeld. In 2018 he was living in southern Oregon, writing books.

Ronnie Gray, the African American baby who was removed from the Baby Contest in Casper when he was three years old (see Introduction at pg. 1), was another member of the Wyo Days troupe, bringing his magnificent singing voice to audiences all over the state. Gray's family had moved to Lander when he was a child, becoming the only African American family in that town. To avoid problems during his school days, Gray said in a 2017 interview, he always had to remember his race in social situations. When he enrolled at UW in fall 1963, he found that he didn't quite fit in either the white students' world or the group of black athletes from urban areas across the U.S. Gray graduated with a degree in education, then taught in elementary schools in Cheyenne for many years, while also performing and singing with various musical combos. The Branding Iron on 10/13/1967 carried a photo of Gray playing the xylophone for a group called "The Hybrid Sounds of the Jazz Minority."

The "Wyo Days" article's author explained one of the group's offerings this way: "One act will include a take-off on the Beatles, a singing group from England which has invaded the U.S.

---

[92] UPI, Pittsburgh Press, 5/3/1969; AP Des Moines Tribune, 5/8/1969; UPI Provo Herald 10/18/1970 (the day of the Wyoming-BYU game). An African American male cheerleader at West Virginia U. was expelled for giving the salute in November, 1970, spurring a black female cheerleader to resign in protest. Pittsburgh Courier 11/21/1970.

by storm. To make the act complete, wigs have been ordered for the Wyo Days act." The Beatles had made their first U.S. television appearance on the Ed Sullivan Show 12 days earlier.

On March 6th, the Branding Iron carried a photo of music professor and band director Charles Seltenrich wearing a Beatles wig during a Cowboys' basketball game. BI Society Reporter Sharon Willmschen's article on "the four wailing Liverpudlians" quoted a UW coed as saying the Fab Four's popularity was due to their haircuts and manner of dress. "If they would have stayed in their black leather jackets, no one would have noticed them," she said.

An estimated 10,000 people greeted the Beatles at Stapleton Airport in Denver on Aug. 26, 1964. They stayed at the Brown Palace and played at Red Rocks. Diane Sabo of Cheyenne won a ticket through KIMN 950 radio station in Denver, home of DJs named Pogo Poge and Jay Mack.[93]

Page one of that 1964 BI issue reported that about 500 students had jammed the Union Ballroom to hear English Professor Tom Francis discuss *Lord of the Flies*.

On April 17th, the BI carried a photo of legendary UW geology professor Dr. Samuel H. Knight in front of the life-sized model of a Tyrannosaurus rex which the retired professor spent two years creating with copper plating over a steel frame. On April 11, 2014, UW students ate cake and signed a large 50th-year birthday card to the campus icon, still standing beside the Geological Museum.

1964: Civil Rights, the "Green Book" and War Drums

On June 21st, the U.S. Senate passed the Civil Rights bill by a 73-27 vote. Milward Simpson, R-Wyo., and Barry Goldwater, R-Ariz., were the only western senators to vote against it, joining 20 Southern senators. Republicans Wallace Bennett of Utah, a Mormon, and Len Jordan of Idaho voted for the measure.[94]

The Act, signed into law on July 2nd, barred discrimination by race at public facilities such as motels. For 30 years, the "Negro Motorist's Green Book," an annual publication from New York City, had listed facilities safe for African American travelers. Originally covering only New York, the Green Book quickly expanded its listings to all U.S. states. The 1939 edition showed these Wyoming listings: Tourist Home owners Mrs. J. E. Edwards and H. Keeling, both on North Grant St. in Casper, Mrs. I. Randall and Mrs. M. Herman on West 18th in Cheyenne and Mrs. R. Collins on 6th St. in Rock Springs. Also listed was the Barbeque Inn at 622 W. 20th in Cheyenne. The 1947 edition listed G. Anderson on N. Lincoln St. in Casper in addition to Edwards and Keeling. Also shown was the Yellow Front at 111 E. Front in Rawlins, with these notations: "See The Golden West / Barbeque Served Every Day / Robert Westbrook Mgr."

---

[93] In 2009, PBS station WNET in New York premiered a documentary titled, "How the Beatles Rocked the Kremlin" (viewable on-line at thirteen.org). Numerous people who were young USSR citizens when the Beatles burst forth are quoted in the film as saying that the Soviets' severe suppression of the Beatles played a significant role in alienating the young and producing the eventual demise of the Soviets. One of those Beatle lovers, Sergei Ivanov, was deputy prime minister when the film was released. "Hearing the Beatles music I'm sure now it helped me to learn English language properly," he said.

[94] According to a Drew Pearson syndicated column published Nov. 5, 1966 in the West Palm Beach Post, Jordan had renounced his membership in the LDS Church.

The 1962 Green Book listed the Blue Spruce Motel at 1914 E. Yellowstone in Casper, the Minnehaha Motel at 1905 E. Lincolnway in Cheyenne and two places in Rock Springs: Collins Tourist Home at 915 7th Ave. and the Liberty Motel on U.S. Hwy. 30.

On August 7, 1964, Congress approved the Tonkin Gulf Resolution after the Defense Department and President Johnson claimed North Vietnamese torpedo boats had attacked U.S. destroyers three days earlier. Military authorities already had suspicions that the attack reports were mistaken, but the Resolution was used as justification for waging the Vietnam War without a declaration of war from Congress.

In November, Wyoming's Democratic party rode the coattails of the Lyndon Johnson-Hubert Humphrey presidential ticket to one of the party's greatest victories in state history. LBJ won Wyoming's three electoral votes by a 56-43% margin over conservative Republican Barry Goldwater. According to an article by Prof. John T. Hinckley of Northwest Community College in Powell, published in the Western Political Quarterly in 1965, the Democrats entered the election with only one incumbent above the county level, U.S. Sen. Gale McGee. But the election gave the Democrats control of the state House, reduced GOP control of the state Senate to one vote and turned out popular Republican U.S. Rep. William Henry Harrison in favor of Teno Roncalio, the childhood shoe-shiner from Rock Springs. Sen. McGee was re-elected and soon became one of the primary Senate "hawks" supporting LBJ on the Vietnam War.

Hinckley attributed the astonishing electoral revolution in part to state Republicans focusing their efforts almost entirely on defeating McGee and taking for granted victory in the other races.

1964: Two Wyoming Women Go South for "Freedom Summer"

More than 1,000 volunteers from out-of-state, almost all of them white and two of them from the University of Wyoming, joined thousands of black Mississippians to do voting rights and educational work in the summer of 1964 . Some Freedom Summer volunteers, including Mario Savio, would play major roles in the Free Speech Movement at UC Berkeley that fall.

Cynthia Small of Laramie, a 1962 graduate in English and 1964 drama graduate Pam Thomas of Evanston, a former Miss University of Wyoming, pulled a camp trailer to Oxford, Ohio, for a one-week orientation session at Western College for Women, where they met Freedom Summer organizer and civil rights leader Bob Moses.

They then went south to the towns of Milltown and Canton where they lived with a black family and set up a Freedom School at a local church. Pam also organized a dance class.

On June 21, 1964, James Chaney, a black resident of Meridian, Miss., and two white civil rights activists from New York, Michael Schwerner and Andrew Goodman, were killed by Ku Klux Klan members near Philadelphia, Miss., while participating in voter registration activities as part of "Freedom Summer." Their bodies were found 44 days later, buried in an earthen dam. Their story became the basis of the movie "Mississippi Burning."

On occasion, Cynthia and Pam were instructed by their host to get under the bed when whites were expected. Another time they went with civil rights leader David Dennis to a meeting in another town and on their way back after dark Dennis told them "you gotta get down" a couple of times because blacks who were with whites in cars after dark could be attacked. The Wyoming women were aware of the murder of the three Freedom Summer activists but never were attacked themselves. At Chaney's services, Dennis saw Chaney's little brother Ben crying in the audience and became very emotional. He talked about the "living dead", all of those who were not standing up against the violence and discrimination. He condemned the pattern of perpetrators of violence on blacks being found not guilty by juries. "Don't bow down anymore," he pleaded to the mostly-black audience. "Hold your heads up. We want our freedom now. I don't want to go to another memorial. I'm tired of funerals."

In August, Small's parents made a surprise visit to their town. Mary and Harry Small were worried about the two. Harry owned a couple of pool halls in Laramie and made extra money with "football parlays" and poker in the back room. When Cynthia was 10, the Small family and many other fans, along with Wyoming's new Shetland pony mascot Cowboy Joe, went by train to the 6th Gator Bowl played at Jacksonville on New Year's Day 1951. Wyoming completed its season with 10 wins and no losses, defeating the Washington & Lee Generals 20-6. Quarterback Eddie Talboom of Tennessee, a 29-year-old WWII vet and father of three, led the Cowboys in passing and rushing, and linebacker Doug Reeves (see the chapter on the Treagle Train) was among the defensive players singled out for praise by Coach Bowden Wyatt. In the Jan. 2nd issue, the Casper Tribune Herald's sports editor claimed the game's "news significance" eclipsed the inauguration that same day of the new Republican Governor Frank Barrett.

Twenty years after their life-changing experience in Mississippi, Cynthia attended a reunion and met up with some of their hosts again. The host family's young daughter, who didn't talk when they lived with the family, had become a television reporter for a Jackson TV station. A former student had become a highway patrolman.

Cynthia worked for a year as publicity coordinator for the Free Southern Theater during which time they performed Raisin in the Sun by Lorraine Hansberry, the first play by a black woman to be produced on Broadway. She then entered grad school at UW and in October, 1965, she and Thomas appeared at a Student Education Association event at the Education Auditorium, discussing their Freedom Summer experience and the status of African Americans in the South.[95] Thomas said many blacks had been injured or fired from their jobs for attempting to register themselves or other blacks to vote.

Small earned a graduate degree in international relations from Denver University and taught for many years at then-new Community College of Denver. She became a feminist and moderated a panel on women's issues on KMGH in Denver.

Pamela Thomas Riley taught drama and dance at Colorado College for 11 years. Her husband was president of CC. In August, 2017, the couple traveled from their home in Philadelphia to Colorado Springs to team-teach a class on philosophy in literature. They reunited with Small at her home in Golden at the time of the 2017 solar eclipse.[96]

---

[95] Branding Iron 10/15/1965; Small and Thomas response 10/22/1965.

[96] Another remarkable event in summer 1964 was the signing of the Wilderness Act by President Lyndon Johnson on Sept. 3rd. On the day before the signing, Secretary of Interior Stewart Udall's office called Mrs. Margaret (Mardy) Murie of Moose, Wyoming, inviting her to fly to Washington to be present for the signing. Her husband, Olaus Murie, had done ground-breaking research on the wildlife of Alaska and of the Greater Yellowstone ecosystem for the U.S. Biological Survey and was one of the organizers of the Wilderness Society which had lobbied for years for the wilderness act. Olaus had died less than a year before his vision became a reality and his associate, Howard Zahniser, director of the Society, died just four months earlier. An AP wirephoto of the signing ceremony shows 15 male members of Congress or the cabinet alongside Mardy Murie and Mrs. Zahniser. Mardy was a champion of protecting the great lands of the caribou in Alaska, influencing the passage of the Alaska National Interest Lands Conservation Act signed by President Carter in 1980. In 1998, Mrs. Murie was awarded the Presidential Medal of Freedom by President Clinton. She died in Moose in 2003 at the age of 101.

1968: "Guess Who's Coming to Dinner" at UW-Interracial dating

In the UW student newspaper, The Branding Iron, on November 11th, reporter Jeff Haag addressed some of the problems faced by black athletes at UW. "There are 20 to 25 Negro men on the campus and one Negro woman," the article said. "Many coeds on campus say they would not mind dating a Negro but are afraid of losing friends and dates with other men." Several white male students told Haag that "they would not take out women who have been known to date Negroes."

The article said "there is a great deal of unrest among the Negro men on campus", citing an interview with one black athlete. "He commented that Negroes are often left out of campus activities because they don't have dates."

Haag quoted Mrs. Virginia Wiley, house mother at Tri-Delta, as saying "that the problem has never arisen in her sorority and she hopes that it never does." Mrs. Marie Heckendorf, a girls' dorm house mother, said interracial dating "is something everyone seems to be adjusting to and that it 'should be taken in stride.'" The article said Mrs. Bessie Gietz, director of another women's dorm, "commented that it is entirely up to the woman, but [Gietz] feels the parents of the coed should be made aware of it." Margaret Tobin, Dean of Women, said UW had no policy on the issue, according to Haag's article.

1965: THE LIGHT WITHIN - JAMES REEB OF CASPER

I want to participate in the continuous creation of a vision that will inspire people to noble and courageous living. I want to share actively in the adventure of trying to forge the spiritual ties that will bind mankind together in brotherhood and peace.
   --James Reeb

Our city and our county has been subjected to the greatest pressures I think any community in the country has had to withstand. We've had in our area outside agitation groups of all levels. We've had Martin Luther Coon ... uh ... King, Martin Luther King ....
   --Mayor of Selma, Alabama, Joseph Smitherman 1965.

For those who attended Natrona County High School from 1942-45, the tragedies occurring during the civil rights struggle in the South came home in a personal way in March, 1965.

After relocating with his family to Casper from Russell, Kansas, James Reeb entered NCHS as a sophomore in September, 1942. He had been a New Year's Day baby, born to Harry and Mae Reeb in Wichita in 1927. Seven years before that, Mrs. Reeb had almost died when she caught the flu after giving birth to a stillborn child. According to the book by Rev. Duncan Howlett, *No Greater Love: The James Reeb Story,* she had prayed as she recovered: "O Lord, if thou wilt heal me and give me another child, I will give him to thee."

But after the birth in 1927 it was James Joseph who became ill. He continued to have health problems during his childhood. At age six he suffered from rheumatic fever in the wake of flu and was confined to bed for two years. Although poor, the parents devoted themselves to caring for him, battling to keep him safe during the awful dust storms that blew across Kansas. The doctor told them James was not strong enough to take the whooping cough vaccine, and thus he contracted that disease at age 11. On the advice of the doctor, his mother took him to New Mexico until she nursed him back to health. Mrs. Reeb and a friend tutored him so that he kept up with his classes.

After being laid-off in Kansas, Mr. Reeb landed a job with Western Oil & Tool Manufacturing Co. in Casper. James thrived in high school, enjoying particularly the teaching of Miss Frances Ferris in English and Miss Margaret Shidler in Latin. He demonstrated even at this early age a concern for the poor and disadvantaged in society, working with a Boy's Club in North Casper.

As WWII raged on, Jim joined the Junior ROTC unit and was elected to be commander of the unit as a senior. He was also deeply involved in the Presbyterian Church and talked about becoming a minister. Although he would have been exempt from the draft if he had gone into a ministerial discipline after his graduation from high school, he accepted induction into the U.S. Army in June, 1945, while the Pacific War appeared headed for a brutal land invasion of Japan. Stationed in California, he became increasingly absorbed in his religious studies.

But then he was transferred to Anchorage, Alaska, and until his release in December, 1946, he was moved mystically by the mountains and the northern lights.

Returning to Casper, he became one of the first students at the Casper Junior College, formed a few months earlier by citizens wanting to provide an education to the returning servicemen under the "G.I. Bill". The college was initially located on the third floor of the high school. During his one semester there he met Marie Deason, a senior in high school who would eventually become his wife.

1947: Into the Ministry
In fall of 1947 Jim was one of many applicants to St. Olaf College, a Lutheran school in Minnesota, but a letter from a Lutheran minister in Casper caught their attention and he was admitted. He devoted himself to his studies there and also attended both sessions of summer school at the University of Wyoming in 1949. He listed his address as 730 Kirk St. in Casper. Reeb graduated cum laude from St. Olaf in 2 ½ years, leaving much of his G.I. Bill benefits for graduate schooling.

After graduating from Casper College, Marie joined Jim as a student at St. Olaf, and they were married in August, 1950, at Casper's First Presbyterian. Then they piled into the 1947 Nash his parents had given them and headed for Princeton, N.J. and Princeton Theological Seminary. As part of one course there he visited the East Harlem Protestant Parish in New York, where Jim was shaken by the urban decay he observed.

During the latter part of his time at Princeton, Reeb was selected to participate in a hospital chaplaincy at Philadelphia General Hospital where he received first hand an education on the problems facing the poor, mostly black, families who were served at that institution. When his mentor in the program moved to the Presbyterian Hospital, Reeb replaced him at Philadelphia General.

He was ordained by the Casper Presbytery at First Presbyterian in 1953.

The family's vacations from his position in Philadelphia usually involved driving back to Wyoming, where Jim became interested in looking for fossils and human artifacts in central Wyoming. He also was becoming increasingly interested in psychiatry and his connection to his traditional Christian faith was weakening as he came to believe that working to improve social conditions directly was more important than prayer.

By January, 1956, he had made the difficult decision that he had to leave the ministry, finding that he had "become much more of a humanist than a deist or theist." By March of 1957, he had decided that the Unitarian Church's principles were more in line with his own and he sought to become a minister in that church.

In a sermon in 1961 he said:

For as long as I can remember, ... what I have always thought of as the light within has been of more importance to me than anything else in life. ... [I]t makes no difference what one calls this inward light, if you call it God, or if you don't. It is not increased by the names we give it nor is it diminished if we do not give it any name at all."

Consideration of his application was a long, slow process. In response to a questionnaire more than a year later, Reeb explained why he wanted to become a Unitarian minister: "Because the members of the Unitarian Church are not bound to a creed or to certain conceptions held to be absolute truths, except that the pursuit of truth is always of ultimate importance, they can respond to new ideas and truths no matter what their source nor how evidently they contradict previously held beliefs."

During this process Jim obtained a position as youth director at the Philadelphia West Branch Y.M.C.A. He told the executive secretary that one reason he had given up the hospital chaplaincy was because he wanted to move from praying with the sick toward addressing "the causes of the human misery he faced in the hospital."[97]

The youth director at another branch was an African American from the South. Reeb pressed him to tell his story, but he resisted at first. Eventually they became friends.

Reeb became like a father to a number of the boys at the Y and established a pre-delinquency program to reach boys headed for trouble. When some were calling for the death penalty for a group of black boys charged with killing a Korean student, Reeb circulated a statement reminding people that everyone shared some responsibility because of prejudice which forced these young men to live in deteriorating, overcrowded sections of the city.

In March, 1959, some Unitarian ministers from Philadelphia met with the Rev. Duncan Howlett at All Souls Church Unitarian in Washington D.C. When Howlett mentioned he was having trouble finding an assistant minister, they recommended Reeb. The folks at the West Branch Y were sorry to see him go, presenting him with a plaque recognizing "his unswerving devotion to the youth of our community and his inspirational leadership."

He would spend five years at the church, deeply involved in the social problems affecting the people, both collectively and individually. Then he decided it was time to move on, and in 1964 he accepted a position doing community development work in a slum area of the Boston

---

[97] Howlett at 106.

suburb of Roxbury. The program was sponsored by the Quakers' American Friends Service Committee.

In his final sermon at All Souls in July, 1964, he spoke at length about the racial unrest in the South which was moving northward. He spoke about the long history of indignities towards the African Americans. They have "a new sense of self-dignity out of which will be born a greater sense of taking responsibility for their own future, but out of which must also be born our sense of understanding of what it is that is involved. We must not misinterpret the situation. We must not let the backlash, as it were, increase because we continue to see that Negroes do what people call 'push'. ... It is up to us to contribute understanding, to try to interpret to the community as a whole what is happening, why things are as they are." Neither blacks nor whites, he said, "must permit [themselves] to be inhibited by the bigots or the racists lest we all go down the drain in a sea of hatred." He said no one could take a vacation from the struggle for justice.

He also spoke about Vietnam. "It is an ugly war, and it contributes to the belief that violence is the way to solve international problems."

In August, he took his wife and now four children to Boston. By the beginning of the new year he had gotten the program off the ground and was working to improve conditions in the area. He was living in the ghetto and his children were going to the neighborhood schools. After a fire in which four people died and thirty families were left homeless, his AFSC project undertook to investigate whether the building complied with legal requirements such as those for exits. He visited a city fire official about improving the codes and received a hostile and threatening response. He issued a report on the fire dated March 3, 1965.

1965: Bloody Sunday brings Reeb to Selma

The front page of the Casper Tribune of March 10th carried the grim news that the son of Mr. & Mrs. Harry Reeb of 265 S. Washington in Casper had been beaten in Selma, Ala. and was in critical condition at an Alabama hospital.

His road to Selma began on Sunday night, March 7th, when James Reeb and his wife watched the 11 o'clock news in Boston. A young African American (and future congressman) named John Lewis had led a voting rights march that afternoon, starting in Selma and planned to end at the state capitol 50 miles away. Gov. George Wallace had vowed that the march would not happen.

Various organizations over two years had made little progress in registering voters. Of the 15,000 blacks old enough to vote, only 130 were registered, and more than 80% lived in poverty. The previous month, a state trooper had shot and killed Jimmie Lee Jackson during a voting rights march in nearby Marion. This killing was also a focus of the Selma-to-Montgomery march.

Some 600 blacks and a few whites started out of Selma across the Edmund Pettis Bridge. At the other end they were met by Alabama state troopers and a sheriff's posse, who knocked marchers to the ground, beat them with nightsticks and fired tear gas. The television newsreels carried footage of severely injured marchers, bloodied and suffering from the gas, while mounted troopers rode into the crowd. Sixty people were injured, some with broken bones and head wounds. Seventeen were hospitalized.

Gov. Wallace stated he had ordered state troopers to use "a minimum amount of force" to stop the march so as to keep the marchers from getting hurt along the highway to Montgomery at the hands of "an element of people in Alabama which sometimes is uncontrollable". He called for an investigation of Communist infiltration in the civil rights movement. And in a statement that would be reused four years later by University of Wyoming officials and U.S. District Judge Kerr to justify the dismissal of the 14 blacks from the football team, Wallace said: "These people had been told they could not march."

Wallace and the Selma mayor complained about the outside agitators. In October 1969, many state and university officials in Wyoming recycled that excuse also, even though there never was a shred of evidence that the black football players' visit to the coach's office on that Friday morning was provoked by any outside agitator.

As a result of the beatings, King and other leaders issued a call for clergy from across the country to join them in a second march to be held on Tuesday. About noon on Monday Reeb received a call from the Unitarian Universalist Association informing him of the plea.

Later that day he told Marie that there had been a tremendous response to King's message and that he wanted to join those going to Selma. Marie soon realized that there was no use in trying to dissuade him. She drove him to the airport, where he met more than 100 Unitarian ministers and lay persons from the Boston area going on a chartered flight to Atlanta. There they sat themselves in cars provided by King's Southern Christian Leadership Conference for the drive to Brown A.M.E. Chapel in Selma. Reeb expected to be back at his desk on Wednesday.

Although a federal judge had issued an injunction against the march, King concluded by mid-day Tuesday that he could not call off the march after so many had responded to his call. But he agreed to a compromise: the march would continue to the other side of the Pettis Bridge and would then turn around.

The march began at 3 p.m. with King in the lead, but only the top leaders knew of the agreement. They were stopped at the other end of the bridge once again, but were granted permission to pray. Then, although the police forces moved aside, King held to the compromise, turned around and led the marchers back into Selma. They were relieved, but confused as to whether anything had been accomplished. Reeb ran into a Unitarian official from Atlanta and accepted his offer of a ride back to Atlanta later that night, after further meetings at the Chapel.

King urged those at the church to remain until Thursday, when he expected the same federal judge to issue an injunction to allow the march. Reeb then decided he would stay overnight.

According to the Duncan Howlett book, this is how things unfolded from there: Having had little to eat in 24 hours, he joined two other colleagues in a walk to SCLC headquarters to ask where they might get dinner. They said they would like an integrated restaurant and were directed to Walker's Café around the corner. Another group of white ministers felt hostility upon entering a different nearby white restaurant, and they decided to go to the overcrowded Walker's.

Reeb called his wife to tell her he would not be home that night. The three then started walking back to the church. They had gone only a few steps when four whites on the other side of the street, who saw them coming out of the restaurant, ran toward them shouting racial slurs. Two of the ministers increased their pace but Reeb did not. The Rev. Clark Olsen, a Berkeley,

Calif., minister, looked around just in time to see one of the thugs hit him from behind with a pipe or club. Reeb fell to the pavement. The Rev. Orloff Miller followed the civil rights protocol, dropping to the sidewalk and placing his hands on the sides of the head. The attackers began kicking and pummeling him.[98] Olsen was also attacked by one of the four, who pounded him with fists and broke his glasses.

Then the attackers ran off. Reeb was conscious, but dazed, without apparent injury otherwise. He was not coherent. They got him to his feet and helped bring a staggering Reeb back to SCLC headquarters to get him help. A hearse from a black funeral home next door was brought over and a black infirmary was called and informed. At the infirmary the physician noted that Jim's eyes were glazing over. He directed them to take Jim to Birmingham 90 miles away where a neurosurgeon might be found.

First they had to talk to the police and to get a deposit check required by the hospital. A police car escorted the ambulance carrying the three white ministers and the black doctor, driver and attendant, to the edge of town. Out on the highway a short time later they had a flat tire. In that it was dangerous for a bi-racial group to be out together at night, they drove back into Selma on the rim and called for a second vehicle. They finally got Reeb to the University of Alabama Medical Center by 11 p.m. and surgery began within 30 minutes, after doctors found in their initial examination that his skull had been crushed on the left side and a large blood clot had developed. The doctors held out little hope.

Shortly after Unitarian officials had informed Marie by phone that night, news of Jim's injury was on the national TV news. Plans were made for Marie to meet Jim's father in Birmingham and for both of their mothers to go to Boston from Casper to care for the children.

The next day, the name James Reeb was on the front page of every newspaper and at the top of every newscast.

Howlett, Reeb's associate from All Souls in D.C. (and soon to be his biographer), also headed for Birmingham and joined Marie on the flight from Atlanta. The doctors knew, after the surgery, that he would not be able to recover from the severe brain damage. The machines were simply keeping him alive.

At 7 p.m. on Thursday night, Jim's heart stopped and this time no efforts were made to restart it. The word quickly spread to the crowd at the Brown Chapel in Selma, which included two little African American girls who were neighbors in the nearby George Washington Carver Homes: Sheyann Webb, then 8, and Rachel West (later Nelson), 9. In a 1980 memoir, Sheyann recalled:

> I just kept thinking how even though he had been white, he had been one of us, too. I kept thinking that he had come to help us, just because he was a good man who couldn't stand by and watch injustice continue. ... And Rachel, kneeling there with her head covered with her coat parka, turned to me and I saw she had a puzzled look on her face. And she had tears in her eyes and she is shaking her

---

[98] Three years later, on April 7, 1968, Rev. Miller was one of the speakers at a memorial service for Dr. Martin Luther King Jr. at the Natrona High Auditorium in Casper.

head and she says to me, 'Why they have to do that, Shey? Why they have to hit him like that?' I didn't know.[99]

In accordance with his wishes expressed in a letter Jim had written to Marie in 1961, he was cremated and his ashes were scattered in Shirley Basin, south of Casper, Wyoming.

Shortly after he died, President Lyndon Johnson called and expressed his condolences to Marie and then to Reeb's father. He said a private plane would be sent to take them to Boston and then to Wyoming when they were ready to go.

1965: Reeb's murder pushes passage of the Voting Rights Act

"With the announcement of Jim Reeb's death," Howlett wrote, "a cry of rage rose from all over the nation and echoed around the world."[100] Several thousand clergy came to Washington for a protest meeting. Their representatives met with LBJ and asked that the U.S. Army be sent to Selma to protect the marchers.

On the day after the attack, hundreds of marchers were stopped by police in Selma as they moved toward the county courthouse. They kept a vigil day and night at the "Selma Wall" until a compromise was reached to allow the Reeb memorial march on Monday March 15th. The Rev. Martin Luther King led more than 3,500 people through the streets of Selma to lay a wreath at the courthouse door and pray for Reeb. King's aide, the Rev. Ralph Abernathy, said the spirit of Rev. Reeb "will dwell at the Dallas County Courthouse until every Negro is free to vote."

In his eulogy at Selma, Rev. King said:

> The world is aroused over the murder of James Reeb. ... James Reeb was murdered by the irresponsibility of every politician who has moved down the path of demagoguery, who has fed his constituents the stale bread of hatred and the spoiled meat of racism. ... He was murdered by the brutality of every sheriff and law enforcement agent who practices lawlessness in the name of law. He was murdered by the timidity of a federal government that can spend millions of dollars a day to keep troops in South Vietnam, yet cannot protect the lives of its own citizens seeking constitutional rights. Yes, he was even murdered by the cowardice of every Negro who tacitly accepts the evil system of segregation, who stands on the sidelines in the midst of a mighty struggle for justice.[101]

---

[99] Webb, Sheyann and Rachel West Nelson, *Selma, Lord, Selma*, University of Alabama Press 1980, 115-116. The frontispiece of the book is a photo of the two girls with Martin Luther King taken 10 days later before the start of the second march to Montgomery.

[100] On January 11, 1966, Howlett lectured on "the current revolution in religious thought" at the University of Wyoming Commerce & Industry auditorium. His talk was sponsored by the First Person Coffeehouse and the Laramie Unitarian Fellowship. The Branding Iron report on the speech does not indicate whether he made mention of his colleague James Reeb.

[101] The use of the word "sidelines" soon took on a deep irony in Wyoming. Four years later, after the Black 14 were booted from the UW football team, Coach Eaton and many of his supporters expressed consternation and anger about the players' arm band protest. Eaton went ballistic, seeing the action as pure ingratitude by young men who should not have been involved in any demonstration called by their fellows in the Black Student Alliance. Most Wyoming people seemed to agree with him, saying: "Why would they do such a thing when, at taxpayer expense, they were being given an opportunity to get an education and play a game they loved. Wasn't that enough?"

In Washington on March 15th, President Johnson spoke to a joint session of Congress, appealing to them to enact legislation guaranteeing voting rights to all Americans, and particularly to African Americans who had been excluded from registering to vote in the South by the imposition of barriers such as literacy tests:

> At times, history and fate meet at a single time in a single place to shape a turning point in man's unending search for freedom. So it was at Lexington and Concord. So it was a century ago at Appomattox. So it was last week in Selma, Alabama. There, long suffering men and women peacefully protested the denial of their rights as Americans. Many of them were brutally assaulted. One good man--a man of God--was killed.
>
>   ...
>
> This time, on this issue, there must be no delay, no hesitation, no compromise with our purpose. We cannot wait another eight months [the time it took to pass the Civil Rights Act of 1964 which, as finally passed, did not include a voting rights provision]. We have already waited a hundred years and more. The time for waiting is gone.

Thousands poured into D.C. for a memorial service, and similar services were held across America. In Worcester, Mass., the official Roman Catholic diocese newspaper proposed sainthood for Reeb.

In Casper, mourners marched from the center of town to NCHS where high school classmates Dr. Joseph Murphy, Attorney Frank Bowron and Mayor Patrick Meenan spoke, along with Roy Wilkins, Executive Director of the NAACP who said Reeb was a "20th Century Good Samaritan". Fred Devereaux, President of the Casper NAACP, was among those who greeted Wilkins at the Casper Air Terminal.[102]

Mrs. Myrtle N. Rucker and Mrs. Johnetta Moore of Casper, officers of the National Association of Colored Women's Clubs Inc.'s Wyoming chapter, joined with their national organization in resolving "that Rev. Reeb has not died in vain. We share his mortal loss with family and friends. We pledge to finish the task he so nobly began."[103] Al Foreman, secretary of the Casper NAACP branch, said leaders from Montana, Colorado and Wyoming were expected to "join the march and sing freedom songs."[104]

In a March 11th editorial in the Casper Tribune, the author called the attack on Reeb "an inexcusable and savage act of terrorism". The author noted that the demonstrations in the South, while peaceful in concept, almost invariably led to violence. But regardless of how one views the strategy of the current struggle, the author wrote, "this determination to stand for principle at all risks must arouse a degree of admiration." An editorial the next day said Reeb's death was felt

---

[102] Casper Tribune, 3/15/1965. Devereaux's son Mike became a major league baseball player and had 24 home runs and 107 RBIs for the Baltimore Orioles in 1992. In 1995 he was a key player in the Atlanta Braves' World Series championship run. He grew up in Casper and attended Kelly Walsh High School.

[103] Casper Tribune 3/17/1965.

[104] Wyoming State Tribune, 3/14/1965.

more deeply in Casper because "it was here that he grew up. It was here that he preached his first sermon."

Gov. Cliff Hansen agreed to be chairman of a statewide fund drive to help the family. In short order, more than $100,000 was raised nationally in other fund drives to provide for Reeb's family, and much more was raised for the civil rights movement itself, including $100,000 from a single show called "Broadway Answers Selma" put on by some of the country's best known entertainers. The nationally-syndicated Washington Post cartoonist Herb Block drew a panel titled "A.D. 1965" showing a new grave and gravestone bearing the name "James J. Reeb – Selma, Alabama" with a wreath of thorns leaning against it.

After an overflow crowd attended Sunday services at All Souls in D.C., they marched to Lafayette Park where 15,000 gathered to pay respects to Reeb. Howlett relates that Jim Reeb himself had played a role in organizing a similar march after the three black girls had been killed in the Birmingham church bombing in September, 1963. An estimated 25,000 people gathered at Boston Commons.

That week, after a memorial service at Arlington Street Church in Boston (the Reeb family's church that would become the site of a landmark Vietnam War protest three years later involving a Cheyenne East graduate - see the Oestereich chapter at p. 142), Mrs. Reeb and her four children boarded President Johnson's private plane and flew to Casper for a memorial service there. On March 20, the family was shown in an AP photo at the Boston airport enroute back to Casper, which was to become their home once again.

On March 25, about 30,000 people completed the march from Selma to Montgomery under the protection of federalized Alabama National Guard troops. They stood on the steps of a state capitol which was crowned by a Confederate flag.[105]

Later on March 25 near Selma, a 39-year-old white mother and Unitarian named Viola Gregg Liuzzo, from Detroit, was returning to Montgomery after dark with an African American in the car. She was part of a team shuttling marchers back to Selma. Ku Klux Klan members pulled up beside Liuzzo's car and shot her dead.

When three men were charged with her murder, Art Hanes became one of the defense attorneys. Hanes was a staunch segregationist who served as mayor during the tumultuous 1963 period in which police commissioner Eugene "Bull" Connor used fire hoses on African American protesters. The three defendants were acquitted in state court but were later found guilty in federal court and were sentenced to 10 years in prison.

Fifty years later, in May, 2013, Sally Liuzzo-Prado accepted the Ford Freedom Humanitarian Award on her mother's behalf.

In Washington on July 15, 1965, Rep. Teno Roncalio, D-Wyo., said House passage of the voting rights bill was "a monument to the dedication of the late Rev. James J. Reeb of Casper."

On Dec. 10, 1965, an all-white jury took only 90 minutes to find three Selma men not guilty of the murder of James Reeb, even though at the trial one of the ministers who was with Reeb that night identified one of the three defendants as the lead man in the assault. The defense

---

[105] On October 18, 1969, the day after coach Lloyd Eaton had cast off the 14 black players from his team, a spectator held up a Confederate flag at the top of the student section at UW's Memorial Stadium for three quarters of the BYU game. The flag was pictured in the Branding Iron the next Friday, but the unfurler of the flag was never identified. Amid all the assertions that the Black 14 incident was caused by "outside agitators" such as the Black Panthers, one has to wonder whether the Confederate flag flyer was the only actual outside agitator at the game.

attorneys had claimed that Reeb's own friends had let him die because the civil rights movement needed a martyr, according to a UPI report from Selma.

At some point shortly after Reeb's murder, a James Reeb Memorial Park was dedicated at Winter Memorial Presbyterian Church in North Casper. In 2011, the Casper Young Professionals began a project to rehabilitate the park into a community garden.

At the University of Wyoming at the end of March, the Student Senate sponsored an appearance at the A&S Auditorium by Lawrence Weiss, a Denver Post editorial writer and civil rights advocate. An article about the appearance in the student newspaper on March 26th said: "the recent death of a Unitarian minister in Alabama has prompted" two grad students in counselor education to urge students to attend the speech and learn how "the individual belief in equal rights for all men can be felt all the way to Selma, New Orleans or Laramie." The article did not mention Reeb's connection to Wyoming.

In 2015, Reeb's widow Marie, one or two of his children and a granddaughter were still living in Casper. Two of the granddaughters traveled to Selma to visit the scene of their grandfather's beating, and Leah Reeb has spoken at a Casper NAACP meeting, according to Casper schools' teacher and administrator Mel Hamilton, one of the Black 14.[106] Family members, including sons Dr. Steven Reeb of Cheyenne and John Reeb of Casper, traveled to Selma and participated in the 50th anniversary activities there.[107]

1869-1965: MIXED RACE MARRIAGE LAWS - LIMITS ON LOVING LIFTED

On December 7, 1869, almost exactly 100 years before the Black 14 catastrophe at Laramie, the legislature of the 17-month-old Territory of Wyoming passed -- over Gov. John A. Campbell's veto -- a law declaring that Caucasians could not "knowingly intermarry with a person of one-eighth or more negro, asiatic or Mongolian blood." Violation of the law was a felony punishable by no less than three and up to five years in prison. The law also made a criminal of the person solemnizing the marriage or issuing a marriage license to the couple.

Campbell vetoed the bill because it did not "bear equally upon all races," in that marriage to American Indians was not also prohibited. His veto message explained:

> How far it may be expedient or well to attempt to govern social life and taste by legislative prohibitions and restrictions is not easily answered; but there can be no doubt that any bill of this character should be formed so as to bear equally upon all races of men. If it be a wise policy to prohibit intermarriage between persons of different races, on account of the supposed or real moral and physical deterioration of the issue of such marriages, I can see no reason for excepting any race from the operations of the law.

---

[106] According to an article in the Casper paper on March 22, 1965, "Mrs. Gaurdie Bannister ended the First Presbyterian service in Casper for James Reeb, slain in Selma, Ala., while supporting Martin Luther King's efforts to extend the vote to Alabama's black citizens. She sang "'We Shall Overcome.'"

[107] Many photos of Marie Reeb and other members of the family in Selma by Casper Star-Tribune photographer Ryan Dorgan published March 14, 2015 and updated August 29, 2019 (also available on-line).

Another possible reason for the anti-miscegenation law was that by "prohibiting Negroes and Chinese from marrying whites, competition among Wyoming men for the few available white women was reduced."[108]

1882: Repeal and William Jefferson Hardin

Thirteen years later, Wyoming's first black legislator, William Jefferson Hardin (who had married a white woman while living in Colorado) played a role in a successful effort to repeal the law.[109] Repeal was supported by a remarkably forward-looking editorial in the Cheyenne Daily Leader on February 12, 1882:

> [The repeal bill] proposes to wipe out a law that is one of the musty and mildewed relics of a barbaric age, and should have no favor or place among the laws of the youngest and most progressive territory. The law aims to do something which statutory law should never attempt to do--regulate purely social matters. The matter of choice of a husband or wife should be left to the consciences and tastes of those desiring to marry.

> ... The miscegenation act aims to prevent 'the corruption of blood' on the principle that Negro, Asiatic or Mongolian blood is so vastly inferior to Caucasian blood that it is a felony to commingle them. ... Is it the right spirit to punish as a felon a colored man who may chance to wed a white woman, when that man stands equal in the eyes of the law with a white man? equal in his right to public office? equal in his right to become president of the United States if the people choose to elect him? In miscegenation laws we subvert the very spirit and principles which have caused the U.S. to advance more rapidly during twenty years than any other nation that ever existed since the day when our *colored* progenitors, Adam and Eve, were driven from the Garden of Eden. [Emphasis in original].[110]

The repeal bill was adopted in March of 1882, but according to a thesis cited in the Kaufman article, the repeal was passed principally by a fear that the law might slow the population growth that was needed to qualify Wyoming for statehood. Whatever the reason, interracial marriages were legal in Wyoming for the next 31 years.

1913: Interracial marriage becomes a felony again in Wyoming

Wyoming did become a state in 1890, and in 1913 the legislature chose to reinstate "the musty and mildewed relic of a barbaric age." The Laramie Republican reported on February 12th that "the house might be said unanimously to have embraced" a bill to make illegal "all marriages of white persons with negroes, mulattoes, Mongolians or Malays" (but not including marriage to persons of "asiatic blood" this time). The bill was signed into law late on Feb. 22nd, the last night of the Legislature. It provided that anyone entering into or solemnizing a prohibited

---

[108] Hardaway, Roger D., "Prohibiting Interracial Marriage", 52 *Annals of Wyoming* (Spring 1980).

[109] "Discrimination in the 'Equality State'" by Reagan Joy Kaufman, *Annals of Wyoming*, Winter 2005.

[110] The editorial does not identify its author. At the time, J. C. Baird, an attorney and businessman, was managing editor and Frank H. Clark was city editor.

marriage would be penalized by a fine of up to $1,000 and "imprisonment of not less than one year nor more than five years". According to an article about Wyoming's miscegenation laws by Roger D. Hardaway in Annals of Wyoming, Spring 1980, passage of the act was part of a white supremacy movement spreading across the country.

In early March, an article was printed in several state newspapers erroneously saying that Gov. Joseph M. Carey had vetoed the bill. This prompted the Natrona County Tribune editor to condemn the governor in an editorial on March 3rd. The author was outraged about a marriage solemnized in Sheridan the previous week between a wealthy Helena, Mont., restauranteur Wang Toy, a "Chinaman", and Emma Waddell, "an American girl". The editorial said:

> Wyoming, the mother of the right of women to the elective franchise, is one of the
> very few states in the Union, if not the only one, where such a thing could occur.
> A Chinaman cannot become a citizen of the United States, will his half-breed
> children be citizens? Israel Zangwill's "Melting Pot" is a tame comparison with
> the indecency, the untold shame, which fastens itself upon our great state because
> such misalliances are allowed within its borders. ... This veto emphasizes again
> the fact that ... the men and women the people elect as their representatives are
> asinine incompetents and should go to Lander or Evanston [site of Wyoming's
> mental hospital] rather than Cheyenne.

The editorial said the bride and groom came to Wyoming from Helena because their marriage was barred in Montana. But on March 18th, the Wyoming Tribune in Cheyenne reported that before issuing the marriage license the Sheridan County Clerk had wired the governor's office asking whether the bill had been signed into law. In reply the clerk was wrongly informed that the governor had vetoed the bill, so the marriage license was issued and the marriage performed. Shortly thereafter the governor's office informed the clerk that the bill had indeed become law on Feb. 22nd. The article said ""Emma Waddell of Helena, Mont., is still Emma Waddell. ... County Attorney Diefenderfer will endeavor to get in touch with the couple and notify them that their marriage was illegal."

1965: Finally, repealed again in Wyoming

The anti-miscegenation statute remained on the Wyoming statute books for the next 52 years.

A UPI article appearing in the Laramie Boomerang on January 16, 1965, reported that the Wyoming House "passed as a committee of the whole today a bill permitting interracial marriages in Wyoming." The bill -- as passed on first reading -- would have recognized interracial marriages created outside the state but would have continued the prohibition on such marriages within the state. The bill, introduced by Rep. Vern Vivion, R-Carbon, was amended at some point to simply repeal the 1913 statute completely. The repeal passed by a 51-8 vote in the House and by 21-3 in the Senate. The "nay" votes in the House were cast by seven Republicans (from Big Horn, Campbell, Fremont, Goshen, Johnson and Sublette counties) and one Democrat (a future governor from Lincoln County). In the Senate the ayes included Sen. J. W. Myers of Uinta County (See the 19-year-old vote chapter at pg. 172). The three nay votes were by Republicans from Park, Sheridan and Converse counties.

According to Kaufman, "The repeal had more to do with the law being unconstitutional than being morally repugnant."

Indeed, the U.S. Supreme Court in 1967 in a case most appropriately titled *Loving v. Virginia*, ruled that anti-miscegenation laws were unconstitutional. (388 U.S. 1). In his opinion for the unanimous court, Chief Justice Earl Warren noted:

On January 6, 1959, the Lovings pleaded guilty to the charge, and were sentenced to one year in jail; however, the trial judge suspended the sentence for a period of 25 years on the condition that the Lovings leave the State and not return to Virginia together for 25 years. He stated in an opinion that:

Almighty God created the races white, black, yellow, malay and red, and he placed them on separate continents. And, but for the interference with his arrangement, there would be no cause for such marriage. The fact that he separated the races shows that he did not intend for the races to mix.

The Supreme Court found that marriage was a fundamental freedom and its prohibition on racial grounds was "directly subversive to the principle of equality at the heart of the Fourteenth Amendment." The opinion concluded that Virginia's law prohibiting interracial marriages was a law "designed to maintain White Supremacy."

In 2002, Alabama became the last state to remove its anti-miscegenation law when its voters adopted a constitutional amendment placed on the ballot by the initiative process.

1964-66: REVOLVING DOOR AT OLD MAIN BRINGS WILLIAM D. CARLSON

1964: Duke Humphrey retires and Fey says 'Hi'

University of Wyoming students of the mid-60s who were still around to witness the "resignation" under pressure of UW President Robert Sternberg in fall 2013 -- after only four months at the helm -- were justified in saying, 'this is all *deja vu*'.

The 1960s version of the same story began on April 22, 1964, when the University of Wyoming trustees announced that UW's president for 19 years, George "Duke" Humphrey, would be retiring as of June 30th. Humphrey had come to UW in 1945 after serving 11 years as president of Mississippi State. In 1975, State's large, newly-built basketball arena was named Humphrey Coliseum after him.

Less than 24 hours after the retirement announcement, Trustees President Harold F. Newton announced that John T. Fey (pronounced as in the song "fie on goodness"), president of the University of Vermont for six years, had been appointed to replace Humphrey.

A native of Virginia, Fey, 47, had an undergraduate degree from William & Mary, a law degree from Maryland, an M.B.A. from Harvard and a doctorate in law from Yale. After practicing law in Maryland and serving in that state's legislature, he became a professor of law and then, four years later, the dean at George Washington Law School. A BI article by Editor Kathy Karpan on April 24, 1964, reported that Fey had been married to the former June Keseler Gerber for 17 years and they had a 15-year-old son, John Jr.

In 1956 Fey had been named clerk of the U.S. Supreme Court. Two years later he left that position to become president at Univ. of Vermont. He was only the third clerk in the history of the high court to resign.

Why did Fey come to Wyoming in 1964? An obscure UPI news report printed in the Bridgeport, Conn., Telegram on July 22, 1964 (three weeks after he became UW president), may partly answer that question because some concern had arisen at UW when Fey showed up with his girlfriend instead of his wife. The news item read as follows: "CRAFTSBURY COMMON, Vt., (UPI) -- University of Vermont President John T. Fey was married here Monday to a 36-year-old Wellesley, Mass., divorcee, it was disclosed Tuesday. University officials said Fey and Mrs. Barbara Jaffee Barnet, a ski clothing designer, were married at the United church here. The university said the couple applied for a marriage license last week in Burlington. It was Fey's second marriage. His first marriage ended in divorce."

1965: UW Civil rights group takes on racial and gender discrimination

In the spring of 1965, a UW organization called the Student Non-Violent Coordinating Committee (SNCC) was formed, and an engineering graduate student from New York, Louis Dell'Osso was elected president. The group's aim was to eliminate all forms of discrimination against minority groups on campus, the BI reported, including removal of "white only clauses" in the constitutions of any fraternity groups. The group decided not to affiliate with the national organization of the same name. Dell'Osso called on students to stand against humor based on racial stereotypes and language, and to not support businesses and groups that discriminated on the basis of race.[111] He also called upon UW to remove from its approved housing list any landlords who discriminated against minorities. (This effort was still being pressed by student groups three years later).

At their first meeting of the fall semester, members of the group -- now calling itself the Student Committee for Civil Liberties -- passed a resolution praising Sigma Chi fraternity's national convention for removing all references to race, color, religion or national origin from its pledge forms and dropping the requirement that a photo be included with the form. SCCL also decided to set up a table in the Union adjacent to the Marine recruiting table and pass out a Quaker pamphlet about obtaining conscientious objector status. A cartoon by John Catterall in the BI October 29, 1965, indicated that serious opposition to the Vietnam War was occurring elsewhere. It showed a Marine Vietnam veteran carrying a flame thrower and asking a bearded man holding a draft card, "Ya' need a light, buddy?" A letter to the editor in the BI October 22nd blasted war protesters, saying they were cowards and "babies who are afraid to put down their bottles, leave home and find the meaning of the word FREEDOM."

Also in fall 1965, the SCCL sponsored a campus appearance by Dale Gronemeier, western regional director of the National Committee to Abolish the House Un-American Activities Committee. He also spoke at a "Unitarian buffet" where his topic was "John Birch, Jim Crow and HUAC." At UW he said it was "a great crime that we allow a small group of politicians to determine what is or isn't 'un-American'". The House committee's only real purpose, he said, was "to place social disgrace on the accused" without due process, not to consider litigation.

In October, after law student Bob Bergstrom outlined his argument that UW's curfew requirements for female dormitory students were unconstitutional and "the truest expression of the double standard", the SCCL adopted a resolution opposing the "hours" rules. "Women should be given the chance to exercise their freedom of choice as part of their education to prepare them for life after college," the resolution said.[112] But at an open meeting on the issue all

---

[111] BI, April 4, 1965.

[112] BI 10/22/1965 pp. 1 and 2.

remarks from the floor, from male and female students, including officers of the Associated Women Students, supported the curfew. Bergstrom listed the many reasons set forth for the curfew, such as promoting good study habits and protecting health and morals. The only reason which did not apply equally to men and women, he suggested, was "that the girls are the ones who carry the babies." At this point Dean of Women Peggy Tobin and several house mothers staged a walk-out. The AWS president, Mada Petranovich, told the BI reporter later that a poll of 800 coeds showed only 10 percent supported the SCCL's effort.

1966: Fey says "bye-bye"
In the spring of 1965, UW President Fey announced that two new science buildings would be built on the west end of Prexy's Pasture.[113] This led to widespread criticism from many alumni and students and the Trustees reversed themselves a month later. Former Branding Iron editor Kathy Karpan remembered this controversy in the fall with a take-off on a Sir Walter Scott poem in the October 22nd BI: "Breathes there an alum with soul so dead/Who never to himself hath said/This is my own, my Prexy's Pasture?"

On December 11, 1965, newspapers carried wire service articles saying that three Selma, Alabama men had been acquitted of murder in the death of James Reeb, a white Unitarian minister from Boston who had gone to Selma in March to join the Rev. Martin Luther King in his voting rights march to Montgomery. Reeb was a 1945 graduate of Casper Natrona High School.

On that same day, Wyoming's newspapers also carried stories saying that the president of the University of Wyoming, Dr. John T. Fey, had announced his resignation effective July 1, 1966, so as to take a position as president of a life insurance company in Montpelier, Vermont.

Trustees expressed "deep regret" and said a search for a replacement would begin immediately. According to then-A&S Dean E. Gerald Meyer, in a 2013 interview, Fey "put UW on the road to becoming a highly reputable research university during his short tenure in Old Main."

After leaving Laramie, Fey served seven years as president of the National Life Insurance Co. in Montpelier, then became chairman of the Equitable Life Assurance Co. in New York. He retired to Stowe, Vt. and was a member of the UVM board of trustees from 1982-85.[114]

1966: John E. King crowned as President of UW
The man selected to replace Fey and become UW's 15th president was Dr. John E. King Jr., but his term at the helm was destined to be short and controversial.

King had been president for the previous 13 years at what was then called Kansas State Teachers College. That institution had been founded as Kansas State Normal School in 1863. A fascinating time line of the college on its website notes that in 1874, "A grasshopper invasion

---

[113] BI, March 5, 1965. The plan called for eliminating the streets and parking areas around the pasture so as to retain the same square footage of the historic pasture despite the new buildings. A drawing of the layout appeared in the BI on April 23, 1965.

[114] A 2008 report of donors to Simmons College in Boston shows Barbara Jaffee Fey as a 1949 graduate. In a 2012 report from the Classics Department at the University of Colorado, the department chairman expressed appreciation to Barbara Fey who had donated funds to finance the curation of "a spectacular collection of Roman gold and silver coins" which her brother, the late Wink Jaffee, had willed to CU.

causes already meager faculty salaries to decline by 18 percent." In 1887, the time line says, "the front parking at the school is extended 10 feet -- to provide a line of hitching posts."

In 1889, KSN's enrollment was nearly double that of both the University of Kansas and Kansas State. KSN graduated its first two African American students in 1898 (the University of Wyoming has not determined who its first such graduate was). KSN's name was changed to Kansas State Teachers College in 1923 (and then to Emporia State University in 1977).

King was reared in Texas and was a Navy lieutenant during WWII. He was a graduate of North Texas State, Arkansas and Cornell. After a stint as a professor at Cornell in the early 50s he was provost at Minnesota-Duluth and went to Kansas from there. Enrollment at KSTC increased six-fold during his 13 years as president, and the art-theater-communications building at Emporia was named King Hall in his honor.

Dr. King arrived in Laramie on Aug. 3, 1966, to a "Wild West welcome".

In a speech to new students at mid-term that fall, he provided his pointers for success at college. "If you are worried about Dad's reaction to your downslips, simply sit down after church and write home explaining that things are now O.K. because you have changed your advisor and are in the process of dropping all uninteresting courses. And of course you have signed up to donate blood to the Red Cross." He advised it was better to have a "B" average in 12 hours of courses than a "C" average in 16.

Law student Jon Brady of Casper responded with a letter-to-the-editor saying King's advice to take 12 hours per semester could result in an immediate Vietnam War draft call for the male students. Brady had graduated from Natrona County High in 1956, went to UW for two years before earning a master's in international studies at Denver University. He then became an officer in the U.S. Navy and was aboard the U.S.S. Coral Sea in 1965 when the U.S. forces began to bomb North Vietnam.

In a 2018 interview, Brady said his first personal experience of prejudice came at UW when a fraternity brother brought a potential pledge to the house for a visit. "He was from South Korea and there was lots of negative reaction to him because he was Asian."

Brady left the Navy in 1965 and enrolled in law school at UW. As he learned more about the deceptions used to involve the U.S. in Vietnam he became an opponent of the war. Brady eventually became a professor of political science and international studies for 29 years at Casper College. One of his students there was Steven Reeb, son of James Reeb who was killed in Selma, Ala. while supporting Martin Luther King's voting rights movement.

Brady said that while he was in law school he received a call from a Navy officer he had known in the service who had since become an FBI agent. "He learned where I was and called and asked to meet," Brady said. "He traveled to Laramie. I thought it was only to be a social call, but he actually wanted me to supply information about people at the university speaking against the Vietnam War."

1967: Protest over "Loco" parentis rules at UW

At the end of February, 1967, as some of their fellow students were headed off to Vietnam and student anti-war protests across much of the nation intensified, the UW Student Senate was busy challenging a policy prohibiting visitation between the sexes in dorms. The policy submitted for Trustees' consideration allowed visiting hours with the opposite sex from 3-6 p.m. on Sundays provided two-thirds of the wing in question's residents approved the idea. The policy provided that dorm room doors must be left "wide open and present an unobstructed view of their room." (This was eventually changed to require doors to be open by two inches).

Furthermore, it said students "should maintain proper conduct (no necking, petting or excessive noise) and proper dress. Girls will wear dresses or skirts and sweaters, and boys will wear slacks and sportshirts." Guests must not be exposed to disorderliness "or pin-ups and other displays of bad taste," the policy stated.

At the same time, the "coeds" at UW were pushing for withdrawal of a UW dress code. Clarine Dunder of Laramie, a 1964 graduate, remembers walking to campus wearing a dress or skirt in sub-zero temperatures because the dress code prohibited women from wearing pants. The women protesters in 1967 presented a petition with 500 signatures to the Senate, asking for a resolution stating: "The dress policy for women students at the UW should be left to the discretion of the individual woman student. Girls will wear some form of skirt to Sunday meals."

The group also sent a letter to Dean of Women Margaret "Peggy" Tobin warning that if their resolution was not approved, "the women of this institution will unite on Thursday in open violation of this regulation."

University officials managed to avoid the demonstration, but the fuss showed that the long-applied *In loco parentis* college management philosophy was alive and well at UW, even into the late '60s. It included a strict curfew for women dorm residents (the so-called "hours" policy) and prohibitions on PDA ("public displays of affection").

A sophomore named Peggy Jo White wrote a letter to the editor of the Branding Iron in November, 1967, complaining that the university was contradicting the state's image as the "Equality State" by trying to impose morality on women students with the hours rules. "Is this institution afraid to recognize the new trend that women no longer seek just the security of home and marriage, but they also wish to attain worthwhile positions as individuals?"

In March of 1968, the Associated Women Students were drafting proposals to liberalize the "hours" policy. If approved by Dean of Women Peggy Tobin and the Trustees, the changes would allow freshmen dorm women to be out until 10:30 Monday through Thursday, 1:30 a.m. Friday and Saturday and midnight on Sunday. Sophomores and juniors could be out until midnight Sunday through Thursday. The proposal would also allow 10 extensions to midnight on weekdays to freshmen women during their first semester and, to those who turned in at least a B-minus grade point average, 15 permits would be allowed during the second semester.

The hours debate was still smouldering in March, 1969. Dan White, a candidate for the ASUW Senate from McIntyre Hall, called for "abolition of women's hours and the point system." Noting that only one of the current 25 senators lived in a dormitory and a large majority were from fraternities and sororities, White advocated changing the Senate election system to insure that dormitory and married student housing residents were represented.

1967: Presto - King dethroned
In December of 1966, a UPI article was printed in numerous papers about the KUWR "Christmas tree" composed of lights strung upon the antenna tower and guy wires on top of the Union. The display was conceived by Ken Haines, a graduate student and the student manager of

KUWR who also worked at KLME radio downtown. The Christmas tree article appeared in the Denver Post, set in type that was arranged so as to form a profile of a perfect Christmas tree.[115]

In late-February, 1967, Haines came into possession of a leaked letter addressed to the trustees and signed by all the deans, expressing a lack of confidence in President King and demanding that he resign or be fired. Suspicious it might be a spoof, Haines began attempts to verify it.

But a few days later, the state's newspapers reported a bolt out of the blue: the resignation of President King after only seven months on the job and the appointment of emeritus engineering dean Hajalmar T. Person as acting president. Person, who had retired as dean in 1964, was to be UW's fourth president in four years, after Duke Humphrey had served for 19.

The resignation resulted from what one active participant many years later called "an incident that probably never happened before or since in the halls of academia."[116]

In the announcement of King's resignation, as is usually the case, the trustees, the deans and Gov. Stan Hathaway (who was only three months into his term) made diligent efforts to withhold from the public all details about the reason for the resignation. King would only say that the resignation "is not the aftermath of action by Gov. Hathaway and the Wyoming Legislature concerning our budget proposals for the coming biennium."

As to his plans for the future, King said, "I'm going fishing." But he added, "I really believe in this place."

The Laramie Boomerang, however, carried an article by Gene Bryan at the same time saying that the resignation had resulted from a petition sent to the Trustees and signed by UW's 10 academic deans and one non-academic dean calling for King to resign.

"These facts came to light as the result of a newscast Wednesday night by radio station KLME News Director Ken Haines," the Boomerang article said. "Haines reported the deans had sent a letter to the board dated February 24th expressing ... 'a complete lack of confidence in the academic philosophy and administrative ability of Dr. John E. King Jr.'"

The letter expressed a desire to meet with the trustees on Friday, Feb. 24th.

Haines said the petition had been provided to him on Sunday evening, Feb. 26th. The resignation came after a day-long meeting of the board -- including ex-officio member Hathaway -- on Wednesday March 1.

---

[115] KUWR was a very low power station when it first went on the air in September, 1966, broadcasting from the tower of the Wyoming Union. The UW Trustees had approved the station based on a proposal under which the Student Senate promised not to play rock and roll music. Only a couple of weeks later speech professor John McMullen, the faculty advisor of the station for decades, heard a female DJ playing Rolling Stones tunes during what was billed as a "folk music" program. McMullen shut the station down, which drew the ire of Tony Yuthas, a student senator from Superior who chaired the Senate radio committee. After graduation, Yuthas landed a teaching job in Nebraska, but was unable to avoid the draft. He served in Vietnam, got a law degree from Denver U. and practiced law in Denver for many years. Toward the end of KUWR's first year, Ken Haines produced an "audio yearbook", an LP record documenting all the programs and voices of that year. McMullen served as KUWR faculty sponsor for many years and was beloved by many of the students who worked at the station. McMullen retired to Santa Fe and died in 2017.

[116] Interview in 2013 with E. Gerald Meyer, who was Dean of Arts & Sciences in 1967. The interview occurred not long before the same sort of coup at UW: the "resignation" of President Robert Sternberg after four stormy months at the helm.

Board president Joe H. Watt said King's resignation was accepted "with deep regret" and he wished King happiness and success in the future. Nothing was said about the deans' petition in the UW press release or press conference.

The article said "there had been rumors the past week of personality conflicts, but King, Trustees and faculty members would offer no comment."

In a May, 2013 interview, Dean Emeritus Meyer – still working in a little office in the Arts & Sciences Building – did not recall that the petition had been leaked to the media. He also disputed UW's official line nearly 46 years earlier that the resignation had nothing to do with UW's treatment by the legislature in the session that had just ended. "During that session, the UW representative called me over and told me that King's presentation was a disaster," Meyer said.

As to the petition, Meyer said the deans had come to a decision to move forward with it after they all agreed that King was not providing the right leadership and was difficult to work with. They also agreed that none of the deans would aspire to become president. "We made only the number of copies we would need to give one to each of the trustees and keep one for each of us. We sealed them in envelopes and we stood in front of Old Main and handed them to the board members as they came in."

Meyer said the deans met the next morning at College of Law Dean Frank Trelease's house. Dean Neal Hilston of Agriculture told them he had spoken to Board president Watt during the basketball game the previous night. Watt told Hilston that the deans were making a bigger issue of this than they should and that they should resolve their differences with King and not bother the trustees again.

At the dean's meeting, according to Meyer, "Trelease then said, 'they don't understand how serious we are about this,' and he said he would call Bill Jones" (a new trustee and a Wheatland lawyer who had been a student of his). Trelease later reported back to us and said that Jones had told him, 'when I got that envelope I thought it was tickets to the game. That's the last envelope I'm going to accept while I'm on the Board.'"

But Jones told Trelease that the deans deserved an answer, Meyer recalled. "Jones called the governor, who called a special meeting of the board. With King sitting at the table, each of the deans came in separately to give their reasons for signing the petition," Meyer said. During his turn in the hot seat, Meyer cited about a dozen instances of King not performing as a UW president should, in Meyer's opinion.

"He was rather puritanical," Meyer said. "He once saw some college boys across from Wyo Hall playing tennis without shirts on. He went over to them and told them that was indecent." (The irony in this arises from the fact that within a couple of months these same shirtless men could have found themselves in a shooting war in Vietnam).

"Another time," Meyer said, "there was an ad for Dean's Music Box in the Branding Iron which said, 'Make Love Not War' and King called an emergency meeting to find out who was overseeing the Branding Iron".[117]

King's wife seemed to have similar leanings. In a brief article in the Branding Iron on December 9, 1966, Mrs. King was asked how she was liking UW (her first name, Glennie, was not given in the article, but it said she was from Prosper, Texas, and was an alumna of Chi Omega). "The campus is lovely, especially with the flowers in the fall and spring," she said. "The enthusiasm and support given to the University by the people of Wyoming are very encouraging."

The BI reporter concluded the little article this way: "Mrs. King feels that the students on the whole are good looking and wholesome, 'not the beatnik type.'"

The final straw for President King in 1967 may have come in a meeting with the deans when the problem of keeping UW grads in the state was being discussed. Hilston made a comment which King didn't like and so he told Hilston, 'if one of my deans at Emporia had said something like that I would have taken him to the woodshed."

Meyer said the process that led to King's hiring in the first place was almost as bizarre as the procurement of his resignation.

"The faculty committee did not like King from the start, but they had not come up with a viable candidate of their own," Meyer recalled. "Another of the candidates failed to show up for his scheduled interview. He didn't realize that the plane from Denver to Laramie stopped first in Cheyenne, so he got off in Cheyenne."

"In the end, Trustee Jack Jones of Rock Springs, who had learned about King at an Association of Governing Boards meeting, told me he decided upon King mostly because the enrollment at Kansas State Teachers was about the same as at UW," Meyer said. "But the University of Wyoming -- as a doctoral institution -- is a far different situation from Emporia State. King wouldn't learn, didn't take time to learn. He would say simply, 'at Emporia we did it this way.' "

After UW, King turned up as a visiting professor at Southern Illinois University-Carbondale and moved up to become chairman of the higher education department there from 1970 to 1983. He died in West Columbia, S.C. on June 28, 2008 at the age of 94, survived by Glennie Beanland King -- his wife of 71 years -- and by two daughters. Glennie followed him in death four years later in Lexington, S.C. She was nearly 101 years old.

---

[117] These incidents are reminiscent of the statements and actions of UW President A.G. Crane in December 1931 which provoked a student strike and a demand for an apology. Crane noticed that a large number of students had left the Engineering Ball and gotten into vehicles parked nearby. He opened a number of the car doors and, according to the students, chastised the women students by saying, "You come out here for all your drinking and petting. You ought to go to First Street [Laramie's 'red-light' district] where you belong." Crane refused to apologize and issued an edict barring protesting students from campus and their residence halls and firing them from any university jobs. The students relented. In a subsequent report to the trustees, Crane said that since the end of WWI "there has been a general tendency toward license and laxity of conduct .... The youth movement, the doctrine of natural development, the relinquishment of parental control, the misuse of automobiles, Bolshevism, student strikes, and bizarre modernism have all contributed their share to the frenzied abandon of youth." The Trustees supported Crane. "'The board is convinced the differences arose out of a misunderstanding and misinterpretation of Dr. Crane's remarks,' board members said." *Saratoga Sun* 12/17/1931; Hardy, Deborah *Wyoming University*, 1986 p. 129-30.

1967: Reaction of State Media

The reactions of Wyoming newspaper editors to what one of them called the "King-Dean crisis" were compiled in an article published in the March 10th Branding Iron. Editor Richard Redburn of the Sheridan Press said the loss of two presidents in such a short time had people asking "what's going on down there?" The answer, he said, "is not helped by the attitude of silence maintained by both the board and the resigned president. ... There ought to be an explanation. Without it the university will be damaged by rumors ... and the university will have forfeited an obligation it has to the public from which it receives its financial support...."

The "turmoil of another change" in the UW presidency, the Riverton Ranger argued, showed the importance of continuity on the board. The Ranger said nine of the 12 board members had served two years or less and for four of them it was their first meeting. "There's no winner in the precipitous action such as that taken in Laramie this week. Wyoming and education lose."

Editor-publisher William Missett Sr. of the Casper Star-Tribune suggested that it takes at least two years for a new president to become acclimated. "Now comes the problem of refilling the position again with someone who it is hoped will stay...," Missett wrote. His editorial then endorsed Casper College president Tim Aley for the job at UW.

The Branding Iron, in an editorial by Lee S. Catterall, took strong exception to the secrecy and called for the state legislature to enact an open meeting law, noting that Wyoming was one of only nine states without one. "Wyoming newspapers have demanded to know what happened behind closed doors last week. But unfortunately, they can't expect the truth when it is merely up to the board to determine which public business should be made public and which should not."

An article in the Branding Iron on March 17, 1967, said UW Faculty Senate leaders refused to release any information about that body's "rumored unanimous endorsement" of the deans' actions.

1967: Dr. William D. Carlson of Fort Collins, Colorado moves north

The King "resignation" paved the way for Dr. William D. Carlson, head of the veterinary radiology department at CSU and a national leader in the field, to be appointed UW President.[118] U.S. Sen. Clifford Hansen (R-Wyo) recommended Carlson to the UW search committee and some felt that his ties to U.S. Sen. Gordon Allott (R-Colo.) "would stand him in good stead as a university fundraiser in Republican Wyoming."[119] Thus, Carlson, along with almost all of the other leaders involved in affirming the dismissal of the Black 14, and deciding their lawsuit, had strong Republican ties.

The announcement of Carlson's appointment came on September 17, 1967, setting the stage for his involvement in the Black 14 incident just over two years later. Carlson shut the revolving door on the UW president's office for 11 years.

Carlson's schooling from grade school through veterinary school occurred in his home town of Fort Collins, Colo., home of CSU. As a junior in 1945, he helped the Fort Collins High School Lambkins win the state football championship. He played in the backfield as a substitute

---

[118] A different William D. Carlson served as dean of Nevada Southern (now UNLV) from 1957-1964.

[119] Bullock, Clifford, master's thesis, *Color, Conscience and Conflict*, May 1, 1991, on file at UW Coe Library microfilm collection, p. 15, based on "Presidential Files 1969-70". See also Bullock's article on the Black 14 titled "Fired by Conscience", *Wyoming History Journal*, Winter 1996, p. 4.

and in the semifinal game he kicked three PATs. The next year he made key plays as a runner and receiver in a victory over Loveland High to put Fort Collins into a tie for the Northern Regional title with Boulder again.[120]

After earning his bachelor's and DVM, Carlson obtained a Ph.D. at nearby Colorado University. While serving on the faculty of CSU he was one of the founders of the American College of Veterinary Radiology.

After UW, Carlson was CEO of St. John's Hospital in Jackson, Wyo., and then finished his career with the U.S. Department of Agriculture in Washington D.C. Carlson retired to Denton Texas where their daughter lived, and he died in 2003 at the age of 74.

On Thursday, October 16, 1969, Carlson was in Denver with his son Earl, 17, who was being treated for "serious kidney problems that he had off and on throughout his life".[121] Earl was a student at the UW College of Education's "University Prep" school at the time. On that day he was called by his assistant and informed that the Black Students Alliance had delivered a letter calling for a demonstration against LDS policies before the BYU game in two days.

Shortly after seating himself in his office the next day he received word that all of the 14 black players had been dismissed from the football team. What happened then is discussed below.

1967-70: AUTHORITIES ATTACK THE LONG HAIR EVIL

Hair and dress codes in the schools

In the late Sixties, high school administrators and district trustees became exorcised about some of the students violating school dress and hair codes. One administrator in Casper previewed the feelings of many at UW and around the state after the Black 14 were booted, saying essentially that rules have to be followed whether they are constitutional or not and whether violating the rule actually causes any harm or not.

[During the 1967 meeting, S. Kelly Walsh, Casper's assistant school superintendent] said it probably didn't make much difference how his hair was,

---

[120] Loveland's quarterback in that game, William "Bud" Davis, suffered a jaw fracture and dislocation late in the first half while defending a point after attempt. Sixteen years later, while serving as Colorado University's alumni director, Davis was named interim head football coach. Although the Buffs had gone 9-1 and played in the Orange Bowl the previous season, coach Sonny Grandelius was fired for violating recruiting rules. Davis authored an article in *Harper's* in October, 1965, which said the Buffs lost 35 key players because of the scandal. "Newspapers stopped referring to us as 'The Golden Buffaloes' and substituted 'The Vanishing Herd,'" he wrote. CU won two of eight games in Davis' only year at the helm, although they upset heavily-favored Air Force in his last game. "I was all choked up as I launched into my final speech to that squad. 'Lads,' I said, 'if you beat the Air Force today, I'll resign after the game.'" In March, 1963, Davis was named assistant to the president for student affairs at the University of Wyoming. From 1965-1975, Davis was president of Idaho State University. In 1972 he won the Democratic nomination for the U.S. Senate but lost to Jim McClure in the general election.

[121] Phone interview with Dr. Carlson's wife Beverley in Denton, Texas, 2/20/2017. Earl followed in the footsteps of his father by earning a DVM degree from CSU in 1977 and working for many years for the State of Colorado as the animal welfare veterinarian overseeing the safety of racing animals and studying racetrack surfaces and safety (similar to the work that 1969-71 UW halfback Frosty Franklin DVM would perform in California). Earl received a kidney transplant before veterinary school (kidney donated by his mother). He died in 2009 at the age of 57. His obituary said "his true passion was the University of Wyoming Cowboys, serving as a Northern Colorado representative for the Cowboy Joe Club."

but the school had regulations which must be followed. He said the boy was
defying the principal and school rules and that this sort of thing leads to anarchy.
"Mother, Armed with Federal Judge's Ruling, Will 'Talk' to School
Board", Casper Star Tribune 3/5/1969.

But U.S. Supreme Court Justice William O. Douglas, in a dissent when the high court
refused to take an appeal from a dismissal-for-hair case, said the U.S. Constitution could not be
ignored in issues regarding personal preference:

It comes as a surprise that in a country where the States are restrained by
an Equal Protection Clause, a person can be denied education in a public school
because of the length of his hair. I suppose that a nation bent on turning out robots
might insist that every male have a crew cut and every female wear pigtails. ... I
had supposed that it would be an invidious discrimination to withhold fire
protection, police protection, garbage collection, health protection, and the like
merely because a person was an offbeat nonconformist when it came to hairdo and
dress as well as to diet, race, religion, or his views on Vietnam.
Justice Douglas, dissenting to the denial of certiorari by the U.S. Supreme
Court in *Ferrell v. Dallas Independent School District*, 393 U.S. 856 (1968).

In Wyoming in the '60s, school attendance was mandatory through the 16th birthday or
completion of 8th grade. In the fall of 1967, "Larry", a 14-year-old 9th grader at Dean Morgan
Junior High School in Casper, was sent home. His hair, an inch below his ears, violated the
school district's grooming rules.
Larry told his mother, his only parent at home, that he didn't want to cut his hair and that
this was so important to him that he would stay home if the school did not relent. In October, his
mother informed the school board that her son's person and his clothes were always clean. His
long hair, she said, was his symbol of identity. She argued that parents who ignore their children
or who are too strict deny them their identity which often causes them to turn to violent behavior.
Walsh said at the 1967 board meeting that the suspension was justified in part because
"the other youngsters in school tease [Larry] about his hair being long". He said Larry was
defying the principal and school rules and that this sort of thing leads to anarchy.[122]
Dr. N. E. Fowler, board president, and several other board members agreed that the rule
requiring boys' hair to be above the collar line was a reasonable rule, although they
acknowledged it was difficult to draw a distinction on what was a long haircut and what was not.
School authorities refused to change the rule, and thus Larry was barred from the Casper
schools for at least the next two years.
In the spring of 1969, Larry's mother again appealed to the authorities after U.S. District
Judge James E. Doyle in Madison, Wis., ruled that "freedom to wear one's hair at a certain length
or to wear a beard is constitutionally protected, even though it expresses nothing but individual
taste." The University of Wyoming's student newspaper carried a full-page article with pictures
about Larry's plight and an editorial titled "The making of automatons." The editorial noted that a

---

[122] Casper Star-Tribune 3/5/1969.

98

school board member in Massachusetts had brought barber's shears to an appeal hearing involving a 17-year-old student expelled for long hair.[123]

The Wisconsin ruling prompted the Casper school board to seek a legal opinion from Casper attorney Robert A. Burgess, a WWII bomber pilot. On April 28, 1969, he reported that other courts had ruled for the school board in such cases. "[W]ith present problems of disorders in schools the permissive view of school discipline will remain in the minority," Burgess wrote.[124] "A reasonable rule as to the length of hair is justified upon factors of health, safety, or school discipline or decorum.... It would appear to me that a boy's hair below his shoulders would certainly be a distraction to other junior high students and a source of teasing and torment to the wearer."[125]

In a dissent in a U.S. 5th Circuit Court of Appeals decision in Texas in 1968, Judge Elbert Parr Tuttle (a Republican appointed by Eisenhower) had cut to the heart of the matter and suggested that views like those of Burgess and the board were backwards: "They [the students thrown out because of long hair] were barred because it was anticipated ... that their fellow students ... would do things that would disrupt the serenity or calm of the school. **It is these acts that should be prohibited, not the expressions of individuality by the suspended students**." (*Ferrell v. Dallas Indep. School Dist.*, 392 F.2d 697, cert den. 393 U.S. 856 (5th Cir. 1968). A

---

[123] An ironic case in California arose from the 1963 transfer of a civics teacher at John Muir High School in Pasadena to home teaching because he insisted on wearing a beard. The irony arises from the fact that it is hard to find a photo of the famous wilderness advocate John Muir in which he is not sporting a long, unkempt beard. To justify the transfer, the school authorities contended that a bearded teacher would encourage students by example to violate school rules against beards and long hair. Apparently the authorities were particularly concerned about black students wearing beards. One of the remarkable arguments advanced by the school authorities was "that a larger percentage of male Negro students than other male students want to grow beards and moustaches." The trial court judge found that the transfer was justified because a teacher with a beard "would cause undue and extraordinary comment thereon, and would be disruptive of the educational program of the school." The 3½-year legal battle concluded in 1967 when the California Appeals Court ruled that the authorities had violated the teacher's freedom of expression protected by the First Amendment. *Finot v. Pasadena Bd. of Educ.*, 58 Cal.Rptr. 520 (Calif. App. 2nd Dist. 1967).

[124] The opinion letter is available from the Casper College Western History Center.

[125] A federal court in Alabama in 1969 reversed the dismissal of a student based solely on the fact that his hair was "blocked" in back instead of being "shingled or tapered". *Griffin v. Tatum*, 300 F.Supp. 60 (M.D. Ala. 1969). That court was not impressed by the school board's lame, sexist excuses: "The school authorities offer as justification for the haircut regulation the following reasons: boys' haircuts that do not conform to the regulation cause the boys to comb their hair in classes and to pass combs, both of which are distracting; cause the boys to be late for classes because they linger in the restrooms combing their hair; cause the boys to congregate at a mirror provided for girls to use while combing their hair; in some instances, cause an unpleasant odor, as hair of a length in excess of that provided by the regulation often results in the hair being unclean; cause some of the boys who do not conform to the haircut regulation to be reluctant about engaging in physical educational activities (presumably because they do not want to 'muss' their hair); and, finally, cause resentment on the part of other students who do not like haircuts that do not conform to the school's haircut regulation."

judge in Chicago made a similar ruling, saying "We can't mold people who are going to run the world in the 1980s into the shapes of the 1920s."

Following the Burgess opinion, four UW law faculty members and 38 law students sent a petition urging reconsideration. "We do not believe the school board has offered any reason which is compelling and justifies" the dismissal, the petition read. The faculty members were Peter Maxfield (of Torrington, a future Democratic candidate for Congress), K. R. Simmonds, William Knudsen and Catherine Mealey.

In October, during the week after the Black 14 were kicked off the Wyoming football team, another petition was sent to the state schools superintendent and the Casper board asking that they "end the tragic absence of a harmless 16-year-old from the 'free public education' supposedly available in this state." That effort was headed by philosophy student Corbin Fowler and journalism major Sue Crist.[126]

Larry and his mother were berated by almost everyone moved to write a letter to the editor. One Mrs. Thompson of Paradise Valley said she "read with interest and much disgust" the article about Larry's situation. "I certainly hope the School Board surrenders no ground to this boy. ... This boy is going to have to learn that the United States is not governed by eccentrics, but by people with well-rounded and open minds. He does not want to conform to the majority but wants us, the majority, to conform to him." A woman identifying herself as a former teacher of Larry's derided his mother for sending him to school too dressed up. "I often wished that he would come to school in jeans and shirt like the other boys," she said.

One writer compared his request to wear long hair as equivalent to growing fingernails as long as a student wished. Another, Dean Alexander, said "Fortunately for him, nudism wasn't his 'bag.'"[127]

Almost everyone accepted the idea that the teaching of tolerance was a one-way street in Larry's case: he had to learn to abide by the rules, but everyone who followed the rules was free to harass and denigrate him.

Letter-to-the-editor writer Dyan Talkington, however, supported Larry. "The fact that so many Casperites became irate because of a trivial matter is appalling. ... If the School Board dedicated as much time to the educational system as they do to rules and regulations, we might have a wiser society – one capable of tolerating individuals."

No one commented upon the elephant in the room: gender. Defenders of the hair rule cited possible danger in shop classes, but apparently there were no rules prohibiting girls from wearing long hair, even though unrestrained hair presumably posed a risk in home economics classes.

And no one expressing concern for Larry's health and safety seemed to see the irony that within a year or two he could be sent off to be killed in Vietnam. The authorities in Casper and many other school districts took the position that the solution to teasing and bullying and even physical harm was to expel the victim.

Nearly 50 years later, Larry posted this quote from Daniel Webster on his social media page: "Good intentions will always be pleaded for every assumption of authority. It is hardly too

---

[126] In 1982, Fowler was a philosophy professor at University of Wisconsin-Oshkosh after earning a doctorate from the University of Nebraska. At UW-O he led efforts to raise student awareness of the nuclear weapons threat. Oshkosh Northwestern 4/23/1982.

[127] An expression at the time meaning "his thing", as in the 1967 James Brown tune "Papa's Got a Brand New Bag".

strong to say that the Constitution was made to guard the people against the dangers of good intentions."

Sheriff Ogburn of Rawlins, Wyoming

During the late '60s and early 70s, many young people disillusioned by what they saw as the unconscionable Vietnam War became intrigued by the "counter-culture" in all its manifestations: alternate lifestyles, tie-dyed and bell-bottomed clothes, long hair and beards, mind-altering drugs, Vietnam and draft protests, communal farms, liberal sexual mores. And at every turn, it seemed to many of them, their elders -- "The Establishment" or "Big Brother" -- brought the power of the state and the law against them, often with extremely disproportionate life-crushing punishments for offenses such as possession of relatively small amounts of marijuana. Unlike the lawmakers and enforcers, marijuana users immediately saw that putting marijuana into the same category as heroin and cocaine in the drug laws was ridiculous (and they remain in the same schedule in many jurisdictions today, including the federal Controlled Substances Act -- 21 U.S.C. Sec. 811 – which regards marijuana as highly addictive and having no medical value).

The rancor which many in "The Establishment" held against the young can be illustrated by a remark once made by Gov. Ronald Reagan of California: "A hippie is someone who dresses like Tarzan, walks like Jane and smells like Cheetah."[128] In June 1970, the Jackson, Wyoming, City Council passed an ordinance commonly referred to as the "Hippie Ordinance." Mayor Abi Garaman said transient hippies had caused the drafting of the ordinance, but he said "long, clean hair and bell bottom pants should not be associated with this hard core group of transients." The proposed ordinance, according to news reports, prohibited sitting on sidewalks, sleeping on public benches, climbing trees, peddling, damaging public vegetation, erection of structures without city permits and use of profane language.[129] Gov. Stan Hathaway sent a letter supporting the ordinance. "This is positive action to control the environment of a beautiful resort town," Hathaway wrote.

The pervasiveness of the alienation between the generations extended even to the children of rich, powerful or prominent fathers. UPI released an article in August of 1970 detailing the drug arrests (mostly marijuana) of the sons or daughters of many politicians and entertainers, including the 16-year-old son of the late Robert F. Kennedy, the daughter of Sen. George McGovern (South Dakota senator who would be the 1972 Democratic candidate for president), the son of Oregon Gov. Tom McCall, the son of New Jersey Gov. John Cahill, the children of actors Maureen O'Sullivan, Henry Fonda, Lana Turner and Robert Taylor, along with Jeffrey Ford, the son of singer Tennessee Ernie Ford, arrested at Breckenridge, Colo., on marijuana charges.

Many young people took to traveling around the country by hitchhiking and when they settled somewhere they returned the favor by giving rides to others. Since hitchhiking was illegal under the laws of many states, including Wyoming, law enforcement often gave the hitchers a difficult time. Word was spreading that if you were arrested in Carbon County, Wyoming, the local sheriff, C. W. Ogburn, would transform your appearance into that of a Marine recruit as soon as you arrived at his jail.

---

[128] See Morrison, Pat, "Remembering the Summer of Love," Los Angeles Times, 6/14/2017.

[129] UPI report in Lubbock Texas Avalanche, 10/16/1970; Jackson Hole Guide 6/18/1970;

This practice brought some national exposure to Ogburn in June, 1968, when the Rev. Maurice McCrackin, the 63-year-old pastor of the Community Church of Cincinnati and a prominent leader of a "Christian-oriented" group called "The Peacemakers", complained to Gov. Hathaway and talked to the press about the long jail sentences imposed by an elderly Justice of the Peace and Ogburn's treatment of the two young men in jail at Rawlins.

An AP report of June 28th said "two members of a pacifist organization had their heads shorn and beards shaved off in a Carbon County, Wyo., jail after they were picked up on a hitchhiking charge, an Ohio minister said yesterday." McCrackin identified the two as Graham Lucom, 25, of New York City and Charles Matthei, 20, Wilmette, Ill.

McCrackin said "Matthei has rather strong religious beliefs about these things and refused to be fingerprinted or photographed and would not stand up in the courtroom." He was sentenced to 90 days for resisting arrest, 15 days for hitchhiking and was serving $59 in fines at one dollar per day. McCrackin was able to visit him at the jail after Hathaway called the sheriff. He said Ogburn had not allowed them to write or telephone during their first week in the jail.

The article quoted Hathaway as saying that the law enforcement officers "have acted fairly, have upheld the law and their responsibility." McCrackin said the authorities had "gone far beyond exacting a penalty" for the offense.

Lucom, the article said, was released after serving 14 days of a 30-day sentence and was "studying with a United Church of Christ minister who is a campus chaplain at the University of Wyoming."

That minister was Rev. Dick Putney, who had recently moved his family from Ohio to Laramie for his work with the University Common Ministry. Five years earlier, on Nov. 22, 1963, Putney was taking a group of students from Athens, Ohio, to Cincinnati to participate in a housing fix-up program developed by McCrackin when they heard of JFK's assassination in Dallas. "So the focus changed when we got there," Putney recalled in a phone interview in 2017. "We spent most of our time talking about violence."

McCrackin called Putney and enlisted his aid in helping the two young men in jail. "They apparently were stopped by the Highway Patrol and decided to lie limp on the ground," Putney recalled. "A deputy sheriff was called and the two were maced and taken to the jail. At some point they told the sheriff they were vegetarians and couldn't eat the hot dogs and beans being served. The sheriff refused to alter the menu, so we organized an effort by Laramie people to take vegetarian food to them every other day. "We talked to the governor's office and the media, trying to get them released," Putney said. "Hathaway was upset with all of the media from both coasts calling him about these guys and began to put pressure on Ogburn and the county commissioners to release them."

"When Lucom was released I got a call that he was on a bus to Laramie," Putney recalled. "I met his bus just a half hour before my wife and young kids arrived from the west on a train. So I had to warn them that the guy with funny-looking hair in the car would be staying with us."

Lucom stayed with them for about a month until Matthei was released.

Numerous internet pages reveal that Chuck Matthei died in 2002 of cancer after a remarkable career which began with participation in the civil rights movement and evolved into a lifetime commitment to improving the economic conditions of people in the U.S. and worldwide through community land trusts, affordable housing, family-run farmlands and community loan programs. Shortly before his death he reflected upon a concept put forth by the famous Dorothy Day, founder of The Catholic Worker in Chicago, "the duty of delight". "We can keep hold of the only 'possession' that cannot be taken from us: our dignity, integrity, soul, call-it-what-you-will," he wrote. "That is the decision that defines us, the first important 'life lesson' we should teach our children."

McCrackin died in December, 1997 and was called "the conscience of Cincinnati" in his front page obituary on Dec. 31st in the Cincinnati Enquirer. Earlier that month he had been awarded the St. Francis Xavier medal at Xavier University for his lifelong commitment to non-violent protest of racial segregation, war, nuclear arms, the death penalty, homelessness and poverty. "He was just a great person – very intelligent and kind and loving," the Rev. Ben Urmston, Xavier U.'s director of peace and justice programs said. "Some people thought some of the things he did were extreme, but I think some of the things we do are extreme – our lack of care for the earth, for the poor."

Ogburn was the county sheriff for 25 years. He died in 1993 at age 71.

1967: MUSIC AND RADICAL SPEAKERS AT U DUB

On November 3, 1967, Branding Iron editor Mike Bryan of Cheyenne (who went on to a career in the U.S. Army) presented a strong defense of the U.S. role in Vietnam. His editorial was accompanied by a cartoon by UW student John Catterall showing a Viet Cong guerrilla marching right behind a bearded war protester and his girlfriend.[130]

An article by Emily Howard in the Branding Iron a week later profiled Paul Jeffryes, one of the very few students at UW to identify himself with the counter culture. Paul was a home-grown "hippie" who had longish hair and could be seen occasionally carrying a guitar on campus. He was a Laramie High graduate and in the fall of 1967 was living with his family at home and walking to classes. He was also the editor of "The Horse's Mouth," a campus opinion/literary magazine that had been published for about five years.

But during the previous summer Paul had traveled to San Francisco where he distributed the "Haight-Ashbury Tribune" to tourists and made some money singing folk songs in a North Beach place called "Coffee and Confusion." At UW he was involved with the First Person Coffee House where the anti-war students congregated. When asked by the reporter why someone would become a hippie, Paul said: "They want to try living for the first time according to a value system nobody has imposed on them. I'd call it an experiment in living. They aren't afraid to question things that don't make sense to them--to step out of the framework."

1965-1967: Two trios and The Rhythm Method

The Kingston Trio (and Bob Shane's famous solo "Scotch and Soda"), entertained a crowd of 3,200 at Memorial Fieldhouse in late October, 1965, their second UW concert. The November 3rd Branding Iron featured an unsigned article reporting that following the concert, the Trio signed autographs at Gene's Bar in downtown Laramie. Nick Reynolds told the reporter that the Vietnam War was causing an increasing popularity of protest songs.

---

[130] John Catterall grew up in several towns in Wyoming where his father worked in the oil industry, graduating from Powell H.S. He went on to a career as an artist and art professor at Montana State, New Mexico State and the University of Florida. In a 2017 interview from his summer home in Story, Wyo., Catterall said this pro-Vietnam cartoon was created a year earlier when he was fresh out of the Marines. He said he was in graduate school at Washington State when this cartoon appeared and his view on the war had changed significantly. "They were *rerunning* the cartoon to service the piece on the war," he said. John is the brother of Lee Catterall, the Branding Iron sports editor and editor in the late '60s.

Bill Stoval of Casper, chairman of the Senate Public Exercises Committee, said a previous concert by the Lettermen and the Trio concert had brought in enough funds to schedule Peter, Paul and Mary and Peter Nero the next semester.

Indeed, on March 18, 1966, Peter, Paul & Mary, one of American folk music's greatest groups ever, made their first appearance at UW, singing at Memorial Fieldhouse. "They took it a bit easy, as Mary was pregnant," UW student Dennis Tangeman recalled in an e-mail 50 years later. They were early activists for racial equality and peace. Without PP&M making big hits with their versions of his songs, Bob Dylan may never have become an icon of 20th Century pop music. Mary gave birth to her second child three months after their UW appearance.

Thirty-three years later, in October 1999, PP&M returned to the campus, this time appearing in the Arts & Sciences Auditorium. It was an emotion-filled performance dedicated to gay UW student Matthew Shepard, 21, who was pistol-whipped, tied to a fence just east of Laramie and left for dead on Oct. 7, 1998, by two young men later sentenced to life terms in prison. Shepard died five days later in a Fort Collins hospital. Peter Yarrow visited the fence on the day of the concert and said, "my heart broke."[131]

In spring 1966, Don Riske, a junior in education from Cheyenne, went to see a performance at UW by a traveling musical troupe called "Sing Out 1966!" or "Up With People," sponsored by Moral-Rearmament. He and Chuck McGee, a fellow member of a local band called "The Jesters", dropped out of school, joined the group and toured the U.S. until late August when they returned to UW and joined Ray Edens, Bob Dudley and Donn Hayes in a popular band called "The Rhythm Method."[132]

1967: Loren Watson and Corky Gonzales come to UW

As excitement built around the Cowboys' Sugar Bowl invitation, UW students experienced two radical minority group leaders from Denver at the end of 1967. Loren (or Lauren) Watson and Don Hubbard of the Black Panthers in Denver presented their call for overthrow of the system, by violence if necessary. "There is no other way," Watson said. "This nation has been racist since it was founded. We've tried our peaceful marches and where did it get us?" He alleged that the U.S. government was "practicing genocide" against young black men by forcing them to fight in Vietnam.

On December 7th, Denver boxer-turned-activist Rodolfo "Corky" Gonzales, 39, brought his "Crusade for Justice" to the West Union Ballroom. He also spoke of armed revolution, in coalition with Black Power and the radical left. He said his people should be called Mexican-Americans instead of Spanish-Americans. "The establishment is protected by its laws," he said, "but if you are outside the society, why obey its laws?" Thirteen years earlier, on June 16, 1954, the Casper Tribune-Herald carried a photo of "Corky Gonzalez, former fifth ranking featherweight in world fight competition", being shown a jet airplane at the 140th Fighter-Bomber Wing headquarters at Casper. Corky, wearing a suit coat and tie in the photo, was in town to participate in a three-round exhibition match with another Hispanic boxer from Denver.

In 1966, Gonzales had publicly questioned the Vietnam War. "Would it not be more noble to portray our great country as a humanitarian nation with the honest intentions of aiding

---

[131] AP report, Jackson (Tenn.) Sun, 10/12/1999.

[132] During his legal career in Cheyenne, Riske joined three other lawyers, including Supreme Court Justice Bill Hill, in a band called "The Law North of Crow Creek" which has produced three CDs for private distribution.

and advising the weak rather than to be recognized as a military power and hostile enforcer of our political aims," he asked.[133] In March, 1969, he convened the first Chicano youth conference. He died in 2005.

1967-1971: BETRAYAL IN CHEYENNE

> I know that I only voice the real sentiments of all the people of this community when I say that they accept this noble gift with feelings of deep gratitude. Let us be willing at all times to contribute generously towards its support, making it a power for good and the advancement of all that is best in this community.
>
> Supreme Court Clerk Robert C. Morris of the Carnegie Public Library executive committee, speaking to Cheyenne High School students on February 5, 1902.

In late-summer of 1967, Cheyenne's civic leaders began a public relations campaign to secure voters' approval at a special election of a $690,000 bond issue to build a new county library. The Wyoming State Tribune on Sept. 7th carried a story with the headline, "City to Keep Old Library." Mayor Herb Kingham was quoted as saying "the City Council has no intentions of demolishing the 66-year-old Carnegie Library Building" if the bond issue was passed.

On Sept. 9th, the Wyoming Eagle carried a story with a similar headline: "If New One Built, Present Library Not to Be Demolished." Again, Mayor Kingham said passage of the bond issue "would not mean the present Carnegie Library building would be demolished."

The library had been built with a $50,000 gift to the city in 1899 from steel magnate Andrew Carnegie. This was the first and by far the largest of the 16 Carnegie library grants to Wyoming communities. (As of 2010, five of these buildings were still being operated as libraries: Lusk, Newcastle, Rock Springs, Wheatland and Lander).

The elegant building was dedicated on May 19, 1902. The building was described by Robert Morris as possessing "the highest ideals (of Greek architecture). It is an almost perfect type of Ionic architecture described by Dr. Lord in his Beacon Lights of History as a modification of the Doric, its columns being more slender and with a greater number of flutes, and the capitals more elaborate, formed with volutes and spiral scrolls, while its pediment, the triangular facing of the portico, is formed with a less angle from the base, the whole being more suggestive of grace than strength."

---

[133] The Black Commentator, Issue 135, April 21, 2005.
http://www.blackcommentator.com/135/135_gonzales.html

The assurances from the government officials in Cheyenne led to the passage of the bond issue and construction of a new library at Central Avenue and 29th Street. But almost as soon as the building was completed and the books moved, the City sold the building to Capitol Savings and Loan, a subsidiary of First Cheyenne Corp., which then announced the venerable old library would be razed to make way for a high-rise condominiums or apartments building. In 1973, Capitol Savings' Stanley Hunt announced that a six-story office building with a parking structure alongside would be built.[134] Neither of these projects ever happened. Eventually the site was sold to the Wyoming Catholic Diocese which erected a one-story office building on the site.

Cheyenne architect Frederic Hutchinson Porter was among a few residents who protested. "That is and has been the most beautiful piece of architecture in Wyoming. It's a classic. It's a museum piece. I could just weep to think we're going to lose it." A Cheyenne resident appeared on a KRAE talk show urging citizens to protest, without much effect.

Two months after the Carnegie building's columns were bulldozed to the ground in April, 1971, and as the U.S. continued in its sixth year of massive technological destruction of Vietnam and its people, Republican State Supt. of Public Instruction Robert G. Schrader spoke to VFW members in Laramie, castigating the young people protesting the Vietnam War and the use of napalm and agent orange there. "It will not be the wild-eyed revolutionaries who take over," Schrader told the group, "partly because the people of this country refuse to be terrorized by violence, and perhaps more importantly, because the radical fringe has no constructive program-- not a desire to build, but only a desire to destroy."

1968: COACH EATON AND THE GREAT APRIL SNOWSTORM

Tuesday April 2, 1968, dawned warm and sunny, and the students and staff at the University of Wyoming were beginning to feel they had put the worst of another brutal winter behind them.

UW football coach Lloyd Eaton drove to Cheyenne where he met the American Cancer's Society's state director Byron Stogsdill, and the two of them headed for Torrington where Eaton was to speak at an ACS function. Chris Humphreys, a junior in physics, and his fiancé Maryanne Marietta headed to the foothills just east of Laramie for an afternoon drive. Another student, Jay Knisely, picked up his date and headed for the Diamond Horseshoe -- a mile north of town on old U.S. 30 -- for his 21st birthday dinner.

In the afternoon, the warm sun went under clouds, snow began to fall, thermometers plunged and the wind turned into a gale. Soon, all roads in southeast Wyoming were accumulating drifts of five feet or more. The pelting wet snow continued without abatement for nearly a day and eventually measured 18 inches in Laramie.

Coming back from Torrington, Eaton and Stogsdill followed a snowplow for a while until their windshield wipers stuck. While trying to address that problem the engine stalled. They had only light topcoats with them. So they stuffed Cancer Society literature under their suit pants and shirts and waited out a very cold night. After 24 hours in the car without heat, National Guardsmen reached them 16 miles north of Cheyenne and took them to Cheyenne's Memorial Hospital, passing the stuck snowplow on the way. Eaton had frostbite on one foot. He said he was "lucky to be alive" and urged Wyomingites to have heavy coats and sleeping bags in their cars, "even in spring."

---

[134] Casper Star Tribune 5/3/1971; 5/23/1973.

At the Diamond Horseshoe, 250 people slept on the floor in a building without heat or power. Knisley decided to attempt a return to town but could not move his car. At 2 a.m. his car ran out of gas. He was only 1000 feet from the Horseshoe and, after three hours, frostbite was threatening. So he and his date decided to walk back to the restaurant.

As they fought their way, the blowing snow froze his companion's eyes closed and Knisely carried her although he too was barely able to see. They reached a station wagon and knocked on the window. "Can we get in and get warm?" "No" was the answer.

They plunged ahead and reached a pickup with the engine running. The driver opened the door. "If he had not let us in, we would have lain down and died out there," Knisely said later. "We could go no farther."

Humphrey's car became stuck near the stone quarry 2 ½ miles from town. Fortunately he had followed his father's advice and stowed two sleeping bags in the trunk. He also turned on the two-way Ham radio in his car and tried to contact his friends, also Ham operators, who lived on the 12th floor of McIntyre Hall. He finally received a response from a man in Springfield, Mo. He asked the welcome voice to phone his friends in McIntyre and have them turn on their receivers. The Missouri man called, but no one was home. Finally, Humphreys heard the voice of his friend, John Nunley, who was worried about Humphreys and had hiked to the Union about 11 p.m. to use the Ham Radio Club's equipment.

A Jeep convoy organized by Nunley was stopped by sheriff's officers at the edge of town. During the early morning hours the next day, crews on snowmobiles tried to locate the car. The antenna, topped by a black cloth which Humphreys had attached, was the only part of the car visible. At one time that morning, a snowmobile drove over the hood of the car and didn't see it.

About 4:30 a.m. a snowmobile rammed into the top of the car and took the two to the highway. They returned to Laramie 31 hours after their departure. Humphreys could not retrieve his car until three weeks later.

The snowfall also caused a Brooklyn, N.Y. draft board to call authorities in Wyoming for confirmation after Ed Pollard, who came to UW in the fall of 1965 to play basketball, reported that the snow had prevented him from undergoing his draft physical in Denver. Pollard became one of the founders of the UW Black Student Alliance.

1968: MARTIN LUTHER KING KILLED IN MEMPHIS - RESPONSE IN WYOMING

As the tragic year of 1968 dawned, Wyoming's newspapers were congratulating Coach Eaton and his football team after Gene Huey, Jim Kiick, Paul Toscano, Vic Washington and company had nearly defeated Louisiana State in the Sugar Bowl on New Year's Day. On its front page on Jan. 2nd, the Casper Star-Tribune headlined its story "New Orleans To Remember 'Poke' Fans," and reported that "The Jung Hotel, official headquarters for the Wyoming Alumni Association, was totally unprepared to satisfy the thirsty needs of the free-spending Wyoming fans."

Also in that issue, an editorial demonstrated that McCarthyism still reigned in the Cowboy State. "The Star-Tribune Thinks" editorial said recent anti-war demonstrations were "Communist-inspired stuff, basically. ... It is a cardinal Red tenet that nobody but Reds should have freedom of speech, because Reds possess all truth and all wisdom."

In the outside world, U.S. aircraft resumed the bombing of Hanoi in Vietnam.

On March 18, 1968, Dr. Martin Luther King, who had become a leading critic of the war, told reporters he had no intention of running for any political office. But he said he would not vote for re-election of Democratic President Lyndon Johnson in the fall. Thirteen days later, the heavy weight of the never-ending Vietnam War forced Johnson to withdraw from his re-election campaign, opening the field to Sen. Robert F. Kennedy. Many expected a rerun of the 1960 Kennedy vs. Nixon race, but this time Vietnam War critic Robert would be the Kennedy involved.

At the end of March, UW students were enjoying two "snow days", a very rare occurrence for the university -- even though it sits at 7,220 feet. Dr. Martin Luther King, 39 years old but a major figure on the world stage, was in Memphis in support of a sanitation workers' strike. The workers had been on strike for seven weeks, seeking higher pay and safer conditions after two of them had been killed in a trash compactor. On Wednesday night, April 3rd, King delivered his last speech, saying "I've seen the Promised Land. I may not get there with you. But I want you to know tonight that we, as a people, will get to the promised land." The next evening, while standing on the balcony of his room at the Lorraine Motel, King was shot and killed by escaped convict James Earl Ray, who was staying in a rooming house across the street, just waiting for an opportunity.

Editorial response in Wyoming varied.

The Laramie Boomerang's editorial on April 6th, headlined "A Leader Is Lost," said the death "shows to what lows the moral level of the United States has fallen. Before the summer is over, the white population of the United States may well suffer as the Negro and other minority groups have been made to suffer in the past. . . . Perhaps the death of King will serve to awaken the American people to the equality and equal rights they [African-Americans] claim are granted under the Constitution. Perhaps, somewhere in the not too distant future, a man may be judged on his ability and not on his color or race. Even the Mafia gets a better break now than does the Negro. We hope that Martin Luther King Jr. did not die in vain. We hope that decent Americans will come forward and take up the leadership he gave the Negro people and inspired in many others."

On April 7, the Boomerang reprinted an editorial from the Denver Post which began, "In the history of the world's injustice there are few spectacles more deserving of anger and of tears than the striking down of a man of peace and goodness by forces of violence and hate."

Bob Peck at the Riverton Ranger on April 6th called it a "tragic assassination. ... Dr. King had a decade of leadership including some substantial triumphs dating back to the Montgomery bus strike that removed one of the many painful Jim Crow discrimination signs. He won world acclaim and received the Nobel Peace prize." Peck said Dr. King faced "severe tests when he came north to try to provide leadership to break the grip of the ghettos which imprison the poorest Negroes in some of our cities." He expressed hope that courageous leadership would bring the country out of the violence so that "Dr. King's martyrdom may prove to be his final and greatest contribution toward the cause of brotherhood."

Dave Bonner, editor of the Powell Tribune, on April 9th spoke of "the feeling of fear" that even people in "this relatively removed area of the West" were experiencing as rioting and looting in urban areas followed in the wake of King's killing. The editor noted that two wrongs do not make a right and that no one had to accept rioting because of the assassination. Then the editor said: "But out of the death of Dr. King comes one realization of a debt that is owed. We owe it to a group of people to understand Civil Rights as our problem--not their problem. We owe it to a group of people to square up to the fact that black has been black and white has been white for too long in this country and that the two colors have walked in different lines."

Before the assassination had even occurred, one Wyoming commentator was already complaining about the demonstrations in Memphis. In the Jackson Hole Guide that hit the streets early on April 4th, Floy Tonkin said in her "Riding the Range" column: "THE 'PEACEFUL' PROTEST MARCH' in Memphis called by and led by the Rev. Martin Luther King turned into a looting riot, and the Reverend took off hurriedly in a car. Since Mr. King is planning a peaceful poverty march to our nation's capital, we suggest that business houses there start boarding up their windows." In her column a week later, the same columnist continued, "Then came the news of the assassination of Rev. Martin Luther King and the terrible rioting of negroes in Washington, Chicago and other cities, with looting and burning. The black people lost more than a leader last week – they lost the respect and tolerance of the whites."

James Griffith Jr., editor of the Lusk Herald who would later be elected as both Wyoming state treasurer and state auditor, noted in his column "Jim's Jottings" on April 11th that he had spoken to two Wyomingites living in Washington, D.C., and he "received the same story from both – the looting, burning, sniping at foremen and attacking of policemen and others was largely done by young Negroes who could care little who Martin Luther King was. [T]he assassination ... was an excuse, not a reason, for violence. This action cannot be condoned, must not be tolerated, and should be dealt with forcefully and immediately. . . . However, the [rioters] are not the Negro community, but merely the lunatic fringe of a much larger and responsible group. We as a nation of compassionate people cannot condone or tolerate the hopeless and dire conditions in which many of these people live."

Sadness about the killing of Dr. King was not the dominant theme in other Wyoming newspapers. In Cody, only 24 miles from Powell, the editor had no appreciation for the concept that poverty, poor schools, employment discrimination and bad housing conditions disproportionately limited the ability of African Americans to pull themselves up by their own bootstraps. The editor said the rioting "has done nothing to further the Negro cause". If anything, he said, "even the moderate, tolerant people are being made more 'set in their ways' and adamant than ever before." The editor acknowledged that "the Negro has not enjoyed equality in civil rights," but this concession was immediately qualified by saying "this is not only true here, but true in almost every nation in the world which is not colored. ... Racial prejudice is a built-in part of life in this world." The editor said civil rights such as fair taxation and a jury trial do not include "social rights" or "financial rights." Legislating equal financial rights, the editor argued, was absurd. "They do not exist. The person with more ability, with more property, or with better luck, is normally going to fare better than the one lacking these qualities. ... Social, financial or any other privileges must be earned by the individual himself."

The editor of the right wing afternoon paper in Cheyenne also was looking past the murder itself to the reaction. The editorial on April 5th began with the suggestion that it might have been black radicals who murdered King. Editor James Flinchum then said that if the assassin was white, "he has served only the purpose of the black power radicals ... The fomenters of domestic unrest who have been using the civil rights movement and Negro unrest to create the massive civil disturbances in the United States of the past few years."

The editorial then quoted from King's statements through the years urging non-violence and said, "We are sorry he went to Memphis.... The important point is that his death has removed a major Negro leader, and also one who stood as an opponent of the urban riots."

The next day, the Wyoming State Tribune's editorial was headlined: "A Time for Action." Printed with unusual double-spacing, the editorial warned:

> It is not the first time rioters have swept through the streets of Washington, nor even burned down buildings. But it just might be the last. ... The time has arrived for a stern and fearless leadership that will say to one and all, whites and blacks, young and old, men and women: We must not and we will not tolerate any longer this violence and this lawlessness. It will be put down with every means at our command. ... To those of you who do not [quiet down], we shall deal with you in the harshest possible measures.

Finally, on April 7, the State Tribune condemned the "mass orgy of self-guilt in which America is now wallowing. ... The public display of emotion which has approached that of the Kennedy assassination has entirely obscured the issues .... In the midst of all this wailing, breast-beating and weeping ... some calm assessment of what has transpired and what is needed is in order." The editorial then rejected calls for civil rights legislation and open housing laws, "plus more billions of dollars of free money from Uncle Sam." He said the spending for those in urban "congestion centers" had "intensified if not actually accelerated the problems of the ghettoes."

The editors of the Torrington Telegram, Evanston Herald, the Star Valley Independent in Afton and the Jackson Hole Guide made no mention of the assassination in editorials during the following two weeks.

On Tuesday April 9th, the Casper Star-Tribune said the "recent rioting" in American cities "should assure Senate passage of legislation to make the streets safer for the public" providing funds to "improve police training and crime-fighting techniques." The next day, the editor said "the outpouring of tribute [surrounding the MLK funeral the previous day] was indicative of the basic values of America."

The CST editor continued with a most remarkable thesis, saying all people "took hope from the tragedy that it might provide a gateway to a better understanding." But the work to solve se problems, the editorial warned, "will not be done in a day. It will take a great deal of money .... Above all, it will take the willing cooperation of those whom it is designed to help. The white man alone cannot solve the black man's troubles."

1968: REACTIONS FROM WYOMING'S BLACK COMMUNITY

Six weeks before the assassination, African-American leaders in Wyoming attempted to warn state citizens about the desperation, hopelessness and anger of their people and the lack of concern by Congress and local governmental leaders. On Feb. 27, 1968, a long UPI article appeared in state newspapers quoting Johnnie McKinney, president of the Cheyenne branch of the National Association for the Advancement of Colored People, saying that Wyoming was not free of the conditions which could lead to rioting. "Unemployment in the ghettoes is of depression proportions, and the housing is unworthy of a wealthy nation—and surely an insult to the black veterans of our wars," McKinney said. He added that riots often were started by "hasty actions on the part of the police," a premonition of events 52 years later after George Floyd was killed by police in Minneapolis and Breonna Taylor was killed by police in Louisville, Ky.

In another UPI article two days later in the Casper Star-Tribune and the Rawlins Daily Times, Fred Devereaux, president of the Wyoming-Colorado Conference of the NAACP, said he agreed with McKinney. He said some 700-1,000 African-Americans lived in the north Casper area which he called "a ghetto" and that Casper was more concerned with planning for a civic center than with improving housing conditions. He said he and other NAACP leaders had recently met with Gov. Stan Hathaway and asked for more representation of Blacks, Hispanics and Native Americans on draft boards and on the Fair Employment Practices Commission.

In the same article, however, Cheyenne Police Chief James Byrd, one of the few Black police chiefs in the country, said his city had not experienced racial violence in the past and although "it's impossible for me or anyone else to say flatly it can't happen, I certainly don't think it's likely."

A UPI report in the Casper Star-Tribune the day after the assassination quoted Devereaux as saying the murder of King "is one of the most horrible things that ever happened in this country. It's really a disheartening thing." In an April 11th Casper Star-Tribune report, Devereaux cautioned that the fact that Wyoming's Black people had not engaged in rioting was not an indication that they were happy. They "are no different than the black people in New York, Chicago or anywhere else," he said. "I feel that anyone who lives more or less trapped in an undesirable situation will feel that way. Most white people feel we're pretty much under their heels."

Devereaux joined some of the editors in saying the death of King removed a man "the militants would really respect. Now they will say, 'Look, there's a man who talked about non-violence and they took his life.'"

On Sunday evening, April 7th, the Casper Interracial Council held a memorial service honoring Dr. King attended by 700 people at the Natrona County High School Auditorium. Dr. Robert Fowler of the CIC minced no words in his presentation. He suggested that the motto should be changed to "hate your neighbor as yourself," saying people don't seem to have respect for themselves, much less anyone else.

Another speaker was the Rev. Orloff W. Miller, Director of the Mountain Desert District of the Unitarian Church, who compared King to a modern Moses saying "let my people go." (Three years earlier, on March 9, 1965, Miller was with fellow Unitarian minister Rev. James Reeb, who grew up in Casper, when Reeb was attacked and killed in Selma, Ala., while supporting the voting rights movement. King gave the eulogy at Reeb's service in Selma). Barbara Banister and the Grace African Methodist Episcopal Church choir in Casper honored King's memory with singing. Across the Casper Star-Tribune's front page story on the service ran the headline, "Racial Violence Hits 80 Cities."

Although the editors of the University of Wyoming's student newspaper did not editorialize about the assassination, the April 19, 1968, issue of the Branding Iron did include a letter to the editor and poem by student Ken Cooper, an African American sprinter for the UW track team.

His paean about Dr. King joining "the ranks of fallen men of peace" showed in stark terms the deep sorrow and pain that the black communities were experiencing.

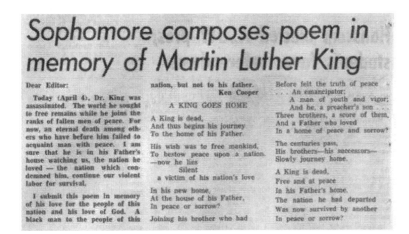

Sophomore composes poem in memory of Martin Luther King

Dear Editor:

Today (April 4), Dr. King was assassinated. The world he sought to free remains while he joins the ranks of fallen men of peace. For now, an eternal death among others who have before him failed to acquaint man with peace, I am sure that he is in his Father's house watching us, the nation he loved — the nation which condemned him, continue our violent labor for survival.

I submit this poem in memory of his love for the people of this nation and his love of God. A black man to the people of this nation, but not to his father.
Ken Cooper

A KING GOES HOME

A King is dead,
And thus begins his journey
To the home of his Father.

His wish was to free mankind.
To bestow peace upon a nation.
—now he lies
Silent
a victim of his nation's love

In his new home,
At the house of his Father,
In peace or sorrow?

Joining his brother who had

Before felt the truth of peace
. . . An emancipator;
A man of youth and vigor;
And he, a preacher's son . . .
Three brothers, a score of them,
And a Father who loved
In a home of peace and sorrow?

The centuries pass,
His brothers—his successors—
Slowly journey home.

A King is dead,
Free and at peace
In his Father's home.
The nation he had departed
Was now survived by another
In peace or sorrow?

Cooper was born in Virginia and raised by his maternal grandparents there until age 12. Earlier, when he was about 6, he had accepted his aunt's suggestion that he pay 25 cents in dues and join her as a member of the NAACP. He began reading that organization's newsletter, The Crisis, and was horrified about the maiming and lynching of 14-year-old Emmett Till of Chicago while visiting in Mississippi in 1955.

By 1959, Cooper was living with his family in Los Angeles. He had developed a lifelong love of music from his musician father's influence, becoming proficient on clarinet, flute and saxophone, and at the same time made himself into a powerful sprinter in track. That is what brought him to Wyoming. As a senior he had sent letters of interest to track coaches in the West and received offers from colleges in Montana and the Dakotas, but his father encouraged him to accept the offer from UW coach John Walker because UW was in the Western Athletic Conference.

After graduating high school, Cooper wanted to hone his speed at high altitude and wound up working for a restaurant in Cody. At UW in September he soon met two other Black sprinters, Araby Jones from Cheyenne, his roommate in McIntyre Hall, and John Mapp of Casper, along with Dwight James, another African-American from Cheyenne who was his floor proctor in the dorm and who became a valued mentor. Cooper was elected to the Residence Hall Council and developed a fund-raising project, bringing in movies to show in Washakie Center.

After track practice on April 4th, 1968, Cooper and Jones went to dinner and learned of the murder of Martin Luther King in Memphis. They were so shocked and angered they went down the hall of their dorm floor and banged on every door, crying out in protest. Then Cooper sat down in his room and wrote his poem.

The author located Cooper in Nevada in 2021 and interviewed him by phone. After reading his letter and poem for the first time in many years, he recalled that his reference to "three brothers" of peace was to Christ, MLK and Medgar Evers, a WWII Army vet who became an NAACP activist and was murdered in front of his Jackson, Miss., home in 1963 by a member of the White Citizens' Council.

Cooper also recalled a response to his poem published reluctantly by the Branding Iron editors a week later. It was from Andrew David Louis, a junior in secondary education who identified himself as being associated as "Lieutenant-Colonel" with Gov. Lester Maddox of Georgia, who had closed his restaurant business because he refused to follow the law and allow blacks equal access.

Louis said in his letter: "I for one, do NOT revere the deceased Dr. King. I do not feel an ounce of pity for the man." He said "the only answer to our national racial crisis is a system of

Apartheid. This system has worked wonders for the people of South Africa." An "Editor's Note" following the letter said this proposal, "like your opinion, is ridiculous."

After his time at UW Cooper attended Sheridan College. In the dorm there he once untied a student from Buffalo who was suspected of being gay and was tied to a bannister one day by other students. Another time he was threatened not to accept an invitation to a dance from a white student, but he refused to be intimidated, went to the dance and nothing happened.

Cooper finished his bachelor's and master's degrees in education in California and taught for several years before beginning a long career as a salesman for 3M Company. Upon retirement to Laughlin he resurrected his passion for music and developed a second career as a solo entertainer playing his own instrumental and vocal "souljazz" numbers in clubs and producing some CDs. When performing live he introduces one song, "Man Ain't Supposed To," as being inspired by his year in Sheridan.

1963-1973: VIETNAM AND WYOMING

We grew up really believing in America and what it stood for. Vietnam came along and most importantly it violated our view of America because we were killing innocent peasants, but also on a very deep psychological level to realize that your elders are prepared to see you die for an unworthy cause, for something you don't want to go die for, threw us into a moral abyss.
Fred Braniman, Dispatch News Service reporter in Laos, in the PBS documentary "The Sixties" 2005.

If we will make the right choice, we will be able to transform the jangling discords of our world into a beautiful symphony of brotherhood.
Martin Luther King, anti-war speech at Riverside Church, New York City, April 4, 1967

I have made the decision. Whatever happens to South Vietnam, we are going to cream North Vietnam. ... For once, we've got to use the maximum power of this country ... against this shit-ass little country to win the war.
President Richard M. Nixon from an Oval Office tape of May 4, 1972.

1963: Into the quagmire

As the Sixties dawned and Sen. John F. Kennedy became president, the country called Vietnam was rarely mentioned in American newspapers. Only two American troops had been killed in Vietnam in 1959, then five in 1960, 16 in 1961 and 53 in 1962.

But by the time the Class of '63 had finished high school, America's involvement in that country was occupying much more of the news space. In a UPI article datelined from Saigon, South Vietnam, on September 4, 1963, for example, officials of the Ngo Dinh Diem government reacted angrily to criticism from JFK. But the officials said they were relieved that Kennedy had said the U.S. would not withdraw from South Vietnam. The article stated that a Vietnamese newspaper had printed reports that the U.S. was involved in attempts to overthrow the Diem regime. The UPI article also stated that the U.S. Embassy was resisting government pressures to release three fugitive Buddhist monks who had taken refuge there a few days earlier. Diem and his brother were assassinated in December, 1963.

In 1963, casualties reached 118, then began escalating. In 1966, for example, 6,144 Americans were killed in Vietnam. One of them was Laramie's 2nd Lt. Gilbert Bush, "hit by hostile sniper fire" on May 8. In a Boomerang article by editor Gene Bryan on May 11th, Bryan said Bush "shipped out for the sweaty, stinkin' little war in South Viet Nam" in January, 1966. Bush's mother was quoted as saying, "we can't help but feel proud. We're so grateful he died bravely." She said in her son's first letter home "he described the horror of seeing all those little Vietnamese children wounded and maimed." After that, she said, he wrote just cheerful letters because "he didn't want us to worry about him."

More than 39,000 of the war's 51,000 fatalities occurred in 1967 through 1969. On March 22, 1967, Lt. Mike Kaul of Rock Springs found himself in "four hours of hell" at Landing Zone Gold in Vietnam.[135] He was a basketball star for the Tigers in high school and played for Bill Strannigan's Cowboys in 1961-62. He became an Army officer through UW Army ROTC before Vietnam became a fearsome word. Early that March morning a large Viet Cong force attacked the U.S. position. Kaul directed his platoon during the long onslaught and prevented the enemy from overrunning the Zone. He was awarded a Silver Star for his leadership that day but he credited his men: "Most of them were young kids. I didn't see one person cowering in a hole, and when their buddies died beside them they just fought harder. That's what I will remember forever." The battle left the U.S. with 140 casualties and nearly 40 men killed. Kaul returned to Wyoming and his wife Jamie and 2-year-old son Dick in September. After a 20-year Army career, he opened the Two Rivers Emporium fly fishing store in Pinedale which he was still operating in 2016.

Larry Wilcox, who grew up in Rawlins, attended UW for a short time in 1966 and then joined the Marines when the draft came calling. He served honorably in Vietnam, emerged as a sergeant, and went on to become one of the co-stars of the famous national TV motorcycle cop show C.H.I.P.S.

In the first week of 1968, 184 Americans died. During the next week 287 died. In these casualty reports the Pentagon always emphasized that many more Viet Cong and North Vietnamese troops were being killed. In a release in early August, 1968, the Pentagon reported that 374,083 "Communists" had been killed in 7 ½ years of fighting.

Nearly 17,000 Americans were killed in the election year of 1968, well more than 300 a week.

---

[135] UPI reports in Rocky Mountain News Sept. 13, 1967 and in Indianapolis Star March 23, 1967.

On August 9th, over an article about Nixon winning the Republican nomination in Miami Beach, the Wyoming Eagle's large banner headline read, "FIRST PRIORITY WILL BE TO END WAR--NIXON."

But in his acceptance speech he actually referred to bringing "an <u>honorable</u> end" to the war, a critical distinction which would result in more than 21,000 Americans dying in Vietnam after Nixon took office in January 1969.

In a 2001 PBS documentary about the late Lady Bird Johnson, historian Michael Beschloss recalled:

> Lady Bird once told me, "You want to know when the Vietnam War really came home to me?" She said she was on a train from New York to Washington, and she saw another train on another track and realized, with a shock, that its cargo was coffins -- the coffins of American boys just back from Vietnam. She said, "That was the moment I knew that this war was going to affect every American family."

Laramie's Sanchez brothers

The Laramie Boomerang on July 10, 2013, carried a long article about four local brothers named Sanchez who had served in the U.S. armed forces. The eldest, Jimmy, declined to talk to the reporter about his experiences in the Korean War in 1952-54. Then Frank Sanchez served in the Army stateside and Rudy served four years in the Navy. The youngest, Roy, was about to be drafted in 1966 and was ready to fight in Vietnam. But because their mother had worried so much about them when the oldest three were away (Rudy was home only once in four years), they eventually persuaded Roy to join the National Guard. He was in an engineers unit and expected to be called up for Vietnam but it never happened.

Roy said he eventually concluded his brothers were wise to keep him from Vietnam. He said 50,000 "kids died in Vietnam for what reason? Iraq, Afghanistan – what's the reason. Big corporations make big money. Politicians don't care as long as their own don't go to war. And what do you think it does to the mamas? That's why I stayed. I did it for mama."

1958-77: UW Prof. Gale McGee and the 1947 Textbook Inquiry

Gale W. McGee was born in Lincoln, Nebraska in 1915, graduated from State Teachers College in Wayne, Nebr., and then taught in high school and college while earning a master's from Colorado and a Ph.D. from the University of Chicago. He joined the faculty of the University of Wyoming in 1946 as a professor of American history.

In late 1947, McGee and several other UW professors protested the textbook inquiry ordered in October, 1947, by UW trustees worried about possible "subversive or un-American" influences in UW's textbooks. The professors argued that this was a blatant violation of academic freedom. A committee headed by the law dean reviewed the social science textbooks in use and reported finding no objectionable material. The faculty and the trustees eventually agreed to a joint statement of principles.

The St. Louis Post-Dispatch in an editorial on Dec. 26, 1947, blasted the inquiry, suggesting to the trustees that they "look at the end-fruits of German book-burning!" In an editorial titled "When Small Men Rule" on January 29, 1948, the Post-Dispatch said "this sorry spectacle" by the UW trustees provoked "indignant editorial comment from ocean to ocean." The inquiry "succeeded only in drawing a cloud over their institution--the cloud of doubt that it was not fully dedicated to the free and honest pursuit of the truth, the feeling that truth must stand second to thought control." The editorial said that "even Marx must be read to be refuted."

A UW graduate from Star Valley, Ernest Linford, was the editor of the Laramie Boomerang at the time and published some editorials opposing the inquiry. The paper, however, was part of a chain of Wyoming newspapers owned by Tracy McCracken of Cheyenne who was also the vice-chairman of the UW Board of Trustees. As a result, Linford was forced to confine his subsequent observations about the textbook inquiry to a column titled "One Man's Opinion." Soon, Linford moved to the Salt Lake Tribune and served as editorial page editor for many years. In the late '60s he returned to UW as journalism department head.

On January 19, 1948, WWII vet Glenn R. "Bud" Daniel of Casper, president of the Associated Students of UW, released a statement saying the trustees' action was a violation of academic freedom. The ASUW requested "immediate clarification" of the purposes of the investigation. The senate's statement said the inquiry had produced "an immeasurable amount of adverse publicity and ill feeling." Daniel later became coach/manager of the Wyoming Cowboys baseball team. [136].

A faculty committee of 15, appointed by Pres. George "Duke" Humphrey, conducted the inquiry and found no evidence to support the fears of the trustees. Under pressure from the faculty, the Board accepted the joint statement on academic freedom of the American Association of University Professors.

In the election of 1958, Prof. McGee surprised everyone by defeating incumbent Republican Sen. Frank A. Barrett, winning by fewer than 2,000 votes. During his third term in the Senate, McGee attended the 25-year commemoration of the textbook inquiry, held at the Wyoming Union on campus. He began his remarks by saying, "At the time of the inquiry I was the only member of that committee without tenure, and as I look around the room today I see I am still the only one without tenure." Indeed, he lost his next reelection bid -- to Sen. Malcolm Wallop of Big Horn.

After his election in 1958, McGee served with Sen. John F. Kennedy in the Senate and became a friend and supporter. He accompanied President Kennedy on the Wyoming portion of JFK's western tour in September, 1963.

One of the items in Vern Shelton's "2 cents worth" column in the Boomerang on Feb. 22, 1962, reported: "According to Mrs. Gale McGee, everyone is twisting back in Washington ... and everyone's got a stiff back." The reference was to "The Twist" dance craze engendered by Chubby Checker.

McGee supported the liberal domestic social programs of Kennedy and Johnson, but he was also a hawk on the Vietnam War. In a speech in early 1965 he defended the intervention in Vietnam as part of a global policy of refusing to make concessions to Communism in any part of the world that it threatened.[137] McGee said "the domino theory is valid" and "if Vietnam goes, Cambodia goes, Thailand goes, Malaya goes, Indonesia goes, the Philippines go." Vice-president Richard Nixon had made a similar statement in 1953 and JFK likewise advanced the theory.

---

[136] Many years after Cowboy baseball was brought to a close by the UW trustees, Daniel contacted as many of his players as he could find and collected their memories. These stories were woven into a book by Ryan Thorburn, author of *The Black 14*, titled *Lost Cowboys, The Story of Bud Daniel and Wyoming Baseball*, Burning Daylight, 2010. Daniel has also published a book titled *Cowboy Down: A WWII Marine Fighter Pilot's Story*, CreateSpace 2014.

[137] Stone, Gary, *Elites for Peace: The Senate and the Vietnam War*, Univ. Tennessee Press 2007.

In an editorial by James M. Flinchum in the Wyoming State Tribune (the Republican paper) on March 25, 1966, the editor strongly opposed the opening of diplomatic or trade relations with China or admitting China to the United Nations. Flinchum's editorials usually included a quotation within a shaded border at the top. For the editorial on March 25th Flinchum had chosen this attempt at humor: "A doctor says that today's wives outlive their husbands. Maybe that's because they don't marry women."

In his editorial the next day, the Tribune editor had no trouble blasting both Sen. McGee, a Vietnam war "hawk", and in the same editorial denigrating all those protesting the war. Flinchum decried the rapidly escalating protests against the War, calling for "a potent United States role in Asia countering (1) Moscow and/or (2) Peking. ... Any American counter-thrust against global Communist purposes poses the threat of frustration of the latter, regardless of whether it is initiated by the Russian or the Chinese Communists." Flinchum proclaimed that "the protests and demonstrations are one vast, giant conspiracy against this country. ... It is a one-way street these marchers walk. It is Peking's avenue. It is Moscow's boulevard. Peace is their sham."

Flinchum said it was necessary to remind "Wyoming's Senator McGee that [the war protesters] are not the conspiratorial right-wingers that he constantly shouts about being a danger to this country. These are the left-wingers...."

Most books about the Vietnam War include references to Wyoming's Sen. McGee. For example, one historian of the war identified McGee as "a loyal Johnson supporter" who challenged Sen. Frank Church (D-Idaho) when in February, 1965, Church spoke out against President Johnson's bombing campaign shortly after eight Americans had been killed and a hundred more wounded at Pleiku.[138] Church rejected the domino theory and warned that American policy had swung too far toward interventionism. "In the end," he predicted, "after a tragic trail of casualties out of all proportion to our real national interest, we will have to negotiate a settlement with the Communists..."

In February, 1965, Sen. McGee characterized those expressing any reservations about the domino theory this way:

> I hope it will not be interpreted wrongly if I were to suggest that the hope that may be expressed and is expressed daily in the press by some, that China really will not be up to anything very serious, reminds us of the speculation that went on about what Mr. Hitler might do, or what Mr. Mussolini might or might not do, in the time previous to World War II.[139]

In the book *Why the Senate Slept* by Ezra Y. Siff, , the author included an extended quotation from McGee's speech in response to Church and then described what McGee's speech represented: "So Senator McGee, an intelligent, perceptive man, still clutched onto the need of a policy of containment of what he perceived as a monolithic communist movement."

Only a week prior to McGee's speech, 36-year-old Capt. Carlton "Jake" Holland of Casper became Wyoming's first fatal casualty of the Vietnam War. He suffered fragmentation wounds while with the 48th ARVN Infantry in Phuoc Long Province, South Vietnam. He was

---

[138] Mann, Robert, *A Grand Delusion: America's Descent into Vietnam*, Basic Books 2001, 7-8.

[139] Cong. Rec. S2886 (Daily Ed. 2-17-1965).

awarded the Distinguished Service Cross and is buried at Arlington National Cemetery. Nine days after Holland's death, 47-year-old Marine Sgt. Robert W. Grove, also of Casper, became the state's second casualty, killed at Khanh Hoa. Air Force Capt. Dennis Cressey of Cheyenne, 25, was the last Wyoming casualty, declared missing and presumed dead May 12, 1972. In all, 119 servicemen with Wyoming home addresses died in the war.[140]

Three years after his 1965 speech, the nebulous and contradictory explanations for U.S. involvement in Vietnam were demonstrated in another speech by Sen. McGee on the Senate floor. According to a UPI report of January 25, 1968, McGee stated flatly that the war was NOT a war against "unified and monolithic world communism." McGee said U.S. troops had been in Korea partly "to prevent South Korea from moving north by force of arms." Likewise, he said, "the American commitment in South Vietnam is aimed at getting the North out of the South at the same time its goal must be to keep the South from ravaging the North by force of arms." But McGee at the same time didn't seem concerned about U.S. ravaging of North Vietnam by aerial bombing.[141]

At pg. 498 of a book titled *Vietnam: A History* (Viking Press 1991), author Stanley Karnow described President Johnson's machinations as the U.S. involvement in Vietnam escalated. "Increasingly, too, Johnson surrounded himself with congressional loyalists like Senators Gale McGee of Wyoming and Fred Harris of Oklahoma, rewarding them with pledges of patronage and invitations to his informal White House suppers."[142] According to a 2018 biography of McGee by Rodger McDaniel, McGee had been a staunch isolationist prior to WWII

---

[140] Most of their names are etched on a Vietnam War Memorial erected in about 1983 at the Veteran's Hospital in east Cheyenne and at the memorial adjacent to UW's Old Main building.

[141] According to many sources, total U.S. bomb tonnage dropped during the Vietnam War was more than twice what the U.S. dropped during World War II.

[142] According to Myra MacPherson in her book *Long Time Passing: Vietnam and the Haunted Generation* (Doubleday 1984), a 1970 report showed that 234 sons of senators and congressmen came of age after the U.S. became involved in Vietnam. Only 28 of those went to Vietnam (including Harvard graduate and future Vice President Al Gore). Fortunately, only one was wounded. No one on the House Armed Services Committee had a son or grandson who did duty in Vietnam. Sens. Cranston, Goldwater and McGee each had two sons who flunked the draft physical. Hence the line from Creedence Clearwater's "Fortunate Son" in 1969, written by Army reservist John Fogerty: "It ain't me, it ain't me, I ain't no senator's son, no. ... It ain't me, it ain't me I ain't no millionaire's son, no." When his college deferments expired with his graduation from Wharton in 1968, Donald Trump obtained a letter from a doctor about bone spurs in his heel, resulting in a medical deferment that kept him out of the service. (On December 26, 2018, the New York Times reported that the daughters of a deceased Queens, N.Y., podiatrist were claiming that their father gave the bone spur diagnosis as a favor to the doctor's landlord, Donald Trump's father). In the 2016 election, Trump took 68.2% of Wyoming's vote, far and away the highest of any state in the nation except for West Virginia. Trump won at least a 60% share in 21 of Wyoming's 23 counties. Teton County was the only county going for Hillary Clinton (60% to Trump's 32.2%) and Albany County, home of the University of Wyoming, turned in only a 46-42% win for Trump. The rest of the "Top 10 states" for Trump were Oklahoma (65.32%), North Dakota (62.96%), Kentucky (62.52%), Alabama (62.08%), South Dakota (61.53%), Tennessee (60.72%), Arkansas (60.57%) and Idaho (59.26%). An independent candidate named Evan McMullin took 21.54% of the Utah vote and 6.73% in Idaho. McMullin, a former CIA officer, was on the ballot in many states, but not in Wyoming. He was born in Provo, Utah, and graduated from Provo's BYU. If all of his votes in Utah and Idaho were added to Trump's vote tally, Utah would have been 3rd among the states with 67% and Idaho right behind with 66%.

and had even applied for conscientious objector status. Pearl Harbor transformed him to the opposite extreme.[143]

McGee's fellow senator from Wyoming, Milward Simpson, was also a hawk on Vietnam and had contempt for anti-war protesters. In a speech at UW in April, 1965, he said:

> Everything for which America has fought two major wars in three decades ... is at stake in Vietnam. If we are driven from Southeast Asia we will have suffered a defeat as profound and crippling as any defeat could be.

Simpson praised the patriotism of students at UW, saying they were "nowhere to be found" during the recent student protest march on Washington, which was endorsed, he claimed, "by a hodgepodge of communist front and socialist youth groups."

1966: Charlie Simpson of Cheyenne

Discussions and speakers about U.S. policy in Southeast Asia occurred on campus at least as early as fall, 1965. In March, 1966, professors Quentin Cook and Thomas Kennedy of history, Dennis Ray of political science and Baird Whitlock of English participated in a panel during which Whitlock criticized Sen. Gale McGee's defense of U.S. military expansion, saying "McGee's 19th century power politics doesn't involve a world of the United Nations or the atomic bomb. It's not a world fighting colonialism."

But the first actual demonstration against the war may not have occurred until a UW student named Charlie Simpson distributed leaflets on campus a year later. In the spring of 1965, Simpson and Gene Stump from Cheyenne opened a bookstore called The Brillig Works in the basement of the 121 Tea House on Ivinson Ave. in downtown Laramie. Among ads for English Leather cologne, the formal-attire Military Ball and Scotti's 19-cent fish sandwich, their ad in the Branding Iron in March proclaimed the store was "for the cultured epicurean." Simpson was an undergraduate in liberal arts who had been involved in publication of a student opinion magazine called "The Horse's Mouth." Stump was identified as a "UW expatriate" in a Jim Coates Branding Iron column on Oct. 29th.[144] The enterprise was launched to satisfy "a need by the academic community for an outlet of contemporary literature of high quality and periodicals and quarterlies of a controversial nature," the founders were quoted as saying.

Operating the bookstore required Simpson to travel frequently to Boulder, Colo. where their wholesaler was located. As a result he attended a world affairs conference at Colorado

---

[143] *The Man in the Arena*, University of Nebraska Press, p. 19.

[144] James H. Coates went from the UW Branding Iron to a news and column writing career with the Chicago Tribune. In a June 18, 1973, Chicago Tribune column, writer Bill Anderson said Jim Coates had led the coverage of the wanton killing of bald eagles by some Wyoming ranchers. In an Aug. 2, 1998, column called Binary Beat in the Tribune, Robert Davis wrote: "A few months after I came to the Tribune in 1967, a rangy young cowboy from Wyoming joined the staff. That cowboy was Jim Coates, who now is on the mend from surgery." He said Coates and himself had surprised the younger staffers in the newsroom by their quick embrace of word processors as a "godsend". The younger staff expected they would stick to their electric typewriters. "Old-timers who use computers today are kind of like the people who get indoor plumbing after years of using an outdoor privy," Davis said. On June 12, 2007, Coates announced that after 10 years he was retiring from writing his "Ask Jim" column answering readers' questions about computers and technology. "Nothing ain't forever, as we used to say back home in Wyoming," Coates wrote. "As my beard got whiter and my burdens as a bread-winner got lighter, the time came for this old cyber cowboy to mosey on down the road."

University and met a Students for Democratic Society leader, Jeffrey Shero from the University of Texas. Having had his eyes opened about the war and other issues of the day, Simpson became disillusioned with the educational atmosphere at UW and dropped out of UW for the spring semester. His best friend and debate team partner at Cheyenne Central, Jim Foreman, had rejected scholarship offers in 1962 and joined the Marines. When he returned, Simpson says, he was a totally different person who lived in the Denver area but showed no desire to renew their friendship. Foreman lived on a military disability income.

Simpson, who had a medical deferment from the draft, stood outside Memorial Fieldhouse on the UW campus on May 14, 1966, where 850 students were taking the three-hour Selective Service College Qualifying Examination which was offered to students with a lower rank in their college classes. A good score would improve their chances for a continuation of a college student deferment. Simpson distributed a test of his own -- on U.S. involvement in Vietnam -- as the students filed out. His leaflet also called for students to "help organize nationwide opposition to the Viet Nam War and build a democratic America." He said most students reacted courteously but some refused to take the leaflet and several others "made a show of tearing them up into little pieces," according to a Branding Iron report appearing May 20th.

Simpson said the college deferment system was unfair to those young men who could not afford to attend college or "whose background has not enabled them to get the education necessary for college." He said Vietnam is "a wrong kind of war, not necessary, not just and not American."

His protest, Simpson said in a 2017 interview, soon made him personna non grata in Laramie. He was evicted from his lodgings three times as the powers in the Chamber of Commerce came down on him. He says he heard that U.S. Sen. Milward Simpson emphasized on the Senate floor that Charlie Simpson was not a relative. Simpson eventually moved to Boulder and opened Brillig Works bookstores there and in Denver.

1967: English Professor Ken Craven

The minutes for the April 21-22, 1967, meeting of the University of Wyoming Board of Trustees announced that Robert Kenton Craven had been hired as an assistant professor of English for the following school year "at an annual salary of $9,000 on a 9-month basis; this appointment to be contingent upon Mr. Craven's completing the requirements for the Ph.D." Little did they know that this appointment would soon prove to be uncomfortable for a different "Ken Craven" who owned the Kassis women's clothing store in downtown Laramie.[145]

R. Kenton Craven, born amid the coalfields in Bluefield, W. V. in 1939, did complete his doctorate that summer at the University of Kansas, building upon his bachelor's degree from Wheeling Jesuit University (Wheeling College) in 1960 and his master's from Marshall University in Huntington, W.V. in 1961. His doctoral thesis was titled, "Seward Collins and the traditionalists: a study of the Bookman and the American Review."

Craven brought his wife and three children with him when he relocated from Lawrence, Kan., to Laramie. Although he had participated in a couple anti-war demonstrations at Kansas, Craven did not enter those lists in a public way until Thanksgiving time during his first semester at UW. It began with a letter-to-the-editor of the Laramie Boomerang which appeared on Nov. 26, 1967, just below another anti-war letter from Methodist minister Dave Steffenson (who,

---

[145] The odds against having two persons named "Ken Craven" in tiny Laramie is indicated by the fact that a 2013 search of an on-line phone book showed not even one "Ken Craven" in Los Angeles or Chicago.

along with Rev. Richard Putney and Rev. George Quarterman formed the University Common Ministry). Signed by "Mr. and Mrs. R. K. Craven," the letter listed many things they were not thankful for that year, including "racial discrimination, ... an unjust and senseless massacre in Vietnam, ... massive military aid to underdeveloped lands while people starve in the streets of Calcutta, ... the government policy of consistent lying, the deterioration of the First Amendment, the decline of belief in free criticism as a necessary function of the true, mindful patriot ...."

His letter brought a response from pro-war law professor William Knudsen, which eventually led to a debate between the two. The letter also provoked a letter-to-the-editor from Kenneth G. Craven on Dec. 1st. This Craven identified himself as manager of Kassis Inc. in downtown Laramie and no relation to R. Kenton Craven. "I wish it known that his views are not mine," Kassis Ken's letter said.

In March, 1968, a standing room only crowd in the Education Auditorium turned out for what the BI described as "the first debate between faculty members in 20 years."[146]

Knudsen charged that the North Vietnamese violated the Geneva Accords from the beginning by sending guerrilla forces into South Vietnam. Craven noted that those accords called for elections which were never held. He charged that the U.S. knew that 80% of the South Vietnamese would vote for Ho Chi Minh if the elections occurred, and therefore the U.S. cooperated with South leader Diem in "seeing to it that these elections were never held."

Later in 1968, Craven became state coordinator for Wisconsin Democratic Sen. Gene McCarthy's anti-war presidential bid. "We had an office downtown and Rep. Bella Abzug (D.-N.Y.) was calling me all the time saying we should have a rally in the football stadium because she thought thousands would come," he recalled in a 2013 interview. An article in the Cheyenne Eagle on August 13, 1968 invited persons of all political persuasions to join a "Clean for Gene" day at Vedauwoo in the Medicine Bow National Forest east of Laramie as part of a public service project across America by the McCarthy campaign.

On May 1, 1969, Craven was on a panel with both of Wyoming's U.S. Senators, Gale McGee and Cliff Hansen, UW President Carlson and psychology professor Wilson Walthall in a discussion about the causes and solutions to campus unrest. Describing himself as "a spokesman for the dissidents," Craven said the Vietnam War and the growing military-industrial complex were causing campus protests. He said the only approach that had been taken was "to put down" the dissidents.

---

[146] This was a bold but surely incorrect declaration. In February of 1964, for example, UW nuclear physics professor Burt Muller (who had participated in the Manhattan Project during WWII) and a senior engineering student named Jack Steadman debated world disarmament with Steadman's UW debate teammate Dan Spangler, a law student who had graduated with Steadman from Cody High, and an Air Force ROTC "assistant professor of air science". Steadman and Muller contended their proposed disarmament system combining inspection and a UN peace force was a workable plan. But Spangler argued the international police force would be very unstable. Muller replied that disarmament plans had never been tried. "Therefore, how do we know they won't work." Muller retired after a long career at UW and until his death in 2017 regularly wrote letters to the editor warning about nuclear proliferation. Spangler went on to become a Wyoming district judge. Steadman spent 37 years as a faculty member of the UW Engineering College before becoming dean of engineering at Southern Alabama. He was the 2004 president of the Institute of Electrical and Electronics Engineers-USA. In a 2014 e-mail he said: "It is clear that everything that our Affirmative Team said was right on point and that the ensuing international agreements associated with nuclear arsenal reduction and the non-proliferation agreements are slowly moving us in that direction."

McGee, one of the leading hawks on the Vietnam War in Congress, said that student protests had happened previously in history. But he said that the protests of the '60s were different because this generation of college students was far better informed, more sophisticated, more intelligent and better prepared to participate than the earlier generations. "Many young people are disturbed by a world that may destroy itself by nuclear war," McGee said.

1966-67: Peace Corps, Marines and protesters in the Union

On December 9, 1966, when young Americans were being drafted at a rate of 200,000 annually, UW student Henry Pacheco reported in a Branding Iron article that 15,000 draft-eligible American men had given up their U.S. citizenship by moving to Canada. Pacheco quoted an article in the Winnipeg Tribune by a reporter who had interviewed many of the "draft dodgers." That writer found the men to be "articulate, seemingly intelligent and genuinely troubled by their society's acceptance of what they believe to be an unjust and unforgivable war."

On February 16, 1967, Capt. Robert Fiero of the UW ROTC department told the BI that the Viet Cong did not win a battle in 1966 and were losing their troops by defection at record levels. The U.S. and South Vietnam armies "are making progress against the enemy," Fiero said.

The tables set up by students and others in the Wyoming Union during the week of February 20, 1967, represented the range of influences facing college students across the nation. Near the front door was a table manned by Peace Corps recruiters, hoping to entice students to join that program -- initiated by JFK shortly after taking office -- and provide service to other countries around the world. Terry Deshler of Kemmerer and Barbara Cresswell of Casper were students at that time who participated in the First Person Coffeehouse programs at the Presbyterian Church and became strong opponents of the war. Terry's father was a supervisor for the U.S. Forest Service and Terry had been interested in serving in the Peace Corps from the time it was created. Terry and Barbara married and joined the Peace Corps in fall of 1969, spending two years in Kenya.

At another table close to the front door were the Marine Corps recruiters.

At the end of the hall which ran back toward the UW Bookstore was a table where ROTC "Corpettes" were selling tickets to the military ball.

Next to them were the anti-war activists. Rick Kogan, a senior in political science, and Michael Durgain, junior in American studies, had formed a chapter of the Committee for Non-Violent Action and were offering information on the draft and the Vietnam War. According to an article in the BI on Feb. 24th, Durgain wanted to move his table next to the Marine recruiter, but the Union manager said there was no room for it there.

The article says that a UW graduate named John Pouttu had an exchange with one of the Marines regarding photos of "maimed Vietnamese children" from a current Ramparts magazine feature. The Marine recruiter asked if those were "Viet Cong kids." Pouttu replied, "How do you expect a child of that age to know?" The recruiter pointed out that the Cong used their children in attacks. "Does it take a lot of guts to shoot children," Pouttu asked, according to the BI article. "'Yes it does,' the captain answered, and stormed away."

The Marine told the BI that this was the first time he had encountered this type of dissent in Wyoming.

Casper Democrat Mayne Miller spoke on campus at the end of March and criticized the attempt by the U.S. to "serve as policeman in underdeveloped parts of the world." In an editorial on March 31, 1967, Branding Iron associate editor Lee Catterall joined University of Chicago economist Milton Friedman in calling for abolition of the draft and creation of an all-volunteer armed service.

1967: University of Wyoming Vietnam Memorial

On October 18, 1967, the UW Alumni Association announced that a stone-and-bronze memorial honoring UW alumni killed in Vietnam would be dedicated that Saturday -- after the Homecoming parade -- in the sunken garden area just southwest of Old Main. The memorial would include individual plaques bearing the names of five former UW students.

- Craig Slade Blackner, a 1960 graduate and Air Force officer from Lyman who was killed Feb. 2, 1966 in an aircraft crash at Long An in South Vietnam.
- Navy Lt. Philip O. Robinson, a 1962 graduate and Navy officer from Sheridan who was killed March 25, 1966. Articles about his death were on the front page of the Wyoming State Tribune in Cheyenne on both March 26th and 28th. The UPI report March 26th noted that Robinson had been eligible to return from Vietnam for stateside duty nearly a year earlier. He had extended his service in Vietnam by a year, his father quoted him as saying, because "if we're to stop Communism we'd better do it there rather than on the Montana border." Also on the front page March 26th was an article by Tribune staffer Wanda Banta reporting that in the last of five ecumenical meetings around the state the Most Rev. Hubert M. Newell, Catholic Bishop of the Diocese of Cheyenne, had called for the containment and early termination of the Vietnam War.

The March 28th article about Robinson quoted from a Christmas card Robinson had mailed in December to a Cheyenne woman who was his ATO fraternity housemother during his college years at Laramie. She had just received it a few days before news of his death came. In the card he said, "After being in the country (I am) still convinced we must make a stand here – (it will) be quite a few years though as I see difficulties in (the Vietnamese) accepting civic responsibility."

Also in the March 28th edition was a UPI report from Hattiesburg, Miss., about the FBI arresting thirteen Ku Klux Klansmen for the fire bomb death in January of Vernon Dahmer, a black civil rights worker. Night riders had fired upon and tossed Molotov cocktails into his house and store. His wife and 10-year-old daughter were severely burned. The FBI was still looking for the imperial wizard of the White Knights of the KKK of Mississippi, Sam Holloway Bowers Jr. He had asserted the 5th Amendment in recent testimony before a congressional committee regarding whether his organization had ordered the "extermination" of three other civil rights workers in the summer of 1964. Finally, on the front page of the March 26th edition was a UPI article noting that protests against U.S. involvement in the Viet Nam war "reached its peak today with parades, rallies and demonstrations from Paris to Pearl Harbor and from New Delhi to New York City." Massive parades were planned in New York, Chicago, Detroit and San Francisco, the article said.

- Joseph B. Fearno, a 1963 graduate and Air Force officer from Mena, Ark.
- 2nd Lt. Gilbert B. Bush of Laramie, a UW student from 1959 until 1961 and then an Army officer. He was killed May 8, 1966, at the age of 25 from small arms fire.
- PFC William B. Esslinger, a 1964 Cheyenne Central graduate who entered UW in 1965 and died June 1, 1967, while serving with the Marine Corps at Quang Tri in South Vietnam. Esslinger anchored the Central swimming team in high school.

The inscription on the monument created by the UW Alumni Association honored them by saying: "In tribute to the alumni of the University of Wyoming who have given so much for so many in the distant fields of Viet Nam. If they should die, think not of death, but rather that they

John Aldrich
Elton Anderson
Curtis Ando
Ernest Balland
Robert Barnes
James Barnes
James Barton
Gary Bartz
Michael Beck
Raymond Benson
Craig Blackner
Steven Boal
Edward Braun
Richard Brown
Kenneth Brown
Gilbert Bush
Candelario Bustos
Donald Button
Jerry Byers
Leroy Cardenas
Richard Cazin
Donald Chipp Jr
Merrell Clayburn
Harry Coen
Orville Cooley
Dennis Cressey
Robert Crichton
John Cukale Jr
Frank Darling
Samuel Delios
Lonnie Dykes

Richard Endicott
William Esslinger
Bennett Evans
Lawrence Evert
Allen Faler
Dennis Farris
Joseph Fearno
Terry Fetzer
Donald Ford
Gary Fox
Gary Fuqua
Walis Garst
Harold Gibson
Randall Glasspoole
William Graves
Joe Green
Robert Grove
Robert Guthrie
Edward Haggerty
Walter Handy
Barry Hansen
George Harrison
Joseph Hart
Carlton Holland
Bruce Jensen
Dale Johnson
Richard Kastner
Dennis King
Kenneth King
John Kobelin II
Alva Krogman

Daniel Laird
Victor Landes
Leslie Lantos
Terrance Larson
Elmer Lauck
Edward Lawton
David Lucas
Jose Lujan
Craig Marrington
Richard Martin
Henry Maul
Robert Maurer
Leonard May
William McAtee
Lester McCabe
Earl McCarty
William McCormick
Edward McNally
Emil Miltnovich
Pedro Montanez
Norman Moore
Robert Morganflash
Weldon Moss
Vernon Nix III
Larry Owens
Joseph Padilla
James Pantier
Pablo Patino
Douglas Patrick
Richard Powers
Charles Reberg

Philip Robinson
Douglas Rogers
Robert Rogers
Robert Romero
Charles Roy
Timothy Saunders
Donald Schroeder
Roger Scott
William Selders
Robert Shuck
Thomas Skiles
Benjamin Slagowski
Stephen Slocum
Dennis Smith
Roy Snyder
Stephen Stark
Edward Steele
Ronald Stewart
Alma Stumpp
Richard Sweeney
Richard Tabor
Ernest Taylor
Lawrence Torrez
Joseph Walker
Larry Warnock
Dennis Wartchow
Walter Weshut
Albert Wayman Jr.
William Wilson

UW Vietnam Veterans Memorial Restoration and Addition of Names
March 30, 2012
Presented by UW Alumni Association, Academic Affairs, and Veterans Services Center

have died that freedom may prevail. Youth foregone, dreams unseen, God give them joy of knowing what freedom their death has brought."

Very soon, more individual plaques were added, including that of Lt. Steven Boal of Upton. He was killed while on patrol in Binh Duong Province a week after the Black 14 dismissals. He had served an enlistment in the Army before entering UW, where his major interest was U.S. history. He and his wife Toni Whelan both graduated from UW in 1968. He was the son of a Wyoming legislator who was superintendent of schools in Upton. Boal made the all-state Class B football team for Upton in the fall of 1962.

According to an article published on October 29, 1969, in the Laramie Boomerang, Steven was commissioned as an officer after his graduation and was first stationed at Fort Benjamin Harrison in Indiana where he pursued his studies of Abraham Lincoln. He requested to be assigned to Vietnam. He took special training in jungle fighting in the swamps of Georgia and Florida and then the couple spent his furlough in Wyoming, including a visit with Professor Merlin Stonehouse in Laramie.

The article says that in late July he wrote to his family: "In two days I will take command of an Inf. platoon. I admit a cloud of fear seems to hang inside me. But I am well trained and plan to do a fine job for those troopers under my care. Take away fear, death and sadness, war is very interesting. We are convinced that booby traps kill most of our troops. Our area of operation is mostly in rice paddies."

The website called 212warriors.com explains what happened this way:

Lieutenant Jachowski gives a vivid account of what happened after the "three-quarter-cav" joined up with Alpha. For the 2-12th's third, and final, attack at the bunker complex. "They came through the bush and joined up with us. We got organized and started moving again. The cav platoon had 2 Sheridans and 3 APC's with us moving behind and between them. We followed the [Cav] platoon leaders track in. The Sheridans fired a few main rounds and all the Cav vehicles started firing. It was very thick brush. You had no visibility to the sides - only what was in front. Then we came to a large clump of brush. Two men were shot dead off one of the tracks....." 3/4 CAV troopers Spc4 Robert Aday and Staff Sergeant Henry R. Lambert were shot in their heads by a sniper and knocked off their APC(s), according to later reports. Alpha Company's Lt. Boal was killed - either trying to get to them or someone else.

When he was killed, Steve Boal was within days of leaving for rest and recuperation, expecting to meet his wife in Hawaii.

Another name and plaque added to the monument not too long after its dedication was that of 19-year-old Pfc. Michael Beck of Cheyenne. He was killed March 29, 1966, less than six weeks after his deployment to Vietnam began. The day before hearing the news, his parents had received two letters from him. One read, "I'm scheduled for a patrol in a day or two and am looking forward to it." He was the second Cheyenne man and the third Wyoming serviceman to be killed in Vietnam that week. He was a letterman in football, wrestling and track at Cheyenne Central. His father, a railroad brakeman, told the reporter from the Wyoming State Tribune, "We have no regrets. We believe the sacrifice of our son was necessary."

When the UW Vietnam Memorial was announced in 1968, James Spiegelberg of Laramie, a board member of the Alumni Association, was quoted in the Oct. 18th Branding Iron as saying: "We pray in the future there will be no additions to this roll." Alas, that prayer was returned unanswered. The Memorial underwent a "Restoration and Addition of Names" in 2012. The names added included all Wyoming men killed in Vietnam, resulting in an increase from the original five to 122, .[147]

1963-1971: From Cheyenne to Vietnam - Jim Steadman

Jim Steadman and Don Bartels were both straight-A students, including a math analysis class taught by Paul Zimmerman in their senior year at Cheyenne Central. Paul was born in Meeteetse, where his father had built a drug store in 1914. When that business failed during the Depression, the family moved to Basin. Paul graduated from Basin High in 1946 and then from UW with a B.S. in math in 1950. He was a middle-distance runner on the UW track team. He taught for two years in Rozet (just east of Gillette) where he met his future wife. Then he was called up under his ROTC commission from college and was dispatched to the Korean War (fortunately for his future students he was not on the front lines). After the war he earned a master's from UW and started his teaching career at Cheyenne in 1955. During his college career and later in Cheyenne he starred as a pitcher or outfielder on several state champion fast-pitch softball teams.

---

[147] According to a July 22, 1946 article in the Wyoming State Tribune, 193 UW alumni, faculty and staff died in World War II.

Selections from Cheyenne's three high schools' for Boys State 1962. BACK (L-R): *Bob Hanscum, *Paul Rayko, Bob Gottschalk (mayor of Millbrae, Calif. 2006-2010), John Ratliff, Courtney Johnson, *Ron Ten Bensel. FRONT: Gary Gysel, Daniel Rondeau, *Gil Kelley, *Don Bartels, *Jim Steadman, *Don Riske. *Mentioned elsewhere in this book also.

After earning a degree in aeronautical engineering at UW, Bartels went into the Air Force and was stationed for six months at Phu Cat Air Base in the Central Plains of Vietnam, built by the U.S. in 1966. He then spent six months at Udorn Base near Udon Thani in northern Thailand.

This base was 200 miles northwest of Ubon Airfield in Thailand where, unbeknownst to Bartels, his Central classmate Steadman was based.

At the same time the Vietnam Memorial Wall in D.C. was being dedicated in 1982, another memorial was dedicated on the grounds of the Veteran's Hospital in Cheyenne. One of the names placed on that memorial was James Eugene Steadman, a graduate of McCormick Junior High School and Central High.

Jim, like many others in Cheyenne schools, had come to Cheyenne because his engineer

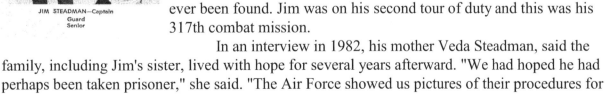

JIM STEADMAN—Captain
Guard
Senior

father was an officer in the U.S. Air Force and was posted to Warren Air Force Base in late 1959 to advance the Atlas missile program. Jim was a brilliant student, a strong football player and wrestler and a trumpet player in the band at Central High.

When he graduated from the Air Force Academy in 1967, he was married and soon had two children. He was a skilled jet fighter pilot. Before our class' 10th reunion in 1973, the author wrote the Air Force Academy to get his address and learned that Capt. Steadman and his co-pilot, part of the 497th Fighter Squadron, went missing in action over Laos on Nov. 26, 1971 while flying an F4 Phantom on a reconnaissance mission out of Ubon Airfield. No trace of them has ever been found. Jim was on his second tour of duty and this was his 317th combat mission.

In an interview in 1982, his mother Veda Steadman, said the family, including Jim's sister, lived with hope for several years afterward. "We had hoped he had perhaps been taken prisoner," she said. "The Air Force showed us pictures of their procedures for searching for planes and eventually you realize that if you look at it realistically and scientifically it's almost senseless to hope anymore."[148]

A report on the mission and the search for these pilots and their plane was put together by Joseph Mortati (himself an F-4 pilot) of GTG Consulting in 2009 (http://www.keytlaw.com/f-4/the-loss-of-owl-08/). It concludes:

> In James Michener's fictional account of fighter pilots during the Korean War – "The Bridges at Toko-Ri" – Admiral Tarrant, upon seeing the selfless and heroic dedication of the men under his command, asks in amazement, "Where did we get such men?" We could ask the same about Jim Steadman and Bob Beutel, well-trained, experienced, combat veterans who understood the risks and yet answered the call to fly some of the most difficult and dangerous combat missions the United States Air Force has ever flown. These men are true aviation pioneers who proved an enemy could no longer hide under the cover of darkness. They gave their very best to their country and earned the right to be called patriots and heroes and should be remembered as such. We solemnly look forward to the day they come home.

This report of Steadman's mission brought back many memories for Bartels, whose job was tied to the F-4D. The APQ-109 radar system pictured on page 12 is the equipment he worked on. Like Steadman, Bartels' oldest son, Clay, is an AFA graduate and flew the F-15, which was the replacement for the F-4. Clay's first trip overseas was to Ubon.

Bartels and Jim Steadman's daughter Karin, and her son Steadman ("Steadie") of Canon City, Colo., were honored guests at the 50th reunion of the Cheyenne high schools' 1963 class in August 2013.[149]

1943-1967: The Tragedies of Two Wars: Curtis Tadashi Ando
Among the thousands of West Coast residents of Japanese descent who were rounded up in 1942 and transported for confinement at relocation camps inland -- most of them American citizens --were Mr. and Mrs. Ushizo Takaki and their children, including their 20-year-old daughter Marguerite. The Takakis were mystified as to why they were being forced into a camp with barbed wire fences and armed guards in towers when three of the family's sons were serving their country in the U.S. armed forces and eventually fought in Europe with the famous 442nd Infantry Regiment composed entirely of men of Japanese ancestry.

---

[148] Casper Star 11/14/1982.

[149] Maj. Douglas "Pete" Peterson, another Air Force pilot flying an F-4C Phantom II fighter as part of the "Night Owl" program out of Ubon, was shot down over North Vietnam in September, 1966 and sustained multiple injuries after ejecting and landing in a tree. Peterson had enlisted in 1954 at age 19. His story had a happier ending than Steadman's, but only after he endured six years as a POW at the "Hanoi Hilton". At Christmastime in 1969, Albert and Mary Peterson of Laramie, the flier's parents who operated the Albany Office Equipment Co., had received no word for three years as to whether their son was alive. Then, in January, 1970, the missing man's wife in Florida received a letter from him saying he was safe. In September, 1970, his wife saw him in films released by North Vietnam. He was freed with the other POWs in 1973 and went on to a remarkable career, serving as a Congressman from Florida from 1991-1997 and then being appointed as the first U.S. Ambassador to Vietnam, a post he held for four years.

Before Pearl Harbor and the resulting influx of internees to the Heart Mountain camp between Powell and Cody, very few residents of the area were of Japanese descent. Sugar beet farmer Charles Ando and others in his family were exceptions. They had been farming from southwest of Billings, Mont., to the Big Horn Basin in Wyoming for many years. The idea of finding a bride of Japanese descent in Wyoming probably never entered Charles Ando's mind, until, almost overnight, a large camp was built near his farm and in August, 1942, thousands of internees began to arrive.

"Man o man they thought they had come to a God-forsaken country with nothing but jack rabbit and sage brush," Ando recalled in an AP article in the Billings Gazette on Dec. 6, 1978. They felt they had been sent out there and dumped at the end of the road, he said. "They were scared and confused, but for the most part local people were real good to them."

Marguerite, born and reared on a farm in California, hated the confinement and soon found authorized jobs in the area. She was hired as a housekeeper for Charles Ando when his mother became an invalid. They eventually married and brought four children into the world.

After the war ended and the camp closed, Marguerite's parents moved back and restarted their lives in California – like most of the internees they probably had to start from scratch.

One of the Ando children was a boy named Curtis Tadashi Ando, born at Powell in September, 1944. Before graduating from Powell High in 1963 he was president of the student council and a three-year letterman in football. On Sept. 30, 1961, the Panthers' junior halfback Curt Ando caught a 27-yard pass to set up a touchdown and help his team to a 20-20 tie against the invading Casper Mustangs.

He attended Montana State in Bozeman for 2 ½ years and then enlisted in the Marine Corps. After training at several bases in the U.S., Ando shipped out of El Toro, Calif., to Vietnam in mid- November, 1966, arriving on Thanksgiving Day.

Six weeks later, the Ando family received the horrible news that their brilliant son had been killed on January 3rd near Da Nang by a sentry, a fellow Marine, possibly because of a password mixup. The boy who had come into being from the circumstances of World War II had tragically become Powell's first serviceman killed in the Vietnam War.

His body was returned to Powell, accompanied by a Marine Corps escort named Lance Cpl. Michio Kusumoto. Powell businesses closed and flags flew at half mast on the day of his services. Even a group of area WWI veterans, members of the Shoshone Barracks No. 1898, attended.

Some of the memorials from the Powell Tribune were entered into the Congressional Record. They were sent to Sen. Cliff Hansen by a former neighbor of the Andos, along with his letter rightfully praising Ando as "an admirable young man, the acme of American youth." But the letter writer also condemned the media attention given "in these days to every communist, crank, crackpot and just plain creep who opposes the disappointing war in Viet Nam."[150] (It took a long time and an incredible toll on the youth of America, but eventually, of course, a significant majority of the American people became opponents of the war and brought the carnage to an end).

---

[150] Powell Tribune, 1/24/1967.

The Ando incident gave rise to some discussion as to whether young men with features that might put them at risk of being mistaken for a Vietnamese enemy should even be sent to Vietnam.[151]

Just over a month later, 31-year-old Sgt. Pablo Patino Munoz, a former Powell resident and the husband of a Lovell girl, joined Ando as a Vietnam casualty. He was the father of eight children and lived in Colorado Springs. His parents still lived in Powell.

1963-1969: From Cheyenne to Vietnam: John William Kobelin II

When the Vietnam Memorial was dedicated in D.C. in 1982, Bill Kobelin and his wife Lorna were still living in their lovely home in east Cheyenne where their son John grew up. Bill Kobelin had been a sprinter for the Thermopolis track team and set a state meet 100-yard dash record in about 1932 which stood for decades. In a 1982 interview he remembered that the team traveled over a dirt road the 180 miles from Thermop to Douglas for the meet.

John Kobelin is pictured second from right in this scratchy photo of attendees at Dan Heist's (second from left) birthday party in 1952 in Cheyenne. Photo courtesy of Dan Heist.

John was their only son, and he was strong and industrious. He worked as a newspaper carrier, throwing papers from his bicycle. Later he worked at the golf course keeping the greens in good shape and then as a switchman for the Union Pacific during his college summers.

He was a member of the first sophomore class in the brand-new East High School. He played tackle on the football team and applied the half nelson on the wrestling team. He earned a business administration degree from UW in 1967.

He joined the Army after graduating. Following a month's leave of absence over Christmas of 1968, he went to Vietnam. Within three months he was dead.

John was a dog handler whose job was to locate enemy bunkers and mines.

---

[151] A letter to the Casper Star printed on Jan. 18th indicates that a CST editorial had raised this question a few days earlier.

On March 6, 1969, he and his dog found a bunker and during the ensuing battle John was wounded in the head. He died in a helicopter flying him out, and came back to be buried in Cheyenne's Lakeview Cemetery.

1968: Tragedy comes even to tiny Hanna

The name Spc. 4 William Joseph McAtee was one of the many names added as part of UW's restoration of its Vietnam Memorial monument. McAtee was the son of Edward F. McAtee and the brother of Edward R. McAtee of Hanna, Wyo. The younger Ed coached the St. Mary's Gaels basketball team in the early '60s in Cheyenne and then returned home to coach the Hanna Elk-Mountain team. One of his star players was James Isaac, who became one of the 14 African Americans whose lives were damaged by Coach Eaton's UW football purge in 1969.

Coach Ed McAtee was the third in a line of Edward McAtees. The first two worked in the coal mines of Hanna. The 1910 census shows Bill's and Coach McAtee's grandfather, Edward (the first), age 40, and wife Helen B. living in Hanna with children Julia age 3 and George, nearly 2. He is shown on the census sheet as an "engineer" in a coal mine. Bill and Coach McAtee's parents, Edward (the second) and Willatta Warburton McAtee, were both born in Wyoming. Ed II (1913-1984) is shown in the 1930 census as a 16-year-old baker's helper and in the 1940 census as a "driller" for a coal mine at Hanna.

Coach Ed McAtee is pictured in July, 2014, standing outside of -- and wearing a hat advertising -- Poulos' Nugget Bar & Grill in Elmo, just east of Hanna, where he ate lunch regularly in his later years. Elk Mountain in the background. Photo by author.

Coach McAtee's much younger brother, William J. McAtee, was born in 1948 and graduated from Hanna Elk-Mountain in 1966. He was an All-state football and basketball player, vice president of the student body and junior class president. Also graduating that year -- from Saratoga's Platte Valley High School 40 miles away -- and also headed to UW was Tony Seahorn. For years, Bill and Tony had been foes in the athletic venues but good friends otherwise. On March 17, 1965, for example, Seahorn scored 24 points in a basketball game against Glenrock and McAtee scored 23 points against Guernsey-Sunrise. They were both named to the Class B all-tournament teams at regionals.

After high school, though, both of them ran out of money, dropped out of college and were drafted.

On January 5, 1967, the Rawlins Daily Times carried a report of a city league game in which Venice Lounge defeated Hanna. Bill McAtee scored 22 for Hanna and his older brother Ed scored four.

The Hanna News column in the Rawlins Daily Times on Feb. 23, 1968, reported:

Guests on Saturday at the home of Mr. and Mrs. Ed McAtee, Sr., and Bill were
Mr. and Mrs. Rudy Aguilar [Nancy Carol Aguilar was Bill's brother] and family

of Laramie and Mr. and Mrs. Ed McAtee Jr. and family. Bill left on Monday for Denver for his physical for the Armed Forces.

On July 24, 1968, Bill began a tour with the Infantry in Vietnam. He was in contact with his friend Tony Seahorn who had gone to OCS and been commissioned a first lieutenant. Seahorn was with a different outfit in Vietnam. They had made arrangements to get together on December 1st. But on that day, Tony was severely wounded for the second time in Vietnam. He had been in a coma for five days when he awoke in a hospital in Japan. Not until he was back in the States a month later did he learn that two days after his injury his friend, 20-year-old Bill McAtee, had been killed.

A note from the Virtual Vietnam Wall says of McAtee's battle:

On 03 Dec 1968 the 116 men of D Company, 217th Cavalry, made an air assault at Landing Zone Eleanor about 15 miles west-southwest of Phuoc Binh, where they were attacked by an enemy force estimated at 400 men or more. By the end of the five hour battle, there were 26 US dead and 50 or more had been wounded.

Clinton Isaac, an older brother of James Isaac (one of the Black 14) and a classmate of Bill McAtee, returned home from Denver to serve as a pallbearer for the service at St. Joseph's Catholic Church in Hanna. James was an honorary pallbearer. In a 2014 interview, Coach Ed McAtee said the friendship between Clinton and Bill caused many to call the pair "Ebony and Ivory".

In a 2013 e-mail, Clinton said: "Bill McAtee and I were very close friends growing up together in Hanna. We were like brothers with different color of skin. Bill was in my graduation class of 1966. I can say he was a friend that never looked at the color of someone's skin. He was always there for me in time of needs. I spent a lot of time with him during my high school years in Hanna and we did things together as close brothers would do. I still miss Bill as a close friend very much until this day. This was a sad day and chapter in my life to lose such a close friend. It seemed to me this was a terrible and senseless shame that we all lost him at a very young age. Only God can answer these questions."

In a ceremony at UW in April, 1969, William Joseph McAtee's parents were presented with his Silver Star, Bronze Star, Air Medal and Purple Heart. The citation for the Silver Star related that when a machine gunner was seriously wounded, "McAtee exposed himself to intense hostile fire as he moved to the machine gun and placed accurate suppressive fire on the advancing enemy."

The issues of the Rawlins Daily Times carrying articles about William McAtee also carried many other stories of tragedy and discouragement. On Dec. 5, the Times reported that funeral services were to be held in Sheridan for another Army Spec. 4, Don Ford, who was killed by a sniper near Na Trang, South Vietnam, the previous week. He had graduated from Sheridan College in 1963.

In the Dec. 6th issue, Paris peace talks negotiator W. Averill Harriman told President-elect Nixon -- who had based his campaign on the idea that new leadership by the Republicans would boost the chances of peace in Vietnam -- that the North Vietnamese attitude toward the new administration would be much the same as toward the Johnson administration. On another page, that issue reported that Sirhan B. Sirhan would go on trial in January for the murder of Sen. Robert F. Kennedy in June, 1968.

The Times sports page on Dec. 7th carried an article about the Hanna basketball team's 45-31 win over Pine Bluffs. The article quoted the team's grieving coach, Ed McAtee: "The boys told me they wanted to win it for my brother who was killed in Vietnam." The lead story on page one was that the North Vietnamese forces had launched simultaneous attacks along the northern frontier against a strategic U.S. base at Dong Ha.

On Dec. 11th, the Times' lead story was from UPI, datelined Saigon, saying that American dead in the Vietnam War had passed 30,000, almost half of them in 1968 alone. Heaviest new casualties were in the Da Nang area along the southeastern coast, the article said.

Subsequently, a VFW organization at Hanna called the "Lucas-Sarr-McAtee Ladies Auxiliary" was established. In 2015, Mr. Seahorn and his wife Janet were living in Fort Collins and maintaining a website about combat PTSD at www.tearsofawarrior.com. They have also authored a book titled *Tears of a Warrior*.

Many young men and women were honored to join the military and serve in Vietnam. But one has to wonder how many of those 122 men listed on the UW Vietnam Memorial found themselves in Vietnam not because they were motivated by the "Domino Theory" but simply because the draft eliminated their freedom to do otherwise.

1968: Dow Chemical-Napalm-Agent Orange

Because Dow Chemical manufactured napalm which U.S. forces were using in Vietnam, college students began to protest Dow's recruitment visits to campuses in October, 1966, a movement which spread to more than 100 other colleges within a year. Dow stopped making napalm in 1969, but it also made Agent Orange, a defoliant that would eventually be linked to cancer and other illnesses among American Vietnam veterans for years to come.

On Feb. 17, 1968, the Laramie Boomerang, in a report by Pete Fetsco, declared that, "A little bit of Berkeley crept onto the University of Wyoming campus Friday when a small group of student pacifists set up camp outside the Commerce and Industry Building where officials of the Dow Chemical Co. were interviewing job applicants."

The article said 25-30 students participated, bearing placards with messages such as "Do Vietnamese Burn Well?" and "Been Burned Lately? Try Dow's Super-Efficient Napalm." Without identifying the student by name, the article quoted a spokesperson as saying that Dow was the only company to make napalm and should be targeted by anti-war demonstrations.

Campus police chief Don Miller said the event "was nothing big. There was no disturbance or anything like that. We never even sent a man over." UW President Carlson said the students did not violate university regulations and "I don't believe any disciplinary measures will be taken."

The article says that "onlooking students, apparently pro-Vietnam, milled around and jeered at the demonstrators, but there was no violence."

1968: Jackson Hole and My Lai: Stanley Rogers Resor

The *Jackson's Hole Courier* on December 11, 1930, reported that "in spite of the depression ..., Jackson Hole has forged steadily ahead," as evidenced by building projects at the Teton Lodge near Moran and "at several of the Dude Ranches. The Stanley Resor summer home above Wilson was built and is one of the finest in the valley at the present time. Mr. Resor is one of the latest eastern business men to become interested in this section."

The Circle R ranch on the west bank of the Snake River (later called the Snake River Ranch) had been purchased sight unseen in 1929 by Stanley Burnet Resor (1879-1962), an advertising executive in New York who lived in Greenwich, Conn. His 11-year son Stanley Jr. (1917-2012) had visited Jackson Hole and told his father about its striking beauty.[152] In October, 1931, the *Courier* reported that "the most modern barn in Jackson Hole" was nearing completion at the Resor ranch. In late March 1935, father and son made a winter visit to the ranch and "saw a lot of game," the *Courier* recounted. In August, 1934, Stanley Resor Sr.'s Hereford bull took first place and the next year his draft mare won second place at the livestock show and rodeo in Wilson. For several years, Resor donated the steers for a free barbeque for visitors to the show. The steers were cooked whole "to a king's taste" in a "mammoth earthen pit."[153]

In late September 1940, Stanley Jr., his sister Helen and Charles Pillsbury of Minneapolis climbed the 13,766-foot Grand Teton. They had to camp overnight at the "cave camp when a snow storm made altitude work difficult." By this time, Resor was in the midst of his studies at Yale.[154]

In 1942, Resor married Charles' sister Jane Lawler Pillsbury, daughter of John Pillsbury, former chairman of the Pillsbury Flour Mill Co., and they raised seven sons in Connecticut and Washington. Jane Resor was actively involved in many Jackson Hole activities such as the annual Wilson rodeo celebration and the county library's collection development during her summers on the ranch.

The younger Resor's summers in Wyoming were interrupted by WWII. The *Courier* on Sept. 2, 1943, reported that Capt. and Mrs. Stanley R. Resor had traveled from Augusta, Ga. for a 10-day visit with his parents at the ranch. He served with the Army's 10th Armored Division, rose to the rank of major and fought in the Battle of the Bulge.

In 1944 Stanley Resor Sr. was chairman of the St. John's Hospital board in Jackson, and as the war was ending, Episcopal Bishop Winfred Ziegler presented Resor with the Bishop's Cross in recognition of his volunteer contribution to the hospital.[155]

---

[152] New York Times obituary, 4/19/2012. In his teens, Stanley Jr. changed his middle name to Rogers "to escape his father's large shadow."

[153] *Courier*, 8/19/1937.

[154] Another Grand Teton ascent made the news two months after the Black 14 incident at Laramie. An AP report in the Riverton Ranger on Jan. 2, 1970, revealed that 61-year-old Paul Petzoldt of Lander and a team of climbers set out from a high camp in -40 degree temperatures at 4 a.m. and managed to reach the Grand Teton summit on New Year's Day. Petzoldt had made the first winter ascent in 1935. His 1970 success came after Petzoldt failed to summit on four successive New Year's Day attempts. One of the climbers whose group was prevented by weather from attempting to summit was 16-year-old Alison Higby of Lander (who became a wonderful artist and married another Teton mountains painter Joe Arnold). In 1974, Alison's step-mother, Helen Higby, a 26-year-old Lander librarian, did summit on Petzholdt's expedition, becoming the first woman to make a mid-winter climb of the Grand. In the fall of 1968, Petzoldt was enrolled at the University of Wyoming and lived and dined in McIntyre Hall. He was the subject of a feature interview in the Branding Iron on Feb. 14, 1969. The 68-year-old founder of the National Outdoor Leadership School in Lander praised the activism of the younger generation. "The old folks condemn youth," he said. "They say, 'well, you should be content. Look at all the things we have given you. You should remember that education is a privilege and not a right' and all that sort of stuff. These old folks are voices in the wilderness. They don't count anymore. Because they don't have the slightest idea of how to solve the problems of the world."

"These kids nowadays are just wonderful," he continued. They're so much more mature than we were at the same age. Morally, they're so much better than we were. They have more concern for their fellow men, for the world and for their country. Old people want more cops and less justice."

[155] Jackson's Hole Courier 8/23/1945.

In July 1944, the elder Resor wrote to the New York Times urging passage of "the Barrett bill" which would annul Pres. Franklin Roosevelt's executive order creating the Jackson Hole National Monument adjacent to Grand Teton National Park (the Monument was eventually annexed to the Park).[156] Secretary of Interior Harold Ickes, a white man who once was president of the Chicago NAACP, played a major role for years in the Teton park expansion effort.

After WWII, Stanley Rogers Resor joined a prominent New York City law firm and then in 1965 Pres. Lyndon Johnson appointed him Secretary of the Army. During his six-year term in that position he oversaw the buildup of Army troops in Vietnam from 117,000 in January, 1966, to 360,000 in 1968.

According to the New York Times obituary appearing April 19, 2012, after Resor's death at age 94 in Washington D.C., "the divisiveness of the Vietnam War led to a two-year program under Mr. Resor in which antiwar politicians and activists were spied upon. Army spokesmen at first denied that the program existed, but Mr. Resor later released a letter acknowledging it."[157]

He also had to deal with a horrible chapter for the U.S. Army during that war.

The My Lai massacre in March '68 became public 20 months later through a Seymour Hersh article appearing Nov. 12, 1969. Resor had ordered an investigation of the incident by a board headed by Lt. Gen. William Peers, and on Dec. 5th appointed two civilian lawyers from New York City as special counsel to assist in an investigation of a possible cover-up in the original field inquiry of the massacre.[158] The committee compiled 20,000 pages of testimony and recommended that dozens of men be prosecuted.

Two weeks after Hersh's article broke, the Army charged Lt. William Calley with the premeditated murder of 109 South Vietnamese civilians. U.S. troops had killed between 347 and 504 unarmed Vietnamese civilians, according to the New York Times' obituary. Resor "ended up not prosecuting top officers, including Gen. William C. Westmoreland, the Vietnam commander," the obituary said.

The Nixon administration was enraged at the media outlets that carried Hersh's expose. "It's those dirty rotten Jews from New York who are behind it," Nixon railed.[159]

---

[156] The bill was sponsored by U.S. Rep. Frank Barrett R-Wyo. Future governor Cliff Hansen, a Jackson rancher and county commissioner at the time, also opposed the monument and was among the group who on May 2, 1943, drove cattle onto monument lands without a permit as an act of defiance. According to Robert W. Righter in his book on Grand Teton National Park titled *Crucible for Conservation* (Colorado Associated University Press 1982) at 114, this "publicity stunt ... was the invention of the imagination of Stanley Resor." Sen. Milward Simpson denounced the Monument in a Jackson hearing on Aug. 17, 1943. The Barrett Bill passed Congress in 1944, but FDR pocket vetoed it. After the war, Barrett tried again. In April, 1947, Resor and Hansen testified before a House public lands subcommittee. Barrett told the committee "that virtually all of Wyoming's population" wanted the monument abolished. Famous naturalist Olaus Murie of Moose testified against the bill, which never emerged from committee. Many years later, in Ken Burns' National Parks PBS documentary, Hansen admitted "I'm glad we lost that fight."

[157] For more on the Army's program see New York Times Service and AP reports in the Detroit Free Press, the Pensacola Journal and elsewhere 2/19/1971.

[158] Fond Du Lac (Wisc.) Reporter, 12/5/1969.

[159] New York Times article about historian Robert Dallek's research into the Nixon and Kissinger duo 4/17/2007.

Of 26 originally charged, Lt. William Calley, a platoon leader, was the only person convicted. Although originally sentenced to life in prison at Fort Leavenworth, Nixon ordered him transferred to house arrest at Fort Benning, Ga. He served only 3½ years of house arrest.

In May, 1971, Resor demoted and censured a former West Point superintendent, Maj. Gen. Samuel Koster, for not conducting a more searching investigation of the massacre. A New York congressman said the punishment was little more than a "slap on the wrist."[160]

In later years, Resor became involved in efforts to reduce international arms and was a founding board member of the Jackson Hole Land Trust. A 1987 photograph of Stanley and Jane with numerous grandchildren appeared with Resor's obituary in the *Jackson Hole News & Guide* on April 25, 2012.

1969: Vietnam Moratorium in Wyoming

The Black 14's dismissal occurred just two days after 664 UW faculty, students and townspeople marched from Washakie Center to downtown and back in the largest Vietnam War protest ever in Laramie. Many of them wore American flag arm bands. Millions of people across the world also participated in the protest which had a theme of "no more business as usual until the war ends."

English professor Ken Craven was asked why he had his three children in the march. "Because a million and a half children have died in Vietnam already – that's reason enough." Two Army veterans carried a sign saying: "I have been there and watched people die! It is all wrong." The marchers returned to the Vietnam Memorial on campus and completed a 24-hour vigil there at midnight. In a Boomerang report, a student named Jacqueline Volz asked, "How long can we be the police force of the world? We just keep putting more lives into it, to retain some sense of honor, but it's impossible to claim we'll ever come out on top."

A bystander downtown told the Branding Iron reporters, "I've never seen so many unpatriotic people. It's called aiding and abetting the enemy." A counter protest by Andrew David Louis attracted 10-15 followers.

Vietnam protesters and supporters sponsored large advertisements in the local newspapers. The ad placed by Moratorium supporters carried 320 names, including that of Al Wiederspahn of Cheyenne, the late husband of Wyoming's conservative Republican U.S. House member Cynthia Lummis in 2016. The ad first noted that both in 1964 and in 1968 "we elected a President who told us he would end the war in Vietnam." It said that "our involvement in Vietnam has been from the outset a tragic mistake. An immediate end to the war is essential if our country is to regain its sense of national priorities and purpose."

At Casper, 175 persons heard Casper lawyer Ernest Wilkerson ask, "How many more bodies do you want before we, as we inevitably will, get out of Vietnam?" Wilkerson, a Marine Corps veteran of WWII who was in combat on Guadalcanal, Bougainville and Saipan, ran unsuccessfully for governor as a Democrat in 1966. He told the crowd that the U.S. seemed to be staying in Vietnam until "we have sacrificed the required number of additional lives to satisfy those who insist that we remain to preserve our national honor, to save our national face, and all of the other blithering and mindless cliches. ... In the history of the United States, and possibly in the history of the world, there has never been a more exemplary piece of national military madness than Vietnam."[161]

---

[160] AP report in Muncie (Ind.) Star, 5/20/1971.

[161] UPI. Northern Wyo. Daily News, 10/17/1969.

In Dubois, Mayor Arden Coad told his local news outlet that he supported the Vietnam moratorium. He then had to deny rumors that he had been removed as mayor and that a VFW convention scheduled in Dubois in January had been canceled.[162]

In Washington on October 14th, President Nixon stated that "under no circumstances whatever will I be affected by the Oct. 15 Vietnam moratorium." On Wednesday of that week, Sen. Gale McGee (D-Wyo), a hawk on the Vietnam War and a member of the Senate Foreign Relations Committee, said he was "apprehensive" about the Moratorium, cautioning students at Earlham College in Richmond, Ind., against "letting advocacy of a policy and the means of exercising it sweep you into a movement whose consequences could be harmful to our democracy. ... The nation cannot follow an emotion-ridden path that could lead to serious political pitfalls."[163]

In a long letter about the Moratorium march in Washington D.C., sent to his hometown's paper, the Powell Tribune and published October 24, George Washington Univ. student Brec Cooke said he was amazed by the sophistication of the planning that led to "the greatest movement of a body of people that I have ever witnessed." He said Pres. Nixon had promised to end the war, which appeared to be at a stalemate, and the people were impatient to see it end. Admitting that the war could not be won, Cooke also questioned the wisdom of immediate withdrawal, noting that Sen. McGee had spoken on national television on the night of the march, warning about "creeping isolationism in American foreign policy." Cooke said, however, that Vice President Agnew's "running-off-at-the-mouth" and calling the marchers 'misfits' showed a lack of farsightedness and an inability to consider opposing views. He said the phrase "Our country--right or wrong" was incomplete. It should mean, he said, "Right to keep it right, wrong to make it right again."

1969: The November Moratorium

Four University of Wyoming students drove 32 hours straight-through to Washington D.C. to join more than 250,000 marchers in the Nov. 14-15 Moratorium marches. They were Peggy Burwell, Al Hendricks, Helen Cooke and future Wyoming Secretary of State Kathy Karpan, who wrote a reflection on the events for the Dec. 17th *Free Lunch*:

> By the banks of the Potomac we waited to march for the dead. It was midnight and cold. Behind us was the City of the Dead, Arlington National Cemetery; before us Memorial Bridge.... The continuing procession of candles stretched around the Lincoln Memorial. ... At the Capitol there were eight wooden boxes, two of them opened. Each marcher took off his placard [with the name of a Vietnam War casualty], placed it in the coffin and blew out his candle.

---

[162] The 18-hour PBS Vietnam documentary that debuted in September, 2017, included two mentions of Wyoming. In his ABC nightly news report on the Moratorium Oct. 15th, anchor Frank Reynolds said that thousands had participated, "from New York with eight million people to tiny Dubois, Wyoming with 800 people". The documentary also included a TV news report of reactions to the conviction of Lt. Calley for his participation in the My Lai massacre in March 1968, in which between 200 and 500 Vietnamese civilians were deliberately murdered by U.S. soldiers, including 109 by Calley. The news reporter in the documentary said "a Cheyenne woman" had written a letter saying "what the jury did to Lt. Calley is a disgrace to this nation."

[163] UPI. Casper Star-Tribune, 10/19/1969 p. 22, adjacent to the report that Michigan State's trustees had chosen black economist Clifton Wharton Jr. to be the school's president.

The next day the huge Moratorium march ended at the National Mall. They heard Peter, Paul and Mary and Arlo Guthrie sing and Coretta Scott King and Sen. McGovern speak.

The only speaker to truly arouse the crowd was Dick Gregory who questioned President Nixon's belief that the march wouldn't affect him. "If that's what he really thinks, he ought to place a long distance call to the LBJ ranch." Thousands stood and cheered. ... Folksinger Pete Seeger provided the high point. He started with "Bring the Boys Home" and patiently repeated verses until thousands joined in. ... When Seeger strummed the first chords of "Give Peace a Chance," a roar of approval went up.

Back in Laramie, the November 15th Boomerang carried a full-page blast at the Moratorium. "Fly Your Flag Today!" was the headline at the top, and below, in all-caps type, the paper urged its readers to "not help prolong the war by participating in the moratorium. ... The blows are being well-timed, the poison is being administered in small doses. ... We are weakening before the relentless determination of ever present minority of evil people whose goal in life is to drag others down to their level."

1968-69: War opposition not healthy for Wyoming clergy
The first opposition to the Vietnam War on the UW campus involving more than a handful of people occurred during the governor's review of ROTC troops in early May 1968. The protesters, many of the male marchers in coats and ties, stood along the railing on the east side of Memorial Stadium while the cadets paraded on the field.

Prior to this event, Rev. George Quarterman, Episcopal chaplain of the University Common Ministry and a chaplain in the Wyoming National Guard, received an ultimatum from the Adjutant General of the Guard in Cheyenne. Quarterman's commanding officer told him that the Adjutant General had ruled that "if you participate in any of that stuff then they request your resignation." In response, Quarterman resigned from the Guard, saying in his letter: "I can't see why the military should make a chaplain agree with the administration. If being part of the Guard means agreeing with military policy, then I couldn't be a chaplain. A citizen has a private right to participate in personal politics."

In a UPI report in the Boomerang on October 1, 1968, the pastor of the Casper Presbyterian Church said his dismissal was due in part to sermons urging the U.S. to find alternatives to expansion of the Vietnam war. The Rev. Garrett Carpenter was dismissed Sept. 27th by the Presbytery of Wyoming. One presbytery official said the dismissal was carried out "in the hope of resolving personality conflicts and re-establishing peace and harmony within the church."

1970-Elver Barker of the Fellowship of Reconciliation in Wyoming
On July 28, 1970, the Rapid City Journal carried an article by Mrs. Royal Bock, its correspondent in Newcastle, Wyo., saying that Newcastle native and artist Elver Barker was abandoning his art career and moving to Des Moines, Iowa, to support the American Friends Service Committee's anti-war efforts . "Art is a luxury," he said, "but the abolition of war in the nuclear age is an imperative, practical necessity. If mankind does not end wars, nothing else is worth doing."

Barker was the son of a cattle ranch foreman and a homemaker in Newcastle. After graduating from Denver University with a degree in education, Barker taught fifth grade in

Aurora, Colo. and then was a social worker in California, studying painting in his spare time. He returned to Newcastle to care for his aging father, Amos Barker, following the death of his mother, Roadifer. During the '60s he made a living through private group art instruction in Osage and other towns in northeast Wyoming and in 1968 he published a book titled *Finger Painting in Oils*.

Barker also entered his unique paintings in art shows in the region, including a one-man show at Black Hills State College in Spearfish in 1968 and in other locations in Wyoming. During this time he was editor of the Wyoming Fellowship of Reconciliation's newsletter and was in Washington D.C. for the November Vietnam Moratorium march in 1969, which he regarded as the greatest religious experience of his life.

In May of 1969, a letter-to-the-editor from Barker defending Martin Luther King was published in the Rapid City Journal. This prompted Al Moore of Newcastle to submit a reply published May 15th saying "the followers of [King] are doing more to further the cause of communism in the U.S. than many actual party members."

As he headed to Iowa, Barker said he would be earning just enough to avoid having to pay any income tax. He said 68 percent of federal taxes went to waging war.

During much of his adult life Barker was an organizer and writer -- often under an assumed name -- for the Mattachine Society, which advocated for the rights of gay people. He returned to Denver in 1972 and died there at age 84.

1963-73: Propaganda on progress in Vietnam

Prior to 1968, when President Johnson and others pushing the Vietnam War realized that the U.S. would not be able to "win" the war, the Pentagon issued many releases seeking to reassure the American public that the U.S. forces were making great strides in Vietnam. For example, an article in the Wyoming State Tribune on March 25, 1966, said a government spokesman had reported that the Communist death toll in the previous six days was 1,811 with hundreds more wounded. The government stated that 86 "starved enemy troops" were killed when they attacked U.S. Marines guarding rice fields near Da Nang. "At least five Viet Cong battalions have been mauled in recent weeks in rice raids," the government said. American losses were reported as comparatively light.

Cpl. Harrod, Free Lunch photo

Many returning Vietnam vets spoke out against the war. Even though he had two years left in his Marine Corps enlistment, Corporal Lawrence F. Harrod from Lander visited UW in December, 1969 and held a press conference. He told Jacki McMurray of the Branding Iron that only the "career men" in Vietnam were bitter about the peace marchers in the U.S. "It's about time someone started caring about what's happening over there," he said, noting that some of the lower-ranking soldiers wore peace symbols with their dog tags. During his 13 months in Vietnam Harrod had been wounded three times and had received the Bronze Star and several other medals. His view on the war had changed completely. "If I had to go back to Vietnam, it would be as a conscientious objector," he said.[164] Harrod lived in Gillette, Wyo., for a period of time after his service and died in 1991 in Leesburg, Va. at the age of 41. His obituary in the Gillette News-Record on Sept. 8, 1991, reported that "the cause of death is being investigated in Virginia."

[164] BI, 12/12/1969; Free Lunch, 12/16/1969.

Lt. Lee Alley, a graduate of University High School in Laramie who was awarded the Distinguished Service Cross for bravery in Vietnam in 1967, was asked by a Branding Iron interviewer in November, 1970, whether the U.S. had helped the Vietnamese people. "Not really," he replied. "I now think we should get out of Vietnam as quickly as possible. ... If there has been a gain in Vietnam, it has been made by the American capitalists who have thrived on the money poured into Vietnam."[165] Alley said the purpose of the Veterans for Peace was good, but that the group lost his support by "setting up a table in the Union manned by individuals with long, shaggy hair, headbands and Vietnamese flags on their clothes."

Alley was one of three Wyoming residents and Vietnam veterans appearing in a Wyoming PBS program filmed to coincide with the Lynn Novick/Ken Burns Vietnam documentary in fall, 2017. When he returned to UW after his service, Alley related, he once went into a military service club in Laramie where a WWII veteran told him, "'We won our war.' I didn't go back to the VFW or Legion for 30 years."

But bitter criticism of the opponents of the war by the "establishment" in Wyoming continued almost to the day the war was over. For example, in April of 1972, James M. Flinchum, editor of Cheyenne's Wyoming State Tribune, wrote: "Again we are treated to a manifestation of the compulsory nature of the leftwing antiwar activists, most of them young people and students. It becomes clear they are advocates of force and violence which they loudly decry and which they contend is being employed within the military context in Vietnam. ... The bombing of Hanoi and Haiphong, which apologists for these revolutionaries claim has sparked the current wave of demonstrations, merely provides them with a pretext for doing their ugly, frightening and disgusting thing."

1964-1973: THE DRAFT - EVERY WAKING MOMENT

A UPI article published December 7, 1970, reported that three recent Supreme Court rulings required the Justice Department to dismiss several hundred criminal cases where young men were wrongly reclassified and ordered to report for induction as a retaliation for engaging in antiwar activities. The Justice Department's lawyer for Selective Service violations reported that prosecutions for refusing to report for induction had increased from 325 a year in 1965 to 325 a month at the end of 1970. This was despite the stiff penalties available for refusing induction or aiding or counseling that act: five years in prison and a $10,000 fine.

The effect of the Selective Service Act -- the draft -- played out in several ways in Wyoming in the "1960s".

In the early '60s at UW, two years of ROTC was mandatory for male students, unless they had taken three years of training in high school ROTC. Some young men at UW continued to Advanced ROTC to obtain financial help for college, never suspecting that a brutal war across the Pacific would soon confront them. An article in the UW Branding Iron on Dec. 6, 1963, reported that 75% of UW male students in a cross-section poll favored making ROTC voluntary as had been done at Colorado State College. But the Army officer in charge of the program warned that ROTC might go out of existence altogether if made voluntary, citing a poll of 30

---

[165] BI, Nov. 13, 1970. Alley, who went on to a career with the Post Office in Wheatland and wrote a book on his Vietnam experience called "Back from War", was selected as grand marshal of UW's 2012 Homecoming Parade. In an Oct. 8, 2012 article in the Boomerang he said he was "a lost soul" when he returned from the war. While the Army trained him well for combat, he said, "there was absolutely no training on how to turn off the switch"

graduating cadet officers which showed that only one of them would have taken ROTC if it was voluntary.[166]

As film of the Vietnam War carnage started appearing regularly on the evening TV news shows, many young Wyomingites were drafted (or enlisted under pressure from the draft) and wound up in Vietnam. Others went to Canada, some got medical deferments, many received student deferments.

After graduate student deferments were abolished in 1967 or early 1968, advanced ROTC numbers rose as law students and other post-grads joined the corps to avoid being drafted.

This chapter focuses on some significant stories involving the draft and Wyoming during those years.

A Cheyenne East High School basketball starter in the 1961-62 season was the plaintiff six years later in a lawsuit regarding the actions of the Cheyenne draft board -- a lawsuit that resulted in one of those major U.S. Supreme Court decisions.

Future U.S. defense secretary and vice-president Dick Cheney of Casper obtained four student deferments and then a married-with-child-on-the-way deferment during the early and mid-1960s. In an interview during his confirmation process for Secretary of Defense many years later he said he had other priorities than military service during that time.

In 1970 the U.S. District Court of Wyoming was the location for two criminal trials involving the draft laws with Assistant U.S. Attorney Tosh Suyematsu doing the prosecuting. Recollecting these proceedings provides the opportunity to mention a previous draft resistance trial in that same court back during WWII. It was a mass trial 25 years earlier of 63 young American men of Japanese descent who had been removed from their homes along the West Coast and interned at the Heart Mountain Internment Camp near Powell, which suddenly in 1942 became the third-largest city in Wyoming.[167]

1967: Gen. Hershey and Cheyenne East's James Oestereich

On New Year's Day in 1962, Cheyenne Central outlasted the East Thunderbirds 48-37 before a crowd of 3,000 at Storey Gym. Bob Fintus and Don Illingworth ("East's bespectacled 6-3 senior" according to the Wyoming Eagle report by Mike Christopulous) scored eight points apiece for East, and "southpaw Jim Oestereich" scored six points. Dick Sherman, who would go on to an impressive basketball career with the University of Wyoming Cowboys, led Central to its 9th straight win with 14 points. A Colorado High School coach who was scouting Central at the game told Christopulous that Sherman was a powerhouse in scoring and rebounding. "The best way to play Central is to score a free throw early and then hide the ball," the coach said. In his senior year at UW, Sherman averaged a double-double (21.2 points, 10.4 rebounds/game).

Following the loss to Central, the Eagle printed the East High statistics showing that Oestereich had played in all nine games for the T-Birds, had scored 35 points and pulled down 15 rebounds. Coach John French lamented the lack of a consistent scoring attack by the East team to

---

[166] In February, 1965, a faculty committee -- with the concurrence of the UW Army and Air Force ROTC commandants -- recommended to the trustees that the two-year ROTC requirement be made voluntary. A report in the Branding Iron on Feb. 12th said that of the 16 colleges in the Rocky Mountain area, only UW and one other school still had compulsory ROTC.

[167] On Feb. 5, 1943, Gov. Lester Hunt signed into law a bill providing that internees "under any national emergency ... shall be prohibited from voting in any election in the state of Wyoming." Mackey, Mike, *Heart Mountain: Life in Wyoming's Concentration Camp*, Western History Publications, Powell, Wyo., 2000, p. 94.

that point, averaging only 45 points per game. Jerry Davey led the team in scoring (95 points) and Illingworth led in rebounding (66).

On January 8th, 1962, the Eagle reported that East had taken the lead over Casper after halftime with a basket by Oestereich, and hung on to win 50-45. Davey was the leading scorer with 14 points, while Oestereich scored 10. Elsewhere on that sports page was a box score indicating that Ed McAtee had scored 15 points for the Gasateria team in city league action at McCormick Junior High gym. McAtee was the basketball coach at Cheyenne St. Mary's at the time, but by 1966 he had returned to his native Hanna where he coached James Isaac, who would become one of the Black 14 in October, 1969. In another city league game, the players on one team included Paul Zimmerman, geometry and calculus teacher at Central, Meredith "Skeet" Weston, principal at Churchill Elementary in the early 60s and Jim Brisson, who years later as principal at Central High would crack down on students and faculty violating the dress and hair rules, and then in 1972 on students protesting the Vietnam War and racial inequities. (See Brisson chapter at pg. <u>270</u>).

After graduation in 1962, Oestereich went on to the Newton-Andover Theological School near Boston. His Cheyenne Selective Service Board had classified him as 4D, a statutory exempt status as a divinity student, which was more than a mere student deferment.

When President Johnson increased the number of troops in Vietnam to more than 185,000 by the end of 1965, the monthly draft requirement rose from 9,000 to more than 25,000. During 1967, 1968 and 1969, the Selective Service drafted 300,000 men a year. After more than 30 people staged a sit-in at a draft board in Ann Arbor, Mich., in October, 1965, Gen. Hershey revoked the deferments of 13 male students in that demonstration. He argued that "reclassification is quicker at stopping sit-ins than some indictment that takes effect six months later." (Foley, *Confronting the War Machine* p. 39). Many men then went to Canada, became fathers or enrolled in college to obtain deferments, leading Hershey to again institute a qualification test to remove deferments of the lowest-scoring college students.

On April 16, 1967, after 170 men burned their draft cards in New York as more than 100,000 marchers participated in the Spring Mobilization to End the War, Dr. Martin Luther King appearing on Face the Nation stated he opposed the war. "In the true spirit of non-violence, I have only advocated doing what we do to resist it openly, cheerfully, and with a desire to reconcile rather than to estrange, and really appeal to the conscience of the nation on what I consider a very unjust and immoral involvement" in Vietnam.

By 1967, James J. Oestereich had become strongly opposed to the Vietnam War himself and he decided to participate in the protest to be held at Boston's Arlington Street Church on October 16th. Along with 356 others, he decided to go up and turn in his draft card to the Rev. William Sloan Coffin Jr., chaplain of Yale University, for return to the Selective Service System.

On January 5, 1968, Dr. Benjamin Spock, author of the famous guide to child-rearing used by millions of parents of Baby Boomers, along with Rev. Coffin Jr., Marcus Raskin and Mitchell Goodman (all signers of "A Call to Resist Illegitimate Authority") were indicted by a federal grand jury for "conspiracy to counsel, aid and abet draft resistance." All but Raskin were convicted in June, but in 1970 an appeals court overturned the verdict.

Three weeks after Oestereich turned in his draft card, Oestereich's draft board in Cheyenne, acting on orders from Gen. Hershey, reclassified him as 1-A for failure to have his registration certificate in his possession and for failure to provide the board with notice of his local status. He was ordered to report for induction on February 26, 1968. Oestereich contacted the American Civil Liberties Union and its director, Melvin Wulf, who agreed to challenge the reclassification in court. Another of the attorneys who appeared in the case for Oestereich was John A. King of Corthell & King in Laramie, one of Wyoming's oldest law firms. Wyoming U.S. Attorney Robert N. Chaffin was one of the attorneys appearing for the Justice Department.

Oestereich's suit was filed in the U.S. District Court in Cheyenne in January, 1968. Judge Ewing T. Kerr quickly dismissed it, and the 10th Circuit Court of Appeals affirmed the dismissal with a one-paragraph per curiam opinion.[168]

1968: Oestereich goes to the U.S. Supreme Court

The lower courts' rulings against Oestereich were based on Sec. 10(b)(3) of the Military Service Act of 1967 which stated: "No judicial review shall be made of the classification or processing of any registrant by local boards, appeal boards or the President, except as a defense to a criminal prosecution instituted under section 12 of this title, after the registrant has responded either affirmatively or negatively to an order to report for induction...." This meant that judicial review of a classification was limited to a defense in a criminal prosecution or to habeas corpus after induction. On the other hand, Sec. 6(g) provided that ministers of religion "and students preparing for the ministry under the direction of recognized churches or religious organizations, who are satisfactorily pursuing full-time courses of instruction leading to their entrance into recognized theological or divinity schools in which they have been preenrolled, shall be exempt from training and service ... under this title."

In an article in Wyoming newspapers in early February, Mrs. Maurice Oestereich of Cheyenne, James' mother, stated that her son was wrong and that he had been led down his path by the Boston seminary and by the ACLU.

On Feb. 26th, a crowd of 350 people were at the Boston Army Base to support Oestereich and another resister who were expected to refuse induction. In a leaflet prepared for the event, Oestereich explained why he had chosen to jeopardize his exempt status by resisting the draft: "I have chosen to take a stand against the Selective Service System which presently functions as an

---

[168] One member of the 10th Circuit's three-judge panel for the case was Judge J. J. "Joe" Hickey of Wyoming, a central figure in the bizarre events surrounding a U.S. Senate seat eight years earlier. In the 1958 race for governor, Hickey had upset Republican Milward Simpson (father of future U.S. Sen. Alan Simpson). Two years later Hickey found himself in a sensitive situation when Republican three-term U.S. Representative Keith Thomson, 41, died of a heart attack on December 9, 1960, shortly after being promoted by the voters to the U.S. Senate in the 1960 election. The law at the time placed the duty upon the governor to select someone to serve the first two years of the Senate term. Hickey offered the position to Tracy S. McCracken, publisher of newspapers in Cheyenne, Laramie and several other towns in Wyoming. McCracken had been Democratic National Committeeman for 18 years and, with Edward "Ted" Kennedy at his side, had cast Wyoming's votes for John F. Kennedy at the 1960 Democratic National Convention, securing for JFK the nomination for President. McCracken rejected Hickey's offer because he wanted to live in Wyoming and because "I love newspapering more than any form of endeavor." Only a few days later, however, the 66-year-old McCracken became ill at a Christmas party and died of an intestinal problem. Hickey then resigned as governor, allowing Democratic Secretary of State Jack Gage to become governor. Gage then appointed Hickey to the vacant U.S. Senate seat. Republicans blasted the move and -- 20 years later when Democrat Mike Sullivan was governor, overrode Sullivan's veto and changed the law to require the governor to appoint someone of the same political party as the person elected. On October 15, 1962, as the new Sen. Hickey campaigned to win election to the remaining four years of the term, Hickey himself suffered a heart attack -- a mild one -- and was ordered to rest by his doctors. This time he lost to Simpson, forcing Hickey to return to the practice of law in Cheyenne. In 1966, however, he was appointed to the 10th U.S. Circuit Court of Appeals. Thomson's widow, Thyra, was elected Wyoming Secretary of State in 1963 and then won re-election to five more four-year terms. Jack Gage was the author of a book titled *Ten Sleep and No Rest*, an account of a 1909 raid just south of Ten Sleep, Wyoming, in which seven cattle ranchers attacked a sheep camp, killing two sheep raisers by setting fire to their wagon and shooting and killing another. See an article about the raid by John W. Davis at wyohistory.org.

accomplice to mass murder. It is very clear to me and the thousands who stand with me that this war is wrong – and we will not return to our everyday lives until the war is over."

During the proceedings on the base, Oestereich was informed that the Supreme Court had granted a stay of the induction until the high court decided whether to accept the case. The court granted his petition for certiorari in May, setting the case for oral argument in the fall.

As the court's term opened in October, the case drew national attention because the Justice Department supported Oestereich's argument, pitting the Department against Gen. Hershey at Selective Service. Earlier that year, Hershey had taken the unusual step of submitting a memorandum to the high court claiming the Justice Department had failed to afford him adequate legal representation in this case. The memo was "lodged" with the court but not filed because of the objection of the Solicitor General, who by law is in charge of Supreme Court litigation for the United States government.

The Justice Department told the court in its brief that the local boards had been using the draft machinery to punish protesters illegally and probably unconstitutionally. At the same time in other federal courts, African-American registrants from New York and San Francisco were challenging the whole concept of student deferments which clearly favored those families able to pay college expenses for their sons.

On December 16, 1968, the Supreme court issued its stunning decision in Oestereich v. Selective Service System Local Board No. 11, reported at 393 U.S. 233. In an opinion by Justice William Douglas for the 6-3 majority, the court found that the System had no authority under law to revoke a deferment status provided by statute because of actions the board deemed to be delinquent. To hold otherwise, the court ruled, "would make the Boards freewheeling agencies meting out their brand of justice in a vindictive manner. ... The conduct of the Cheyenne Local Board," the opinion stated:

> is basically lawless. It is no different in constitutional implications from a case
> where induction of an ordained minister or other clearly exempt person is ordered
> (a) to retaliate against the person because of his political views or (b) to bear down
> on him for his religious views or his racial attitudes or © to get him out of town so
> that the amorous interests of a Board member might be better served.

The opinion concluded that to require a person deprived of a statutory exemption to either commit the crime of refusing induction or submit to induction and then raise objections through habeas corpus would be to construe the Act with unnecessary harshness.

Thus did the actions of a former basketball player for Cheyenne East High School result in a major decision from the highest court in the land. The decision was followed a year later by two more decisions extending the ruling beyond just those with a ministerial exemptions and holding that punitive reclassification by local boards was unconstitutional.[169]

1968: Gen. Hershey and Kevin McKinney

On July 31, 1968, during the final stages of the presidential primary campaigns, the 75-year-old Director of the Selective Service System, Gen. Lewis B. Hershey, came to Cheyenne as part of a tour of draft boards in the Rockies. Hershey was appointed by President Roosevelt as director of Selective Service in 1941 and he served in that position until the war -- and the draft

---

[169] The case of David Earl Gutknecht was one of them, reported at 396 U.S. 295. UPI report in Laramie Boomerang 1/20/1970. See also *Davis v. United States*, 417 U.S. 333 (1974).

for a short time -- ended. When the draft was reinstituted he was appointed by President Truman as Director and served until 1970.

While in Cheyenne he sat for a press conference and one of the reporters in attendance was Kevin McKinney, a summer staffer for UPI following his freshman year at UW. (Several years later, McKinney replaced Bill Young as UW Sports Information Director and then became a senior associate athletic director. For many years he has also been the color commentator part of the UW football and basketball radio broadcasting team with Dave Walsh. Kevin's father John McKinney assisted Larry Birleffi of Cheyenne's KFBC radio on hundreds of football and basketball broadcasts from the 1950s to the 1980s).

UPI Bureau Chief Pete Kelly had sent McKinney to the press conference with a question, and directed him to phone in with Hershey's answer. What happened next demonstrated that on very rare occasions even a skilled, experienced national bureaucrat might drop his guard and blurt out an answer that produces unwanted scrutiny.

During the press conference McKinney asked Hershey, "Of all the political candidates now, who do you think you could work with best?" At the time, Vice-president Hubert Humphrey was running against anti-war Sen. Eugene McCarthy for the Democratic nomination and former Vice-president Richard Nixon was being challenged by Ronald Reagan and Nelson Rockefeller for the GOP nomination. Segregationist Gov. George Wallace of Alabama was the nominee of the American Independent Party and was running the strongest third-party race since 1912. (In the general election that year Wallace actually won five states with 46 electoral votes from the deep South. His vice-presidential candidate, retired U.S. Air Force General Curtis "Bombs Away" LeMay, had suggested in a 1965 interview about Vietnam that the U.S. should "bomb them back into the Stone Age." During the 1968 campaign he said that unlike many Americans he did not fear using nuclear weapons in Vietnam).

After the press conference, McKinney called the UPI bureau in the Tribune-Eagle Building at 110 East 17th St., and UPI filed a story quoting Hershey as saying he felt Wallace would make "a good president." According to a Washington Post report that appeared in newspapers three days later, UPI bureau chief Kelly said that a corrected version was filed an hour later, simply quoting Hershey as calling Wallace "the best candidate for my office to work with."

When this report, as well as AP reports of the mention of Wallace, began getting nationwide attention, two things happened: 1) Hershey, first in Denver and then in Washington, denied that he favored any of the candidates and declared that his remarks had been misinterpreted; and, more sensationally, 2) Hubert Humphrey in Detroit promised to fire Hershey if Humphrey were elected president. "General Hershey understandably has his own preference for President," Humphrey said. "I have my own preference for Director of the Selective Service Administration."

In response to Hershey's denial of the news reports, the owner of KRAE radio in Cheyenne, Tom Bauman, came forward with a transcript of a tape recording he had made of the exchange at the press conference:

Reporter: Of all the political candidates now, who do you think you could work with best?
Hershey: Oh, I haven't the slightest idea. There has been some rumor about some that I wouldn't necessarily have to plan on. But I don't get into political campaigns. And I, ah, you might be surprised if I told you some that I have

worked with very, very – to me, and I think to him – very successfully. Now that isn't why 'cause I'm for him. And he's a guy you probably wouldn't think of.

    Reporter: Who would that be?

    Hershey: George Wallace.

    Reporter: Wallace?

    Hershey: Well, he is the governor – and anybody who's been governor of a state – and, of course, you said well, what about Rockefeller. Well, I don't have any quarrel with Rockefeller. ...

Thus did McKinney's question provoke a national debate about whether Hershey favored Wallace for president. For example, in an editorial in the Delta Democrat-Times of Greenville, Miss., the editor wrote: "About the only incontrovertible fact in the whole situation is that Gen. Hershey is a public speaker of the Dwight D. Eisenhower school. You can't tell what he's saying by listening to what he says. ... Did Hershey endorse Wallace? Humphrey says yes, Hershey says no, and we can't tell. Try your own interpretation."

Third-party candidate Wallace tallied 11,105 votes in Wyoming in 1968 (8.7%).

Hershey's mere mention of Wallace's name in answer to the press conference question carried a tragic irony. Hershey's Selective Service System had been drafting African-American men in numbers much higher than their proportion in the general population. A New York Times report in May, 1968, said 50,000 blacks were fighting in Vietnam.

When Wallace took the oath of office as governor only five years earlier, he had said: "In the name of the greatest people that have ever trod this earth, I draw the line in the dust and toss the gauntlet before the feet of tyranny, and I say segregation now, segregation tomorrow, segregation forever." In June of that year, 1963, he stood in the doorway of the auditorium at the University of Alabama in an effort to prevent the enrollment of two black students.[170]

At the same time the news reports of Hershey's mention of Wallace were circulating, Wallace himself brought his red, white and blue campaign to Great Falls, Montana. An article in the Billings Gazette on August 3, 1968, reported that Ralph Zettlemeyer, a 20-year-old Army lieutenant who was wounded during a recent tour in Vietnam, had come from Fort Carson, Colo. to attend the rally. He said he was the son-in-law of Wallace's Wyoming state chairman C. E. Reed. "Wallace is the best candidate to end the Vietnam war the way I think it should be ended -- militarily," Zettlemeyer said.

Nixon won the close election over Humphrey. Ten months after his inauguration he called Hershey to the White House and following their meeting announced that Hershey's 29-year term at Selective Service would conclude in February and he would be reassigned as an adviser to the president on manpower mobilization.

Kevin McKinney's first report of Hershey's answer most likely struck right to the heart of his thinking.

----

[170] Wallace's advocacy for "segregation forever" brings to mind that great turning of tables authored by Ray Durem that goes something like this:

    Hey Mr. Scientist, is it too late
    To make them A-bombs segregate?
    One little change would please me fine:
    Put on there a big "WHITE ONLY" sign.

1962-1967: The Draft and Dick Cheney

Because he brought to UW some credits from Yale and Casper College, Dick Cheney was able to earn a bachelor's degree in political science from UW in December, 1964. In January, 1965, as he worked toward a master's degree, he was an intern at the Wyoming Legislature. He worked with the Republicans only because the other student who won an internship wanted to work with the Democrats.

As he neared the completion of his graduate classes, he was awarded a six-month internship beginning in January, 1966 with Governor Warren Knowles of Wisconsin, sponsored by the National Center for Education in Politics. When that ended he went to work for Knowles full-time as part of the governor's re-election campaign. Cheney's master's thesis, which he completed in July, 1966, is titled, "Highway Acceleration in Wisconsin: A Case Study in Executive-Legislative Relations." (The thesis is available at the Emmett Chisum Special Collections Room at UW's Coe Library).

In January 1966, soon after learning of his wife's pregnancy, Cheney applied for and received his fifth and final draft deferment. On January 30, 1967, Cheney turned twenty-six and was no longer eligible for the draft.[171]

During his confirmation hearings to become secretary of defense in 1989, Dick Cheney had told a Washington Post reporter: "I had other priorities in the '60s than military service." When asked about this by biographer Stephen Hayes he said: "It didn't figure as prominently in my life. ... There were an awful lot of people who were living their normal lives and the war was something that was off there .... We were struggling graduate students living in student housing trying to get our PhDs, and everything else was sort of irrelevant to that basic thrust of what we were trying to do."

While working and attending the University of Wisconsin in Madison, Cheney found the Vietnam War and draft protests to be "an aggravation ... if you couldn't get to class because the protesters were blocking you or there was tear gas released that morning. And we were serious about doing what we wanted to do in terms of pursuing our educations."[172]

2016: Liz Cheney follows her father's path to Congress

Dick and Lynne Cheney's first child, Elizabeth, was born in Madison in 1966 and in 1984 graduated from high school in McLean, Va. and earned degrees from her mother's alma mater Colorado College and from University of Chicago Law School. In 2012 she purchased a home in Jackson Hole, Wyo., listed for $1.9 million, and then in July 2013 announced she would oppose Sen. Mike Enzi in the Republican primary in 2014. This, of course, revived the same "carpetbagger" charges her father had faced when he returned to Wyoming, after more than 10

---

[171] Hayes, Stephen F., *Cheney: The Untold Story of America's Most Powerful and Controversial Vice President* (2007).

[172] Hayes, *Cheney: The Untold Story* at 44.

years in Washington, to run for Congress.[173] Liz Cheney's campaign was rocky from the outset. One of her problems was that she had purchased a resident fishing license shortly after buying the Wyoming home (the license requires a one-year residency). Bumper stickers appeared saying "Liz Cheney for Virginia". After spending a huge amount of money on television ads, Ms. Cheney withdrew from the campaign in early 2014, claiming that the special health needs of her child required her to withdraw. In 2016, however, she jumped into the race for the U.S. House and easily won election to replace retiring Republican Rep. Cynthia Lummis. She quickly rose in the Republican ranks and became chairman of the House Republican Conference, the third-highest position in the Republican Leadership, from 2019-2021. But Liz Cheney soon lost that position and came into the cross-hairs of defeated Pres. Donald Trump when she voted to impeach him for his role in the attack on the U.S. Capitol Building on Jan. 6, 2021, and then became a household name in the U.S. when she accepted the role of co-chairman of the House Select Committee investigating that attack. Back in Wyoming the state Republican Party disowned her, and Trump appeared at a rally for her chief primary opponent on June 4, 2022 in Casper. On Aug. 16th, Liz lost to Cheyenne attorney Harriet Hageman in the Republican primary, winning only 30% of the vote.

1969: Draft Lottery

On the evening of December 1, 1969, the Selective Service System conducted the first draft lottery in 27 years. It was broadcast live by CBS TV. The drawing determined the order of induction for men born in the years 1944 to 1950. Including one for February 29th, the bowl contained 366 capsules, each containing one date of a year's calendar inside.

The young men whose birthday was drawn early in the evening had little hope of avoiding the draft. Those with birthdays drawn hours later could make longer-range plans.

Some statisticians blasted the system of starting with #1 of the draft order and then pulling a date from the bowl, saying this method was not as random as it should have been. In June of 1970 the Selective Service System announced that its next draft drawing for 18-year-olds born in 1951 would involve two bowls: one with the draft order numbers 1 through 366 and the other with the dates of the year.

1970: Randy Kehler and Daniel Ellsberg

The release of the Pentagon Papers by former Defense Department analyst Daniel Ellsberg in 1971 is generally considered to have been a significant factor in finally bringing an end to the Vietnam War and, of course, to the presidency of Richard Nixon. Ellsberg's action had

---

[173] From 1993 until 2000, Dick Cheney was CEO of Halliburton oil service company in Texas and lived in Dallas. But on July 21, 2000 -- four days before becoming George W. Bush's running mate -- he flew to Jackson, Wyo., and changed his voter registration to Teton County, Wyoming. He did this because the 12th Amendment to the U.S. Constitution would have prohibited the Texas electoral college electors from voting for Texas residents for both president and vice-president. Lawsuits in Texas and Florida challenging the sudden change in voter registration were rejected by the federal courts on grounds, among others, that the challengers had no "standing" to bring their suit. This avoidance of the merits brings to mind the Wyoming Supreme Court decision in the 1972 case *Schieck v. Hathaway*, 493 P.2d 759, where some Democrats challenged the eligibility of Dean Prosser to be a member of the Wyoming House of Representatives. At the time of the 1970 election, Prosser owned ranchland in both Wyoming and Colorado but resided in a residence located just south of the Wyoming state line. There was no question but that Prosser would have been fully qualified to be a member of the Colorado legislature if he had run in that state. But the Wyoming Supreme Court essentially refused to address that issue, ruling that the Legislature had determined that Prosser was qualified to serve in the Legislature and that was the end of the matter.

a direct connection to a young man who registered for the draft in Rawlins, Wyo., a few years earlier.

Ellsberg's story is told in a 2009 documentary titled, "The Most Dangerous Man in America." In that documentary, the former Marine and staunch advocate for the war explained how he slowly evolved into a leading opponent of the war and decided to risk many years in prison by releasing the classified documents showing a pattern of lies told to the American people by its leaders for many years.[174]

In August, 1969, as he was reevaluating his position, he attended a meeting of the War Resisters League at Haverford College at Philadelphia where he heard a young man discussing his decision to resist the draft even at the risk of prison. This young man's forceful words turned Ellsberg around. His name was Gordon Randall Kehler, and in the documentary Ellsberg is filmed sitting across a kitchen table from Kehler talking about that day many years earlier.

Ellsberg said Kehler talked very personally about what had caused him to leave Stanford and join the War Resisters' League. Kehler talked about a friend named Bob and about David Harris, husband of Joan Baez, both of whom had gone to prison.

"I was crying," Ellsberg said in the documentary interview. "I left the auditorium. I found a men's room. I was sobbing for over an hour. One of the thoughts I had was, 'the best thing that the best young men of our country can do is go to prison'. When I heard you [Kehler] say these words 'I'm going to prison', it was as if an axe had split my head. But what had really happened was that my life had split in two and it was my life after those words that I've lived ever since. ... And then I thought, 'okay, what can I do to help end this war, now that I'm ready to go to prison.'"

In 2002, Ellsberg wrote a short memoir of the Haverford meeting for a book titled *The Right Words at the Right Time* published in 2002. In it he wrote: "Randy Kehler never thought his going to prison would end the war. If I hadn't met Randy Kehler it wouldn't have occurred to me to copy those papers. His actions spoke to me as no mere words would have done. He put the right question in my mind at the right time."

What Ellsberg did was to begin copying 7,000 pages of classified documents, a project that took months. Then he attempted to get Sen. William Fulbright, a leading opponent of the war, to hold hearings on the papers, without success. Finally he handed the papers to the New York Times and other papers and they were published over the objection of the Nixon administration. A criminal prosecution was brought against Ellsberg, and the administration succeeded in obtaining an injunction against further publication, a ruling later overturned by the U.S. Supreme Court.

---

[174] As the Pentagon Papers were being published in June, 1971, U.S. Senator Gale McGee (D-Wyo) "defended former President Johnson's lack of candor about his plans for widening the war in Vietnam while he was campaigning for the presidency in 1964. McGee said if Johnson had openly admitted his plans he would have 'telegraphed' American intentions to the enemy." *Wyoming Eagle* 6/18/1971.

President Nixon's response was, "we've got to get this son of a bitch." He set in motion a burglary of the office of Daniel Ellsberg's psychiatrist, which led to the Watergate burglary and eventually to Nixon's downfall.[175]

In November, 1969, a few months after Ellsberg heard Kehler's message, the 25-year-old Kehler came to Laramie and visited with local peace activists and groups at the First Person Coffee House and other venues. Kehler had been indicted for failure to cooperate with his draft board and was facing trial in U.S. District Court in Cheyenne on February 9th. He came to the university community to explain what was happening and why he had chosen the path he took. "The process by which men learn to hate and kill goes on," he said. "The draft is, sadly, only one manifestation of that process. And the war in Vietnam is only one end result."[176]

Kehler grew up in Scarsdale, N.Y., the son of a bakery executive. He went to Sunday School every week, became a Boy Scout and later a Scout leader. During his undergraduate days at Harvard he took a year's absence to work as a volunteer teacher in East Africa.

He spent the summer after his senior year in high school working with a classmate in the hayfields of the Silver Spur Ranch near Encampment, Wyo. He turned 18 while there and the ranch foreman, Jim York, took him to Rawlins so he could carry out his legal duty to register for the draft.

At Harvard, Kehler worked with the Harlem chapter of the Congress of Racial Equality (CORE) in that group's poverty programs, including organizing participation in the 1963 March on Washington. After graduating with honors from Harvard in 1967, he began graduate work at Stanford. But he had become increasingly opposed to the Vietnam War, and the draft which fueled it. He dropped out of Stanford after only three weeks and joined the War Resisters' League. He returned his draft card to the Selective Service and became an outspoken opponent of the draft. Although he had a medical condition that could have prevented him from being drafted, and although the feds well knew where he was, the government charged that on or about June 10, 1968, "the defendant did willfully and knowingly fail and neglect and refuse to keep his Selective Service Board No. 4 of Rawlins, Wyoming, informed of his current mailing address." Kehler had refused to apply for conscientious objector status because he felt that would amount to cooperating with the draft and the war.

---

[175] The head of the "Special Investigations Unit", otherwise known as the "White House Plumbers", was Egil "Bud" Krogh, an attorney in John Ehrlichman's firm in Seattle who followed him to the Nixon White House. Krogh coordinated Elvis Presley's visit with Nixon at the White House on Dec. 21, 1970, after Elvis had sent a hand-written letter to the president expressing his admiration for him and asking to help the country as "a Federal agent at large." The photo of Elvis and Tricky Dick shaking hands was for many years the most requested item from the National Archives -- even ahead of the Constitution. (http://nsarchive.gwu.edu/nsa/elvis/elnix.html) Krogh also coordinated the Sept. 3, 1971 break-in of Ellsberg's psychiatrist. When the Plumbers' break-in at Watergate and the subsequent cover-up brought down Nixon's presidency, Krogh became the first of Nixon's staff to be sentenced to prison, pleading guilty to violating the psychiatrist's civil rights. After serving less than five months he eventually was readmitted to the bar and became a lecturer on legal ethics. In a New York Times op-ed in 2007, Krogh said the lawless activity of Nixon and staff evidenced "a meltdown in personal integrity." In 2011, Krogh spoke at the UW College of Law on "Good People, Bad Choices and Life Lessons from the White House," providing insights from his book *Integrity*. Ellsberg wrote the Foreword to Krogh's book, saying the first time he had ever seen the code of ethics for U.S. government workers was in 1971 when he went to visit Randy Kehler, serving time at the LaTuna federal prison near El Paso. The code's first principle was "Put loyalty to the highest moral principles and to country above loyalty to persons, party, or Government department."

[176] UW Branding Iron Jan. 9, 1970.

At his trial before Judge Ewing T. Kerr in Cheyenne's O'Mahoney Federal Building, Kehler represented himself. The prosecutor was decorated World War II veteran Tosh Suyematsu, who as Justice of the Peace had sentenced and castigated the Atlas missile protesters in 1958 (See Missiles chapter at pg. 31 and Suyematsu chapter at pg. 159). The Court had appointed Weston Reeves, a 1969 UW law graduate from Riverton who was working for Graves & Smyth in Cheyenne, to sit at counsel table to assist Kehler if he had any questions. At the same time, Reeves and Charles Graves were the local attorneys for the Black 14 in their suit.

1947: Heart Mountain draft resisters pardoned

On Christmas Eve of 1947, President Harry Truman issued a full pardon of all Americans of Japanese descent who had resisted the draft while involuntarily confined at internment camps such as Heart Mountain between Cody and Powell in Wyoming during the war. Only one of them, who had been sentenced to five years in prison, was still incarcerated. All the others had served their sentences and been released. Forty years later, Congress passed the 1988 Civil Liberties Act, resulting in a $20,000 payment to each survivor of the internment camps.

One has to wonder whether Asst. U.S. Attorney Suyematsu, as he prepared the case against Randy Kehler in early 1970, was aware that the Kehler case might have been the first jury trial of a draft resister in the U.S. District Court of Wyoming since the 1944 mass trial of 63 young American men of Japanese descent who had been interned along with their families at Heart Mountain.

Obviously, Randy Kehler's situation was much different from what had happened to those men, in that he and his family had not been rounded up without any due process of law and transported to an armed internment camp. By the same token, the Vietnam War's effect on Kehler's generation was much different from WWII on their parents' generation. Even so, the story of the Heart Mountain resisters is an important part of the history of draft resistance in Wyoming.

It should be noted that as soon as rumors began to spread about relocating people of Japanese descent from the West Coast to inland camps, some of Wyoming's political leaders expressed strong opposition to the idea. According to Roger Daniels' book *Prisoners Without Trial: Japanese Americans in World War II*, Wyoming Gov. Nels Smith -- while attending a meeting of western governors in Salt Lake City in April, 1942 -- told Milton Eisenhower, War Relocation Authority Director, "If you bring Japanese into my state, I promise you they will be hanging from every tree."[177]

Despite Smith's warning, the camp was built and thousands of persons of Japanese descent were forcibly interned there, beginning in August 1942. Some of them were veterans of World War I and others were parents of sons and daughters serving in the armed services.[178]

Only one editorial voice in Wyoming seemed to discern the injustice of the internment. L. L. Newton, publisher of the Wyoming State Journal in Lander, visited the camp in person shortly after the internees arrived, and then protested the action in a series of articles in late 1942. "They

---

[177] Hill and Wang, New York, 1993 at 57. Mr. Daniels was a history professor at the University of Wyoming in the fall of 1969 and was the faculty sponsor for the Black Students Alliance. The black players immediately reported their dismissal to Daniels, who may have been the first to contact the UW President's Office. At that time, Daniels and a co-author had just finished a book titled *American Racism*, published in 1970. Daniels retired in 2002 after a long career at the University of Cincinnati.

[178] Mackey, Mike, *Wyoming in the Twentieth-Century*, Western History Publications, Sheridan, Wyo., 2011 at 62.

are American citizens born in this country with the full rights of this country, 'even as you and I.' They do not have any other loyalty than to America and are as much our people as second generation German, Irish, Italian or Scandinavian citizens."[179]

News articles routinely referred to the internees as "Japanese", even though most of them were Americans. In early February, 1943, the Legislature passed and Gov. Lester Hunt signed a bill "preventing the 10,000 Japanese brought to it because of the war from voting in any election." The bill resulted from the plain fact that when the internees had resided long enough to become eligible to vote they could have controlled the election for county offices.[180] Another law was passed at the same time, arising from a fear that the internees at the camp would not return to the West Coast after the war was over. It prohibited aliens ineligible for citizenship from owning real property in Wyoming (excepting Chinese aliens because China was a U.S. ally fighting Japan).

The young internees at Heart Mountain who refused to cooperate with the draft, along with more than 200 others in similar camps around the U.S., had taken a position described by an assistant attorney general in charge of the Justice Department's War Division this way: "Many of these individuals refused to serve in the armed forces on the ground that they had been denied their rights as American citizens and therefore had no obligation to serve if the covenant of citizenship was first broken by the Government."[181] The "Fair Play Committee" organized at Heart Mountain also objected to the fact that the government was segregating those who were drafted into units composed entirely of soldiers of Japanese descent. Their position was described in a March 4, 1944 circular that is set out at length at p. 83 of a book by former University of Wyoming law professor Eric Muller titled, *Free to Die for Their Country: The Story of the Japanese American Draft Resisters in World War II*. It concluded by declaring that "until we are restored all of our rights, all discriminatory features of the Selective Service abolished, and measures taken to remedy past injustices ..., we feel that the present program of drafting us from this concentration camp is unjust, unconstitutional, and against all principles of civilized usage." They declared they would refuse to participate in draft physicals or induction.

According to the Introduction to Muller's book by U.S. Sen. Daniel Inouye (D-Haw.), 120,000 people of Japanese ancestry -- 62% of whom were U.S. citizens -- were rounded up along the West Coast in 1942 and incarcerated in ten concentration camps inland, simply because of their heritage. They were held behind barbed wire with armed guards in towers watching them. No one had ever accused them of sabotage or treason. At first, the young men among them who were born in the U.S. -- the Nisei -- were classified by the Selective Service System as "4C" enemy aliens. But then, in January of 1944, the government began to draft these men into the military from the camps where they had been incarcerated originally as suspected subversives.

Most of them answered the draft call, but more than 300 refused, insisting that their civil liberties be restored first. Sen. Inouye says in his introduction: "In this climate of hate, I believe that it took just as much courage and valor and patriotism to stand up to our government and say 'you are wrong'. I am glad that there were some who had the courage to express some of the feelings that we who volunteered harbored deep in our souls."

---

[179] Roberts, Phil, "Wyoming Residents Respond to Relocation," in Mackey, Mike, Ed. *Remembering Heart Mountain*, Western History Publications 1998 at p. 42.

[180] AP report, Casper Tribune-Herald, 2/7/1943, p. 1 and 2/8/1943 p. 1.

[181] Muller pages 100-101.

Without a jail large enough to hold all of them, by March, 1944, 63 Nisei from Heart Mountain were in county jails around Wyoming, awaiting trial. One of them was an internee in his mid-50s who was not, of course, eligible for the draft but was charged with encouraging draft resistance because he had led the Fair Play Committee.

At the time of trial in June, they were all packed into the Laramie County jail in Cheyenne which was so overcrowded that they were not allowed any time outside the cells for exercise. One said it was "a dirty, smelly and depressing place." An attorney named Samuel D. Menin of Denver, who had previously represented African Americans and Mexican Americans in civil rights cases, was hired to defend them. Mr. Menin also had served as attorney in 1940 for several Jehovah's Witnesses who sued 35 citizens of Rawlins for monetary damages after a large mob beat them up and destroyed their property on June 18, 1940 in retaliation for their refusal to pledge allegiance to the flag.[182] As might be expected, no Wyoming jury would even consider awarding money to anyone who did not render unto Caesar, despite Art. 21, Sec. 25 of the Wyoming Constitution which provides: "[N]o inhabitant of this state shall ever be molested in person or property on account of his or her mode of religious worship".

1944: U.S. District Judge T. Blake Kennedy

Judge T. Blake Kennedy, nearly 70, presided at the 1944 draft resistance trial in the marble-lined courtroom of the long-ago razed U.S. Courthouse and Post Office building on 18th Street. Kennedy had been appointed as Wyoming's sole federal judge in October, 1921 (he resigned as chairman of the state Republican Central Committee to accept the position).[183] The defendants had some hope that they might be treated with more fairness by the courts than they had been by their jailers and the executive branch, but that hope evaporated when, according to Muller's book, on the first day of the trial the judge referred to the defendants as "you Jap boys."

In Muller's opinion, the writings and memoirs Kennedy compiled late in life "reveal him as a racist, an anti-Semite, and a xenophobe." For example, Muller discussed an address Kennedy had given to the Cheyenne Young Men's Literary Club before he became a judge. He praised

---

[182] O. L. Clare, a pioneer Rawlins businessman, was forced by a mob of about 1,000 Rawlins citizens, to kiss and carry the flag through downtown. Two Witnesses from out-of-town who had been distributing literature were severely beaten, according to a UPI report June 19, 1940. Their car and trailer were burned. Two women, residents of Rawlins, suffered broken teeth and bruises and were virtually stripped of their clothing by a group of local women who attacked them, according to an INS report transmitted June 20, 1940. Another wire service report in the Corpus Christi Times on June 19th quoted a leader of the crowd as saying, "We'll round up every member of that outfit and make them go through the flag-kissing routine. We don't want any of that kind of stuff in Wyoming." First Lady Eleanor Roosevelt read a news report of the incident and then commented upon it in her nationally-syndicated column "My Day", saying "it is time we stopped and took stock of ourselves. ... Must we drag people from their homes to force them to do something which is in opposition to their religion?" New York World Telegram, June 21, 1940. The four Jehovah Witnesses who sued were denied any damages by a state district court jury in Cheyenne, according to an INS report published April 4, 1941. In another case involving a Jehovah Witness and attorney Menin two years later, the Wyoming Supreme Court agreed with Menin and his co-counsel, Paul Lorenz of Cheyenne, and reversed a public disturbance and profanity conviction of a Jehovah's Witness in Torrington, concluding that the language used was not profane and was not used to insist that those in attendance sign "a petition of questionable character", as required by the statute. *Town of Torrington v. Taylor*, 137 P.2d 621 (Wyo. 1943).

[183] The appointment of Kennedy was reported on page one of the Wyoming State Tribune of Oct. 11, 1921. The headline at the top of the page read: "CONGRESS ARRAIGNS KU KLUX KLAN". U.S. Rep. Tague (D-Mass) demanded an investigation of the KKK. "There is no law to permit men to go out in the dark and take me or my family from my home to punish me whether I am black or white, Catholic or Jew," Tague said.

legislation imposing stiff educational requirements for voting that, the judge explained, would "practically place so high an educational qualification upon the voter that the rank and file of the negros are thereby disfranchised." As a result, he said, the man of the South could vote "without fear that he will be overcome and dominated by the ignorant and illiterate black." He also favored a ban on intermarriage so as to keep the "foreign blood" from mixing with the white.

In another speech -- after becoming a judge -- Kennedy endorsed legislation to allow immigration only to those from northern Europe.[184]

U.S. Attorney for Wyoming, Carl Sackett, was the prosecutor in the four-day trial before Judge Kennedy. The FBI agents who had interviewed the defendants testified that every one of the defendants had indicated a desire to fight for the country if his civil rights were restored, and that they believed each of the defendants was a loyal American.

On July 25, 1944, Judge Kennedy found them all guilty of willfully failing to report for preinduction physicals. He sentenced each of them to three years in federal prison.[185]

On appeal, Menin argued on their behalf:

> If our government cannot trust American citizens of Japanese ancestry so that we can accept them on an equal basis and accord them equal rights, then how can we ask them to fight, and for what do we ask them to fight? Is it to fight for a continuation of relocation centers with armed guards and barbed wire? How can we ask them to lay down their lives in approval of such unconstitutional treatment?

The Tenth Circuit addressed the appeal of the first-named defendant, Shigeru Fujii, and then applied its decision to all the other 62 appellants. The court recognized that Fujii was a native-born American citizen and "was loyal to the United States at all times. There can be no question about this. The agent for the Federal Bureau of Investigation who investigated him after he failed to report testified that his attitude was that of being loyal to the United States, that he indicated no desire to live in Japan, and that he desired to fight for his country if he were restored to his rights as a citizen." But the appeals court quickly disposed of the appeal, saying whether the appellants' constitutional rights were violated by the internment was not relevant to whether, as citizens, they were required by law to answer the draft call.[186]

1944: Prosecution of Heart Mountain's Fair Play Committee

Later in 1944, Sackett put the leaders of the Fair Play Committee on trial for aiding the draft resistance, along with a writer for a Japanese-American newspaper in Denver called the Rocky Shimpo who had written articles about the FPC's activities at Heart Mountain. A. L. Wirin, a Los Angeles attorney hired to represent the FPC's leaders, tried to quash the grand jury

---

[184] The Naturalization Act of 1790 restricted U.S. citizenship to "free white persons", which excluded Japanese immigrants from becoming citizens. A part of the Immigration Act of 1924 was the Asian Exclusion Act which banned the immigration of nearly all Japanese. Thus, most of the Japanese citizens who had immigrated to the U.S. before 1924 (the Issei) and who were interned in 1942, remained as Japanese citizens because U.S. law had prohibited them from becoming U.S. citizens. Their children (the Nisei), however, were born in the U.S. and were U.S. citizens.

[185] Mackey, Mike, Ed., *A Matter of Conscience*, Heart Mountain Wyoming Foundation 2002, at 69,

[186] Shigeru Fujii v. U.S., 148 F.2d 298 (10th Cir. 1945).

indictment on the grounds that it was illegally constituted in that the grand jury did not include any Japanese-Americans.[187] Wirin pointed out that during the previous two years, Wyoming's third-largest city was the Heart Mountain Relocation Camp (which at one time had a population of more than 10,000, nearly 5% of Wyoming's population). But the judge ruled that even though they had probably been brought into the state against their will, they were not permanent residents of the state and therefore were not eligible to serve on a grand jury. If they were not residents of Wyoming, Muller wrote in his book, "it is hard to know where their true residence actually lay. They were stateless ...."

The jury quickly found the seven FPC organizers guilty but acquitted the newspaper reporter. The prominent leaders of the FPC were sentenced to four year terms and sent to Leavenworth, and the less active leaders were sentenced to two years. But these convictions were later overturned by the Tenth Circuit because the judge had not given their proposed "test case" jury instruction. Their chief defense was that their activities were designed to bring about a test case on the legal validity of the draft orders, not to aid draft resistance.

1970: Randy Kehler Trial

Twenty five years later, a very different draft resistance trial occurred in the U.S. District Court of Wyoming, this time in the context of a war which was losing public support.

After the judge's brief voir dire of the first prospective jurors, both Suyematsu and Kehler accepted the jury of eight women and four men. The judge then had the clerk call an alternate juror. The alternate juror who was called, according to a Cheyenne Central classmate of the alternate's daughter, had been a conscientious objector during WWII. As an alternate juror, however, he did not participate in the jury's deliberations after the testimony was over.

Kehler admitted to the jury he had broken the law deliberately. "I feel that the only defense that I can put up before you this morning is a moral defense, an ethical defense, a defense based upon my conscientiously-held principles..."

Mr. Suyematsu had told the jury that the only issue before them was whether Kehler had broken the law. Kehler told them it was not that simple. What the jury had to decide, he told them, "is whether or not you think, after you have heard all the testimony, that I have committed a crime; whether you think that what I have done was the right thing to do or the wrong thing for me to do." He told the jury that they were representatives of the people of this country and the people were the highest authority, higher than Congress or the president or the courts.

Maj. Duane Wheeler of Cheyenne, the Selective Service's state director for four years, testified first. He supervised the files of the 23 local draft boards in Wyoming. An exhibit was introduced showing that Kehler had informed the board of his change of address to 2935 Piedmont Ave., Berkeley, Calif., on April 19, 1968. He also informed the board that during the previous week Kehler had reported to an address in Oakland to undergo a draft physical but that he had refused to submit to it. In his letter, Kehler wrote: "And I was appalled and horrified to see all the other young men who were submitting to it--not because they wanted to go into the army or even felt that they had a duty or an obligation to go in, but simply because they were too scared to do otherwise."

---

[187] Wirin argued internee cases before the U.S. Supreme Court in the 1940s. Twenty years later Wirin was involved in defending Rena Price and her son, Marquette Frye (later known as Marquette Price), who grew up in Hanna, Wyo. Their arrests triggered the Watts riots. See pg. 166. An immigrant from Russia when he was eight, Wirin was an ACLU attorney for four decades. He died in 1978. *New York Times*, Feb. 5, 1978. See encyclopedia.densho.org/A.L._Wirin/ for more on his work for Japanese American clients and groups.

154

Wheeler testified that on July 22, 1964, Kehler had been classified as 1-Y, which he explained as meaning "one who does not currently meet the standards ... for induction into the service."

Also introduced into evidence was a letter Kehler sent, along with his draft card, dated September 29, 1967. The letter read in part: "I cannot honestly say that I oppose all wars. But ... this war is the only one which I have been old enough to seriously think about and try to understand. ... All I can say is that my conscience will not let me support this particular war at this particular time--the war in Vietnam. ... I am objecting to the present selective service system simply because it is the most effective way I can think of to make known my profound opposition to the United States' policy in Vietnam. As long as I continue to possess a draft card, even though at present I am deferred from military service, I am giving my tacit assent to that policy.

"I am also a citizen of this world. And I have obligations to its people, too. ... Just as we declared in the case of the German people who cooperated with Hitler, I feel that cooperation with the United States' activities in Vietnam is a crime against humanity. I want no part of it, and I will do my best to convince other Americans that they should have no part in it either – in the hope that some day soon, enough Americans will have the courage to join me in speaking out against our involvement in this war, so as to bring our government to its senses and the killing to an end.

"I feel that I am a person who has refused to be an accomplice to murder in any way. I cannot see how that is a crime," Kehler said.

On the other hand, Suyematsu told the jury that allowing draft resisters to escape the law would amount to allowing a cancer cell to grow that eventually could destroy this country from within.

Wyoming State Tribune editor James Flinchum covered the trial and could not resist an opportunity to denigrate Kehler's supporters. Flinchum wrote: "The slender, neatly-dressed Kehler [was] in sharp contrast to a University of Wyoming group of hippy-type students who showed up at the trial this morning in support of his defense ...."

The Casper Star-Tribune report of Feb. 10th by Joan Wheelan (who has been capital reporter in Cheyenne for 40 years, most of that time using the by-line Joan Barron; she deserves the Pulitzer Prize for Community Service, single-handedly keeping state government on its toes for decades) noted that Kehler's wife and parents had testified in his behalf "before a courtroom filled with sympathizer students from Laramie, Cheyenne and Denver." The article said Randy's mother Elsie told the jury in a breaking voice, "Randy always had this feeling that all men are brothers." She testified that every day she asked Randy as he grew up, "are you obeying the golden rule."

Joan Barron of the Casper Star-Tribune at her desk in the
press room on the 3rd floor of the State Capitol in 1982.

Even Barron mentioned the appearance of audience members. "Included were ministers
and teachers, and the majority sported beards, long hair and 'Granny glasses.'"

One of the students observing the trial, according to the Star-Tribune article, said he
would not resist induction even though he morally opposed the draft. "I wouldn't have the
courage," he said.

Kehler was quickly convicted by the jury, although in a Casper Star *Wyoming Horizons*
article published October 3, 1982, one of the jurors was quoted as saying she wanted to vote "not
guilty." Wavis Twyford of Cheyenne remembered feeling "very frustrated" because "Judge Kerr
had told us we had to come up with a decision, that we couldn't have a hung jury. I knew from
being with the other jurors there was no way to change their minds and it looked like I was going
to be the only one that would say, 'this law is ridiculous.' Here was a man refusing to kill. It

seemed such a contradiction to put him in jail," Mrs. Twyford said. "I still marvel at what courage it took to do that when he didn't have to. It was very American – what he did – because that Vietnam War nearly destroyed us."[188]

University of Wyoming English professor Ken Craven, who left UW three months later because the Black 14 were not reinstated, attended the trial and spoke to a Casper Star reporter afterwards. He said the guilty verdict reflected the "tremendous fear and insecurity" felt by Americans at the time. The jurors were affected, he said, by the prosecution's argument that dissent against war was going to destroy the U.S. from within. The trial, he said, represented the "best and the worst of the country."[189]

Kehler served 22 months in federal prisons. When he embarked on activities to improve conditions at the low-security prison in Safford, Ariz., the federal authorities transferred him to the LaTuna prison in Texas, just north of El Paso.

Ten years after his release, he became the coordinator of the national Nuclear Weapons Freeze Campaign, which brought him a great deal of national media attention.

In August 1982, under intense lobbying against the measure by President Reagan, the nuclear weapons freeze bill was defeated by only two votes in the U.S. House. A substitute White House proposal that simply supported arms-control negotiations then underway in Geneva was approved.

"We are disappointed," Kehler was quoted as saying in an AP report released August 6th. But he said the close margin "demonstrates the great progress which the freeze campaign has made. The real vote will come this fall." A referendum on the freeze was to be on the ballots of seven states and several cities.

Kehler's refusal to cooperate with war also involved refusing to pay federal income taxes beginning in 1977. He and his wife Betsy Comer paid state and local taxes and donated their federal taxes to charity. In 1989 the IRS began foreclosure proceedings on their home and in 1990 they were arrested for trespassing on federal property. These proceedings regarding the home are the subject of an award-winning documentary film titled "An Act of Conscience".

---

[188] A hundred years earlier, in March 1870, an event occurred in Laramie City, Wyoming Territory that caught the attention of the world. The first women in America served on a jury, in this case a grand jury. The first called was Eliza Stewart, a Laramie teacher. A few weeks later, five other Laramie women served on a trial or petit jury. The Belmont Chronicle in Saint Clairsville, Ohio, published a dispatch about the women jurors on March 10th which included the entire speech given by Wyoming Chief Justice John Howe when he empaneled the jurors, apparently because the all-male juries had been acquitting well-known guilty criminals. Howes said: "I have long seen that women was [sic] a victim to the vices, crimes and immorality of man, with no power to protect and defend herself from these evils." The article said none of the women asked to be excused. Many newspapers condemned the practice of having women on juries. The Philadelphia Press, for example, asked: "Can the sex, ordinarily so quick to pronounce pre-judgments, divest itself of them sufficiently to enter the jury-box with unbiased minds?" The New Orleans Times predicted: "We think the Wyoming experiment will lead to beneficial results by proving that lady jurors are altogether impracticable--that they cannot sit as the peers of men without setting at defiance all the laws of delicacy and propriety – the conclusion may be reached that it will be far better to let nature alone in regulating the relations of the sexes." The Harrisburg (Pa.) Telegraph declared: "its expediency can only be tested by experiment. Let it be tried moderately--and Wyoming is a good place to so try it. If it prove to be a folly and a nuisance, it will not be so likely to be epidemic." The legal establishment in Wyoming apparently found the Laramie experiment to be a folly. With one exception in Bonanza (northeast of Worland, now a ghost town) in 1891, women did not serve on juries in this state again until 1950. Hein, Rebecca, "Those Damn Women: Louise Graf and Women on Wyoming Juries", wyohistory.org.

[189] Casper Star 2/11/1970.

1970: Robert Minick and the Moral Objection to War

In December of 1970, Tosh Suyematsu was back in Judge Kerr's courtroom to prosecute another draft case. Robert Minick of Casper and then Riverton had been indicted for failing to report for induction after his application for conscientious objector status had been denied by the Casper draft board.

Minick graduated from Natrona County High School in 1964 where he was an All-State lineman for the Mustangs. He went to college at Colgate in New York and at some point applied for CO status. At that time, practically the only such applications which received a thorough review were from practitioners of religions like the Quakers or Jehovah's Witnesses who had a long history of refusal to serve in war.

Between 1948 and 1965 only 35,000 men sought conscientious objector status, but the Vietnam War brought 170,000 applications during the next five years.

Minick's application was based on moral, not religious, grounds and therefore was denied by the Casper draft board, headed by local attorney Richard Bostwick who had served in WWII in Europe.

After his indictment for refusal to report for induction, the U.S. Supreme Court on June 15, 1970, issued its *Welsh* decision, ruling that a draft board could not deny an application for CO status solely because it was not based on religious beliefs. Minick then applied for reconsideration, but the draft board ignored it. As a result, draft board officials testifying at the trial had to admit that they had failed to follow their own regulations regarding a petition for reconsideration.

According to an article in the Wyoming State Tribune of December 16, 1970, Judge Kerr instructed the jury on the law of the *Welsh* decision, telling them that persons whose consciences, spurred by deeply held moral, ethical or religious beliefs, would give them no rest or peace if they allowed themselves to become an instrument of war," were entitled to the same consideration as those whose religious training and belief prohibited them from going to war. "You should consider this language in determining whether or not the defendant ... is a conscientious objector...," the court's instruction said. After deliberating for more than six hours, the jury returned a not guilty verdict.

Minick stated in an AP article dated December 17th that he had decided to risk going to jail because it would show that some people "really oppose the war and are willing to do something about it."

The jury's verdict did not bank the induction fires of the Casper draft board.

A UPI article datelined Boston on May 3, 1971, reported that Minick's CO application had been denied again and he had been ordered to report for induction. Minick explained the dilemma he was in this way: "If I don't report for induction, the law has made this a crime. If I do report, I would be saying everything I wrote in my conscientious objector form was false, which is also a crime." He argued that the prohibition against double jeopardy should apply. "It seems that if this procedure is approved, I could be going to court forever. The U.S. Attorney could keep prosecuting me until he can convince some jury, some time."

The article said Minick's father intended to appeal to the state's congressional delegation.

In October, the U.S. Attorney's office in Cheyenne announced it would not attempt to prosecute Minick again. Minick at that time was working for a drug counseling program operated by the district attorney's office in Boston. He obtained a Ph.D. in applied psychology from St. Louis University and worked for 10 years as an industrial and organizational psychologist, primarily for the U.S. Government Accountability Office.

In 2013 he was a Senior Jury Consultant for TrialGraphix in Washington D.C. He had served as the lead consultant on more than 600 cases.

Prosecutor Toshiro Suyematsu from Casper, Wyo.

According to an on-line video memoir produced by one of his nephews, Toshiro was born in 1918 in Oakland, Calif. The records of the Southern Pacific available through ancestry.com show that from October of 1918 through January 1919 a Tsuchi Suyematsu, probably Tosh's father, was a laborer for that railroad in California.

In the video, "Tosh" says that his father was a shoemaker with a shop in the YMCA on First Street in Oakland. He says his father became very interested in Wyoming by reading about the "Cowboys and Indians," and made arrangements to move to Wyoming to work on the railroad. Indeed, the 1920 census-taker's handwritten sheet for a portion of Casper, Wyo. shows Toshiro age 15 months living with his father Tsuchio and mother Masa, who were both born in Japan. It shows that his father was a laborer for "steam railroad."

The 1930 census shows that the Suyematsu family had grown substantially and was residing at 235 East H Street in Casper. The sheet shows Tsuchio, age 42, (he gave his nickname "Ben" to the census-taker), mother Masa, age 31, and the children Toshiro, Kinji, Suvoy, Kiyo, Horo age 20 months and Jiyo, a newborn (those names are ancestry.com's interpretation of the handwriting). The father is shown as a "cobbler" engaged in the "shoe repair" industry. All the children except the newborn are shown as having been born in California. (Daughter Kiyo is shown in the 1943 Casper High School yearbook – available on-line).

During that time, the Suyematsu family became acquainted with George W. and Helen M. Bentley and their children. The 1920 City Directory shows that George was a driver for Casper Laundry Co. and the family lived at 152 N. Jackson. The 1928 Directory shows George working for Troy Laundry and residing at 302 East H, only a few doors down from the Suyematsu family.

The 1930 census shows George and Helen with their three children Vernon, 15, Delwin 11 and William C. age 5. Mr. Bentley was still working for Troy Laundry in 1945, now as a route supervisor. Vernon G. of the U.S. Navy and brother Delwin D. of the U.S. Army are shown with their official residence at 629 E. 12th St., their parents' address.

Tosh graduated from high school in Casper in 1936, and the 1937 City Directory shows him as a helper at Wenner's Bakery, residing on East H with his parents. Later that year, the Laramie City Directory shows Tosh as a student at the University of Wyoming living at 907 S. 9th. Tosh already knew Vernon Bentley, who was in law school when Tosh arrived. He certainly soon made the acquaintance of another law student, Philip White of Cheyenne, who became a life-long friend. Both Bentley and White went on to become state district court judges.

According to the video, Tosh ran out of money for college and joined the Army in Casper on February 24, 1941, hoping to earn enough in a year to allow him to complete his college degree. His brother King Suyematsu, three years younger, joined the same day. By the end of November that year, both of them had been promoted a couple of times. However, on November 30th, Tosh recalled, the first sergeant came to him, said "gee I'm sorry about this" and handed him a regimental order demoting him from tech sergeant back to "buck private." His brother was also demoted. An officer went with them to the commander of the regiment to inquire as to the reason for the demotion. They were only told that "it was in the best interest of the regiment."

A week later, when Tosh was on the rifle range, a soldier came rushing up on a horse and said Pearl Harbor had been bombed. Tosh, his brother and another soldier of Japanese descent from Kemmerer were then transferred to Fort Benjamin Harrison in Indiana and placed in a service company. Early in 1943 the two Suyematsus joined up with the soon-to-be-famous 442nd Regimental Combat Team and were sent to Camp Shelby in Mississippi for training.

In early 1944 the group was sent overseas, landing at Anzio, Italy, shortly after the American 4th Army had suffered heavy casualties in taking the town . Both Suyematsu brothers were wounded as the war progressed. When he was discharged in 1946, First Sgt. Tosh had been awarded a Silver Star, Bronze Star and Purple Heart with Oak Leaf Cluster and several other medals.

And Tosh had also added a bride to his resume, an Italian woman named Marina Fracheschi of Bologna. They were married Sept. 29, 1946, and Tosh remained as a civil employee of the war department until August 1947 when he was called home because of illness in his family.

Marina did not accompany Tosh when he returned to the U.S., but he drove to the East Coast in December, 1947, in a winterized Jeep to bring her to Wyoming. On the way, according to an article with a photo in the Syracuse Post-Standard on December 7, 1947, the couple stopped in Syracuse to visit Rev. Calvin Thompson Jr., who had met the Suyematsu family when he was pastor of the First Baptist Church in Casper in the 1920s. Tosh also took his wife to Niagara Falls.

He returned to the University of Wyoming to complete his degree. Marina became a U.S. citizen in August of 1950 and on October 6th of that year Marina was employed at New Method Laundry. She was looking forward to a planned trip home to Italy.

Tragedy struck the young couple at 7 a.m. that morning as Tosh was driving her to work. A 21-year-old UW student ran the stop sign at 6th and Grand and collided with the Jeep, knocking it onto its side. She suffered a skull fracture and died two days later. Tosh and the other driver were not injured.

Tosh carried through with his college career, earning a B.A. in 1949 and a law degree in 1950. The 1953 City Directory for Laramie shows him as an attorney with Bentley & Suyematsu at 703 University Ave.

At about this time he met Mary Ellen Crowley, an attorney in Cheyenne, and they were married. The 1930 census shows Frank J. (born in Wyoming in about 1883) and Miriam G. Crowley and their daughters Mary Ellen age 13 and Miriam age 12 living at 700 E. 22nd in Cheyenne. He was Chief Clerk for Railway Package Express Co. Ellen graduated with a B.A. from U.W. in 1938 and was admitted to the Wyoming State Bar in 1953.

Several sources have stated that some of Ellen's family and friends were very much opposed to her marriage to a man of Japanese descent, even if he was a U.S. war hero.

On July 28, 1954, Ellen Crowley was among nine persons injured in front of the State Capitol during the Cheyenne Frontier Days parade. Jack Crews, 14, was holding the reins of a horse drawing a sled in the parade when the horse bolted. It ran about a half a block down the street, dumped Mrs. Suyematsu out of the sled when the sled hit the concrete gutter and continued into the crowd. Jack Crews' older brother Jim, who had won the wild horse race in the rodeo the previous day, ran from the crowd and brought the runaway horse under control. Ellen was treated and released, but three others were hospitalized with cuts, abrasions and shock.

The Cheyenne Directory for 1955 shows Tosh as a lawyer with state Democratic leader Walter B. Phelan. The 1957 Directory shows him as a Justice of the Peace. The City Directory for Casper in 1957 shows Ben T. Suyematsu and wife Masa at 810 W. 19th. Ben was running the North Casper Shoe Repair Shop. Kiyo was a secretary at Ohio Oil, living at home, Laro was a beverage distributor living on South Poplar and Sara was a teacher at Casper College living at 235 E. H Street, the address for the family in the 1930 census.

An article published in the Greeley Tribune on October 20, 1956, told of a 73-year-old Pine Bluffs, Wyo., physician being arraigned before Justice Suyematsu. The doctor, who had practiced in Pine Bluffs for more than 31 years, was charged with performing an abortion. The charges arose from the arrest two days earlier of a 22-year-old man and his 18-year-old wife, along with another man from Warren Air Force Base. During questioning on suspicion of robbery, those three alleged that the doctor had performed an abortion on the wife and that they had obtained $565 from him in blackmail by threatening to expose him.

In 1958 Suyematsu sentenced the Atlas Missile protesters (See Missiles Chapter at pg. 31).

On the front page of the Laramie Boomerang of Sept. 26, 1963, was a lengthy article about President Kennedy making a speech at the University of Wyoming. On page 6 was an article written by Danny Nelson, a student at Laramie High who later taught American history at Laramie Junior High for 35 years and served as executive director of the Laramie Plains Museum for 17 years. His column was about the homecoming queens and about Mrs. Williams, the commerce teacher, winning second place in the state horseshoes contest. The last paragraph of the column concerned Tosh Suyematsu's brother and nephew. It said, "We were all sad to hear that one of our teacher's sons, Mr. Taro Suyematsu's Ronnie, had been hit by a truck Monday night. He has a basal-fractured skull, and we all hope that he's feeling much better." (Ronnie did recover).

Tosh was appointed assistant U.S. Attorney in Cheyenne in 1969 and then was appointed U.S. Attorney in 1977 and 1981.

In 1973, Suyematsu became involved in prosecutions involving the February seizure of Wounded Knee, S.D. by 200 Oglala Lakota associated with the American Indian Movement. On May 30, 1973, news reports quoting Tosh Suyematsu appeared in newspapers across the country. Suyematsu announced that the federal government was dropping charges against eight of the nine persons arrested near Cheyenne a month earlier who were allegedly headed for Wounded Knee. The nine had been charged with violating federal anti-riot laws by crossing state lines after they left Fort Collins, Colo., and crossed into Wyoming. The nine allegedly were headed to Wounded Knee to "aid and abet" Indians who held the hamlet for 70 days.

On February 2, 1974, Suyematsu announced that conspiracy charges against AIM leader Vernon Bellecourt and two others had been dismissed at the request of the Justice Department. He termed the dismissal "prosecutorial grace" based on the fact that no violence was involved.

Suyematsu was the federal government's attorney in a 1977 suit involving 6,500 acres of land along a 22-mile stretch of the Snake River north of Jackson. Sen. Clifford P. Hansen (R-Wyo) and Laurence S. Rockefeller were among the 128 landowners along the Snake who were sued by the U.S., seeking a declaration that the land was part of the national park and national forest lands. Suyematsu explained that the government claimed the land along the river because the course of the river had changed and because of inaccurate surveys going back to the previous century.

Tosh's colorful life and career came to a tragic end when he died in an auto accident in 1994 on a dirt road east of Cheyenne not far from his home near Burns.

1967: THE BLACK 14'S JAMES L. ISAAC OF HANNA

James Lonnie Isaac was a special member of the Black 14 for two reasons: 1) he was the only one of the 14 from Wyoming; and 2) his life was cut short only seven years after his football dreams at the University of Wyoming had been shattered by the coach.

James Isaac, Sept. 25, 1969

James was the son of Clinton and Louise "Lovie" Watkins Isaac. His father was born in Ansley, Louisiana in 1923. The 1910 U.S. Census records show Lovie's parents, Eugene and Margaret Watkins, living with sons Tait age 2 and Turner, age 1, in Bienville, Louisiana, where Eugene was a farmer. The 1940 census again shows Eugene, now 64, and Margaret, 54, still in Bienville living with their daughter Reathy, her son Fred and daughter Louise (age 15) in the household.

In 1943 Clinton married Lovie in Ansley. In 1946, after Lovie's mother died, they were invited to move to Wyoming by Lovie's sister Reathy and her husband, Oscar Humphrey, in hopes Clinton could join Oscar as a laborer for the Union Pacific Railroad.

At first the Isaacs, including their one-year-old daughter Jeanie, lived with the Humphreys at their section house located at the Dana section, ten miles west of Hanna. After Clinton was hired as a section hand, the family moved to a small section house at Como, about ten miles east of Hanna.

"The houses were right along the tracks and had no running water or electricity in those days," Clinton Jr. recalled in an interview in 2013. "We carried water from a well and used kerosene lanterns". Sometimes the children would walk into Hanna for school.

Soon their family had expanded to six children. Twins Clinton Jr. and Bessell were born in 1948, James L. came along in 1950, followed by Ada Mae in 1951 and Charles in 1952. All would eventually graduate from Hanna-Elk Mountain High School.

Sometime in the late 50s, the Isaac family moved into a house in Hanna.

Clinton Jr. participated in high school sports before James, and Charles did likewise after James. But Clinton says James was the best athlete of the three. Clinton says he didn't experience much racism growing up in Hanna, Wyoming. "Sure we got called names occasionally, but we didn't pay attention to it because it wasn't enough to be alarmed. We didn't see much racism from the older folks."

The name-calling, Clinton recalls, was worst in Pinedale, Saratoga and Lyman, and one time "we were refused service in a Rock Springs restaurant. But Coach [Ed] McAtee stood up for us and said, 'if they can't eat here, nobody will eat here.'"

In a Casper Star article by Ryan Thorburn published Nov. 7, 2009, McAtee recollected about the Isaacs:

"I remember one game we were playing Mountain View and a big running back kept going through our line and running over our players. That player said to James, 'We're going to get you black boy,'" legendary Hanna basketball and assistant football coach Ed McAtee said. "The other boys on our team stood up for him. There was no prejudice in Hanna. We all liked the Isaacs. They were just the nicest kids in the world."

All during the 1966-67 school year, James L. Isaac, a junior at the Hanna, Wyo., high school, was making headlines in the sports section of the Rawlins Daily Times newspaper. He ran the opposition ragged in football and continued his exploits on the basketball court.

On January 9, 1967, he scored 19 points for his Hanna-Elk Mountain basketball team. On January 23rd, Isaac scored 20, and in a game the next weekend he posted 21 points. On February 21st he scored 27.

One of Isaac's teammates during Isaac's junior year was senior Tom Patterson, who went on to become sports editor of the Denver Post. Sixteen years after playing with James L. in Hanna, Patterson contributed a memoir about his black teammate to a major feature by Post sports writer Rick Reilly about the action of UW's Coach Eaton in 1969.[190]

In the fall of 1967, James L. Isaac was a senior and was phenomenal on the football field. In the first game of the season, the Rawlins Daily Times reported, "Hanna Miner back Jim Isaac put on a one-man show" in a 39-0 win over Goshen Hole. He had 150 yards rushing and four touchdowns.

On September 18th that fall, the Trustees of the University of Wyoming announced that Dr. William D. Carlson had been selected as UW President. Two years later, Carlson proved to be completely ineffective in defusing the situation after football coach Eaton booted James L. and his 13 black teammates off the football team.

On September 21st, Hanna's Isaac racked up more than 200 yards rushing and three touchdowns from his halfback position. On October 12th he ran an interception back 60 yards for a touchdown, ran in another TD from scrimmage and kicked two points after touchdown. Later that month he turned in 19 tackles from his linebacker position in one game, and then he had three touchdowns and 27 tackles in another. An article on October 27th identified Isaac as the "top small school track man last year."

Guided by first-year coach Dick Stein, the Miners won eight of nine games.

James L. Isaac's exploits continued into his senior basketball season. On Dec. 8th he scored 32 points in a win over Pine Bluffs and three days later scored 31 in another game.

On January 5, 1968, Hanna suffered its first loss of the basketball season at Mountain View near Evanston. The Daily Times reported: "But it was hard-driving Jim Isaac who copped scoring honors for the night with 26 points. The 5-10 Miner also got his share of rebounds despite the height advantage of his opponents."[191]

On February 2, 1968, Isaac scored 33 points in a game against the league-leading Glenrock Herders.

Later that year, James L. would receive a scholarship to play football for UW. The Isaac family was very proud of their son and brother.

---

[190] Rick Reilly went on to become a sports reporting celebrity for Sports Illustrated and ESPN.

[191] Leading scorer for Mountain View was 6-2 forward Mark Hopkinson, who went to Arizona on a football scholarship. The Sept. 19, 1969, edition of the Tucson Citizen showed the rosters for both teams in a preview of AU's game at Laramie. Hopkinson was on AU's roster and Isaac on Wyoming's. Hopkinson did not win a football letter, apparently because he got crosswise with the law. He served time in federal prison for a 1971 drug conviction. He returned to his Bridger Valley home in the mid-70s and soon was terrorizing anyone who stood in his way as he attempted to develop a trailer park. He was eventually convicted of ordering the dynamite murders of Evanston attorney Vincent Vehar, his wife and son, and hiring the murder of a witness against him. He was executed by lethal injection at the Wyoming State Prison at Rawlins on January 21, 1992. His was the first execution in Wyoming in 26 years, and no one has been executed subsequently.

SECOND GRADE – Back row: Debbie Korkow, Larry Sanchez, James Isaac, Mary Ruth Poulos, and Paula Braun. Second row: Connie Shipman, Orrill Dean Briggs, Kenneth Mills, Clinton Withrow, and Randy Scott, Ronald Leathers, Philip Cook. Front row: Donna Burns, Kathy Tabor, Rosie Vigil, and Mary Aragon. (Here we are in a figure "2".)

James Isaac in his Hanna Elementary 2nd grade classroom in 1958.

He played on the undefeated UW freshman football team in the fall of 1968 along with fellow African Americans Jerome Berry, Lionel Grimes, 17-year-old Henry Powell of Conneaut Lake, PA (Isaac's roommate), and Wendell Jackson of Cheyenne.

Powell and Jackson both abandoned their UW football careers before the 1969 season started. In an interview 40 years later Powell said he returned to Laramie for the 1969 season but left before the first game:

> Trouble started brewing. Eaton wanted everybody to be clean shaven. Some of the black players got together and said we are not going to do that. I went ahead and shaved. But this was only part of the problem. Those were stressful times and Laramie was a rough place to be in 1968-69 out west for a young black person. Very few minority females.

Hanna coach McAtee told Thorburn for the 2009 article: "Everyone in the state knew about James from the regional and state track meets. If the Black 14 hadn't happened, he would have had an outstanding career at Wyoming and possibly played professionally. He was that good. He loved to hit, and he had speed."

The other Isaac siblings

After graduating from high school, each of James Isaac's siblings left Hanna and made their way in the larger world. Jeanie attended the University of Wyoming in the 1963-64 school year. She is pictured in the '64 WYO yearbook. She then moved to Denver and went to Central Business College. After their high school graduation, Clinton and Bessell moved to Denver to live with their sister.

164

Clinton Jr. graduated from the Parks Business College in Denver and was hired at an engineering company in 1968 where he worked for 42 years until he was laid off without warning in January of 2010 in the wake of the Wall Street debacle at the end of the George W. Bush administration.

Charles also went to Parks College and worked in Denver. Jeanie wound up in California, Ada in Denver and Bessell in Casper.

Hanna 1963 yearbook

Jeanie was one of only two African Americans pictured among the freshmen in the 1964 UW WYO Yearbook

1969-70: Tragedies strike the Isaac family

Following the Black 14's dismissal, his former coach Ed McAtee at Hanna helped James Isaac enroll at Dakota Weslyan University in Mitchell, S.D., where he played football and competed in the long jump, triple jump and sprints for the track team, helping the 440-yard relay team set a school record. He missed most of the 1970 football season with a broken leg.

After graduating from Dakota Weslyan, James held a teaching job in Arizona where he met and married his wife. At some point they separated, James returned to Hanna and was working in the mines. According to his brother Clinton, James' wife persuaded him to rejoin her, now living in San Bernardino, Calif. Early on Christmas day, 1976, James' wife shot and killed him with a .32 caliber revolver. She was originally charged with murder, but accepted a plea bargain reducing the charge to manslaughter. She was sentenced to six months in jail with three years supervised probation to follow.

Only 11 months after the death of their son and brother, the Isaac family was shaken to its core by another tragedy. Over Thanksgiving in 1977, Clinton Sr. and Lovie were in Rock Springs visiting with their daughter Ada Mae and her husband, then 32 years old. On Friday night, an argument erupted and Ada's husband shot and killed Clinton Sr. Only 54 years old, Mr. Isaac died at the scene from a single .32 caliber wound to his chest. His son-in-law was arrested that night and served time in prison.

Clinton Sr. and Lovie at that time had 10 grandchildren. He also was survived by three brothers and six sisters.

That Thanksgiving weekend, Ed McAtee's Miners swept past Midwest, Wind River and Shoshoni to win the Class B Guernsey Tournament, but his thoughts must have been with the Isaac family.

In 1986, Bessell's son and James L.'s nephew, Robbie Jackson, scored 62 of Casper Kelly Walsh High's 70 points in an opening-round state tournament victory over Green River at the Events Center in Casper.[192]

Robbie's daughter Britney Jackson, lettered in basketball, volleyball and track at Natrona County High School. From 2007-11, she starred as a multi-event competitor for the University of Wyoming track team. In her junior year she posted team highs in the high jump (5-feet, 7 inches), triple jump (36-5) and heptathlon (3,388 points, the highest mark in UW women's history at the time).

In May, 2019, two siblings of James Isaac visited the Black 14 mural created by Adrienne Vetter in downtown Laramie. Posing below their brother's image, Clinton and Jeanie Isaac were joined by Clinton's daughter Jocelyn and her husband Sean Rice of Denver area.

1944-1965: Marquette Frye: From Hanna to the Watts Riots

Two other young black men who grew up in Hanna had preceded James Isaac in becoming involved in a racial episode -- a big one -- in the Sixties.

In 1944, C. L. and Rena Price moved with their four children from Oklahoma to Hanna. Marquette, the youngest, was one year old. At Hanna, the Prices divorced and Rena began a relationship with Wallace Frye, an African American who also had four children from a previous

---

[192] According to Randy Tucker of the Riverton Ranger, that stood as the most points by a Wyoming high school basketball player until 2012 when John Sounding Sides of Wyoming Indian High School hit 17 three-pointers on the way to a 65-point total in a regular season win over Shoshoni. Eight years earlier, his sister Diana hit 14 of 16 three-point shots and scored 55 points for the Lady Chiefs in a win over Big Piney.

marriage. The 1951 Hanna Miner yearbook[193] shows Marquette Price in first grade and Ronnie Frye in second. When the economic situation in Hanna deteriorated in 1957, Marquette, age 13, moved to Los Angeles with his step-brother Ronnie and the rest of the family.

Eight years later, on Aug. 11, 1965, Marquette (now using the last name Frye) and Ronnie were driving along South Avalon Blvd. when a motorcycle police officer pulled Marquette over for reckless driving. As police were giving field sobriety tests, Ronnie ran to their house nearby and brought Rena to the scene. More police arrived, tensions rose, Marquette resisted arrest and punches were thrown as a crowd gathered. Rena and Marquette were both arrested and jailed overnight. They didn't know until the next day that the incident had sparked the disturbance known as the Watts Riots. During the next week 34 people were killed and more than 1,000 were injured, with tens of millions of property damage.[194] A state commission found the riots were caused by unemployment, inadequate schools and resentment of the police.

In an interview for the book *Burn, Baby, Burn*, Marquette said he had difficulty adjusting after moving from Wyoming:

---

[193] Courtesy of Daniel Sanchez of Laramie who lived for a few years in Hanna as a child and knew some of the Frye and Price children.

[194] "Rena Price is Dead at 97", New York Times, June 29, 2013.

People there were much better. The school curriculum was better. The kids' vocabularies were better. When I came to California the kids here resented my speech, they resented my intelligence. In Wyoming, a human being is a human being. There were only about eight Negroes in the school where we went and we were accepted by the whites. When we came to California, we got into an all-Negro school. It was all new to us. I'd never been to an all-Negro school before.

He dropped out of high school as a senior and had minor run-ins with the law prior to the fateful traffic stop. In a 1985 interview with UPI he said the incident ruined his life. He grew tired of being referred to as "the man who started the Watts riots"[195] and used the last name Price at times. He warned children of the dangers of drinking, drugs and gangs.[196] He died of pneumonia in 1986 in Los Angeles at the age of 42.

His mother Rena died in June 2013 at the age of 97. According to a Los Angeles Times obituary on June 22, 2013, she "enjoyed visiting friends and family in Oklahoma and Wyoming".

Shortly after the Watts situation calmed down, a UW law student wrote a remarkable letter to the editor of the Casper Star. John W. Davis pointed out that the unemployment rate among blacks in Casper was three times the overall rate. He said no blacks were employed by either the fire or police departments or any other city agency except the sanitation department. He said that Fred Devereaux, president of the Casper NAACP, had recently attempted to rent three homes on the south side of the tracks, the white area of town. "In each case he was told that 'we don't rent to Negroes'", Davis wrote. Although Casper had not experienced any racial strife, Davis argued, "it is necessary that responsible city officials acknowledge the situation and attempt to take some sort of preventive measures now."[197]

1967: THE WORLD OUTSIDE OF HANNA

The bloody war in Vietnam was on the front page of Wyoming's newspapers nearly every day in 1967. On July 22nd, 27-year-old Capt. William Boyd Graves of Douglas and his co-pilot died when their OV-1C Mohawk crashed in the jungle while flying a reconnaissance mission in Vietnam. During his two months in Vietnam, Capt. Graves taped reports of his activities which he sent home to his wife and three young children, and they sent tapes back to him. On his last tape he said: "We were kind of on alert last night. We were expecting some trouble so we had to double all the guards and have the airplanes ready to move out and all that kind of junk. So, I was up rather late."[198]

Because the UW Cowboys went undefeated in the fall of 1967 and were ranked in the top 10, the name of Coach Lloyd Eaton appeared frequently on the same Daily Times sports pages with James Isaac. On Sept. 20th, next to an article about the Hanna Miners preparing to play

---

[195] New York Times, 12/25/1986.

[196] blackpast.org/aaw/frye-marquette.

[197] Casper Star, 9/5/1965. Many years later, Davis authored several books about Wyoming history such as *Wyoming Range War* about the big cattlemen and their hired guns escaping legal consequences for murdering a homesteader near Kaycee in 1892. Davis has authored an article about the "Johnson County Invasion" at wyohistory.org.

[198] Excerpts from these tapes are available at the Wyoming State Archives or wyohistory.org.

Glendo, was a UPI article saying that UW's Vic Washington, an African American from New Jersey, was selected as the Western Athletic Conference's "Back of the Week". The article said Washington had returned a punt 48 yards for a touchdown and on defense had four unassisted tackles, three pass saves and a fumble recovery in the season-opening 36-17 win over Arizona. In 1966, the article added, Washington had led the nation in punt returns and had capped UW's WAC title win over BYU with a 95-yard kickoff return. On the same page was an article reminding readers that UW Coach Lloyd Eaton was to be the featured speaker at that night's Rawlins Quarterback Club meeting.

Also on the news pages of the Daily Times that fall were articles about a jury trial in Meridian, Miss., of several Ku Klux Klan members charged with killing some white civil rights workers a couple years earlier.

On October 20, 1967, the Daily Times carried an article about a different "James L." A congressman from Tennessee was calling for the resignation of Dr. James L. Goddard, Commissioner of the Federal Food and Drug Administration, who two days earlier had lectured at the University of Minnesota.   In an interview afterwards Goddard said that if possession of marijuana were not a federal offense, he would not object more if his 18-year-old daughter smoked marijuana than if she drank a cocktail. He said of marijuana, "I don't think it is any more dangerous than alcohol." Dr. Goddard was then featured in an article in Time a week later. It would be a long while before politicians could tolerate this sort of deviance from the politically-productive war on drugs, including marijuana. Not surprisingly, Dr. Goddard left the FDA a few months later.

Also on October 20th, the Daily Times carried an article quoting novelist John Steinbeck's son as saying that 85% of American troops in Vietnam used marijuana. The University of Wyoming Branding Iron in early November mentioned the comments of Dr. Goddard. In an article on legalization, Dr. Martin Wollmann, director of the UW Student Health Service, cautioned that while marijuana may not be physically addictive, the psychological effects were of concern. "Because of the distortion in perception and mood, if a user has a shaky personality to begin with, it can cause a personality distortion. They will do things they never would do otherwise," Wollman said.

BI reporter Bonnie Warner concluded her article by saying: "Most UW students are not concerned with marijuana and feel no need for its legalization". Five months later, Goddard's position was cited by Branding Iron editors Larry Armstrong and Jeff Haag in an editorial urging the legalization of marijuana. "Nothing alienates the youth of this nation more than outdated, useless laws that, when enforced, seem to be an attempt to harass individuals who do not conform to the norm," they declared. Laws classifying marijuana as a hard narcotic were idiotic, they said, noting that even Time Magazine had recognized that the arrest of "increasing thousands of young Americans each year" was having no deterrent effect. Armstrong and Haag asked: "A lessening of the laws against marijuana is inevitable. The only question is how long it will take the lawmakers to see the light."[199]

In November, the Rawlins newspaper carried articles about African Americans winning mayoral races in two major cities, about U.S. forces suffering "severe losses" in a battle for Hill 875 near Dak To, and about racial demonstrations at Central State University in Ohio.

---

[199] Branding Iron, April 26, 1968. Nearly 50 years later the same question is still being asked in Wyoming as possessors of marijuana are being sent to prison, years after legalization in neighboring Colorado did not result in a complete collapse of civilization there. Famous anthropologist Margaret Mead told a U.S. Senate committee on October 27, 1969, that the law's punitive view of marijuana "is a new form of tyranny by the old over the young."

In December the paper carried an article about the first black astronaut being killed in a crash, and about anti-draft-and-Vietnam War demonstrations.

1966-67: Assembling the Black 14 cast - Hathaway becomes governor

A March 23, 1966, UPI article said Wyoming Republicans would select a new State Chairman to replace Stan Hathaway, a Torrington attorney, during a central committee meeting in Casper. The man selected was attorney C.A. Brimmer of Rawlins. A week later, Hathaway announced he would be a candidate for governor. Earlier, Sen. Milward Simpson had announced his retirement and Gov. Cliff Hansen of Jackson said he would seek election to replace Simpson.

A Nov. 25, 1967 UPI report had Chairman Brimmer of Rawlins predicting that Wyoming voters, regardless of political affiliation, would turn to the Republican party the next year "because it offers them sensible and responsible solutions without crash spending programs that result in higher taxes, taxes upon taxes, inflation ...." Brimmer pledged to devote himself to strengthening the state GOP organization from top to bottom.

As governor in October, 1969, Hathaway essentially made the final decision to ratify Coach Eaton's dismissal of the 14 black players.[200] As Wyoming attorney general four years later, Brimmer succeeded James Barrett in defending the dismissal of the Black 14 in the federal court suit brought by the players. While the case was still in litigation, Barrett was appointed to the U.S. Tenth Circuit Court of Appeals. Brimmer was later appointed as U.S. District Judge for the District of Wyoming and heard cases for nearly 38 years. And presiding over the Black 14 lawsuit was U.S. District Judge Ewing T. Kerr, himself a former state Republican chairman. He ruled against the players at every opportunity during the next three years. (See the Ewing T. Kerr chapter at pg. 262).

On November 14th, the Rawlins paper carried an article about the editor of the magazine produced by inmates at the Wyoming State Prison in Rawlins. The "Best Scene" magazine included columns with names like, "Pardon Me, Governor" and "Here Today, Here Tomorrow." The editor, who was in prison for a non-violent crime, would reappear two years later as the main reporter covering the events of October, 1969, for the Laramie Boomerang.

But Wyoming was agog that fall about the UW Cowboys, who on the last day of 1967 were in the Fountainbleu Hotel in New Orleans preparing for their battle with LSU in the Sugar Bowl the next day. The Cowboys were the only major college team to go undefeated during the regular season, setting 47 school records along the way. Their top players included African Americans Vic Washington, Hub Lindsey, Dick Speights, Tom Williams and Gene Huey. For the second year in a row, cornerbacks Washington and Speights had been selected to the all-WAC first team.

1968-69: Black Students Alliance formed at UWyo

In the fall of 1963, a basketball star from Brooklyn Technical High School named Bob Jefferson joined the basketball team at the University of Wyoming. Two years later another Brooklyn Tech grad, Ed Pollard, followed Jefferson to Laramie. Each of them earned a UW letter in their sophomore seasons but then left the basketball program. Jefferson worked as a head resident in the dorms while finishing his degree and became an architect in New York. Pollard became a college basketball referee and administrator.

---

[200] According to Hathaway in his interview in the UW documentary on the Black 14.

During Christmas break of the 1968-69 school year, Pollard and Jefferson were among a group that gathered at the home of accounting student William Johnson and his wife Alberta in Laramie and began discussions that led to the formation of the Black Students Alliance.

"I walked in the snow from the dorms to 4th and Canby for the dinner," Pollard recalled in a 2016 interview. The other black students who participated were Ike Aycock, Willie Black and Dwight James.[201] "Recognizing that UW had no program for the black students, they had no black magazines like Jet or Ebony in the library, we decided we needed to get some kind of organization together," Pollard said. "We decided to call it an 'alliance' rather than a 'union'. Alberta said she would find out how to apply for recognition as an official student organization. The primary purpose was to be education of all students."

This was reflected in an article in the April 25, 1969 Branding Iron, reporting that the Student Senate had voted 16-4 to appropriate $2,030 of student monies to the newly-approved BSA for seminars, speakers, black publications and cultural programs. The vote was the culmination of a three-hour committee of the whole discussion during which the BSA's Chancellor, Willie S. Black, told the students and senators, "this will be the education of the whole history of black people in this country. This area has been largely ignored and distorted."

Black said the Senate "stands at an important point in the history of this University and you have the opportunity to prevent the type of unrest into which many universities have been plunged."

Little did anyone know that before the BSA could even launch its educational programs in the fall, the football coach would bring the national spotlight on civil rights issues to Laramie and the UW campus.

1969-70: ATTEMPTING TO LOWER THE VOTING AGE

"Old enough to kill [and be killed], but not for votin'"[202]

Even as late as 1968, only four states had a voting age lower than 21. Georgia and Kentucky allowed citizens to vote at 18, Alaska at 19 and Hawaii at 20. At the same time, thousands of young men who were not old enough to vote in most states were being drafted and sent to an unpopular war in Vietnam. Hundreds of them were being killed or wounded every week.

By early 1969, this inequity was spawning legislative efforts in 40 states to lower the voting age. In March, 1969, for example, student body presidents from seven Utah high schools wrote to the Utah Senate in favor of a 19-year-old vote measure, pointing out that 12 million young people paid large amounts in taxes but had no voice in how the money was expended. The students also pointed out that "the average age of those who fight and die in war is under 21. These men and women rightfully deserve a voice that determines whether there be war." Because of improvements in education and communications, the students argued, their generation was better informed than young people were when the age was set at 21 many years earlier.

---

[201] Dwight was one of the all-African American starting lineup for Cheyenne Central's basketball team at times in 1965-66. The others were Barry West, Percy Johnson, Jerry Gadlin and Ronn Jeffrey. Dwight earned a law degree and then a medical degree and practiced in California. Ronn Jeffrey was a founder and director of a troubled-youth counseling program in Cheyenne and also served as a lay judge in a drug court for juveniles. In the Powell Tribune of 10/17/1969 (same day as the Black 14 dismissal), Gadlin was pictured as a returning letterman for the Northwest Community College Trappers.

[202] "Eve of Destruction" 1964 by P. F. Sloan, recorded by Barry McGuire in 1965.

Even in Wyoming, a bill to place before the voters a constitutional amendment which would lower the voting age to 19 was under consideration in the Legislature. Because of Sen. J.W. Myers of Evanston, the Wyoming Legislature's discussion of that issue would soon provide a laugh for newspaper readers all over America.

The implications of these measures were presented in an Associated Press article in April, 1969. It was estimated there were about 11 million Americans between the ages of 18 and 21, equivalent to more than 15% of the total number of people who voted in the 1968 presidential election. Lowering the voting age to 18 would make nearly a million young people in California and about 800,000 in New York into eligible voters.

Minnesota's governor said he would sign a bill to lower the voting age if a bill came to his desk. "It is time to quit preaching at the young to become interested while blocking them from becoming involved," he said. "Let us let them in."

But legislators in many states objected to lowering the voting age while thousands of those potential voters were actively demonstrating against the Vietnam War. Thus, the opponents of the war were faced with another "Catch-22." They could not vote on their representatives in Congress and, if they wanted to gain the vote, they had to be careful not to upset legislators with their methods of expressing their opposition to the draft and the war. Many politicians were oblivious to the hypocrisy of calling on young people to stop demonstrating and "work through the system" when they couldn't even vote.

Some lawmakers took the opposite approach, suggesting that denying young people the right to vote could drive them to show their displeasure through campus demonstrations. "If we continue to deny the right of young people to vote, it's possible they'll be even more inclined to join militant minority groups," a Wisconsin senator said.

A young Democrat from San Francisco in the California Senate, George R. Moscone, had introduced a bill to lower the voting age for the third straight year. Passing the bill, Moscone said, "would be a clear admission on our part, on the part of the Establishment, that we realize times have changed." But because of student disorders at San Francisco State and UC-Berkeley, the Senate rejected the bill.

The motivation of some opponents thus showed itself to be something like, "we aren't going to give you young people the right to vote until all of you are going to vote the right way."[203]

1969: Wyoming stuck in Myers' embarrassing mire

Wyoming made the national news that spring while the legislature was considering a bill to allow the voters to decide on a constitutional amendment that would lower the voting age to 19. Sen. J.W. Myers proposed an amendment which quickly made Wyoming a laughing stock. Myers apparently didn't care so much whether Wyoming's young men favored or opposed the war, so long as they looked like they supported it. Instead of "America: Love It or Leave It," a frequent admonition from war hawks at the time, Myers' bumper sticker might have read, "Look Like You Love It ... or Leave It."

---

[203] In 1975, Moscone won election as mayor of San Francisco, defeating future U.S. Senator Dianne Feinstein in the primary. He survived a recall election in 1977, but on November 27, 1978, former city supervisor (councilman) Dan White walked into City Hall and shot Moscone dead, along with liberal supervisor Harvey Milk. Feinstein, as president of the Board of Supervisors, was in the building at the time, heard shots and discovered Milk's body. She announced the assassinations to the public and, because of her position as president, succeeded Moscone as mayor.

Myers' amendment would have required 19 and 20-year-old men, before they could vote, to meet the "same standards of personal grooming and hair styles ... as are acceptable in the military services." According to the February 7th Wyoming State Tribune, the amendment first "provoked an outburst of titters in the Senate, but Myers jumped to his feet and said: 'This is a very serious amendment. If these young people are going to be given all the responsibilities of citizenship, then they should look like citizens.'"

The amendment was passed unanimously by a voice vote in the Senate on Friday, February 7th, but was removed the next day. The next week Myers was asked by the UW student newspaper, the Branding Iron, whether one could determine fitness to vote by hair length. "If 99% of the people have well-groomed hair, the other one per cent does give an indication," he replied. "There is a certain group that would never take any responsibility in any government or in the army and pretty soon you wouldn't have a country. Most parents are a little reluctant to have their children getting off in left field that way, away from the generally-accepted appearance. If you can't tell a boy from a girl except by a physical examination, why there is something wrong here," the livestock rancher said.

"It's these people who look like an English sheep dog who we're talking about here," he said. "I, and most people, don't think this type is ready for full citizenship."

Articles about Myers' amendment made the front pages of newspapers all over America, including the Moberly (Missouri) Monitor, the Mitchell (South Dakota) Republic and the Fergus Falls (Minnesota) Journal. The headline on the front page of the Mexia (Texas) News on February 9, 1969, said, "Short Hairs Can Cast Ballot At 19 in Wyoming".

The Lubbock (Texas) Avalanche-Journal ran a UPI article that same day under the headline, "Shorn Locks Required For Voters."

The AP article under the Mexia headline explained the event this way: "The Wyoming Senate amended a proposed constitutional amendment Friday, giving 19-year-olds the right to vote – if, in the case of men, they don't have long hair."

Myers' amendment and quotes were also included in the April AP article about efforts to lower the voting age around the country, and thus gave readers from the Fresno Bee to the Uniontown (Penn.) Evening Standard another round of amusement at Wyoming's expense.

1970: Wyoming Supreme Court: "Take a walk"

After the Myers proposal was removed from the bill, the Legislature did pass an act placing the proposed constitutional amendment lowering the voting age to 19 on the 1970 general election ballot. On election day, 53,997 Wyoming citizens voted "YES" on Proposed Amendment Number Two, and 48,418 voted "NO", nearly a 53-47 split. However, the total number of voters who voted in the election, including those who voted neither for or against Amendment Number Two, was 122,354.

Based upon a 1909 Wyoming Supreme Court case, the state canvassing board headed by the governor ruled that the constitutional amendment had not been approved in the election. In that early case, the court ruled that an affirmative vote by "a majority of the electors", the phrase used in the amendment section of the constitution, Art. 20 §1, required that "yes" votes be cast on the amendment by a majority of those who cast ballots in the election, whether or not they voted on the proposed amendment. The practical -- but absurd -- effect of this ruling in many Wyoming elections during the past century has been that the ultimate deciders of proposed constitutional amendments have been those who did not bother to actually vote on the amendment.

In the hope that the Wyoming Supreme Court might reconsider the 1909 decision, two separate petitions were filed in the high court asking the court to revisit its ruling. These petitions noted that the Idaho Supreme Court in 1896, interpreting identical language to Wyoming's constitution, had taken the position that only those who actually vote on the particular constitutional amendment should be counted. That court concluded (emphasis added):

> Experience has shown that it is almost, if not quite, an impossibility to secure an expression from every elector upon any question, and, above all, upon a question of an amendment of the constitution; and it is equally difficult to ascertain the actual number of electors at any given time. To rely upon the vote cast upon some other question at the same election would be entirely unsatisfactory, and such a construction is, we think, at least impliedly negatived by the provisions of section 3. While it is true that some ten thousand or more electors would seem to have been entirely indifferent upon the question of the adoption of this and the other amendments, still all were--must have been--fully advised as to the importance of the questions submitted, and **should their indifference be taken as conclusive of their opposition to the amendments? Upon what rule of honesty or righteousness can this be claimed? Is it not more reasonable, as well as more righteous, to say that in a matter about which they manifest such indifference their silence shall be taken as assent?** We hold that the amendment under discussion is adopted, and has become a part of the constitution of the state of Idaho.

By a 2-2 tie vote, the Wyoming Supreme Court in 1970 refused to even allow briefing or hear oral argument on the question. In a perfunctory order reported at 478 P.2d 56, Justices Glenn Parker and Norman "Tiny" Gray (called "Tiny" because he was a large man), simply took the position that the court could not reconsider the 1909 decision. Justices John McIntyre and Leonard McEwan, on the other hand, voted to allow briefing and argument.[204]

Justice McIntyre suggested that the two judges who wouldn't even allow argument were acting improperly: "If, after some 60 years, we close our eyes to the circumstances and reasons for an earlier decision and consider ourselves so bound by such decision that we are not willing to listen to counsel, it seems to me we fail in our duty to the public who elected us. It hardly needs to be said that the entire membership of the supreme court has changed in the meantime and the number of justices has been increased." Justice McIntyre also asserted that Gray and Parker were misleading the public by citing two cases McIntyre felt were inapposite.

---

[204] Justice McIntyre was the 1946 Democratic candidate for U.S. Representative. He lost to Frank Barrett, father of James Barrett who was Wyoming attorney general at the time of the Black 14. At some point in 1970, Justice McEwan spoke to the Laramie County Bar Association and, unlike all other state political leaders, acknowledged what should have been obvious: that racial discrimination was involved in the dismissal of the Black 14. He said that Coach Eaton was not the best choice for "Man of the Year" in 1969. McEwan was also one of the dissenters to the high court decision in 1972 allowing Republican Dean Prosser to serve in the Wyoming House of Representatives even though Prosser lived in a ranch house located in Colorado since 1940 and he would have unquestionably been qualified to serve in the Colorado Legislature. *Schieck v. Hathaway*, 493 P.2d 759 (Wyo. 1972). Wyoming statutes required residence in a Wyoming county for at least 12 months to be eligible to run for the Legislature. Dean Frank Trelease also spoke at the 1970 Bar meeting about the Black 14, saying the UW administration had instructed him that law professors should not make statements which would prejudice the state's case. He said many among his law faculty believed the coach's action was an infringement of the players' free speech rights and inconsistent with university rights but they felt muffled. "Maybe I could replace them. Maybe find some little grey mice who would always please the dean and whoever else was listening to them," Trelease said.

Justice McEwan agreed with McIntyre that the rule of *stare decisis*, which means that prior decisions on point are generally to be followed, should not be so harshly applied as the other two justices had done. "This is particularly true when previous court decisions involve only questions of public interest not affecting property rights. I would hope that we are not so rigid that we cannot at least listen to the arguments of petitioners to determine if the previous opinion is wholly illogical and unsupported by reason and, therefore, subject to correction."

Even though a strong majority of Wyoming voters who actually voted on the 1970 19-year-old vote amendment had approved it, and even though half of the Supreme Court justices wanted to at least hear arguments, the amendment went down. Democracy in Wyoming would not include those being forced to fight in Vietnam. No sir.

Still today, the fates of proposed constitutional amendments are being decided in Wyoming by voters who do not vote on the particular amendment. By not voting on it, they are essentially voting "NO" under Wyoming law. The Supreme Court's decision more than 100 years ago has never been overturned by the Legislature. Doing so would require -- you guessed it -- a constitutional amendment.

1970: Congress acts to lower voting age

Because Wyoming and numerous other states did not act to correct this hypocritical situation regarding the voting age as opposed to the draft age (which was lowered from 21 to 18 by Congress and President Roosevelt early in World War II), the job fell to Congress. In 1970, the Congress began the process of allowing all citizens 18 years of age and up to vote when an extension of the 1965 Voting Rights Act was adopted. In a 1970 decision, however, the U.S. Supreme Court on constitutional grounds ruled that the act did not apply to state and local elections. This ruling complicated voting procedures across the country and soon led to a final resolution. On July 1, 1971, the Twenty-sixth Amendment to the U.S. Constitution was adopted, barring the states and the federal government from setting a voting age higher than 18. Presumably, Sen. Myers back in Wyoming was pulling his hair out about this.

1969: SPRING LECTURE SERIES ON AFRO-AMERICAN LIFE AND CULTURE

During the fall semester at UW in 1963, the Student Senate considered whether to bring James Meredith and Alabama Gov. George Wallace to campus to speak about civil rights issues. Just over a year earlier, on October 1, 1962, Meredith had become the first African American to enter the University of Mississippi after federal troops had been deployed to protect him. On June 11, 1963, Wallace stood in the doorway of a University of Alabama building to block the enrollment of two black students. His effort was unsuccessful because U.S. Army troops had been sent to the campus to insure their matriculation.

A Branding Iron article published Dec. 13, 1963 included warnings from several students and faculty that these speakers might not attract much of an audience at UW. A senior in commerce said she would not attend either speech. "It's not of interest to Wyoming, the University or myself," she said. But others polled by the BI showed considerable interest. An Arts & Sciences junior said, "Sure, I'd be all for it. I'd say that Civil Rights is one of the most pressing problems we have in America today." A female student said she would like to hear the speakers. "After all, what happened in the South could very easily happen here someday." A "UW official" said the incidents happening in the South "are closer to us than we realize" and it would be beneficial "to hear both sides of the question before we'd ever have to make a move here in Wyoming."

It does not appear that either of those figures from the South or any other civil rights leaders appeared at UW until late 1969 when James Farmer came, and in November, 1970 when Julian Bond made a speech. But a series of lectures on "Afro-American" history, literature and sociology by white UW professors did occur in the spring of 1969, .

Considering how important a winning Cowboy football team was to the leaders of the state, and considering how important African American players had been to the team's recent success, one of the most surprising facets of the Black 14 event was how ignorant the coach, the athletic director, the UW president, the governor and the trustees were to the civil rights struggles of that decade and to the sociological and psychological makeup of their black players, many of them from urban areas.

This deficiency was also remarkable because it occurred within an institution of higher learning.

Perhaps the angry dismissal of the players might not have happened at all if those officials had attended the series of lectures sponsored by the American Studies Department and the Associated Students Speakers Committee six months before the coach's excision of the players. The Feb. 28th Branding Iron included a preview of the series and an editorial encouraging attendance. Below a stanza of the Oscar Hammerstein song "You've got to be carefully taught" the editorial said:

> You have a responsibility to be there. No matter what pinnacle of material and mechanical excellence we reach, the effort will be for naught unless we can force a change in the sad, shameful history of the white man's inhumanity to other human beings for so long.

In the first lecture, presented to an overflow crowd in a classroom, history professor Roger Daniels said most white Americans were largely ignorant of the contributions of black people in American history and many of them still believed that blacks were inherently inferior. By refusing to grant African Americans full membership in society, the whites had caused the militance, the "ethnic crisis" occurring in the country, Daniels said.[205]

The next week the lecture series was moved to an auditorium. More than 100 people heard anthropology professor Thomas Brockmann say inbreeding in a race is dangerous because it cuts down the number of variable genes in the population, slowing the process of evolution and causing inheritable diseases such as diabetes. He also said that social class, not race, was the strongest factor in intelligence tests, pointing to a test that showed "northern Afro-Americans scored higher than southern Euro-Americans."

In the third lecture, English professor Robert Hemenway discussed the "Great Migration" of African Americans from the south to northern cities between 1890 and 1920, leading to a literary movement called the Harlem Renaissance." He said it was a "travesty of American literary scholarship" that distinguished black writers such as Langston Hughes, Jean Toomer and Countee Cullin "have been so long excluded from the anthologies, the critical studies, the literary histories and the classroom."

---

[205] Millsaps, Betty, "Daniels presents informative opener", Branding Iron March 7, 1969. Other articles about the series appeared in the BI each week in March and April.

One indication of the effect of these lectures was visible in the first through seventh issues of the Branding Iron that fall. The weekly "Who's Whose" column had been replaced by a column titled "Racism Is".[206] On the other hand, one indication that not everyone in the university community had attended the lectures was visible on the front page of the third issue that fall: a photo of a Laramie license plate on a car parked in an employee lot behind the Wyoming Union. Below the bucking bronc and rider on the official plate, another metal plate was attached showing a caricature of a very pregnant black woman with thick lips and pigtails alongside these words in red: "I went all de way wif L.B.J.", a stereotypical reference to the idea that all black women lived by having babies and collecting LBJ's "Great Society" welfare.

Northwest Community College in Powell also presented a program on prejudice in spring 1969. Classes were dismissed for the hour and students were encouraged to attend the panel and open discussion. Moderator and student Steve Blood opened by saying "there's one problem we won't sweep under the rug on this campus and that's prejudice. We need to develop tolerance," he said, "in other's dress, color, ideas ... we need to do away with judging by classes or groups." African American NWCC basketball players Larry Green and Mike Childress were on the panel and said they could sense prejudice against them on campus.[207]

100TH YEAR FOR COLLEGE FOOTBALL - 100TH WIN FOR UW'S COACH

UNION PACIFIC RAILROAD
OCTOBER 1969

SUN	MON	TUE	WED	THU	FRI	SAT
			1	2	3	4
5	6	7	8	9	10	11
12	13	14	15	16	17	18
19	20	21	22	23	24	25
26	27	28	29	30	31	

1869 1969
Centennial

"You can't run a football program without discipline. If Wyoming is ever hit by student unrest, I hope the administrators have guts enough to see it through."
--Coach Lloyd Eaton speaking in Casper in September, 1969, quoted in a Casper Star article by sports editor Chuck Harkins on October 19, 1969.

"University of Wyoming students do not advocate violence or vicious confrontation. They come to us to talk things over."
-- UW President William Carlson, speaking to the Casper Chamber of Commerce directors, October 15, 1969, two days before the Black 14 were purged from the team for trying to talk to the coach.

---

[206] Also in the spring of 1969 the UW students adopted a Student Bill of Rights, which included this provision: "Students ... shall be free to examine and to discuss all questions of interest to them, and to express opinions publicly and privately. They shall always be free to support causes by orderly means which do not disrupt the regular and essential operation of the institution." This provision, except for the Student Senate, was also ignored in October.

[207] Powell Tribune 5/16/1969.

177

1969: Great expectations

In January of 1969, coach Lloyd Eaton interviewed at Pittsburgh, Pa., and was offered the head coaching position for the Pitt Panthers. Wyoming Cowboys football fans were relieved when he turned Pitt down and returned to Laramie. "Pitt was a tremendous challenge, but we, as a staff, decided to stay at Wyoming," he said. [208]The fans were bursting with excitement as the 1969 season approached. It was the 100th year of college football nationally, and Eaton was hoping to reach a personal milestone: his 100th win as a head coach. It was also the centennial year of the completion of the transcontinental railroad, marked by the driving of the golden spike at Promontory Summit, Utah Territory, on May 10, 1869.

The Cowboys wound up 1969 spring practice with an intra-squad game at Sheridan. A sports column about that game by Dave Bonner in the Powell Tribune on May 13th mentioned five players who would be among the Black 14 five months later. Bonner mentioned the speed of Ron Hill (two receptions for touchdowns) and he noted that "[Ivie] Moore, who may be the key to the defensive secondary, displayed his 9.7 speed with a good game coverage-wise." Bonner also mentioned Jerome Berry, Tony McGee and Guillermo Hysaw.

Heading into fall practices, Wyoming had won three consecutive Western Athletic Conference championships, had won 31 of its previous 36 games overall and 16 of 17 WAC conference games. UW had defeated Florida State in the Sun Bowl on Christmas Eve in 1966, and had very nearly upset LSU in the Sugar Bowl on Jan. 1, 1968, after going undefeated during the 1967 regular season. During the previous decade the Cowboys' 72-win, 23-loss, 4-tie record ranked sixth in the nation. Arizona State coach Frank Kush had the 5th best career winning record among major college coaches, but his teams had lost to UW three times in three years.

During the '60s, Wyoming had lost only once in 10 games to BYU (loss coming in 1962), posting an average margin of victory in the nine wins of 23.5 points. But after winning the 1969 game minus the black players, Wyoming won only two of the 10 games against BYU in the 70s, with an average margin of a minus 22 points in those eight losses. Even in the 80s Wyoming won only three of the 10 games. In 1984, when BYU went undefeated and was named national champion, Wyoming lost at Provo, but only by three points.

As the season began, Eaton's record as a head coach, including seven years at UW, was 97-40-5. His popularity in the state was very high. People said he could easily be elected as governor or to some other office if he went into politics.[209]

In an interview on Sept. 7th, Eaton said his biggest challenge was re-shaping the defensive secondary after losing three starters from the previous year. He mentioned sophomore Jerome Berry and JC transfer Ivie Moore as the keys to solving that problem.

The "Chicago 8" trial opened in September, 1969. Several of the leaders of the protests during the 1968 Democratic convention in Chicago were on trial. One of them, Black Panther Bobby Seale, was shackled to his chair and gagged in late October when he persisted in presenting his own defense. (Another defendant, Jerry Rubin, sponsored by the Associated

---

[208] Sioux Falls Argus-Leader 2/2/1969.

[209] In November, 1964, legendary Oklahoma Sooners' coach Bud Wilkinson barely missed in a bid to ride his football popularity into the U.S. Senate. Running as a Republican with support from former President Eisenhower, he lost in a close race to Democrat Fred Harris. At the time, registered Democrats outnumbered Republicans in Oklahoma by four-to-one. In that 1964 election, the LBJ sweep also allowed Democratic Sen. Gale McGee of Wyoming to win re-election. But by 2016, Oklahoma had turned into a solid Republican/Trump state. Oklahoma had about 15% more Republicans than Democrats. In Wyoming, 69% of the registered voters on Jan. 1, 2016 were Republicans, only 19% were Democrats.

Students, spoke at the UW Arts & Sciences Auditorium on Dec. 15, 1969. His calculatedly outrageous, shocking statements provoked protests in Thermopolis and Green River over paying such radicals to speak on campus. In January, 1970, ASUW President Hoke MacMillan defended the speech, saying the Student Senate tried to present speakers of varying viewpoints. "I doubt very seriously if many people listening to the speech agreed" with Rubin, MacMillan said, "but his speech was very educational in that it provided an entirely different point of view." He said the senate would be sponsoring conservative William F. Buckley later that semester.[210]

The escalating Vietnam protests may be what Larry Birleffi was referring to in his Cheyenne and Laramie sports column on Sept. 16th, following his participation in the "Skywriters Tour" of the Western Athletic Conference football teams. He wrote: "You really sensed that athletics, one of the last citadels of discipline, may be more important than ever before."

The University of Wyoming expected about 8,300 students to enroll that fall.

Two days before the football season opener, articles at the top of page ten of the 9/18/1969 Laramie Boomerang offered a glimpse of the world that fall. At the top right, UPI reported that Dr. Stanley F. Yolles the director of the National Institute of Mental Health, told a Senate juvenile delinquency committee that marijuana was "a mild drug" and that classifying it as a narcotic carrying stiff jail penalties was not warranted. He said the U.S. had for years based its drug laws on "fables," ignoring facts well documented in science.[211]

In the middle of the page was a report quoting the Clergy and Laymen Concerned about Vietnam saying that two Denver men, one a graduate of Regis and the other from the Colorado School of Mines, would refuse to report for induction. One of them said he would not "participate in the killing in Vietnam or cooperate with the draft system which makes this killing possible."

On the left side of the Boomerang page was a photo showing a crane lifting a station wagon to a height of 40 feet above a used car lot as a promotion for Carlisle Motors of Laramie. Inside the car was Bob Borino, a recently-returned Vietnam vet who was a radio announcer at KLME and a UW English major. Borino stayed in the vehicle for six days, occasionally doing remote broadcasts from the car. In a 2015 interview he said a bucket tied to a rope was used by fans to hoist food, whiskey and even some contraband to him. "My legs were like rubber when I got down and I needed some assistance walking for the first 50 yards or so. It was back when radio was fun, a very distant memory."

Wyoming 23, Arizona 7

In the season opener before a sellout crowd of 20,400 and a regional TV audience on September 20th, UW hoped to wreak revenge on the Arizona Wildcats, a team which had rebounded from an 0-7 deficit at the half to defeat Wyoming 14-7 in UW's last game of 1968 at

---

[210] AP in Billings Gazette, 1/2/1970. In 1986, Yippie Abbie Hoffman, another Chicago 8 defendant, spoke to a large crowd at UW. Noting that Rubin had become a stockbroker, the 49-year-old Hoffman said not all of the '60s protesters had joined the establishment. "I'm pretty proud of my generation," he said. "It's true that with age you get kids, taxes, hemorrhoids, doubts. But that doesn't mean you have to eat your political soul with a shovel." Hoffman committed suicide in 1989 and Rubin died in 1994 after he was hit by a car while jaywalking in Los Angeles.

[211] Yolles resigned in June, 1970, to avoid being fired by Nixon. The Director of the Bureau of Narcotics and Dangerous Drugs, John Ingersoll, also recommended to the committee that first-time possession of marijuana should be reduced to a misdemeanor. AP, Riverton Ranger, 10/20/1969.

Tucson, knocking the Cowboys from bowl contention even though they still were WAC champions. (In those days the number of bowl games was minuscule compared to today. For example, ASU had a won-loss record of 8-2 in 1967, 1968 and 1969 and yet received no bowl invitations).

During the second period, Cowboys' split end Ron Hill, a sophomore from Denver, thrilled the 20,000+ crowd at Memorial Stadium in Laramie when he caught a pass and took the ball 24 yards for UW's first touchdown in the college football centennial year.

In the third quarter, a sophomore safety from Tulsa, Jerome Berry -- dubbed "Jerry Berry" by UW's Poke Pigskin Press Guide -- intercepted an Arizona pass on his own 12 and returned it 88 yards for another touchdown. Berry also had ten tackles, eight unassisted and two for losses. Cornerback Ivie Moore, a junior college transfer from Arkansas, had six unassisted tackles and three passes broken up. Hill, Berry and Moore were playing in their first game as a member of the UW varsity.

Ron Hill #81 and Frosty Franklin 1969 Arizona game. Photos by John Henberg, courtesy of Wyoming State Archives.

Defense rests against Arizona: Ivie Moore #33, Larry Nels, Rich Trautwein and Steve Adamson.

UW 27, Air Force Academy 25 at Falcon Stadium

Defensive end Anthony McGee, a junior from Battle Creek, Mich., keyed the Cowboys' second-half comeback win at the Air Force Academy by tackling the AFA quarterback for losses seven times. Joe Williams had a 20-yard touchdown run and led UW rushers with 74 yards. Tony Gibson added 36 yards rushing as the Cowboys came back from a 12-point deficit at the half. Mel Hamilton, an offensive lineman who also played on special teams, performed an extremely unusual feat: he reached up and caught a low-flying Air Force kickoff to give UW good field position. A photo in the Boomerang showed sophomore James Isaac of Hanna tackling a Falcon receiver. The cutline said Isaac "made several fine saves for the Cowboys in the defensive backfield." The next week, coach Eaton discussed the 149 yards in penalties assessed against the Cowboys. "My kids work real hard every week for two years, then they get these calls that make them so discouraged they don't know what to do," he said. When asked if he was complaining about the officiating he said, "Sure. But then I've been complaining about it for 25 years."

UW 39, CSU 3

Tied 3-3 at the half, Wyoming exploded for 36 points in the second while the defense held CSU scoreless, giving Eaton his 100th career win. It was Wyoming's largest margin of victory in the 61-year history against CSU.[212] With tri-captain Joe Williams sidelined by an injured ankle, Ted Williams, a junior college transfer from Port Hueneme, Calif. who, like those previously mentioned, would soon become one of the Black 14, came to the rescue and led all rushers with 89 yards. One of the two touchdowns scored by the defense was a 24-yard interception return by Jerome Berry. The defense was so dominant that the Cowboys ran 99 plays on offense during the game, still a school record in 2019. CSU's running game, led by Lawrence McCutcheon who had set a school record with 213 yards on the ground the previous week, was held to a minus 44 yards.

Ted Williams
24

Tony Gibson. Photos courtesy of UW Athletics.

UW 37, UTEP 9

John Griffin, a junior college transfer from San Fernando, Calif., caught six passes for 57 yards and a touchdown to help lead Wyoming from a 9-3 deficit late in the second quarter to 28 straight points and its 20th home win in a row. UW had 15 first downs by passing, a new school record, and 24 completions, tying a school record.

On Tuesday October 14th, the Boomerang's preview of the upcoming BYU game quoted Eaton as saying that both Mel Hamilton and Earl Lee had been doing "yeoman's jobs at that offensive tackle spot." Hamilton was starting in front of sophomore Conrad Dobler (a white

[212] Casper Star-Tribune 10/5/1969.

181

player from 29 Palms, Calif., who was drafted after the 1972 season and made three Pro Bowl appearances during his 10-year career in the NFL). Griffin, Hamilton and Lee were also soon to be among the Black 14.

The Cowboys were ranked 12th in the nation in the UPI coaches' poll and 16th in the AP sports writers and broadcasters ratings as they prepared for BYU. They led the nation in rushing defense. On October 10 the Trustees approved the design for an 8,500-seat addition to the west side stands at War Memorial Stadium. The $1.1 million project was to be the first phase of a long term plan to add a similar addition to the east side and enclose the end zones. "When these phases have been completed, the stadium may be covered through the use of cables and inflatable dome," UW announced.[213]

Construction underway on the west side addition 1970. Jon Henberg photo courtesy of Wyoming State Archives.

On October 11, 1969, the Madison (Wisc.) Capital Times reported that Wisconsin Athletic Director Elroy "Crazy Legs" Hirsch was considering Eaton to become the Big Ten team's next coach if Hirsch decided to make a move after the season. Shortly afterwards Hirsch and Eaton denied any contact between them].

But Eaton pulled the curtain down on his own future on Friday morning, October 17th, when he summarily dismissed the players mentioned above -- and the other African American

---

[213] Gillette News-Record, 10/16/1969.

players on the UW varsity -- when they appeared at his office as a group wearing black arm bands on their civilian clothes.

The coach's action not only damaged the players' lives and promising football futures. It would soon cause the demise of his own coaching career also.

Protest comes to Laramie

The Black 14 dismissal occurred just two days after well over 600 UW students and townspeople had marched downtown and back, and had conducted a 24-hour candlelight vigil at the Vietnam Memorial at Old Main, as part of the worldwide Vietnam Moratorium protest. It was the largest Vietnam action in Laramie up to that time. On that same day, in the ultra-conservative town of Powell in northwest Wyoming, some high school students joined the

> Page 4—THE BRANDING IRON, Thursday, October 23, 1969
>
> ## Editorial commentary . . .
>
> In our system, state-operated schools may not be enclaves of totalitarianism. School officials do not possess absolute authority over their students. Students in school as well as out of school are 'persons' under our Constitution. They are possessed of fundamental rights which the state must respect. A student's rights . . . do not embrace merely the classroom hours. When he is in the cafeteria, or on the playing field, or on the campus during the authorized hours, he may express his opinions even on controversial subjects. . . .
>
> U.S. Supreme Court (per Fortas, J.) in Tinker v. Des Moines School District, Feb. 24, 1969

protest by wearing black arm bands to school. The principal, Ken Mullan, told the Powell Tribune that no action was taken against the students. "We don't interfere with personal expression of protest – like the black armbands – as long as it doesn't disrupt school," he said.

At the University of Wyoming, the state's only four-year and graduate institution of higher learning -- where passing a class on the U.S. and Wyoming constitutions was a prerequisite for all students -- an entirely different armbands scenario was about to play out.

A week before the BYU game, Willie Black, a 32-year-old doctoral student and teaching assistant in mathematics with a wife and four children, all living in student housing, had learned that under the tenets of the Church of Jesus Christ of Latter Day Saints (the Mormons), which owned BYU, African American men were prohibited from becoming priests in the church. As

Willie Black 1993

Chancellor of the Black Students Alliance, he informed the members, including the black players, of this information on Monday of the BYU week and in mid-week he delivered a statement titled "Why We Must Protest" to the UW president and athletic director, announcing a demonstration at the stadium before the BYU game.

The BSA's release said: "Our Humanity Demands: ... That all people of good will--whatever their color--athletes included" protest this policy. The release also called on UW and all WAC schools to stop using "student monies and university facilities to play host to [BYU and] thereby, in part, sanction those inhuman and racist policies...."

This BSA initiative should have come as no surprise to UW's leaders at either end of the campus. "Overall, there were over one hundred publicized examples of black college athletes registering complaints in 1968 alone, and most involved football players."[214]

---

[214] Demas, Lane, *Integrating the Gridiron*, Rutgers Univ. Press 2011, p. 111.

183

In April, 1968, eight black members of the Texas Western track team (UTEP) refused to participate in a meet against BYU, prompting Joe Watts, sports editor of the Provo Herald, to produce a column urging Texas Western's president and athletic director to support the coach's dismissal of those athletes. "If the athletes are allowed back on the team the entire structure of authority is destroyed," Watts wrote. "The purpose and objectives of college athletics would be thwarted."

"The negroes don't make sense on the situation," Watts continued. "That's not unusual. It's getting to be commonplace in the civil rights movement."[215]

The LDS church's tenet had been challenged by a Mormon in Look Magazine almost exactly six years before the Black 14 were dispatched from the Cowboys' roster.

An article by a 20-year-old LDS student from Utah appeared in the October 22, 1963 issue of Look Magazine and called for a change in the church's policy prohibiting blacks from serving as ministers. This "Memo from a Mormon" by Princeton University junior and former BYU student Jeff Nye set forth how African American boys as young as 12 years old were barred from passing the sacrament as white boys did and also from entering the temple to perform the covenants, which many Mormons consider to be "their choicest earthly blessing." Nye said "the Mormon Church taught me that the Negro was not equal to the white in terms of religious rights and opportunities. It taught me that the Negro was cursed with loss of God's priesthood and that the evidence, or mark, of this curse was his dark skin."

Nye's article called for "a new view. If we Mormons believe that God is directing our Church, we can hope that God is preparing a new revelation that will revise our present Negro doctrine. If we do not believe this, we can hope that the more liberal element of the Mormon leadership will produce a doctrinal change as the problem intensifies."

Nye quoted from a statement of a high Mormon official, the "doctrinarian" Joseph Fielding Smith, who stated in the Mormon-owned *Deseret News* that the Latter-day Saints have not described Negroes as belonging to an "inferior race." Smith admitted in the quoted article that "the work of the ministry is given to other peoples" but said that criticism from Christian churches on this point was hypocritical. "How many Negroes have been placed as ministers over white congregations in the so-called Christian denominations," he asked. Nye said Smith's comments were "just the opposite of what I had learned throughout my teen-age years as a member of the Church. ... The Negro is *not* equal to the white in the Mormon Church and equality is impossible as long as the Church denies the priesthood to the Negro."

Nye's article prompted the Utah NAACP to announce a picketing at the church's 133rd semiannual general conference. The organization said that Utah was "the only state outside the South that doesn't have a single civil rights law on its books". The announcement brought about a first-of-its-kind meeting between the NAACP and LDS leaders, including Church President David O. McKay. The church issued a statement supporting civil rights for all, resulting in the NAACP cancelling its picketing.[216]

---

[215] One of UTEP's black athletes was Bob Beamon who set a world record in the long jump at the 1968 Mexico City Olympics.

[216] AP articles in Idaho State Journal 10/4/1963 and in Ogden Standard-Examiner, 9/29/1967. The LDS statement may not have been approved by all church leaders. LDS Apostle Ezra Taft Benson, Secretary of Agriculture in the Eisenhower administration, said in 1967 that "the so-called civil rights movement as it exists today is a Communist program for revolution in America." He said the racial issue would be used to create violence, anarchy and sabotage.

In another AP article in October, 1963, Adam Mickey Duncan, a white Mormon attorney and chairman of the Utah Advisory Committee to the U.S. Commission on Civil Rights, said he considered himself a good Mormon "but I am constantly and repeatedly embarrassed by the church doctrine on Negroes. I don't believe in it." [217]

As the 1969 season began, the University of Wyoming's administrators on both the athletic and academic side should have been fully aware of the growing willingness among black athletes across the nation to risk severe personal losses to show solidarity with the civil rights movement and to seek fairer treatment within the colleges.[218]

In May, 1968, an Associated Press report by Ted Smits appeared in newspapers from coast to coast reporting that African American athletes at 10 major universities had presented demands including appointment of black coaches and faculty members, instituting black history courses or adding at least one black female cheerleader. Fourteen black athletes were boycotting spring football practice at Cal Berkeley, the article reported, but several of the universities had taken steps to address the issues raised. That same month, another AP report said black athletes at Iowa State had threatened to boycott all athletic teams unless 1) a black head coach was appointed to at least one major sport, and 2) a policy was implemented to require that lineups be determined strictly on the basis of ability, not a "black-white quota." The article said black athletes had protested practices at five of the Big Eight schools that spring.[219]

In April 1969, the black football players at the University of Iowa announced they were boycotting spring practice, claiming the graduation rate of black athletes was poor. Head coach Ray Nagel said the boycott amounted to "self-dismissal from the squad." The players released a statement saying "the black athlete is the gladiator who performs in the arena for the pleasure of the white masses." The *Iowa City Press-Citizen*'s sports editor recounted Iowa's long history of firsts for black athletes. But the editor then recognized that in assessing the black players' action, "one should realize and respect that today's black man does not want to be patronized with yesterday's history. Nor does he want to be judged just for what he is, or does, in the arena."[220] On Aug. 29, 1969, 12 of those 16 black players pleaded their cases for reinstatement in front of a jury composed of the 57 white players, who voted to allow seven of them to return to the team.

An African American football player at Eastern Washington was dismissed in September when he displayed a clenched fist salute at the start of a game despite the adoption earlier that year of an athletic code provision barring the salute.[221]

---

[217] AP, Pocatello Idaho Journal 10/27/1963 (this article also contains an extensive discussion of housing discrimination in Utah). The *Look* article and other materials are set forth in a blog: http://thoughtsonthingsandstuff.com/jeff-nye-memo-from-a-mormon/. This blog says Nye advocated for equality for all people during his life and marched with Dr. King. He died in 2010. See a response to the Nye article at http://www.blacklds.org/look.

[218] See the three-part series in Sports Illustrated by John Underwood which ran 8/25, 9/1 and 9/8, 1969, discussing various racial issues including whether coaches could control players' hair length and facial hair. See also facial hair problems discussed at p. 164 and p. 235

[219] Santa Fe New Mexican 5/19/1968 and Oshkosh Northwestern, 5/23/1968.

[220] Iowa City Press-Citizen, 4/21/1969.

[221] In the Black 14 lawsuit, the state never produced an actual written document containing Eaton's rule prohibiting participation in demonstrations.

The Black 14's visit to the Fieldhouse in 1969 occurred only 11 days after an Associated Press article was printed in the Riverton (Wyo.) Ranger and many other papers under the headline "BYU's Racial Policy Is Under Fire Again," reporting that an Arizona State black student group had asked black students to boycott the Sun Devils' WAC game against BYU that week because of alleged discrimination against blacks at BYU. The article said the protest arose from "the Mormon Church's policy against admitting Negroes to leadership positions, including the priesthood."

The article said black students at Texas-El Paso, New Mexico and San Jose State "staged similar protests against BYU last year." San Jose State's black football players boycotted the team's home game against BYU on Nov. 30, 1968. " Protestors marched outside the stadium gates, their placards reading, 'By attending this game you are silently supporting the racial bigotry of Mormonism.'"[148] Even without their black players, SJS beat the Cougars 25-21. The black players boycotted the game but "university officials then worked out a 'rights of conscience' authorization for any player to sit out a game without penalty if he first notifies the coach."[222]

In March 1969, the University of New Mexico athletic council rejected demands from the Black Students Union and the Student Senate that UNM sever all relations with BYU.

But incredibly, UW coach Eaton testified at the 1971 trial that he had not heard of any previous protests against BYU in the conference prior to the day the 14 players appeared at his office. (Tr. 325:6).

Appointment with destiny

Then peace will guide the planet
And love will fill the stars ...
Harmony and understanding,
Sympathy and trust abounding[223]

After practice on Thursday afternoon, October 16, 1969, Wyoming tri-captain Joe Williams had some discussion with coach Eaton about the BSA letter. On Friday morning about 9:15, the 14 black players gathered at Washakie Center, donned arm bands and walked to the football office in Memorial Fieldhouse. "We wanted to talk to him about our beliefs," senior tailback Joe Williams said in a Denver Post interview two days later, "but we didn't get a chance to say anything. It didn't necessarily have to be armbands, but we did want to show our beliefs. We just feel that you shouldn't be punished for your beliefs."[224] In 2013 interviews, Hamilton and Griffin stated that the players were united and that none of them expressed opposition to or reluctance about going to see the coach.

Upon seeing them together wearing the arm bands, coach Eaton led them into the upper seating area of the Fieldhouse and immediately told them that they were all off the team. After that, according to the wife of a faculty member who was doing her regular walking exercise on

---

[222] AP report in Riverton Ranger 10-24-1969, quoting SJS football coach Joe McMullen.

[223] From the 5th Dimension song "Aquarius/Let the Sunshine In", the highest ranked song for 1969 by Billboard. During the two weeks before and after the Black 14s dismissals, the #1 hit on those charts was "I Can't Get Next to You" by the Temptations and #2 was "Hot Fun in the Hot Sun" by Sly and the Family Stone.

[224] Article by Irv Moss, Denver Post sportswriter, 10/20/1969.

the Fieldhouse floor below, the coach insulted the players in an angry manner. "It was pretty belligerent talk," Annie Marie Walthall recalled in a documentary on the Black 14 produced by University of Wyoming Television. She said she felt embarrassed for the young men hearing this tirade.

In an interview with Pat Putnam of Sports Illustrated the next week, Joe Williams described what happened this way:

> The whole problem is that no one understands us. If Eaton had, none of this would have happened. His story of a racial plot is ridiculous. We knew about the rule against protest and we went to him on that Friday morning only to see if we couldn't work something out. We felt very deeply about this, but we just wanted to talk to him. We wanted to see if we could wear black armbands in the game, or black socks, or black X's on our helmets. And if he had said "no", we had already agreed that we would be willing to protest with nothing but our black skins. ... He said our very presence defied him. He said he has had some good 'Neeegro boys'. Just like that.

That Eaton's lecture had infuriated the players was obvious in their comments in the immediate aftermath. The team's leading receiver, John Griffin, said "we didn't tell him we were not going to play the game; he just assumed it. He wouldn't even let us talk. He just said, 'forget it, your scholarships and all.' I have no respect for the man." In another UPI article printed on the afternoon of the BYU game, lineman Don Meadows was quoted as saying: "I came to Wyoming because of Lloyd Eaton, and I'm leaving because of Eaton".[225]

Shortly after he reached Laramie for the emergency Trustees' meeting at about 8 p.m. that night, Gov. Hathaway sensed the polarization. At the 1971 trial he testified: "Frankly, Mr. Reeves, when I arrived the situation had solidified itself so much that there wasn't much area to see a compromise." (Transcript at 365). This situation was created by the coach, but the governor was only looking to the players to compromise, not understanding that it was ridiculous to expect that some of them, even though still stinging from Eaton's words, might turn their backs on their brothers.

In an article in the Tucson Daily Citizen on October 20th, Eaton extolled the importance of discipline: "I feel that we have won here at Wyoming with team and individual discipline. That's why we've won three titles and been in two bowl games. There's no substitute for discipline." To Eaton and the state's leaders, the presence of the 14 players on the football team was solely due to the generosity of the state. They would soon learn from the crucible of the football field that Eaton needed these talented black players at least as much as they needed him.

---

[225] Albuquerque Journal and Ogden Standard Examiner 10/18/1969.

Trustee Gordon Brodrick of Powell[226] and some of the other trustees participated by conference call in the marathon Board meeting from Friday evening stretching into the early morning hours. "Brodrick said Eaton told the board that the troubles which fanned into open revolt on the Cowboy squad were stirred by Black Panthers from Denver", according to an article published in the Powell Tribune on the following Tuesday. Brodrick said the 14 "had their day – or night – in court. We heard them completely...."[227]

At the trial in Sept. 1971, the players' attorney Weston Reeves attempted to show the unfairness of the proceedings that night, but Wyoming Attorney General Clarence Brimmer objected, claiming the burden for insuring that due process procedures were followed rested upon the players, most of them 19 or 20 years old and not far out of high school. Brimmer called Carlson to testify that the players had never asked for an attorney. Brimmer argued as follows:

> The Plaintiffs never protested at any time during the proceedings on Oct. 17th to shortness of notice, and they never protested to lack of a recording, or lack of a court reporter, or lack of a transcript, they never protested for any of these other items of due process that counsel is trying to imply now, to make this something less than a hearing that was fair and of due process." (Tr. Vol I, 195:1).

The players "emphatically denied any part of Black Panthers in their protest," the Powell Tribune article said. In an Associated Press article published in the Riverton Ranger on October

---

[226] Brodrick must have been battling distraction and worry during this meeting. Only three days previously, on October 14th, the Powell Tribune published an article and picture about Gordon's son, Navy pilot Lt. Gary Brodrick, who was flying a fighter-bomber off the USS Hancock near the coast of Vietnam. On Oct. 4th, a tire had blown when his plane was being catapulted off the deck on take-off and a strip of the tire remained attached. Upon return to the ship after the mission, the left tire assembly collapsed on impact because the strip had fouled the brake drums and frozen the assembly. So Brodrick jerked the plane back into the air to avoid an uncontrollable skid and went aloft for refueling while the carrier's crew removed all but one landing cable and erected a nylon barricade. Without flaps now, Brodrick hit the deck at 25 mph above the usual 140, caught the cable and came to "a screeching halt" at the barricade, saving both himself, the ship and the plane. Gary, a 1966 UW graduate, joined his father at Gordon's car dealership in Powell after his Navy service and eventually bought the Chevrolet dealership in Riverton, where he met and married a teacher from South Dakota who had graduated from UW in 1972. Marlene Brodrick has served on the UW Foundation board and the Athletics Hall of Fame board. Gary died in 1992 and Marlene still resides in Riverton. In a 2016 interview she said that Gary's buddies filmed the arrested landing and presented him with a VHS tape which he occasionally showed at Rotary meetings.

[227] Judge Kerr adopted this argument, ruling that this informal meeting "afforded procedural due process to all of the interested and affected parties, and was fundamentally fair in the light of the total circumstances of this case." (333 F.Supp. at 113). But the "hearing" that night can hardly be considered a fair due process hearing (no independent hearing officer presided, no court reporter or tape recorder was present, no witnesses were sworn in, the players had no opportunity to confront or cross-examine the most important witness against them, the coach, and certainly the UW Board could not be considered an impartial decision-maker. No minutes were ever recorded, other than the press release. The U.S. Supreme Court in 1967 and previously had recognized "the various procedural due process protections (notice of charges, right to counsel, right of confrontation and cross-examination, privilege against self-incrimination." (507 U.S. 316). And it certainly was not a level playing field. The governor and several members of the board, including Al Pence of Laramie, Joseph Sullivan of Douglas, Eph Johnson of Rawlins (who died less than seven months later) and William Jones of Wheatland, were lawyers. With only a couple hours' notice, the 14 players had no chance to find legal counsel to advise them and protect their interests. Remarkably, at the end of Trustee William Jones' deposition, he surprised the Black 14's lawyer, Weston Reeves, by asking Reeves: "Well, don't you think they have a right to do that as individuals [publicly express dislike for the Mormon Church's tenet]?" Reeves answered, "Yes" and Jones said, "So do I." (47:16) Too bad Jones didn't express that view on the night of the Trustees' meeting when it might have mattered.

24, 1969, under the headline "Black Athletes Weren't Puppets," UW President Carlson said charges of Black Panther involvement were unfounded. "I'm convinced their decision was on an individual basis." Carlson also said the UW Black Student Alliance "has acted in a most responsible manner" following the dismissal.

In 1993, Carlson created a memoir of his time as UW President, with several pages addressing the Black 14. In that memoir, Carlson contradicted his own statement that the players were not puppets. He acknowledged that the coach's rule was "possibly too harsh at that period of time in the universities," but then charged the rule "was exploited by outsiders to accomplish certain 'political goals' at the expense of a lot of innocent people." He admitted the obvious: "there were no winners, we were all losers", but like almost everyone else, Carlson ignored the coach's angry and denigrating comments to the players. He says he told the players during the long Trustees meeting that Friday night "that the university had to back the coaches because they were legally and morally correct."

Carlson's memoir was obviously created from memory, without much research. It has numerous factual errors, such as the assertion that the murder of Don Meadows' brother Mel at a theater in Denver "was determined to be a case of mistaken identity" (See p. 250) and the assertion that two of the 14 were brothers.

Carlson also adopted the false story line that "the players told the coach that they all were going to wear black arm bands during the game" and that "they informed him that they would wear black arm bands or not play." Even coach Eaton never contradicted the players' unanimous assertions the day before the game that Eaton dismissed them as soon as he saw them wearing arm bands in violation of his rule, before the players had any opportunity to make any demands. However, Carlson correctly analyzed the situation: "There was no give and no leverage since the coaches were heroes in the state."

To coach Eaton, to the Casper Star-Tribune's editorial department and to many Cowboys' fans who wrote letters to the editor to express their firm support of the coach, it was all a matter of rules and discipline. "Freedom of speech doesn't apply to scholarship football players", they essentially were saying.

An AP article appearing on Dec. 28th said the Casper Quarterback Club had issued a statement immediately after the dismissals in which they deplored the actions of some faculty members and students because of "apparent disregard of the importance of proper discipline on a football team."

After being ejected and belittled -- as a group -- by Eaton, the players' faculty advisor contacted UW President William Carlson, who invited them to come to his office in Old Main at noon. Before they arrived, Carlson met with Eaton and the assistant coaches. At the Sept. 1971 trial, Carlson testified that none of the coaches said the players had demanded to wear black arm bands at the game. (Tr. Vol. I 166:16)

At the Temporary Restraining Order (TRO) hearing on Nov. 10, 1969, Carlson testified that after meeting with the coaches he asked the athletes "What can I do for you?" and they asked to meet with Eaton. Carlson testified he made efforts to accomplish this, but that Eaton said "he would be glad to see these young men on an individual basis but he did not care to talk to them as a group."[228] As a result, Athletic Director Red Jacoby met with the black players, BSA members and student leaders, including the Branding Iron editor, but his comments showed not a scintilla of understanding of the players' motivations and their race's traumas. Jacoby should have been informed enough to understand that calling the players "you boys" -- as he had always innocently referred to his players black or white – was simply not appropriate or helpful in that situation.

A secretary in Old Main was heard to say during that snowy Friday afternoon: "The next thing they'll be demanding is black snowflakes."

Guillermo Hysaw, a wide receiver from Bakersfield, Calif., was visibly outraged by the coach's action and the harangue which followed in the Fieldhouse that morning. "We're just beasts," he said at a meeting a few days later. "Throw on a uniform, go out, hit, get bloody, go back to the dorm and don't have anything to say."[229] Other players appeared to be in shock at seeing their football and education dreams crumbling before their eyes, and at hearing and seeing another side of the coach to whom they had given their best efforts.

In a letter to the editor published in the Branding Iron Oct. 23rd, BSA sponsor and history professor Roger Daniels excoriated the coach for not allowing "dialogue at even the primitive first grade level." He said the 14 players had acted "in a conciliatory, moderate, responsible manner. Nobody did anything impolite, much less make any non-negotiable demands or threats."

That Friday evening, the 17th, the Trustees and Hathaway conducted a special meeting that lasted from 8 p.m. to sometime after midnight. The State's Answer and Counterclaim in the resulting lawsuit says the meeting concluded at 12:15 a.m., but news reports say it went until 2 or 3 a.m. Only one of the 14 black players commented to the media as they left the meeting. Mel Hamilton described the proceedings tersely: "It was all white."[230]

Following the meeting, UW's PR director Vern Shelton issued a press release, approved by the Board, saying the trustees had confirmed the dismissal of the 14 players for the season. The release said the players "will not play in today's game or any during the balance of the season" and that "**The dismissals result from a violation of a football coaching rule Friday morning**."

Board President Gerry Hollon testified at the 1971 trial that UW's attorney Joe Geraud and Vern Shelton prepared the press release, after which the draft was passed around the Board room and trustees made corrections and additions. "It was satisfactory to the board." Tr. Vol. I, 117:16; 263. In his testimony, UW President Carlson agreed that the press release "as nearly as anything ... puts in writing what the decision of the Board was." (Tr. 189:20). But shortly thereafter Brimmer told the court that the press release "does not reflect the real reasons for the decision that was made by the Board of Trustees that night...." In essence he was saying that the press release was false.

The release, which the state introduced into evidence at the 1971 trial, quoted Athletic Director Jacoby as saying: "Ample notice was given to all members of the football team regarding rules and regulations of the squad, some of which cover a ban on participation in

---

[228] Tr.112:2. At that hearing, Carlson was able to avoid answering a question posed by the players' attorney William Waterman as to whether Jewish students would have a right to protest against a religion with a dogma of genocide against the Jewish people. He was also asked whether players were required to waive any of their constitutional rights if they accepted a scholarship. "They are required to play under the coaches' rules," he testified in response. Tr. 136-141.

[229] Branding Iron 10/23/1969

[230] AP article, Greeley Tribune 10/18/1969.

student demonstrations of any kind. Our football coaching staff has made it perfectly clear to all members of the team that groups, or factions, will not be tolerated and that team members will be treated as individuals. There was no recourse, then, when the 14 players, as a group and not as individuals, came to the meeting with the coaches this morning. We had no choice but to drop them from the squad. It is unfortunate this happened, but **an open defiance of a coaching staff regulation cannot be tolerated.**"[231]

The writers of the press release then had the temerity to add a statement which their action had just belied: "The University recognizes that the black student has a deep involvement in current issues that may result in actions of a new nature, trustees said."

On Tuesday October 20th, the Casper Star carried an article based on the UW press release saying the dismissals resulted from a violation of the rule against participation in demonstrations. In a UPI article which appeared on October 21, Eaton said he had warned the athletes not to wear the armbands because that would violate his rules against players participating in student protests. He then summed up his reason for the dismissal: "They did it and it was an open defiance of the rules."

In response to the dismissals, the UW Student Senate met early Saturday morning and by a 15-3 vote, adopted a resolution saying the Senate "expresses its shock at the callous, insensitive treatment afforded 14 Black athletes.... [T]he actions of coach Eaton and the Board of Trustees were not only uncompromising, but unjust and totally wrong." The resolution called for a freeze on student fees going to Athletics unless Eaton met with the players to discuss "their rights as individuals and also their reinstatement".[232] Four days later, while on the Homecoming Week tour, Student Sen. Robert Anderson of Riverton, who presumably voted against the resolution, did his best to neutralize it. Speaking at a Rotary meeting in Powell, he said the resolution "was passed in the spirit of withholding judgment until all the facts were in." He said the resolution did not mean that the Senate wanted Eaton fired. "We love Eaton," he said, "just as you do. We respect him and what he has done for athletics at the university."[233]

The Faculty Senate the next week voted 37-1 in support of a resolution asking that the 14 be placed on temporary suspension pending an investigation by a student-faculty committee. Faculty members of this ad hoc committee were Chairman Don Anderson (statistics), Arthur Burman (adult education), Claude Edmiston, Robert McColloch, James Hook, Oliver Peters and E. George Rudolph. Student members were ASUW President Hoke MacMillan, Alan Kirkbride

---

[231] An Associated Press report datelined Laramie and printed October 20th in newspapers across the country declared that "The existence of an anti-demonstration rule is disputed here. White players on the team Sunday agreed with the BSA that there was no such rule." In his second decision in the players' lawsuit, Judge Ewing T. Kerr ruled: "The action and order of dismissal by the Board of Trustees of the University of Wyoming was not predicated upon the existence or non-existence of any football coaching rule ...." This directly contradicts the UW press release that the Trustees' approved at the end of their late-night meeting.

[232] The Student Senate's vote was surprising because 10 days earlier the same Senate had separated itself from its counterparts across the nation by voting 15-10 against a resolution to endorse the National Vietnam Moratorium protest planned for Oct. 15th in Laramie. Senators voting in favor were Gary Fisher, Corbin Fowler, Art Hanscum, Greg Maag, Larry Sackman, Jim Robinson, Carolyn Wallace, Dan White, Al Wiederspahn (sponsor) and Ron Weinberg. Thirteen years later, Democratic state representative Wiederspahn led an attempt – also unsuccessful – to obtain the Legislature's endorsement of the Nuclear Freeze (see Kehler chapter at pg. 147). In 1983 Wiederspahn married arch-conservative Republican Cynthia Lummis who served as Wyoming's sole representative in the U.S. House from 2008-2016. Wiederspahn died in 2014.

[233] Powell Tribune 10/24/1969.

of Meriden, Al Wiederspahn of Cheyenne, Bob Schuster and Dan Burke, both law students from Casper, and Dwight James, an African American from Cheyenne. MacMillan asked students to avoid protest while the committee tried to work out a resolution. But in the end the committee could not penetrate the polarization injected by Eaton and reinforced by the Trustees.

Dwight James (second from left) was among Black 14 players and supporters making signs prior to the San Jose State game on October 25, 1969. The players shown are Jerome Berry, left, Ivie Moore center and Guillermo Hysaw making a sign. Third and sixth from left are Paul Melinkovich and his sister Mary from Rock Springs. Paul became a pediatrician at Denver Health and Hospital and a professor at the CU School of Medicine. Mary became a nurse. Photo courtesy of Art Shay archive.

One of the 600 UW faculty at a meeting in the Union Ballroom the day after the BYU game predicted that their voices would have no effect. Nothing would be done about Eaton, he said, "until he has an 0-10 season." (He was almost right. The one-win season in 1970 would bring Eaton's coaching career to an end).

During the trial in federal court in Cheyenne on September 27, 1971, Hamilton testified that he never told trustees he would not play against BYU without an armband. Regarding the meeting with Eaton earlier that day, Hamilton testified, "Eaton agreed to speak with us at our request, but then told us: 'Gentlemen, you can save time and breath. As of now you're off the football team.'"[234]

In an interview in 2009, Tony Gibson, one of the 14, told Ryan Thorburn, author of *Black 14 -- The Rise, Fall and Rebirth of Wyoming Football*, that the players were not going to demand that they be allowed to wear armbands on their uniforms the next day. "If Eaton didn't let us, we would just play the game. That's the part that was never brought out enough after the fact."

In an article with many photos in Jet Magazine November 13, 1969, Joe Williams was quoted as saying that Eaton booted the players "before we had a chance to talk." In an interview with *Sports Illustrated* the week following the dismissal, Eaton claimed he had given the players ten minutes to speak. But Joe Williams disputed that: "Like hell he gave us ten minutes. He came in, sneered at us and yelled that we were off the squad."

---

[234] UPI report in the Wyoming Eagle, 9/28/1971.

In a UPI article printed on Sunday, October 19th, starting defensive end Anthony McGee, 20, was quoted as saying: "We went in there to talk intelligently and to discuss the way we felt about the game. He [Eaton] cussed at us and didn't even try to find out what we wanted to talk about." He said the players were met with abuse from Eaton.

Another UPI report on Oct. 19th included this statement: "Eaton said when the 14 athletes came into his office Friday wearing the armbands, there was nothing to talk about."[235]

In that same article, Eaton admitted the incident would hurt recruiting among black football players. "They will probably not want to have anything to do with Wyoming," he said. "They would have to follow the rules."

Berry said he joined the group not so much to protest LDS beliefs but because he had heard that Wyoming's black players had been mistreated at Provo the previous season. "We wanted to play BYU in the worst kind of way," he said, and he saw the visit to Eaton as "a starting point for negotiations." But Eaton, Berry said, "opened his statements to us by saying 'were it not for him we would all be on Negro relief.'"

Testifying at the hearing in Cheyenne in September, 1971 Eaton confirmed making nearly all of the statements which the Black 14 complained about on the day they were dismissed. He was asked by the state's attorney general, Clarence Brimmer, "why didn't you give the 14 players the opportunity to speak at length?" The coach's response: "There was nothing to discuss. The rule was clearly cut. (i.e. the rule against players participating in demonstrations). ... They left the dormitory, they came as a group wearing the arm bands, and they were in an action of demonstration as of then."[236]

Knowing that Judge Kerr would be receptive to the argument, Eaton and state attorney general Brimmer emphasized that the coach had warned his players several times "that the rule against participating in any kind of demonstration must be strictly observed."[237]

Eaton also confirmed that he had made what could only be considered by an unbiased observer as racially-tinged statements which the players were mentioning to Carlson and Jacoby within minutes of their dismissal, to no effect:

> He testified he did tell the 14 if they did not think the UW program was fair ...
> they should consider attending Morgan State or Grambling – two predominantly
> black universities. He also said he told them if they rejected their football
> scholarships and took some form of grant when they were capable of earning their
> keep on the gridiron, it would be like taking "Negro relief."[238]

---

[235] Ogden Standard-Examiner 10/19/1969.

[236] Tr. 305:11.

[237] Wyoming State Tribune, Sept. 28, 1971, p. 1. That newspaper's front page "flag" each day included a short quotation. On Sept. 28th, the quotation was: "...But I will defend to the death your right to say it. -- Voltaire".

[238] Laramie Boomerang October 3, 1971. Trial Tr: 295:18. One of the Black 14, Earl Lee, did later earn a master's degree in education administration from Morgan State University, according to his obituary in the Baltimore *Sun* on 1/17/2013 which was still available on-line in 2018.

Eaton testified on cross-examination that he could not see why the "Negro relief" comment might be offensive to the players. He confirmed that he had told them to shut up.[239]

Eaton acknowledged that previously, players had been involved in drunken driving, fist fights and assault or dorm infractions where the player was not expelled. The players' attorney Weston Reeves asked him "why was it necessary to take so much more serious action with regard to these 14 than it was with these other violations?" Attorney general Brimmer objected and the court sustained the objection.

But Eaton's angry statements and the players' understandable fury were ignored by the governor, the trustees and the people of the state. The free speech right of students -- even in junior high as recognized in the *Tinker* case[240] -- were ignored by the state's attorney general, the highest law enforcement officer, with a sworn duty to uphold the Constitution. The state's leaders simply did not have the strength of character to explain to Eaton that his rule and his dismissals were illegal and could expose the public coffers to monetary damages under the federal civil rights act. Instead, Hathaway and the trustees expected those young men to immediately forget and forgive the insults Eaton had hurled at them that morning and meekly beg the trustees and the governor to make them Cowboys again. But the Fourteen knew they had done nothing objectively wrong and did not deserve such a severe punishment. They had not sexually-assaulted anyone. They had not been charged with aggravated assault after a drunken brawl outside a bar.[241] They had simply exercised their right to free speech and assembly, and yet the governor and the trustees supported Eaton's decision to chastise them for their ungratefulness while administering the "death penalty" to the football careers of almost all of them.

Much of the criticism directed at the players from every quarter of Wyoming during the ensuing weeks seemed based upon a belief that the players knew that UW's football success was a product of Eaton's strict disciplinarian philosophy. Overlooked in all of that was Eaton's own lack of discipline, his failure to recognize that these 14 black players were not defying him on a personal level. None of the UW leaders understood that these players could not totally ignore the urging of their brothers in the BSA to protest the LDS tenet "in some way". Even though they had made themselves into proficient, polished football players, they were not devoid of feelings about the long history of injustices, violence and hatred inflicted upon their race in this country.[242] Since the Birmingham church bombing in 1963 in which four young black girls were

---

[239] Tr. 319:6; 294:9.

[240] *Tinker v. Des Moines Ind. School Dist.*, 393 U.S. 503 (1969).

[241] In December, 2012, two UW basketball players got in a brawl outside the Buckhorn Bar downtown. One of them, a starting guard who had scored 25 points in a game 11 days earlier, kicked and injured a man who was already on the ground, resulting in charges of aggravated assault and dismissal from the team. The Cowboys were undefeated after winning all 12 non-conference games to open the season, and won another game without the suspended player, the best start in UW history. Bismarck (N.D.) Tribune, 1/15/2013. Wyoming won only four of 16 conference games after the incident.

[242] Amid all the talk about discipline, nobody mentioned that the coach had some responsibility in that regard also. Certainly, the discipline to keep one's head in the pressure-packed final minutes of a close football game is critical. But the same thing could be said about a football coach confronted with a crucial situation that could profoundly affect not only the black players, but also his assistant coaches and their families, the white players, the athletic director, the university and the state. If only Eaton had followed his own and oft-repeated "Coaches' Prayer": 'Lord help me keep my big mouth shut.' If only he had counted to ten, or at least talked to Athletic Director Jacoby before taking this extreme action.

killed, and since 1965, when Casper's James Reeb was clubbed and killed in Selma, the Rev. Martin Luther King had been entreating his people to stand up and resist prejudice and discrimination, to not "stand on the sidelines" anymore.

If only Eaton had remembered his response in an interview published in the Branding Iron two years earlier when he was asked, what do today's players expect from their coaches?

> They want the truth right down the line and they want to be treated fairly, regardless. You don't fool college football players today. They are very intelligent and sensitive. They don't want a lot of baloney. We feel this combination of fairness and truth will establish an excellent rapport and relationship between coaching staff and player.[243]

Same day: Clifton Wharton Jr. named president of Michigan State U.

The morning after the BYU game, the Casper Star-Tribune's front page was dominated by news of the dismissal of the Black 14. But tucked away on page 22 of that edition was a short article that dramatized how Eaton and the UW Trustees had launched the university and the state down a regrettable, regressive path.

UPI's report declared:

> EAST LANSING (UPI) - The year 1969, the year when man landed on the moon and the Mets won the World Series, has also become the year a Negro became president of a major American university.[244]

The article reported that on the same day UW was dispatching its black football players, the Michigan State University Board of Trustees was naming economist Ph.D. Clifton R. Wharton Jr., 42, an African American, to be that university's next president.

Wharton, the article said, would become the first black president of a major, predominately-white American university. Only 4% of MSU's 40,000 students and about 1.6% of the faculty were black.[245]

Wharton said he had never knowingly accepted a position where race was the primary factor. "In each case, the situation was one where I could utilize and demonstrate a set of skills and competencies. Meeting racism and white competition on these terms--and beating them--is what I call positive militancy," he said.

Wharton was the son of the first African American named as an ambassador after rising through the ranks of the Foreign Service (Wharton Sr. was ambassador to Norway 1961-64). Dr. Wharton served as MSU president until 1978 when he became the first African American to head the largest university system in the nation, the 64-campus State University of New York serving 345,000 students. Michigan State's Wharton Center for the Performing Arts was named for him and his wife.

---

[243] BI October 20, 1967.

[244] Holland (Mich.) Sentinel, 10/18/1969. News of Wharton's appointment was on Page One of the New York Times on October 18th.

[245] New York Times, 10/18/1969, p. 1, 16. UW had no black faculty members at all.

1936-1979: TREAGLE STAG FOOTBALL TRAIN

On the morning of the BYU game, many of Cheyenne's male business and political leaders, together with special guests, gathered at the Union Pacific Depot for the 34th annual running of the "Treagle football special train" sponsored by Cheyenne Newspapers Inc., the publishers of the Eagle and Tribune. As the invitees gathered up their tickets, their "Eagle-Tribune" hatbands and slim bamboo canes, everyone was talking about the events that had transpired in Laramie the previous day. Former U.W. history professor and by then U.S. Sen. Gale McGee (D-Wyo.), purportedly said that "At least there will be one McGee at the game today," a reference to the absence from the playing field of the Black 14's Anthony McGee, a probable future All-American selection if his Division One college career had not been crushed by Eaton and the Trustees.[246]

The Treagle, a promotion of the McCracken family who owned the Cheyenne, Laramie, Rawlins, Rock Springs and Worland newspapers, had always been a stag affair since its first run in 1936. Among the features of the chartered train ride were free beer and a four-page spoof tabloid newspaper called *The Treagle*.[247] A preview of the football trip on Oct. 26, 1939, said "Wyoming's most novel newspaper, the 'Treagle', will be read by the 350 Cheyenne business and professional men (including Gov. Nels Smith) invited aboard, keynoting the trend of fun and frivolity." Post-trip reviews on Oct. 29th and 30th reported that the participants "forgot their dignity" as soon as they climbed aboard and "happy voices mingling in football and medleys" were heard on the trip over the hill. "Everywhere a 'Treagle' man went, fun followed."

Elsewhere on that 1939 Wyoming State Tribune front page were several reports about the Nazis. One told of the capture of a German pilot shot down over Scotland and another said a Cheyenne woman was hoping for Hitler's fall. She had a nephew fighting for Germany on the western front and five sisters and her aged mother were still in Germany.

The 1939 edition of *The Treagle* contains evidence of the racism and misogyny of that era. For example, the paper attempted to explain the purpose of the excursion this way: "Reasons which are partially responsible include our desire to fraternize with our esteemed neighbors in the Gem City, to get away from our wives in one of the very few 100 per cent masculine debauches remaining in this democracy ...."

A front-page article in the Wyoming Eagle on October 4, 1958, proclaimed that the 600 invited guests included U.S. Sens. Barrett and O'Mahoney, Rep. Keith Thomson, Gov. Milward Simpson and "all state officers and candidates for state office, **excluding the ladies**." This exception had to be stated because the State Auditor in 1958 was Minnie A. Mitchell, the first woman to serve as Wyoming's State Treasurer and State Auditor. Neither Mrs. Mitchell nor

---

[246] On Aug. 14, 1963, the Casper Star ran an AP article datelined Cheyenne in which the NAACP's regional counsel said Sen. McGee had voted for only one of "nine or ten issues in 1962 which the NAACP considered important to us as Negroes." Although the Fourteen's dismissal should not have been a joking matter, it should also be recognized that in 1964 and 1965 McGee voted for Johnson's civil rights acts. He also was a Vietnam "hawk". A month after his depot statement, McGee was back in Cheyenne, addressing the first session of a series of foreign affairs seminars at the new Laramie County Community College. McGee said withdrawing precipitously from the Vietnam War "would almost certainly sow the seeds for a new world war in Asia." McGee argued the U.S. must stay with South Vietnam until it can assume responsibility for its survival on its own "because this may well be our last chance to at least help set the stage for a more peaceful world." Powell Tribune, 11-18-1969. Orwell's Big Brother had stated it this way: "War Is Peace."

[247] The 1939 version of that paper is available to view at the Wyoming Newspaper Project web site.

Thyra Thomson was ever invited to ride on the Treagle train. Mitchell was one of the top five state elected officials from 1952 to 1971 and Mrs. Thomson, U.S. Rep. Keith Thomson's widow, was the first woman elected as Wyoming's Secretary of State, serving in that office from 1963 to 1987.

The 1958 article indicated that Cheyenne Newspapers Inc. would again treat the guests to lunch in Laramie after being welcomed by UW President George "Duke" Humphrey and State Rep. Oscar Hammond[248], and also provide dinner before the return trip. The meals for the large crowd were divided up between the streamliner's diner cars, the Connor Hotel and other downtown restaurants.

The 1963 Treagle brought 600+ participants, including JFK's brother Sen. Edward M. Kennedy, to the Laramie depot, where they were greeted by a three-round cannon salute, the UW band, cheerleaders and the pony mascot Cowboy Joe. The previous day, Kennedy had been flown from Denver to Cheyenne by Cheyenne lawyer, banker and future U.S. Rep. Teno Roncalio, a pilot.[249]

At the football game, Kennedy met four Wyoming football players from Massachusetts: guard Bob Hickey, tailback Rick Desmarais, center Ken Spires and guard Bill Levine.

U.S. House Minority Leader Charles Halleck (R-Ind.) was also a guest on the Treagle. Speaking at a Cheyenne luncheon the day before, Halleck said Pres. Kennedy's administration had failed on just about every campaign promise, including keeping the Communists out of the Western Hemisphere and "throwing Hoffa out of the Teamsters' Union."[250]

In 1965, astronauts Gordon Cooper and Pete Conrad were guests on the Treagle.

The famous "Washington Merry-Go-Round" syndicated columnist and investigative journalist Drew Pearson was invited aboard the Treagle on Sept. 30, 1967. In his column carried from coast to coast by hundreds of newspapers, Pearson remembered that 20 years earlier, just after WWII, he had "traveled through Wyoming [on the Friendship Train] collecting boxcars of food for Western Europe." One of the people who greeted that train in Green River or Rock Springs (and was now on the Treagle with him), was future U.S. Rep. Roncalio[251]. Pearson noted that in 1964 Roncalio had defeated incumbent U.S. Rep. William Henry Harrison, grandson and great great-grandson of two U.S. presidents. Also on the train, Pearson said, was John Banner, "the bulky TV Sergeant Schultz of 'Hogan's Heroes.'"

In his column, Pearson mentioned Cheyenne lawyer George Guy "who studied under Judge Thurman Arnold, the old trust-buster, at the University of Wyoming Law School." (It was no surprise that Pearson mentioned Arnold because Arnold's son George had married Pearson's daughter Ellen. One of the children of that marriage is the "plein air in thin air artist of the

---

[248] Father of long-time Boomerang sports editor Bob Hammond and Vietnam vet Dave Hammond.

[249] The next week, Dr. Martin Luther King said in a Birmingham, Ala. speech that he would turn out more black people "than any man can count" for a protest march unless the city hired more black policemen. "We are tired," King said, "tired of being denied equal employment." According to a Nov. 5, 1965, Casper Star-Tribune report, the NAACP Regional convention of the Wyoming-Colorado Conference approved a resolution put forward by Fred Devereaux of Casper, urging the Casper city administration to "follow the lead of other Wyoming cities in the hiring of Negroes" in police and fire departments. This employment issue was still in the headlines more than 50 years later with the "Black Lives Matter" movement in 2016.

[250] UPI, Boomerang, 10/12/1963.

[251] Roncalio ran for the Senate in 1966 and lost, but regained the House seat two years later. He served five terms. He died April 1, 2003 at age 87 in Cheyenne.

Tetons" Joe Arnold of Laramie. In the 70s, Joe's father George Arnold also was a UW law professor. A couple of Joe Arnold's large pastel paintings hang in the addition to the UW College of Law building).[252]

Finally, Pearson said he had seen -- at the Cheyenne depot grounds -- one of the 49 railroad boxcars sent full of gifts by the French people to each U.S. state in 1949 in appreciation for Pearson's "Friendship Train". The "Merci Train" cars were suitable for 40 men or eight horses ("quarante hommes, huit chevaux"). They were used in WWI, Pearson wrote, when "Capt. Thurman Arnold was marshaling the Wyoming National Guard up the faltering railroads of France to the muddy battlefields of Verdun, Chateau-Thierry and the Argonne." Pearson said the brightly colored coats of arms designating the French provinces had been stolen from the car. Today, with those coats of arms replaced, the railroad car can be seen at the American Legion Post #6 at 2201 E. Lincolnway in Cheyenne.[253]

Bill Moyers, former press secretary to LBJ, deputy director of the Peace Corps and editor of Newsday, who then produced PBS specials from 1971 to 2010, was a guest on the 1970 trip. He probably was not impressed by *The Treagle*, which featured "cheesecake" photos of women and an ad showing the Budweiser Clydesdales above the question, "What's Your'n? It's Horse Beer." Moyers has received more than 30 Emmy awards.

The 1969 Treagle arrived in cold snowy weather and was to be greeted by dignitaries such as UW President William D. Carlson, according to a Boomerang Treagle preview on October 14th. If Carlson was actually there he could have been nodding off. He was in the emergency Trustees meeting regarding the black football players until around 3 a.m.

1979: Men only ... or no Treagle at all

I hear the Treagle comin', it's steamin' round the bend,
Free beer and Cowboys football and back to Chey again.
But aboard you won't see Thyra or Shirley or Lynn
'Cause this McCracken junket, it carries only men.

The exclusion of women politicians and advertisers from the annual Treagle Train began to rankle some women in Cheyenne in the late 70s.

An editorial setting forth the history of the special train appeared in the Wyoming Eagle on Sept. 26, 1979, saying the train had been run every year since 1935 except during WWII. The staff of the newspapers, it said, were "pleased to be able to extend this kind of a 'thank you' to our news sources and newspaper advertisers". The editorial made no mention, of course, of the male-only aspect. And because all of the McCracken newspapers in Wyoming carried only the UPI news service, few of the 700 men who boarded the streamliner cars on the morning of Sept.

---

[252] See www.joearnoldstudios.com and https://vimeo.com/162385484.

[253] An article about the restoration of the car in the Wyoming Tribune Eagle April 9, 2017, says that many of the gifts contained in Wyoming's car are in the Wyoming State Museum. One of them is a small display case with a letter dated Dec. 13, 1948, which translated from the French says: "Sir or Madam in America, This little piece was made by one of my workers, and I gift it to you in token of my admiration and gratitude toward your great country. And I wish that all people, instead of using arms, might make war with gifts. My best wishes for the happiness and good health of all."

29, 1979, would have read an Associated Press report describing efforts made by several Cheyenne women to convince male public officials not to ride the Treagle.[254]

Cheyenne attorney Mary Kennedy was quoted as saying, "Public officials should not be involved in private discrimination." Karen Deike, owner of a framing gallery and a former aide to Sen. Malcolm Wallop, organized calls asking leaders, including Wallop, to not participate. Waterbed store owner and Tribune-Eagle advertiser Ellen Fox waited for several hours outside Publisher Robert McCracken's office before handing him a letter asking that he reconsider the all-male policy. "He looked at it, and then he looked at me, and he just sort of balled the paper up and tossed it," Fox recalled.[255]

The women noted that three of the five highest elected state officials were not invited: State Treasurer Shirley Wittler, Superintendent of Public Instruction Lynn Simons and Thomson.

McCracken was quoted as saying the Treagle was "a private party" and the newspapers could invite whomever they chose. He said the newspaper's owners "just haven't given any thought" to changing the policy.

When confronted with the women protesters in the depot, Sen. Wallop remarked: "If this is the most important issue facing us, we're in good shape."

Two weeks later a complaint was filed with the U.S. Dept. of Labor by a female ad salesperson at the Tribune Eagle arguing that because her male co-workers were invited on the train the newspapers denied her an equal opportunity to meet potential male clients.[256]

Joan Barron of the Casper Star pilloried the newspapers and its male guests in a classic 9/30/1979 article, reporting that Ellen Fox had boarded the train and then had been removed by plainclothes UP detectives. Fox had obtained a ticket for the 44th running of the Treagle from a male friend. But Doug Reeves, a former football player for the Cowboys who was advertising director for the newspapers, made sure she was returned to the platform.

According to Fox, Reeves grabbed her ticket and ran. Then the detectives approached and pulled her off the train. She reported that a male passenger said, as she was being removed, "those damn broads are going to mess it up for us." Fox and around 20 other Cheyenne businesswomen and leaders, including Wyoming's first female federal prosecutor Sharon Lyman, picketed the train that morning.[257] Lyman had not been invited, but U.S. Attorney Chuck Graves and Assistant U.S. Attorney Tosh Suyematsu were invited and were at the depot.

Barron's report also set forth the response of U.S. Sen. Alan Simpson: "Before boarding, Simpson turned and muttered to an acquaintance, 'I think I'll hide in the toilet.'"

One of the headlines in *The Treagle* showed that the misogynist theme in the 1939 edition still held sway 40 years later. The headline read: "Butch McCracken's Gang Throws Off Chains of Hard Work, Long Hours and Marital Servitude." Another note in the little paper instructed guests, "Please be sure to take a copy of *The Treagle* home to your wife. It's the only thing she'll get out of this excursion."

---

[254] AP, Great Falls Mont. Tribune, 9/29/1979.

[255] "Taking the Equality State for a Ride," p. 22, Wyoming News Vol. 4, No. 10, Sept. 1979.

[256] *Id.*

[257] Fox was the subject of another AP report in May, 1980. The owner of Grandma Brindel's Waterbeds and Things announced she was closing her store because of slow sales and that she was planning a mock funeral which was to feature a velvet-lined casket with a waterbed and a mirror on the inside of the lid. Lead S.D. Call, 5/24/1980.

In August, 1980, Robert McCracken announced that the annual train and football trip was being discontinued. It was, he said, "a dinosaur that has seen its day." Yes it was, a dinosaur with its record intact: the Treagle never carried a female passenger.

BLACK 14 REACTION ON THE GRIDIRON AND BEYOND

The statistics fans would read in the Wyoming vs. BYU game program on Oct. 18, 1969, showed that the 14 African American players had contributed substantially to the team's unbeaten status. Eight of them had been listed in the starting lineup for at least one game, and the play of three others had been mentioned in at least one game story. John Griffin was the leading receiver, Ron Hill led in kickoff returns and tri-captain Joe Williams led in rushing attempts. Mel Hamilton, a junior from Boy's Town, Nebr., had moved into a starting position in the offensive line and Tony Gibson, a junior from Pittsfield, Mass., started at fullback in the UTEP and CSU games. Jerome Berry was starting at strong safety and Anthony McGee at defensive end. Ivie Moore, a Pine Bluff, Ark., defensive back who transferred from a Kansas junior college, was listed as a starter for the BYU game.

In a 2010 phone interview from Beaumont, Texas, Ron Hill recalled a running play named "26 Blast" which "we ran over Mel's position and always made yards because Mel was so strong."

Only one of the 14 was a senior and half of them were under 21, the age of legal majority at the time. Eaton was 51.

Guillermo Hysaw (then known as "Willie"), who had been steered to UW by the same coach at Bakersfield, Calif., who had influenced the Marion brothers to go to Laramie (See Marion chapter at pg. 61), was shown on the 1969 UW track roster for the long jump and triple jump. (That 1969 track media guide also showed that black football player Vic Washington, a star of the 1966 and 1967 football teams, had found time to set one outdoor and two indoor school records for UW track).

First newspaper reports

Because the University of Wyoming had imposed an official news blackout Oct. 17th pending the emergency Trustees meeting that had been called for that night, the initial wire service reports were based on interviews with the players and BSA chancellor Willie Black. "Eaton refused to comment on the situation and said any statement would have to come through the university's sports information department," UPI reported. Eaton refused to meet with the players and with President Carlson that afternoon at Old Main. In fact he told UPI that he would not even attend the "special meeting of the board of trustees called late Friday."[258] The UPI articles quoted Jerome Berry, Joe Williams and John Griffin. Williams said the players went to

---

[258] Eventually, Eaton did have to meet with the board that night. According to Board chairman C. E. "Jerry" Hollon of Lusk, in his interview included in the UW Television documentary years later, Eaton always took his team to a movie on the night before a game. Hollon went to the movie theater and sent the manager in to ask Eaton to come out to talk to him. The manager did so but reported that Eaton declined. So Hollon sent the manager in again and this time Eaton did emerge to meet with Hollon.

his office that morning and "we were going to play the game no matter what, and we hadn't even decided to ask to wear black armbands on the field."[259]

Joe Williams #26 was featured on cover of BYU game program.

The Casper Star-Tribune's October 18th edition reported that the trustees were still in session at 11:10 p.m. and that Gov. Hathaway was in attendance. "There was guarded optimism that the board might be able to resolve the crisis." Sports editor Chuck Harkins opined that "mute silence" from the university "was stark proof that all was not well in the Cowboy fold."

Harkins managed to reach former UW running back Dave Hampton with the Packers at the Sheraton-West in Los Angeles. Hampton said he had just heard about the UW incident "over KIFI while watching the Lakers play on TV. I just finished calling Frank Pescatore in Laramie to find out if it was true."

Hampton said he would not comment, other than to say "that the talk about Eaton being a racist is not true. I've never known him to be a racist in even the mildest form." But he had not heard about the language Eaton had used that morning. In an AP article datelined Green Bay and carried in the Riverton Ranger on Oct. 29th, Hampton called for the Fourteen's reinstatement. "I think athletes are part of the university and should be given the right to participate in campus issues," he said.

Harkins had no sympathy for the Black 14's situation. In a radio interview during the San Jose State game on Oct. 25th, he told Gene Benson the players' action was "a very, very cheap shot. You can't have true democracy on a football field. We can't vote on each play to see whether we go off tackle or around end, vote to see who starts the ball game. It's impossible."

"Cowboys don't need those blacks"

On that cold, dark, snowy Saturday afternoon, the Cowboys, who were suddenly an all-white team like BYU, defeated the Cougars 40-7 while the Black 14 watched from the first rows of the student section on the east side. The cover of the program featured a drawing of #26, Joe

---

[259] This statement of intent from Joe Williams has been much ignored down through the years. One of many examples is the explanation for the Black 14's dismissals in a book about BYU: "Rather than comply with the coach's warning, fourteen black players decided not to participate in the 19 October game and were therefore dismissed from the team." Bergera and Priddis, *Brigham Young University: A House of Faith*, Signature Books, Salt Lake City, 1985, p. 300.

Williams, carrying the ball for Wyoming amidst former Cowboy greats Joe Mastrogiovanni, Jim Crawford and Eddie Talboom. BYU was held to 16 yards rushing.

Outside the stadium on October 18 and the following Saturday, protesters carried signs saying "No More Brown in the Brown and Gold" [the school colors], "Fourth and Inches for Conscience" and "What If God Is Black?" Another carried by Steve Nickeson was a take-off on a gun rights slogan of the time: "When Rights are Outlawed Only Outlaws Will Have Rights." Two white women's sign said "King George in 1776, King Eaton in 1969."

The wife of a young UW zoology professor, Jenny Parker, carried a sign saying: "Esther Morris, Hang Your Head in Shame." (Esther Morris has been credited by some historians with influencing the Territorial Legislature to grant equal rights to women in 1869. A full length sculpture of her on a tall pedestal was located at the entrance to the Capitol Building in Cheyenne for many years. Thus, Parker's sign meant that the dismissal of the Fourteen was a shameful blow to Wyoming's claim to be the "Equality State".

Football fans walk past demonstrators protesting the dismissal of the Black 14 prior to the San Jose State game on Oct. 25, 1969. Guillermo Hysaw, sporting his Kangol hat, is third from right. The full text of the sign on the right was "Fire the Faculty, Burn the Books, Hire the Green Bay Packers." Photo courtesy of Art Shay Archive, Chicago.

Protesters passed out a sheet addressed "To All Loyal Cowboy Fans" attempting to counter the rumors circulating about the black players boycotting the game and making unreasonable demands. "No Black Athlete has quit the team or threatened to do so. ... The only demand being made by the Black Athletes is that Coach Eaton include them in the Human Family."

Supporters of the coach passed out arm and hat bands and bumper stickers supporting the coach before the San Jose State game. These stickers were produced by Don Riddle of Casper, former western states coordinator for the George Wallace presidential campaign. After Democratic national committeeman Teno Roncalio expressed dismay about this connection, the state chairman of the Wallace campaign, C. E. Reed, denied the stickers were connected with the campaign, saying "almost all Wyomingites resent the attempt to smear a great coach." Casper Star 11/19/1969. Photo courtesy of Art Shay Archive.

Two protesters carried signs side-by-side saying "Reinstate the Blacks" and "Discipline Eaton."

Police confiscated all of the protesters' signs as they filed into the BYU game, but did not challenge a man who displayed a large Confederate flag at the top of the east stands for more than half the game[260]. Fans on both sides of the stadium chanted, "We love Eaton."

After the game, Eaton's anger at the black players showed no signs of abating. He told the press: "The victory was the most satisfying one I've ever had in coaching. It was a team effort by a bunch of youngsters who want to play the game the way it is supposed to be played. And I'm so happy for them."[261]

Kicker Bob Jacobs and halfback Frosty Franklin were both quoted as saying the dismissals energized the white players. Jacobs said they wanted to "win more" for Eaton, and Franklin said "we're trying harder than ever for the coaches."

In a letter to UW President Carlson dated the same day as the BYU game and bearing a hand-written "Confidential" at the top, BYU President Ernest Wilkinson thanked Carlson for supporting Eaton's action. "I am frankly happy, in view of the forthright action that you took, that your remaining team members enjoyed a victory." Wilkinson told Carlson he had been told "that at your school you have a rule that Negro students should not date white girls." He asked Carlson if that was true. In Carlson's response dated Oct. 31, he thanked Wilkinson for the

---

[260] A photo of the flag waver was published on p. 1 of the Oct. 31, 1969 Branding Iron.

[261] UPI article in Ogden Standard-Examiner, 10-20-1969, correctly predicting that "It also may prove the costliest".

203

support and said that "our position of standing firm certainly seems to be substantiated more and more as we proceed." Carlson did not answer Wilkinson's question about interracial dating.

The black players claimed that during his outburst after booting them off the team Eaton had told them that "I am the only father some of you ever had." This seems quite plausible, given his statements in an Associated Press report published on Monday, Oct. 20th. Eaton first said that the protest was a "plant job" by the leader of the Black Student Alliance. "Look," he said, "most of these players are only marginal students. They come from split homes and poor families. They are usually 'C' students at best and we're trying as hard as we can to give them an education through football."[262]

Demonstration rule quickly amended, but no reinstatement of the players

On Thursday of the next week, Eaton and Carlson appeared at a news conference at the A&S Building to announce that the coach's rule prohibiting student athletes from participating in demonstrations was being amended to apply only while on the playing field.

Eaton said, incredibly, that the original rule was not intended to interfere with anyone's individual rights of self-expression, according to the Laramie Boomerang report the next day. Eaton said the rule was modified by the football staff "to reduce the chances for future turmoil within the football team."

An AP dispatch printed in the Atlanta Constitution and across the country on October 24th reported that "The coach said he is sticking by his decision to keep the blacks off the team for violating his rule that -- before it was modified -- banned football players from joining any student demonstrations."

According to an AP article printed in the Riverton Ranger Oct. 23, "Eaton left the news conference, ostensibly to attend a coaching staff meeting, when he was asked if the dismissal of the players would have happened if the now-modified rule had been in effect earlier. University information officer, Vern Shelton, said Eaton was not ducking the question but had a previous commitment. Shelton said he would arrange a meeting between Eaton and reporters later in the day so the question could be asked again." But that never happened. The answer was obvious.

Editorials in the student newspaper, the *Branding Iron*, on Oct. 23 and 31 urged reinstatement of the players. "It is only right that at the time of revocation [of the rule], the violator should be freed from his punishment." The BI pleaded with all parties to look deeper than the "it's a matter of discipline" defense. "Nazi Germany thrived on blind obedience to rules," it said.[263]

By revoking the rule, UW was apparently acknowledging that the coach's absolute ban on participation in demonstrations was unconstitutional under the *Tinker* decision from the U.S. Supreme Court eight months earlier. But even so, UW declared that the revised rule would not go into effect until after the football season, apparently believing the state and university had the power to suspend the authority of the U.S. Constitution for several months.

---

[262] AP report printed in papers across the nation, including in the Greeley Tribune, 10/20/1969. Many in the Wyoming power structure, including Eaton primarily, felt the players were pawns in a larger game. But this feeling did not provoke any empathy from Eaton, the Trustees or the governor when it came to imposing a punishment that fit the "crime."

[263] In about 2010, Pete Gardiner, a pacifist living across from UW on Lewis Street, told the author about Sophie Scholl. She was a student and anti-Nazi political activist in Germany who was convicted of high treason and executed at age 22 for distributing anti-war leaflets at her University of Munich.

On Friday Oct. 24 a protest march occurred between the Union and the Coe Library. Among the protesters were 1968 Cowboys' quarterback Skip Jacobson and students Allen Gardzelewski and Doug Shaw (L-R in the foreground of the Jet Magazine picture below, published 11/13/1969). ASUW President Hoke MacMillan asked that the demonstrations cease, assuring the students that a faculty-student committee "was working toward a just result". But in the end nothing came of it. Even the BYU student executive council -- composed of 10 elected students -- protested the LDS tenet. An AP article in the Riverton Ranger on Oct. 23rd said the student leaders presented their administrator with a statement saying: "We do not believe in discriminating against members of any ethnic, racial, or religious group", and asking that the university issue a statement on civil rights.

PROTESTED: SUPPORT GROWING

Black and white students march to Wyoming stadium hours before homecoming game with San Jose State College.

Entire San Jose State team wears multi-colored armbands in support of Wyoming's black athletes.

63

On October 30, 1969, the faculty of UW's largest college, Arts & Sciences, passed a resolution by a vote of 114-38, charging that "fourteen black athletes have been given deep human injury and have been dismissed without a trace of due process by Coach Lloyd Eaton. ... [T]his faculty believes that the action ... was unjust, unconstitutional, and unwise, bringing the entire University into disrepute." The resolution's sponsors included several of the greatest names in UW faculty history: George Baxter (zoology), Anthony Guzzo (chemistry), Herbert Dieterich (American Studies), Marshall Jones (sociology), T. A. Larson (history), Ernest Linford (journalism -- who as Boomerang editor had protested the book inquiry in 1947), Ronald B. Parker[264] (geology), John Mathison (English), Robert Russin (art -- sculptor of the A. Lincoln bust atop the I-80 summit east of Laramie), Wilson Walthall (psychology) and Burton Muller (physics).

English professor Ken Craven stated at the October 19th all-faculty meeting at the Union that he would resign if the players were not reinstated. A Casper Star article on October 21st reported that some Casper businessmen headed by painting contractor J. L. "Dode" Gerdom "had started a fund drive to provide moving expenses for Ken Craven or any other faculty member" who opposed Eaton's action. In what would eventually qualify for a "Famous Last Words" list, Gerdom said: "We don't care if Wyoming wins another game--we stand behind the coach." Gerdom, a 1950 UW graduate in agriculture, added, "If Craven's power play fails, and we think it should, we will be most helpful in assisting him down the road."[265]

Gov. Hathaway also expressed unqualified support for Eaton in an Oct. 21st p.1 article in the Wyoming State Tribune, saying he hoped Eaton remained as coach "for a good long while. ... [D]emonstraters cannot be permitted to run a university." Hathaway, a lawyer himself, then stated an entirely erroneous view of constitutional law: "a demonstration for freedom cannot succeed if it restricts another freedom – in this case freedom of religious belief."

Editor James Flinchum of the State Tribune in Cheyenne echoed this view. "We applaud [the coach's and trustees'] stand and say this: If it becomes a matter of whether Wyoming ever wins another football game or not, or surrenders principle, then we waive all claims to the former and insist that rules being rules, they must be enforced."[266] What was that principle? That African American football players given a scholarship should be seen only on the football field and not heard?

In contrast to A&S, faculty in UW's Agriculture and Education colleges voted overwhelmingly to support Eaton. Several days later, an informal poll conducted by BI editors Monica Miller and Candy Carroll showed that 69% of UW students felt Eaton was justified.

---

[264] After earning his Ph.D. in geology from U. Cal. Berkeley, Parker taught at UW for 17 years and went on to produce several popular books about earth science such as *The Tenth Muse: The Pursuit of Earth Science*, Scribner's 1986.

[265] Casper Star, 10/21/1969. See the Craven chapter at pg. 225 for what happened when Craven tried to take them up on their moving expenses offer. Also on Oct. 21, Jack Kerouac, author of *On the Road*, died of cirrhosis of the liver at the age of 47 in St. Petersburg, Fla. In the summer of 1947 or thereabouts Kerouac hitchhiked from New York to Denver and along the way found himself in the midst of what he called "Wild West Week" in Cheyenne when he disembarked from the flatbed truck which had carried him on U.S. 30 across much of Nebraska and along Lincolnway to downtown Cheyenne. "The stars seemed to get brighter the more we climbed the High Plains. We were in Wyoming now," he wrote in his book. "As the truck reached the outskirts of Cheyenne, we saw the high red lights of the local radio station, and suddenly we were bucking through a great crowd of people that poured along both sidewalks."

[266] Reprinted in the Laramie Boomerang 10/21/1969.

UW's public information director Vern Shelton provided a report to Carlson about the reaction. The report indicated that 1,197 letters favoring the dismissals had been received but only 53 opposed.

During the next week, four black trackmen (two of whom had been conference champions in their main event the previous year) quit the team and left UW in protest of the dismissals. They were Huey Johnson and Grady Manning of Chicago, Mike Frazier of Pueblo, Colo. and Jerry Miller of Battle Creek, Mich. A white track athlete from Willowick, Ohio, Greg Santos, left UW after the semester. In a UPI article dated December 18th, Santos was quoted as saying, "In Wyoming, people say they aren't prejudiced when they are, and they have closed minds when it comes to racial issues."[267]

Coach Bill Strannigan's basketball team was also affected. Guard Rick Bell, a Thornton, Ill. High School star from the Chicago area and a UW letterman the previous year, had followed Leon Clark, Reuben Poindexter and Harry Hall from Thornton to UW's program. Even their high school coach, Bill Purden, had migrated to Laramie to become the assistant coach for Strannigan. On Oct. 22, Bell was quoted in the Arizona Republic as saying the sentiments of the four black basketball players were with the Fourteen. According to a Tucson Citizen article on Nov. 11th, Strannigan told a pre-season media gathering in Denver that Rick Bell, a black guard counted on as a starter, had left school and returned home to Illinois. "He told me it was personal reasons," Strannigan was quoted as saying. "'Family trouble', he said, but I talked with his family and there wasn't any trouble at home. I'm pretty sure it was connected with the football problem up there." Another black player, Mike Bannister of Cleveland, went to Northern Colorado and was leading the Bears in both scoring and rebounding in January of 1971.

Rick Bell joining the Black 14 protests

On Tuesday October 21st, coach Eaton was quoted in an AP article as saying that "there is little chance the 14 players will be reinstated on the team. If I did that, it would be discriminating against the 43 members of the team who obeyed the rules and have been working hard."

That same day the New Mexico Civil Liberties Union urged the University of New Mexico's president to re-examine the school's association with the WAC, asking "whether the university's and the nation's interests are being served by the continued association in a conference harboring racist institutions." According to an AP article of that date printed in the Pocatello Idaho Journal and elsewhere, the letter stated: "The NMCLU's main concern is that the conference may be characterized as a bastion of racism and repression, particularly if the Wyoming action is not rescinded promptly."

---

[267] Apparently Greg Santos changed his mind. He penned a BI article on 2/19/1971 about the Wyoming track team's chances at the WAC championships that weekend. Santos himself was competing in the 60-yard dash.

According to a UPI article printed in the Provo, Utah Herald on October 21st, President N. Eldon Tanner of the Mormon Church refused to comment about claims that blacks could not advance to the priesthood. "I think it would be best not to say anything. My comments wouldn't be understood."

Because the official student newspaper was published only once a week, a group of UW students began producing a daily mimeographed report called "Revelations". The "rotating" editors of Revelations included Lew Pyenson, Rose Korhonen (Mrs. Rose Marie Wright), Terry Brubaker, Steve Nickeson, Cris Hamm, Elbert Belish, Gary Gilmore, Peter Feeney (a future lawyer and judge in Casper), Dale McKay and Lawrence Murrell.[268] The Oct. 27th edition bemoaned the effect the dismissal of the Fourteen would have on the university and state: "It is sad that the 'Equality State' is about to become known as the 'denial of rights state'".

On Wednesday, October 22nd, a group of about 85 UW students called the "Committee for the 14" sent a letter to the San Jose State student newspaper asking for support of the Black 14. On that same day, two black and two white San Jose State players released a statement saying the team would travel to Laramie to play Wyoming that weekend but that all the players would wear either black or multi-colored arm bands. "Our team has had the experience of attempting to reconcile individual conscience and the desire to play football," the statement read. "The plight of the black athlete who is a member of a team which has scheduled Brigham Young University is understandable, we believe."

Also that day, Wiles Hallock, the WAC commissioner in Denver who formerly was the sports information director at Wyoming, said "the whole problem of membership of BYU in the conference" would be discussed during a regular conference meeting Nov. 3-5 in Denver. Hallock said the conference has to "look in all directions and be perfectly honest with each other." He suggested there may be some guidelines the conference could agree to "which may help avoid some of the more drastic things which have happened."

Many articles printed nationally during the next couple of weeks by white writers quoted white officials as saying that the Black 14 action was not racially-motivated. Almost none of the articles mentioned what the players claimed were racially-insulting statements Eaton made to them during their brief meeting in the Fieldhouse. None of them questioned the severity of the punishment. In a UPI article printed around the country on Oct. 22nd, for example, Gov. Stan Hathaway said the dismissal of the 14 athletes was not a racial issue and should not be made into one. He said if 14 white athletes had violated the same rule, they undoubtedly would have been dismissed from the squad. He said Eaton and the other coaches "have repeatedly demonstrated their moral integrity and racial unprejudice." Most officials and citizens naively clasped onto the idea that Eaton's recruitment of black athletes proved that the players' color played no role in the coach's decision and the angry (and polarizing) lecture that followed.

---

[268] Several editions of Revelations can be read on-line from the digital collections at the UW American Heritage Center. (uwyo.edu/ahc). Pyenson was a graduate student at the time and was appealing the denial of his petition for conscientious objector status. As of late 2016, he was a professor of history at Western Michigan U. In an interview he gave his perspective of the near-50 years since the Black 14, saying the incident damaged his assumption "that universities were unlike other parts of society in that they valued reason and truth-seeking above all. The action of the coach and the complicity of the administration shamed the university and needlessly injured the Fourteen. The nation has moved in the right direction over the past half century, but we are neither kinder nor gentler. Universities have not become leaders in making things better, notwithstanding their success in a few areas, such as the exact sciences and medicine. It would help if trustees chose university presidents for their visionary qualities, rather than for their experience as shills."

In a UPI article printed on Oct. 22nd, the BSA's leader Willie Black rejected allegations by Eaton and many other officials that the players were pawns in an effort by outside groups to cause a confrontation. "I am not a troublemaker and I was not sent here by some subversive organization," he said.

When Wyoming's Episcopal bishop David Thornberry retired in 1976, he had a different view than Hathaway's party line: "The affair concerning the black athletes revealed deep racial prejudices in many places in Wyoming where it was unsuspected. People were as much incensed because they were black as they were because they broke the discipline. The people in Wyoming have as far to go as any people in eliminating their racial prejudice."[269]

In a column printed October 30th, Arizona Republic sports editor Verne Boatner said one WAC athletic director "advocates BYU's withdrawal from the conference." The column quoted this director as saying, "If BYU would relax its rules, it would help. But I don't think they are going to do that, as long as its basis is religious belief." A person Boatner described as "one of the leading forces in the founding of the WAC" told him: "These are changing times. They [BYU] need to change with them."

Another AD told Boatner of his concern that the conference "is gaining a whites-only athletic image. He claims both Wyoming and Texas-El Paso have only one Negro on their freshman football teams."

All of the ADs agreed, Boatner said, "that athletes should be allowed to participate in all student activities – including demonstrations – as long as it does not interfere with athletic routine."

Irene Schubert's Letter to UW Personnel Director

Following UW's press conference announcing that Eaton's rule against participating in demonstrations had been modified, Irene Schubert, Documents Librarian at the UW Coe Library, sent a memo to George Fowler, UW Personnel Director. She asked a number of difficult questions about her authority "now and at the end of the football season."

1)   May I, if I wish, require that members of my staff not participate in protests or demonstrations or restrict the wearing of arm bands while they are on duty in my department? ...

2)   Until the end of the football season, do I have the right to restrict their wearing of arm bands and their participation in protests even when they are not on duty?

I would also appreciate a word on the extent of the use of arm bands: does this also apply to the wearing of badges and buttons supporting one cause or another? Would a ban on demonstrating include such activities as participation in Veterans' Day parades?

Fowler responded with a short letter saying her concerns "should first be taken up with the Director of the Library" and if he desired to "bring this matter to the administration then I would feel that it would be his business to do so."

---

[269] Casper Star-Tribune, June 21, 1976.

Homecoming routine unaffected-Memorial to Eaton proposed

During the week after the BYU win, it was business as usual for football-affiliated activities at UW. The Riverton Ranger on October 24th carried two pictures of the Homecoming Queens and entourage's visit to Riverton and Hudson the previous day. The photos appeared alongside an AP story with the headline: "BSA Pushes for Reinstatement".

The photos showed Queen candidates Mary Ann Schwartz of Casper, Julie Henderson of Basin and Linda Lamb of Laramie, along with ASUW Senators Jay Bishop of Lander, Bob Archuleta of Green River and Robert Anderson of Riverton ("director of the tour").

The article about the BSA quoted its chancellor Willie Black as saying that since the rule against football players participating in demonstrations at any time had been rescinded, the players should no longer be treated as if they violated anything. An engineering graduate student named William Daley said a group of about 20 students had formed a committee to oppose reinstatement. The group also claimed the Branding Iron had been slanted toward the Black 14 in its coverage and called on students, faculty and alumni to "reexamine their support of the paper."

The article said the BI editor had announced his resignation, quoting him as saying the majority of UW students "do not want to hear about racism, the Vietnam War" and other issues of the day. "Maybe if the Branding Iron doesn't mention these problems they'll all go away," the editor said.

Coming off its win over BYU, Wyoming was still ranked 12th by UPI, tied with Notre Dame. The Cowboys finished their home slate with a narrow 16-7 victory over a weak San Jose State team (the Trojans went 2-8 that year). A small airplane pulling a banner saying "Yea Eaton" flew over the stadium and the crowd responded with a roar generated by stomping their feet and shouting. Many wore "EATON" arm bands. According to an article in the San Jose Mercury-News the next day, "a banner estimated to be 30 feet long was unraveled along the sidelines, stating, 'Coach Eaton's Million Friends Say Get The Cats Off His Back.'"

Because of the loss of black running backs Joe and Ted Williams and Tony Gibson, the rushing duties fell to sophomore Frosty Franklin of Powell for the rest of the season. He carried the ball a UW-record 31 times in the San Jose State game. According to the game story in the Casper Star, "Franklin said he lost his sharpness late in the game which led to a pair of fumbles. 'I was tired and just didn't have the good reflexes to hang onto the ball,' he said."

On October 21, 1969, the front page of the Wyoming State Tribune in Cheyenne carried a front page article headlined "Battle Lines Forming In University Dispute". The UPI article reported that Campbell County State Rep.

Coach Lloyd Eaton on the sidelines during the San Jose State game, next to #12 Mike Leake, flanker. It was to be Eaton's last home win. Photo courtesy of Art Shay Archive Chicago.

C. H. "Cliff" Davis, the Republican majority whip, had issued a statement supporting the coach and trustees: "[I]f the university backs up in any way on their decision, I would urge other state legislators to be very hesitant in obligating state funds to the university when we don't know if we have a university," Davis said.

The Rock Springs City Council on Oct. 21st supported the dismissals, and former State Rep. Richard Forsgren of that city declared that "Coach Lloyd Eaton should have a memorial built for his fast, decisive action in regards to this black power movement. He stopped it before it got started at the university."

In a UPI article published in the Arizona Republic on October 26th, even UW's conservative Republican political science professor Thomas Parnell acknowledged that the players' constitutional rights had been violated. "When these players are not playing in a game, they enjoy the same rights that all Americans do. Armbands are symbolic of the freedom of speech and their going into Eaton's office as a group is the freedom of assembly."

One of the very few expressions of support for the Black 14 in the Boomerang was an article appearing October 23rd written by a young African American long-time Laramie resident and high school football player about another and much older African American long-time resident and player. Author Bart Parham, in an article appearing on the Boomerang's "Teen-Age Scene" page, quoted Sammie Miller as saying that the dismissal was "uncalled for and that a workable compromise should have been sought." He said Eaton "should have at least heard the men out." Miller also correctly predicted that the dismissals "could be bad news" for UW's recruiting of black players.

Even Larry Nels, one of the white players who was a star at defensive end, told Ryan Thorburn in 2009: "I was in shock afterwards. As you look back you just wonder what could have been done differently and if a compromise could have been reached to appease Coach's strict rules. Maybe a one-game suspension or something. I don't know, but we didn't have any say in the matter. What Eaton said went."[270]

The dismissal of the 14 brought camera crews from the three big TV networks to Laramie, and articles appeared in newspapers and magazines across the land. The November 3rd issue of Sports Illustrated carried an article with pictures, including a photo of 10 of the players on the south steps of the Wyoming Union. The Casper Quarterback Club, the Rock Springs City Council and the Worland-Ten Sleep Chamber of Commerce supported the coach. The Wyoming High School Activities Association through its director Bob Cook expressed its gratitude to and pride in Eaton "for the constructive and wholesome influence he has been on interscholastic athletics in our state."[271] Cook said a claim that any citizenship rights were violated "is truly ridiculous. ... Discipline is an absolute necessity."

The Wyoming Stockgrowers Association, under the leadership of president Van Irvine, a Casper rancher, passed a resolution condemning the use of tax-supported institutions "as a podium for subversive activities and demonstrations." [272]

---

[270] *Black 14*, p. 65.

[271] Laramie Boomerang 10/23/1969.

[272] Wyoming Rural Electric News, January, 1970 p. 4. Irvine pleaded no contest and was fined $679 in July, 1971, on 29 state charges of killing antelope out of season and lacing their carcasses with a poison called thallium sulfate. He testified he was trying to kill coyotes not eagles, but the investigation was sparked when the same poison was found to have killed 50 eagles in Jackson Canyon near Casper.

The UW Alumni Association also climbed onto the Eaton bandwagon. The Association's president Jerry Hand, a Casper lawyer, said the group condemned statements from "allegedly responsible" members of the faculty advocating and therefore possibly teaching individual students to disregard rules and regulations. The real issue, he said, was whether a coach or teacher has the right to establish rules for discipline and enforce them. "We all recognize that some rules may not be proper, but we question the philosophy that an individual has an absolute right to violate these rules without suffering the potential consequences of such violation," Hand said. "If the rule is wrong," he said, "we should follow proper channels to effect a change. Individual defiance is not the answer if we are to have any order in our society unless the individual must also face the consequences of his defiance."

The Cheyenne Quarterback Club on Oct. 22nd issued a statement deploring the actions of some faculty members and students who showed "apparent disregard of the importance of proper discipline on a football team."

Aside from some of the students, the Denver Post and the student newspaper at UW, one of the few expressions of concern for the dismissed players, ironically enough, came from a source close to the BYU board of trustees quoted in the Denver Post on October 24th: "It's most disturbing to think that the Negro athletes at Wyoming could lose their education."

The Casper branch of the NAACP adopted a resolution supporting the 14. President Gaurdie Bannister (who had been a pall bearer in 1961 at services for UW's 1930s black athlete Taft Harris) said, "I don't think a coach can tell someone how to think or act."[273] He said the punishment did not fit the crime and that claims that race did not play a role in the dismissals were wrong. Mrs. Stillman Reynolds acknowledged the coach's right to rule while on the playing field, but said he did not have "the right to be someone's conscience."[274]

The Denver Post carried an editorial on October 21st under the title, "Which Comes First in Wyoming?" It said:

> We hesitate to offend some big-time sports enthusiasts with the heretical notion that football players are human beings with rights like other people. ... For a coach at the University of Wyoming to issue an edict that football players may not take part on their own time in a lawful Vietnam demonstration or may not protest policies they think are racist at Brigham Young University is an outrage.
>
> The power of the State of Wyoming ought not be used by a football coach or anyone else to defy the Constitution. And all coaches should be made to understand that the dictatorship they exercise in athletic matters cannot extend to politics. If Coach Lloyd Eaton of Wyoming cannot accept that, then it is he, and not his 14 black players, who should leave the team.

But in a column the next day on the sports pages, Post sportswriter Jim Graham argued Eaton "is 100 percent right. ... A football team is not a democracy," he wrote. "Either the coach has full, unquestioned authority or you will not have the discipline, self-sacrifice and self-control that a winning team demands. ... The Negro players were warned. They broke the laws. They must accept the consequences. ... And if Wyoming does not stand squarely behind its coach in this

---

[273] AP article, Riverton Ranger 10-27-1969.

[274] Casper Star-Tribune 10/27/1969.

showdown, then it will be the university – and not Lloyd Eaton – who will be the big and final loser." Graham couldn't have been more wrong.

Jack Rosenthal, manager of KTWO Television in Casper, broadcasted an editorial on the 21st that acknowledged that a football team, like the military service, "by its very nature cannot be a completely democratic organization. However, neither football players nor soldiers are vegetables, completely without rights or feelings." Rosenthal wondered whether "those young players, still in their teens or near teens, might have modified their position if the coach, 25 or 30 years their elder, had sat down and counseled with them."

A UPI article in the Riverton Ranger on Nov. 6th reported that the Western Athletic Conference's Council, consisting of faculty representatives and athletic directors, had cut short its meeting in Denver after 50 black students walked into the session uninvited. The article says most of them were from the University of Colorado, a Big Eight Conference school, identifying themselves as members of the Black Student Alliance and wearing armbands with the numeral "14". One of their leaders told a news conference later they intended to mount an effort to dissuade high school athletes from playing for WAC schools.

On Oct. 29, 1969, Whitney M. Young Jr., executive director of the NUL, sent a telegram to UW President Carlson saying "The National Urban League views with deep concern [the dismissal of the Black 14] because they desired to symbolically protest the existence of racism...." The NAACP was involved in obtaining legal representation for the players.

U.S. Rep. Donald Riegle, D-Mich., sent a letter dated Nov. 10 to UW President Carlson and Trustees saying he was "deeply disturbed" about the dismissals. "[I]t appears that this action was arbitrary, provided inadequate safeguards for due process and may constitute a form of political repression. ... [T]hese young men violated what was purported to be a standing ground-rule imposed by one individual. That this rule may have been articulated prior to the incident does not necessarily make it right." Riegle was also concerned about the hypocrisy displayed by UW when the 14 players were not reinstated even though a few days later the rule that led to their dismissals had been modified to permit what they had done. "The First Amendment", Riegle wrote, "guarantees the right of free speech, and there are no provisions within the Constitution that these rights are to be abridged by arbitrary football coaches, or anyone else." Riegle said college students are entitled to the same rights of citizenship as anyone else. "A young man's college and possibly his professional football career ought not to be arbitrarily terminated because he freely exercises rights that are constitutionally guaranteed."[275]

But in Wyoming, the politicians lined up behind the coach. For example, in a speech at Sheridan on Nov. 17th, Republican State Rep. Alan Simpson of Cody recalled his own political activity when he was a UW football player under coach Bowden Wyatt in the 1950s. He said he was putting Eisenhower for President buttons on every player he could find. "Wyatt told me I was either to play football or play politics, one or the other, but not both. ... I played football." Simpson noted that Wyoming has had some "tremendous black athletes, and we are proud of them." He noted that the citizens had raised $40,000 for Dave Marion after he was accidentally paralyzed by a gun shot wound in 1963 and this showed Wyoming "is not a racist state."[276]

---

[275] From the UW American Heritage Center, provided to the author by Black 14 researcher Richelle Rawlings. Riegle served five terms in the U.S. House and then three terms in the Senate. Because of his opposition to Nixon's Vietnam War policies, Riegle switched from Republican to Democrat in the midst of his U.S. House career.

[276] Casper Star Tribune 11/18/1969. For more on Dave Marion see p. 61.

On November 12, 1969, President Kenneth Pitzer of Stanford, acting on recommendations from the campus Human Relations Committee, declared he "today barred any new commitments to intercollegiate competition with institutions sponsored by the Mormon Church." The statement said church officials had confirmed that black men could not become priests. The release quoted a New York Times article saying that BYU had only three black students among its enrollment of 25,000.[277]

BYU's university relations director responded to the move by acknowledging that "no negro of African lineage may have the right of priesthood." However, Heber Woolsey said, "it is the lineage and not color which is used as a determination. Black-skinned islanders are allowed full rights to the priesthood."[278]

On the same day the Stanford decision was announced, the Sun Bowl released the names of 16 teams being considered for that year's game, a list that included BYU. In the end, Nebraska trounced Georgia in the 1969 Sun Bowl and BYU has never played in that bowl.

Within two weeks of the Stanford announcement, BYU physical education dean Milton Hartvigsen announced that BYU planned "to step up recruiting among Negroes."[279] At that time, no African American had ever played varsity football or basketball at BYU.[280] He said the effort was a direct result of the demonstrations against BYU. In 1970, BYU coach Tommy Hudspeth recruited BYU's first black player, Ronnie Knight, from Sand Springs, Okla.[281]

Like other bowl games, the Sun Bowl had segregation policies in its early years.[282] In November, 1948, the Sun Bowl invited Lafayette College of Easton, Penn., to play in the game under the condition that its star running back, David Showell, an African American, could not participate. When this was brought to Showell's attention he urged his teammates to make the trip without him. But the Lafayette College faculty voted to reject the invitation. Student protesters

---

[277] Cal State Hayward, the University of Washington and two other schools followed Stanford's lead, according to Bergera and Priddis, *Brigham Young University*, at p. 300.

[278] Provo Daily Herald 11-13-1969.

[279] AP report in Abilene Reporter News Dec. 7, 1969. The Black 14's Willie Hysaw was quoted in the article saying that the protest was about the LDS policy, not the lack of blacks on the BYU team. He predicted the recruitment drive would not slow protests.

[280] Two blacks had been on BYU's track team 10 years earlier. Denver Post, Nov. 26, 1969, p. 29.

[281] Gary James Bergera and Ronald Priddis, authors of the book titled *Brigham Young University: A House of Faith,* Signature Books, 1985, at p. 301, say the Y's first black player was Bennie Smith who enrolled in 1972. The authors relate that as late as 1969, BYU administrators discouraged blacks from attending, sending letters to applicants advising them that there were few blacks enrolled at the school and "no families of your race" in the community. Applicants were also informed that BYU "does not look with favor upon marriages of any individuals outside their own race, whatever that race might be, and hence frowns upon mixed courtships, which might result in such marriages." This attitude was "not a matter of race prejudice," the letter said, but was based on the difficulties encountered by individuals in such relationships in adjusting to differences in family and cultural backgrounds. *Id.* at 298. As of 1970, only four blacks had ever graduated from BYU. *Id.* BYU's football coach Tommy Hudspeth was quoted in the Provo Herald on Feb. 16, 1970, as saying "we will not allow interracial dating."

[282] "Integrating New Year's Day," *Journal of Sport History* 24, no. 3 (Fall 1997). This article details how Boston College (in 1939 and 1940) and other northern schools prior to WWII had accepted bowl bids and agreed "to abandon their black players in pursuit of athletic success and financial rewards." Earlier in 1939, Boston College had held their black halfback Lou Montgomery out of home games against Auburn and Florida. In 1940, even the Naval Academy had refused to allow a black Penn State champion sprinter to run in a track meet at the Academy.

caused the athletic director to call the Sun Bowl and request that Showell be allowed to play, pointing out that he was a lieutenant in the U.S. Army during the war. The Sun Bowl responded by saying it had already invited another team and could not cancel its commitment. No black player played in the Sun Bowl until 1952.[283] A controversy involving the Sugar Bowl erupted in 1956.[284]

In November, 1958, the 8-1 University of Buffalo team was invited to play in a bowl game for the first time, the Tangerine Bowl in Orlando. The game was to be played in a stadium leased by the Orlando High School Athletic Association, which had a rule prohibiting racially-mixed teams from playing there. Rather than leaving their two African American mates behind, the team chose to reject the bid entirely. A book titled *Brothers Tonight* was written about the team's decision. One of the white players said in an interview at a 50th-year reunion in 2008 that the action was "one of the most rewarding things I have done in my life."[285] The team's star halfback, Willie Evans, was present at the reunion. His black teammate was deceased. Evans recalled his feelings at the time:

> Being confronted with the situation of not being allowed to play because you're black, I'm saying to myself, "Well, I didn't do nothing to these folks". In talking with the fellas, we laugh about it now. And we sum it up and say, "It was just dumb. It was just dumb."

Evans and teammates were in attendance at the International Bowl luncheon one day before the Buffalo Bulls played the Connecticut Huskies in Toronto on January 3, 2009, the first time Buffalo actually played in a bowl game. He expressed joy at having had the opportunity a few days earlier to vote for an African American for President. The Rev. Jesse Jackson spoke at the luncheon, linking the "gallant" stand by the Buffalo football team in 1958 to Barack Obama's election, and crediting athletics with "changing our mind about what matters."

In that 2008 season, the Buffalo Bulls were split about evenly between African Americans and whites and were led by a black coach, Turner Gill, and a black athletic director.[280]

Wyoming editors: The Black 14 were the ones violating people's rights

---

[283] Demas, *Integrating the Gridiron*, 86.

[284] In December, 1955, Georgia Gov. Marvin Griffin, who had vowed "to take whatever steps necessary to preserve segregation" and "the southern way of life", was celebrating Georgia Tech's invitation to play in the Sugar Bowl until he learned that the opponent, Pitt, had an African American player, Bobby Grier. He then asked the Board of Regents to reconsider allowing Georgia public colleges to schedule athletic events with integrated teams. This sparked protests by white students at Tech and other schools, including hanging Griffin in effigy from Georgia to Oregon. The controversy attracted more attention than Rosa Parks and the bus boycott in Montgomery, Ala., according to Ch. 4 of *Integrating the Gridiron* by Lane Demas. Up to that time, even the Sugar Bowl's tickets were segregated, with tickets for whites reading "issued for a person of the Caucasian race." The regents voted against Griffin's request, but limited its decision to the Sugar Bowl game only. They and most of the protesting students still supported segregation in most areas. Grier was the leading rusher in the game. Tech won 7-0 after what Grier always claimed was an unfair interference call against him in the end zone.

[285] Hamburg (New York) Sun, 12/4/2008.

[280] AP, Asheville (N.C.) Citizen, 1/3/2009

In an editorial published on Monday, October 20, 1969, the Casper Star, Wyoming's largest newspaper, set down what was to become the "party line" of Wyoming newspapers. In an editorial titled "Eaton Took the Logical Course", the author argued that to have done otherwise "would have been to tolerate violation of regulations that had previously been established by the coaching staff. These rules, which prohibit players from taking part in demonstrations, were known to the team members." The editorial noted that the black players knew BYU was on the schedule "and if they had any objection ... they should not have enrolled at Wyoming in the first place. Other schools more agreeable to their attitude could have used their talents." The publisher then suggested that "Bigotry is a two-way street, and if the blacks can accuse BYU of such an attitude they also should recognize that they themselves are not guiltless." The editorial concluded by saying the players' accusations of discrimination had no merit because the presence of 14 blacks on the team "was far larger in proportion than the black population of Wyoming has to the rest of the state."

In a response to the editor published October 28th, Thomas Connell of Lander said the Casper Star's stance was hypocritical. "Here we have the spectacle of our leading Wyoming daily paper, one which has heretofore cried loudly for freedom of speech, freedom of expression and all those other freedoms we prize so highly, denying these same rights to students who may wish to participate in athletics. You have implied that these students have willingly discarded their birth rights in seeking a place on the football team and therefore have no right to disobey a stupid rule which should never have been formulated in the first place."

In his editorial on October 21st, Dave Bonner, publisher of the Powell Tribune, was also moved by the claims that the players were warned about the rules. "It's that basic. They broke the rules. ... When they walked into Eaton's office in a group on Friday morning, all wearing black armbands, it was simply viewed as a defiant breach of discipline. ... [A]s the board of trustees affirmed in its support of Eaton's action, the matter of discipline is delegated to the coaching staff. ... Again, it's as simple as that."

The next day, the publisher of the Cody Enterprise wasted no time embracing Eaton's view of the source of the players' protest. The editorial began by asserting that the "suspension" of the 14 players "has caused a stir throughout the state not experienced we are sure since the first Wyoming sheepherder heard that women were going to get the vote 80-odd years ago. ...

"Eaton was made the patsy in what we think was a coldly calculated plan by so-called 'black power' groups to create a panel of martyrs and crack the university which has in the past remained relatively immune to the normal methods of protest by such groups." The editorial said these groups "under the guise of fighting for civil rights for minorities (and they are usually working for the Negro race) have created untold damage, loss of time, upset and riots throughout the country in a well coordinated and we think entirely too-radical an attempt to gain civil rights for the Negro. ... [Eaton] offered them many face-saving chances to back off but evidently they were ordered to become martyrs and too many people now believe they are. Football is non-political, non-racial, non-religious and non-denominational. It is merely a game. To use it as a whipping boy is illogical to the extreme and besides, we think it might infringe on our civil rights (which we are also entitled to)." [281]

Jack Nisselius, publisher of the Gillette News-Record, took a similar tack: "Coach Eaton had made his rules. He was not unfair in any way about them. His players knew the ground on

---

[281] If he had any understanding or empathy for the courageous battle for equality fought by African Americans for decades in the South, the editor might have understood that rejecting the Black Students Alliance's call to protest the LDS tenet could not possibly be "face-saving" for the players. Just the opposite.

which they would be right and where they would be wrong. And in the lingo of the west, 'He stood by his guns' and we are proud that he did. Wyoming university will be stronger because of it."[282] The editorial then praised Vice President Spiro Agnew's denunciation of what Agnew called the "senseless [Vietnam Moratorium] demonstration" organized by "hard core dissidents and professional anarchists." Agnew said the leaders were being encouraged by "an effete corps of impudent snobs who characterize themselves as intellectuals."[283] Nisselius said the Black 14 protest showed Wyoming can be reached by these outside influences.

Publisher Bob Peck of the Riverton Ranger, in an editorial on October 27th, declared that "Eaton's greatest moment came with his willingness to change the rule. This is the mark of a real man." But Peck didn't take the next logical step: wouldn't a "real man" put the players back on the team since the rule they violated had been withdrawn?

Melvin Baldwin, editor and publisher of Evanston's Uinta County Herald, proclaimed in an October 23rd editorial that it would be better to drop athletics altogether rather than giving in to the Black 14's "separate organization". He even used the loaded word "appeasement", which to the minds of the World War II generation meant only one thing: the appeasement of Hitler by Britain's Neville Chamberlain:

> Under Eaton the team is a unit; he allows no separate "clicks" and groups within this unit. When 14 players flaunted the rules, formed as a separate organization within the team and defied the coach, there was no alternative but to dismiss them. Now the racists and militants are grasping the opportunity to blow it up into a racial issue and undermine our state university. The student senate, without time to properly consider their action, fell into the plot, as did the small faculty senate groups. ...
>
> As for this writer: If it becomes a question of abandoning principles such as Coach Eaton personifies, or abandoning athletics altogether, lets do away with athletics. ... There is no room for compromise or appeasement. Peace on the campuses cannot be purchased cheaply.

Immediately below that editorial was a guest column titled "For Candor, Conservatism and Quieter Voices" from the president of the Southern States Industrial Council, in which the writer decried "the national tidal wave toward socialism, moral and fiscal bankruptcy. ... We're for the Constitution. That is, the Constitution as drawn by the Founding Fathers; as named by due process of law. We're for Justices of the U.S. Supreme Court being nominated by the President with the advice and consent of the Senate – not with the advice and consent of CORE, NAACP, AFL-CIO, or CBS." (CORE and NAACP were among the African American organizations protesting the dismissal of the UW black players).

The Star Valley Independent, in the heart of Wyoming Mormon country, put it this way in an editorial on October 23rd:

> Wyoming team members had been warned that if they wore black armbands into the game they would be dismissed from the team, as it had been announced policy

---

[282] 10/23/1969.

[283] AP, Denver Post, 10/20/1969.

that Coach Eaton would not tolerate participation of players in protest demonstrations of any kind. This was not a racial edict, but purely a matter of discipline. It was not aimed at blacks any more than whites.[284] ...

LDS Church members should find it gratifying that to date ... no criticism has been leveled at the church or at BYU in connection with the incident, except by the Black Student Alliance. It is apparent that most people of the state respect the church's right to its religious beliefs, as guaranteed by the U.S. Constitution.[285]

The editor said the incident was "instigated by a group whose purpose went far beyond **the minor religious issue** upon which it was allegedly based." (Emphasis added).[286]

The founder and former editor of the Jackson Hole Guide, in her column called "Riding the Range" on Oct. 23rd, managed to offend both the LDS church and Black 14 supporters. In a paragraph titled "NEVER SATISFIED", the 76-year-old said the fact that "more than a dozen [black] players were getting an education through athletic scholarships" proved "there is no discrimination" at UW. The coach warned them, she said, but they went ahead with "this silly gesture.... When will our black brothers realize that belligerence is not the way to acceptance as full citizens."

The former editor, who died just over a year later, also threw in this off-hand comment: "As is generally known the Mormons DO discriminate against the blacks as an "inferior race." This prompted a local Mormon to write a letter-to-the-editor which appeared a week later, saying: "Negroes are permitted to join our church, they are excluded from our Temples, but so are Catholics, and Jews and Protestants and many Mormons. Some call it discrimination, we call it the right to worship God according to the dictates of our own conscience."

The former editor made one final blast in her Oct. 30th column: "Now that everyone has chosen up sides on the black athletes at Laramie, we will say no more. Our football players seem to be doing okay without them. It has given the white boys a chance to show their stuff anyway."

---

[284] The editor ignored the fact that Eaton did not dismiss them for wearing armbands "into the game".

[285] Not so when that belief was polygamy. See the chapter titled "100 Years Earlier" at p. 230. The editor, like all the other Wyoming editors, failed to see that the student-athletes were not government officials denying Mormons their right to practice their religion. On the other hand, Eaton was a government official denying citizens their free speech rights.

[286] For an understanding of why the LDS belief could not and should not have been considered a minor issue by all right-thinking people, including Mormons themselves, see the "brown eyes, blue eyes" PBS documentary "A Class Divided" at http://www.pbs.org/wgbh/frontline/film/class-divided/. The documentary reunited an Iowa elementary teacher in 1984 with 50 of the students in her class in 1968, centering on what happened in her class immediately after the assassination of Martin Luther King. The teacher recalled that her experiment, in one day, turned "wonderful, thoughtful children into nasty, vicious, discriminating little third graders."

The response of Bernard Horton, editor of the Wyoming Eagle – the Democratic morning paper supposed to balance the right-wing evening paper – was just as obeisant to the football sacred cow as was the State Tribune. Horton, like most other Wyoming editors, placed onto the players the entire blame for the injury to the university and its football team, and accepted the idea that they are essentially second-class students on campus. Like the others, Horton ignored the constitutional guarantee of free speech. Like Judge Ewing Kerr would say two years later, Horton proclaimed that "If [Coach Eaton] had one racist bone in his body, there wouldn't have been 14 black students on his football team in the

first place," Horton wrote on 10/22/1969.[287] "We are pleased to note that [Eaton] has strong and growing support throughout the state. [The players] must have known Coach Eaton well enough to know that rules are rules, and they must apply to all the players." He urged the players to go to the coach and tell him "We made a mistake." Horton suggested that the fans "make next Saturday 'Lloyd Eaton Day' at Wyoming university."

The next day, Horton wrote that the dismissal of the players "was simply a matter of discipline. ... [A player] must expect to abide by the rules. In this instance, there is a rule against Wyoming players participating in student protests. The 14 players had a choice: Protest or play ball." Horton recognized, however, that the controversy "has spread far beyond" the UW campus and "if it isn't curbed could threaten the football program at the university. ... It is tragic because ... distortions, exaggerations and misunderstandings are tending to label Wyoming university as anti-black. That absolutely is not true. Wyoming and its university has never had a racial problem of importance."[288]

Finally, Horton observed that "It is not [Eaton's] job nor his responsibility to try to change Brigham Young university's policies..."

In his sports column in the Eagle on 10/21/1969, Larry Birleffi analyzed the situation this way: "There are a lot of forces at work to separate us in this country. One of the most effective ploys is that the 'establishment' is not 'sensitive' to the Black feeling. Oh, this will come up a hundred times on the University campus this week among faculty and student 'leaders'. To the Black Americans on the University of Wyoming teams, don't fall for this overworked hogwash."

---

[287] And if there had not been world-class African American players on UW's teams the previous three years there would not have been three straight conference championships and two bowl appearances. This fact very soon became obvious.

[288] Obviously, Horton, Kerr and probably 99.9% of Wyoming people knew nothing about the sordid side of the history of African Americans in the state. Prof. T. A. Larson's discussion of lynchings in his *History of Wyoming* first published in 1965 included only what appear to be white vigilantes against white criminals. But see "African American Lynchings in the Equality State" by Todd Guenther, *Annals of Wyoming*, Spring 2009, or "Discrimination in the 'Equality State': Black-White Relations in Wyoming History" by Reagan Joy Kaufman, *Annals of Wyoming*, Winter 2005. Guenther declared that on a per capita basis, Wyoming's lynch rate exceeded that in the southern states.

Thus, the essence of UW's and Eaton's and the Wyoming citizens' defense during the first week after the dismissals could be stated in this manner:

–It is okay for a state government employee to punish a citizen for exercising the constitutional right of free speech if you warn the citizen in advance, and

–It is okay for a state government employee to deny a minority citizen the constitutional right of free speech if you deny that right also to white citizens (Eaton claimed he prohibited some white players from participating in the Vietnam Moratorium march two days before the players were dismissed).

--The race of the players played no role in the dismissals because Eaton showed he had no prejudice against their race when he brought in black players to play on his football team. The fact that he couldn't win without them in his early years as UW head coach is irrelevant.

A VOICE OF REASON IN RIVERTON: STEVE MURDOCK

Ten of the Black 14 had grown up in urban areas from Massachusetts, Tennessee and Ohio to California. But from the governor on down, Wyoming officials and editors displayed a woeful lack of appreciation for the long civil rights struggle from which most of the 14 black players had emerged. The prevailing attitude seemed to be that the players were obliged to lock away their heritage -- and the struggle of their race -- and just play football in exchange for an education.

Surprisingly, one of the few voices writing in any Wyoming newspaper who brought some background to the discussion, and some concern for the players' futures, was the sports editor of the Riverton Ranger, Steve Murdock. He was a 56-year-old career journalist who had come to Wyoming from California only two months earlier.

A week prior to the Black 14 incident, Murdock produced an article for the Ranger about the Native American basketball players at the St. Stephen's Mission near Riverton, founded in 1884. But Murdock immediately saw the larger picture, more important than merely reciting the Eagles' two Class B state championships and 46 consecutive wins in the early '60s.[289] "Father Zummach [the Jesuit priest at the Mission] and Bill Strannigan [cousin of the UW coach -- this Bill coached St. Stephen's and Riverton High basketball teams for 18 years] live in hope of the day when an athlete comes off the Wind River Reservation and goes into the outside world to help give the lie to the horrible stereotype of the Indian that is still the shame of white America." The article spoke about two forms of integration: first, arranging for St. Stephen's teams to play outside the reservation and second, the incorporation of white players into the St. Stephen's lineup. They thought the second step would be difficult but discovered the Indian players liked the idea and "there were white kids who were eager to come to their school." This result, Zummach said, "Lifted up the whole place."

Culture shock in Riverton
On the Tuesday after the BYU game, Murdock's column noted the near unanimity of local opinion in favor of Coach Eaton. In listening to local people discussing the issue, Murdock said he had "to put my own feelings and opinions to the test of values that sometimes have been quite

---

[289] On April 3, 1961, Sports Illustrated carried a long article about sports helping the Jesuit fathers and Franciscan sisters at St. Stephen's to keep their Native American students in school. Much of the article was about Shannon Brown, the star basketball player who led the team to the Class B championships but then quit the team before his senior year. (This SI article is available on-line).

different than my own." He noted also that he had "heard a lot of anti-Negro remarks that would not – in all probability – have been made in the presence of a black person."

After pointing out that the dismissals were triggered by an authoritarian rule of the coach rather than the religion issue, Murdock wrote:

> Without attempting to push a point of view, I would simply urge people to ask themselves whether the young men involved were not motivated rather strongly by principle? There may not be agreement with such motivation, but there should be respect for it.

In his "Steve's Soliloquy" column on Wednesday, Murdock noted the irony in the Cowboys facing off against San Jose State -- his alma mater -- the upcoming weekend in Laramie. "San Jose State has been through the agony of the racial crisis," he wrote, "and it's worked its way to some sort of a solution," including the hiring of a black assistant athletic director. Murdock recalled that the black players on San Jose State's 1968 team refused to play in their game against BYU. "They feel the Mormon religion demeans black people. This point may be open to debate, but there can be no doubt but what this is the feeling of many black people."

Even earlier, Murdock wrote, Dr. Harry Edwards, a former SJS discus thrower and faculty member, started the controversial Olympic boycott idea at SJS in 1967. SJS sprinters Tommie Smith and John Carlos were among the black athletes sympathetic to that proposal. But they eventually participated in the 1968 Mexico City Olympics. Smith set a world record in the 200 meter sprint and Carlos finished third. At the medal ceremony they bowed their heads and raised black-gloved fists. They were immediately suspended from the team.

In contrast to UW and the Black 14, Murdock wrote, SJS did not "take absolute, inflexible, authoritarian positions" on the issue.

Murdock's next mention of the Black 14 incident came in his column on November 13 in which he noted that "some people in the stands at the state high school football championship game in Casper last Saturday were close to tears as their transistor radios told them" UW was losing its second straight conference game. "Arizona State and Utah had proved on successive Saturdays what Coach Lloyd Eaton probably had known all along – that he could not hope to remain undefeated without the 14 black players...." Murdock said that the wins over BYU and SJS had created "some illusions" and that he heard several men saying "we can do it without them." But he said he had also heard "an old man in the stands at Casper say, 'I guess they made a mistake in getting rid of those colored fellows. They had the push.'"

Murdock said it was now clear: "a less precipitous action might have avoided the kind of confrontation that has occurred."

In his column of December 15, 1969, Murdock reported he had just returned from a trip to New York City "for personal reasons." As it turned out, he had gone for a job interview, in part because some people in Riverton, including two members of the right-wing John Birch Society, were making his presence there very difficult.

"Steve's Soliloquy" of December 18th related that someone in the stands at Riverton High had shouted "Miss it, blackie!" when Casper Natrona's African American 6-8 center Ken Morgan stepped to the foul line. Murdock was encouraged, however, because a Riverton varsity football player sitting near him "turned around and shouted at the offender, with all the authority to which his bulk and status entitled him, 'Hey you! Knock that stuff off!.'" Murdock then reported:

I listened to a great many stupid and racially prejudiced remarks during the suspension furor [at UW]. Often I found myself biting my tongue. I didn't want to embarrass the paper by expressing my own view. So it was with a great deal of joy that I heard a young man – obviously moved by a sense of decency and fair play – put down a kind of racist mouthing that in this day and age can be characterized only as stupid.

In an end-of-decade column appearing on Christmas Eve, Murdock referred to a magazine article saying many younger people were losing interest in the traditional sports, perhaps spurred by anti-establishment feelings as the Vietnam War raged on. Murdock noted that among the dictionary definitions of "discipline" was the concept of "self-control ... which suggests authoritarians themselves must be controlled in the manner in which they impose discipline if they are going to earn the respect of those upon whom they impose it."

On January 19, 1970, in one of his last columns for the Ranger, Murdock related a story that again showed the contrast between his consciousness about race and the lack of it among many Wyoming residents. He related that while driving in Riverton he had heard a radio announcer refer to Natrona's Ken Morgan as a "Negro boy."

"I winced," Murdock said, noting that the phone would have rung off the hook if the station had been located in a larger city. Although the announcer was "trying to be complimentary", Murdock acknowledged, "[I]n this day and age you don't go around calling black men boys – even if they are still in their teens. The reason is that for scores of years in the South the term 'boy' was employed as a calculated insult by whites. ... Black men with white hair heard themselves called boy."

His column two days later revealed Murdock, a self-described 'train buff', was in Billings to take a train to NYC.

On January 22, 1970, Ranger publisher Bob Peck noted that Murdock had taken a better-paying job as editor of the monthly magazine of a NYC Hospital Union. That opportunity, Peck said, arose partly because Murdock had written a feature article for *The Nation* magazine titled "The Real World Comes to Wyoming."

Finally, on the 26th, Murdock's last column appeared on the Ranger's sports page, concluding this way:

And so we come to the end of the space and to the end of our time. The train is near the Illinois line. The sun is bright, the world is white with new snow – and my memories of my time in Riverton are bright, too. Good luck all.

Steve Murdock's Journey to Riverton

Murdock was born in 1913 in Alameda, Calif. In 1934 he was a member of the San Jose State mile relay team competing in the West Coast Relays at Fresno. On June 5, Murdock and SJS's other sprinters raced Skip-Jack, a greyhound, over 100 yards. Although the Spartans were given a 30-yard head start, Skip-Jack beat Murdock and all but one of his teammates.

The next year Murdock was sports editor of the San Jose State College Daily, The Spartan.

Steve was a reporter for the San Jose Mercury Herald from 1936-1943 and served a term as president of the San Jose Newspaper Guild. In 1940, his profile of the San Jose city manager was syndicated across the country.

In 1943 he was re-elected as secretary of the C.I.O. Labor Council in San Jose and then became assistant legislative director of the California Council. In 1944 he was a member of the county Democratic Party's executive committee.

A Jan. 13, 1951, article in the Pittsburgh Courier, an African American newspaper published from 1907 until 1966, reported that Steve Murdock was one of three San Francisco authors writing a life history of black San Quentin death row inmate Wesley Robert Wells, according to the Civil Rights Congress. Wells at one point had served the most time of any inmate in the California penal system. Originally convicted at age 19 and sentenced to prison, he later was sentenced to death for throwing a cuspidor at a prison guard. Efforts to forestall that fate drew worldwide publicity. He was the only man in California history sentenced to die as a result of a criminal prosecution that didn't involve a death. That sentence was commuted to life by the California governor in 1954 and 20 years later Wells was released, two years before he died.

In 1953 Murdock married Bay Area artist and civil rights activist Phyllis deLappe and the couple became close friends of the famous author of *The American Way of Death*, Jessica Mitford. They were divorced in 1969.

Following his brief Wyoming experience, Murdock was back in the Bay Area in 1973, working as editor of the International Longshoremen's and Warehousemen's Union's newspaper The Dispatcher.

Three years later, Murdock and second wife Evelyn were living in Ashland, Ore., where he was active in Oregonians For Nuclear Safeguards. He died in 1976. Bob Peck published a memoir in the Ranger, saying Murdock had shown "unusual perception and wit" in his work in Riverton.

Murdock's remarkable *The Nation* article

The Black 14 disaster in Laramie, and an incident with a Riverton teacher, also from California, spurred Steve Murdock to submit an article titled "The Real World Comes to Wyoming" to the prominent national publication *The Nation*. Published as a featured item in the November 17, 1969, issue, Murdock's article first noted that even in conservative Riverton, a town of fewer than 7,000 people, forty young protesters had marched with candles and peace symbols in support of the Vietnam Moratorium demonstration Oct. 15th. And in the "little lumber, hunting and fishing village of Dubois (pop. 800), ... Mayor Arden Coad, a service station operator, caused a statewide furor" by supporting the Vietnam Moratorium. "If [John Lindsay] the mayor of the nation's largest city can back it, the mayor of one of the smallest cities can too," Coad was quoted as saying. One of the mayor's sons at the time was serving in the Army in Germany. "I'm not a pacifist," Coad said, according to Murdock's article, "'I'd give anything to this country, but this Vietnam War has no meaning.' He said he couldn't understand how educated people can pay income taxes to, in effect, have their sons killed."[290]

In Riverton, some high school students and two teachers wore black arm bands to school. Even Bob Peck, the Ranger's publisher, wrote that "Nixon is in the process of getting the United States out of a war, which, in retrospect, most people realize now, we should never have been in. We're witnessing today a reverse transmission of knowledge, from the young to the old."

---

[290] Another feature in that issue of *The Nation* was titled "Integration by Evasion" by two black Princeton graduates. Robert Engs and John B. Williams looked back to the early Sixties "when a handful of blacks like ourselves became anomalies on lily-white campuses. ... White universities, like many other institutions in American society, have been trapped into mistaking changes in appearance for changes in substance...."

Suzanne Hawley Hunsucker's Riverton High "Love Festival"

Murdock's *The Nation* article also discussed the furor a planned "love festival" caused in Riverton. In the immediate wake of the Black 14 incident, Riverton High English and journalism teacher Suzanne Hunsucker -- one of the teachers who marched in the Moratorium protest there -- planned an "Autumn Love Festival" for her students on Oct. 23-24. Wire service articles about the uproar over the festival appeared in newspapers from coast to coast. On October 28, 1969, an AP article in the Billings Gazette quoted Hunsucker as saying her festival was about "love of people, love of animals, love of country, all kinds of love". The students were to discuss literature and present original skits and favorite foods.[291]

But Murdock's article reported that "alarmed school authorities, egged on by parents, ordered her to take the exhibits down." The 24-year-old Phi Beta Kappa from the University of Southern California refused, and then the school board asked her to resign, which she also refused. She later explained that "my armor was up and my Irish blood was defending the deeper principles of academic freedom and educational relevance that I felt were the key issues at stake." Hunsucker was removed from classroom teaching and assigned to correcting papers. School board member Tom Hill accused her of teaching the sexual aspect of love.[292]

At a school board meeting Oct. 27th, Hill said "there are rules and regulations which teachers have to submit to. We can't have 150 teachers each going their own way without uniformity." The Ranger reported, however, that "the majority of the speakers (about evenly divided between adults and students) spoke in Mrs. Hunsucker's behalf."

Hunsucker was still living in Riverton until early 1973 and must have been involved in efforts to obtain the Wyoming Legislature's ratification of the Equal Rights Amendment. She was quoted in a front page article in the Los Angeles Times on March 3rd under a sub-headline saying "Wyoming Women Want It to Stay a Man's State." Hunsucker said, "Wyoming women are charming and hospitable, but basically uninvolved and unsympathetic with their national sisters who are pushing for a ticket to equality." The chairman of the Wyoming Senate committee which handled the bill said the mail, mainly from women, was overwhelmingly against passage. He said it was not necessary to vote on it because "our women have all the rights ever hoped for." UW history professor T. A. "Al" Larson told the *Times* the only reason the Legislature went along with the amendment "was because of our fame as the Equality State."

Secretary of State Thyra Thomson -- the highest ranking woman state official in the country -- was pictured in the article and supported the amendment. "I'm in favor of women having equal opportunity, not being locked in at the lower end of the pay scales," she said.

SUZANNE HUNSUCKER

From 1973-75, Ms. Hunsucker was a reporter for the Fort Collins *Coloradoan*, authoring a music and arts column titled "Foothills Footlights," and then she worked for a Fort Collins advertising firm. On May 19, 1975 the LA Times published an op-ed she had submitted titled "A Mellowing Radical Wonders at the Quiet." This brought her a trip to

---

[291] AP report in Billings Gazette 10/28/1969 and UPI report in Statesville, NC Record, 10/30/1969.

[292] AP report in Arizona Republic 10/29/1969.

New York and an appearance on an NBC late-night show.[293]

Her column in the *Times* asked "What happened to my boxes of dove buttons and those great candlelight peace marches I staged in Wyoming? Ah, remember me, Wyoming? Remember the crazy lady from Los Angeles who infiltrated your wide, open spaces? Wasn't I a treat?"

On March 2, 1976, the *Coloradoan* published a letter-to-the-sports-editor from her, encouraging CSU basketball fans to emit more positive vibes to the players and show more class to everyone. "It's only a game. It should be fun. It should make people feel good. Appreciated. Loved a little. ... If you need to yell negative garbage at somebody, stay home and scream at the TV."

The newspaper reported on March 10, 1978, that a local group had made a movie called "Cocky", a take-off on the Stallone film "Rocky", written and directed by Suzanne Hawley, who also played one of the leading roles. Other actors included Suzanne's father Pat Hawley, who was a bit part actor in Hollywood, and her daughter Kirsten Hunsucker.

1969-70 - ENGLISH PROFESSOR KENTON CRAVEN EXITS UW

Craven risks his academic career

Although the young English professor was well-known on campus as an opponent of the Vietnam War, Ken Craven received national attention after he announced at the all-faculty meeting on the day after the BYU game that he would resign if the Black 14 were not reinstated. Bernie Bever of English and John Lent of Journalism joined him in making that pledge (and in resigning at the end of their contracts).

"The idea of not allowing black athletes their constitutional rights is morally repugnant," Craven told the faculty meeting. The university should not be made "a fief of the athletic department," he added.

"I could not tolerate an association with an institution that permits such injustices to exist," Craven said in an AP article printed widely, such as in the Pocatello, Idaho, State Journal on December 28th. He predicted the Black 14 incident would hinder faculty recruitment for at least ten years.

Ken Perry, an assistant professor of geology, also attracted attention. Perry said he felt the university should de-emphasize "big time sports" and devote more money to education. "It's up to the people of Wyoming to decide whether they want to create a football team they can enjoy four weekends each year, or whether they want to turn their attention to their sons and daughters who must attend this university. At the present time I feel their sons and daughters are being shorted out of the best possible education because too much time and effort is being channeled into big time athletics," Perry said. [294]

A group of 100 graduate students and instructors met to plan protests of the dismissals. Some wanted to teach for free and give their pay to the athletes. Others wanted to resign.[295]

The widespread publicity not only lit up the home phone and mailbox of Ken Craven the English professor, it also spurred "Kassis Ken Craven" into action again. This time he placed a

---

[293] *Coloradoan*, 5/29/1975.

[294] AP report, top story in Riverton Ranger 10/20/1969.

[295] BI, Oct. 23, 1969.

225

large ad with a photo of himself in the Boomerang on October 24th. The text said: "Citizens of Laramie: Do you know that there are two Ken Cravens in Laramie? People are confusing me with Professor Ken Craven of the University. I AM NOT HIM! I am the Ken Craven who is part owner and manager of Kassis. I was born and reared in Laramie, the son of Tom and Edna Craven. I am married to the former Linda Woody and the father of four children, Debra, Tommy, Shelly and John.

"Please, do not confuse me with the other Ken Craven. I do not share his views."

Casper football zealots renege on moving expenses pledge

In late 1969, Craven, 31, announced he would resign at the end of his one-year contract in May. Two other English profs, Bernard Bever and Ronald Gaskill, also resigned. The headline in "Free Lunch", a small alternative newspaper that sprang to life that fall, was "Quoth the Craven: Nevermore." [296] Craven said he was accepting the Casper Quarterback Club's offer to pay his moving expenses. Max Pedon, president of the club, then denied such an offer had been made.

In a speech to the Casper Rotary Club in mid-December, E. Gerald Meyer, Dean of Arts and Sciences, defended Craven. He said evaluations from both undergraduate and graduate students showed Craven to be one of the best professors on campus. Meyer said the lack of violence at any UW protests was "partly due to Craven. He is committed to the ideas of pacifism and has conducted himself peacefully."

An AP article appeared in the Pocatello Journal on New Year's Day of 1970 bearing the headline: "Savant Slates Casper Talk." It said Craven had accepted an invitation from Casper teacher Donn Driscoll to tell his side of the controversy over his moving expenses. When he received a scan of this article in 2013, Craven replied: "I remember this well! Delightful audience! Good old Bob Lange (RIP) was behind it. First and only time I have been called a savant!"

When the moving expenses issue didn't die out, the Casper football boosters found a way to weasel out of their pronouncements from the previous October. "They sent a moving van to my house on a Saturday morning with a couple months remaining on my contract," Craven said. "I asked the driver what was up and he said he had been paid to load all of our furniture, take it to the Colorado state line and dump it."

Craven remembers his days at UW this way: "My best friends were my student Bob Carlson, who later became one of the founders of Wyoming Catholic College; Bob Lange, owner of Lange's Book Shop in Casper; Dr. John Smith (English Department) at UW, who resigned his commission as a Captain in the U.S. Marine Corps to protest the war; and Bernie Bever (also in the English Department), with whom I later worked as a social worker in Kentucky."

---

[296] Whether he actually viewed any of the very few issues of Free Lunch, or not, that little paper certainly stuck in the craw of S. J. Crawshaw, editor of the Wyoming Rural Electric News in Casper. In a January 1970 editorial, Crawshaw ripped into Free Lunch, saying it was produced by "smug, over-indulged neophytes who have never scraped for a penny" and "by a thankfully small group of extremists who hardly agree with anything. FREE LUNCH ... evokes a discussion of our children's new-found pastime of telling their elders how to run the world. ... Those kids are down-right arrogant in their criticism of a society which ... has provided them with more food, clothing, luxuries, and playthings than has ever before been enjoyed by any generation of youngsters. ... [Their elders have given them] too much of the wrong kind of freedom ... the kind of license provided by lack of discipline, restraint, and values properly taught. Theirs is the arrogance of abundance and indulgence." The editorial does not mention the Vietnam War. In an article on p. 4, the editor downplayed the significance of the UW chapter of the American Association of University Professors' resolution calling for reinstatement of the Black 14. The article wrongly says the controversy arose from "the refusal of 14 Negro football players to play against BYU last fall."

On December 5, 1969, the Branding Iron carried a remarkably erudite letter-to-the-editor from Harold Bloomenthal, who taught corporations and investment securities law at the UW College of Law. Bloomenthal said he had never met Craven and only knew of him from his protest speech in the all-faculty meeting on October 19th, but he expressed regret at Craven's departure. He noted that Craven's student ratings were among the highest at UW. "I wonder if the Quarterbacks around the state who have offered to pay his moving expenses have considered how difficult it is to find, recruit and retain exceptional young teachers," he wrote, noting that during the previous year only five Wyoming residents were on the football team but many more residents studied under Craven. (The roster in the BYU game program shows that Wyoming's 62 varsity football players came to Laramie from 24 states, nearly half the Union).

Bloomenthal said that much of the state's antagonism toward Craven arose from his anti-war activities. "If we refuse to inquire as to how we got involved in Vietnam ..., but prefer to permit the Johnson-Rusk-McGee-Nixon-Agnew axis to do our thinking for us, we may never learn that we irresponsibly committed and dissipated our world power and prestige...."

Two UW students at the time, Frank Nelson and Jane Varineau, recalled in an interview many years later that they thought it was a tragedy UW was losing Craven. Nelson said Craven "was partial to Tolstoi and Dostoyevski, and had us keep a journal, which was unusual at that time." Varineau, who later married Nelson, said her honors seminar with Craven "was a great class."

1970: End of tenure track for Craven

Craven never again obtained a tenure track teaching position. All of his teaching jobs were adjunct or part-time. After UW he next taught for one year at Muskingum College at New Concord, Ohio, east of Columbus. Because of the stress involved with taking a leading role in opposition to the Vietnam War and the Black 14 at UW, his marriage broke up during the year in Ohio.

He spent a semester as associate professor at Universidad Inter Americana at San Juan, Puerto Rico, before working for four years as a lecturer in philosophy at the University of Louisville and at three community colleges in Louisville. This was followed by two years as an English prof at Wartburg College in Waverly, Iowa, one year at West Virginia University, a year teaching literary criticism at Kuwait University, two years at Fairmont State University in Fairmont, W.V., and five years teaching business communications at Sultan Qaboos University in Oman.

As the new millennium dawned, Craven taught at Corpus Christi, Texas, and at Tennessee Tech in Cookeville, Tenn.

In 2015 Kampus Ken Craven lived in Sparta, Tenn., reading G. K. Chesterton and advancing a program he started to provide books and counseling to prisoners called "Desert Prison Ministry". Kassis Ken was living in Colorado.

IRENE KETTUNEN AND FRANK SCHUBERT
Irene Kettunen, in her second year as documents librarian at UW's Coe Library in fall, 1969, wrote letters supporting the black football players to several newspapers in Wyoming, noting that allowing the coach to ignore the Constitution's guarantee of free speech essentially nullified the efforts spent in schools "instilling in our children what it means to be an American citizen." Irene grew up in Minnesota and earned a degree in library science in 1968 at the University of Denver.

In a 2016 phone interview from her home in northern Virginia, Irene said "one of my first customers" at UW was a history graduate student from D.C. named Frank "Mick" Schubert who was working with his major professor Roger Daniels on a thesis about the Buffalo Soldiers (African Americans) in Wyoming. Mick Schubert had served in Vietnam and obtained a degree from historically-black Howard University in D.C. Because universities at that time did not want photos to accompany applications and did not ask about race in their hiring processes, so as to avoid allegations of racial prejudice, Irene said, UW would not have known her future husband's race. Mick's application to UW was accepted. "They thought I was black. I fit the profile of a conservative, respectable black person," he said in a 2016 interview. So when Mick arrived on the scene, UW's history department was taken aback to find he was white. "T. A. Larson[297] told me the department had expected they had hired an African American but that the hiring decision was not based on that factor," Mick said.

Irene and Mick married during their time at UW and Mick, along with Mike Robinson, Bill Epstein, Doug Nelson, Gordon Olson, Phil Eidsvog (history and American Studies grad students) and Caleb Sanborn (law) formed a committee that protested the dismissal of the 14 players. Mick went on to obtain a Ph.D. at Toledo in 1977 and worked as a historian in the Department of Defense for 26 years. Irene retired from the Library of Congress. The UW American Heritage Center houses her Irene Schubert Black 14 collection. The Schuberts are the authors of *On the Trail of the Buffalo Soldier II* (Lanham, MD: Scarecrow Press, 2004), giving individual details on the thousands of African American men who served in the Army between the Civil War and World War I.

Frank "Mick" and Irene Kettunen Schubert in Hungary-2018

Doug Nelson's master's thesis was titled "Heart Mountain: The History of an American Concentration Camp", went on to become the president and CEO of the Annie E. Casey Foundation, a major contributor to PBS as part of its programs to advance racial equality and to

---

[297] Larson is remembered as a legendary UW history department head and author of a definitive history of Wyoming, who later served for several terms as a Democratic representative in the Legislature. He was among the professors who signed a strong resolution protesting the Black 14 dismissals.

develop "a brighter future for children at risk of poor educational, economic, social and health outcomes." He served 20 years in that role, and in 2016 Nelson was honored by Living Cities for his work on behalf of children.

Other letters and opinions
Irene Schubert's letters brought some irate rebuttals, such as one from Gerry Seawright in Worland who saw no distinction between a government employee restricting the free speech rights of students and a group of students in civilian clothes making a silent protest against a policy of a church which they deemed racist:

> Granted, the black people have been mistreated and they have every right to try and correct these wrongs, but in fighting for their civil rights, do they have the right to demonstrate against another Constitutional right? While you [Schubert] were reading the Amendments, why didn't you read the [first part of the] 1st Amendment? ... The Black Alliance seems to be degrading the very Amendment that they keep quoting. ... [Coach Eaton] has every right to set any rule for his athletic department that he feels will benefit his team. It's everyone's right to drink or smoke too, but most athletic departments have rules against doing so and would suspend any player caught doing either. [298]

Another Big Horn Basin resident, a UW education grad who was in his first year of teaching civics at Greybull, showed that he had read the entire First Amendment. Donald Amend Jr. sent letters to the Worland and Casper newspapers praising Schubert's stand, saying "Mr. Eaton's rule was unconstitutional and un-American." Identifying himself as "An ex-Cowboy fan(atic)", Amend synthesized in one sentence the flaw in the reasoning the federal judges later used to justify Eaton's action. "May I say that there is an awful lot of difference between protesting the policies of the Mormon church and forbidding the practice of the Mormon religion," Amend wrote. "I don't agree with everything the athletes had to say, but they certainly had the right to speak their minds." Amend concluded his letter by urging "the firing of the coach and the delay of stadium expansion."[299]

In a 2016 interview by phone to Amend in Powell, the retired teacher said he has always been astounded by the 1969 incident because "it showed that the football coach essentially ran the University."

The Worland newspaper on October 28, 1969, carried a letter from UW students Pat Rillihan of Worland and Larry Walker of Ten Sleep, who noted that the Black 14 incident had been featured on the Huntley-Brinkley Report on NBC October 22nd. "We plead with you," the students wrote, "to look at the solution of this problem in the light of 'how it will reflect on the University of Wyoming as an institution of higher learning' not 'will Wyo. make the Sugar Bowl in 1970.'"

Betty Rider Bass, editor of the Douglas Budget, wrote that the athletes essentially waived any concern about racism at BYU when they signed contracts to play football at UW. [300] "The

---

[298] Northern Wyoming Daily News, October 25, 1969.

[299] It took the disastrous 1970 season before Eaton was fired, but stadium expansion was not slowed.

[300] Several of the Black 14 were minors under the law and could not sign a legally-binding contract.

entire issue involves discipline - not constitutional rights, " Rider said. James Bruner, a UW student, responded with a letter-to-the-editor saying "the thing that is relevant and that you don't seem to understand is the fact that the very purpose of a university is threatened by the existence and enforcement of regulations such as the one the athletes disobeyed. ... A university should be a place where minds, sheltered up to this point from reality, are exposed to the processes of free thought and free speech. ... If you want to turn out individuals who are aware and productive in a modern humanistic society then you have to have concerned professors teaching them."

A first-blush reader of a letter to the Boomerang by engineering grad student Wm. Daley would have thought the Black 14 had gone crazy and burned down the campus. "For the future of this country, all must follow sane and legal means of expressing our opinions and working for the changes we espouse," he wrote.[301] In the same issue, two 1950 grads said the coach's action "would have excited little comment and no publicity if those players involved had not been colored."

UW education student Andrew David Louis, a veteran who was an outspoken supporter of the Vietnam war on campus and went on to a career in law enforcement in Colorado, said Eaton's and the Board's dismissal of the players "was an act of collective courage." In another example of "famous last words", Louis said "the worth of these individuals as football players is presently in grave question as in spite of their absence, the football team thundered over BYU." Calling them the "14 agents provocateurs" engaged in a "childish display of pique", Louis said they had "demonstrated the very worst of professional athletic conduct by blatantly issuing a deep offense to our WAC friends at BYU." Louis also implied that the Black 14 had committed some horrible destructive act. "Political activism," he said, "belongs in meeting halls or on the public streets-- with a proper parade permit in hand and Ghandi's non-violent ethic firmly entrenched in the mentality." (Had Louis already forgotten that the whole disaster resulted from a coach's rule forbidding any players from participating in such a demonstration?)

Don Sessions, another 1950 graduate living in Colorado, joined the chorus of voices who apparently felt that the Bill of Rights in the U.S. Constitution had been repealed. In his letter, Sessions said "laws, rules and policies are made to follow – not to break and tear down. ... policies and rules are for everyone to follow." In a letter to the Casper Star on Oct. 20th, Edna Kukura of Evansville asked the black players "If you do not want to be discriminated against because of your skin color, why do you think you should be favored because of it?"

1869: RELIGIOUS RIGHTS 100 YEARS EARLIER: POLYGAMY

In the aftermath of the Black 14 episode, many of the defenders of the coach's and trustees' action asserted that the players' protest of Mormon beliefs violated the First Amendment's establishment of religion clause. Religion was off limits, they argued, when exercising free speech rights under the other clause in that amendment. It is ironic, therefore, that exactly a century earlier the non-Mormon American population and many of their leaders in Washington and Wyoming were engaged in a battle to eliminate the Mormon religion's embrace of the practice of polygamy. "American society spoke through the pulpit and the press demanding legislative action against what it defined as licentious, immoral, and degrading."[302] Another study of that era concluded that "in late 1869, Congress began debate on a comprehensive anti-

---

[301] Boomerang 10/22/1969.

[302] Larson, Gustive O., *The "Americanization" of Utah for Statehood*, Huntington Library, 1971, p. 52.

230

polygamy bill that would have put real teeth in the powers of federal officials to prosecute polygamists."[303]

At the same time the Mormons were being regularly castigated by Wyoming's main newspaper. In January, 1869, Cheyenne's *Wyoming Weekly Leader,* said the polygamy doctrine "teaches the violation of both moral and civil law and the laws of nature." On January 15th, the paper called polygamy a "fanatical doctrine." On July 14, the *Evening Leader* asked President Grant to appoint "a tried and gallant Christian soldier over Utah" so that "the lecherous Brigham's rule will be of brief duration." The practice of polygamy was "a horrid crime" practiced by "Brigham Young and his beastly followers", the *Wyoming Tribune* declared on Jan. 29, 1870.

On August 7th, the *Leader* bemoaned the passage through Cheyenne of five car loads of Swedish immigrants who had converted and were headed toward Salt Lake to "the Mormon church, with its heathenish curse of polygamy."

The 1869 Republican Party of Wyoming platform, printed in the August 28th issue, included this provision: "That the worse than barbarous practice of polygamy in the Territory of Utah should immediately be suppressed and the [federally-appointed] officers of that Territory sustained in the discharge of their whole duty by the power of the Government if necessary."

Mormons were arguing that the efforts of Congress, the president and vice-president and thousands of American citizens to enforce federal laws against polygamy in the Territory of Utah were in violation of the freedom of religion clause of the First Amendment. On October 20, 1869, a defender of the Mormon religion named John Taylor contended that the revelation allowing the practice of polygamy "is one of the most vital parts of our religious faith; it emanated from God and cannot be legislated away." At that time, with slavery recently abolished by the Civil War, government officials and activists from the established religions were blasting the Mormon religion, calling polygamy and slavery "the twin relics of barbarism." U.S. Vice-President Schuyler Colfax told a large audience in Salt Lake City in October, 1869, that "I do not concede that the institution you have established here, and which is condemned by the law, is a question of religion."[304]

When Indiana congressman George Washington Julian introduced a bill to grant women in Utah the right to vote, the editor of the *Leader* in Cheyenne argued that Julian was naive to think that if Utah women could vote they would abolish polygamy themselves. "Does Mr. Julian really fancy, that while the male Mormons can compel women to live in a state of barbarity, they cannot also compel them to vote for it?"

Statehood for Utah Territory was blocked for three decades. "The institution of polygamy, and the temporal power of the Church which insured its survival, became the focal points of attack in the federal crusade to 'Americanize' the Mormon community in preparation" for statehood.[305] Finally, in September, 1890, LDS President Wilford Woodruff, "after praying to the Lord and feeling inspired" and having conferred with his counselors and the Twelve Apostles, issued a "Manifesto" saying: "I publicly declare that my advice to the Latter-day Saints is to refrain from contracting any marriage forbidden by the laws of the land."[306] Although Utah's

---

[303] Gordon, Sarah Barringer, "The Liberty of Self-Degradation, Polygamy, Woman Suffrage and Consent," *Journal of American History*, Dec. 1996, p. 826.

[304] *Id.* pp. 62-63.

[305] *Id.* at 59.

[306] *Id.* at 263-4.

population was well over three times that of Wyoming when Wyoming became a state in 1890, Utah was not admitted until 1896.

1969-70: DESCENT INTO OBLIVION

After six games in 1969, Wyoming's football team was still unbeaten and leading the country in rushing defense. Many fans were convinced the Cowboys could continue their winning ways without the black players. The national polls showed little concern about Wyoming's chances. In the sportswriters and broadcasters' AP poll Wyoming moved up one spot to #15 and in the coaches' UPI ranking Wyoming fell one spot to #13.

But the Cowboys lost their last four games of the 1969 season by lop-sided scores -- while protests against Eaton's action -- as well as the LDS tenet -- followed them on the road.

The victory over San Jose State -- Wyoming's 22nd straight victory at home -- made the Eaton boosters very happy, but it brought an end to the home schedule. Very soon, the die-hard Wyoming fans who cheered the airplane banner and wore Eaton arm bands would be wishing they had directed their energies toward achieving an immediate and enlightened resolution of the situation Eaton created on the morning of October 17th, such as recognizing that even if the players violated Eaton's unconstitutional rule, their innocuous "offense" did not deserve the equivalent of a "football death penalty". In hindsight, it became indisputable that Eaton and Gov. Hathaway and the Trustees and Pres. Carlson had not only acted inhumanely in dismissing out of hand those 14 young men's lives and dreams, they also had set the stage for the complete collapse of the UW football program, the sad demise of a remarkable coaching career and a long period of very unfavorable publicity for the state and its only four-year university. Very soon, the chickens came home to roost, and Eaton defenders became as scarce as those hens' teeth.[307]

After losing to Arizona on Nov. 1 by a 30-14 score, Eaton was asked by an Arizona Republic writer whether the loss of the 14 black athletes hurt Wyoming's speed, which must have seemed like deja vu to October, 1964 (see p. 66). Unlike in 1964, however, Eaton was not comfortable with the subject. "We won't even discuss that. It's just like we graduated 14 players. We have to make do with what we have." He then made the mistake of telling the reporter: "I think we'll defeat Utah next week. Then we'll have a wide open race for sure."

On Nov. 8th at Salt Lake City, Wyoming's tired runners lost four fumbles and allowed a 97-yard interception return in a 34-10 loss to Utah. The Cowboys brought in recently-activated student manager SDU Upton to spell Frosty Franklin at running back in the 4th quarter.[308] In post-game comments, Eaton said, "We fumbled only twice in our first three ball games, but now that some of the players are performing without rest we've been hit with fumbles at inopportune times."

A report in the Daily Utah Chronicle on Nov. 10 said "Wyoming was definitely hurt by the lack of running backs. ... The 5,000 Wyoming fans who drove to the game ended their trip by shouting 'We love Eaton' in unison. Many bumper stickers were seen on Wyoming cars which said 'We Support Coach Lloyd Eaton.'"

---

[307] In a Star Valley Independent article printed October 30, 1969, the Black 14's Detroit attorney William Waterman was quoted as saying that Eaton had made a grievous error and that his friends and counselors had compounded the tragedy by applauding Eaton. Waterman said Wyoming could not be a football power and continue its attitude of isolationism.

[308] Casper Star Tribune 11/9/1969.

The next week, high school star Lee Thompson of Newcastle, who dropped football at UW after his freshman year and became a cheerleader, rejoined the Wyoming football squad as long-snapper after an injury to the first-team center.[309] Although Wyoming was an 18-point favorite and UNM was riddled by injuries, on Nov. 15 the New Mexico Lobos ended their string of 25 straight conference losses by defeating the Cowboys 24-12.

Two protests against UW occurred in conjunction with Wyoming's game at Albuquerque. On the day before the game, some of the New Mexico African American players and other students protested the dismissal of the Black 14. Lobo linebacker Houston Ross prophetically said, "Coach Eaton violated their basic constitutional rights of freedom of speech. This man has made a big blunder." The players read a letter they had sent to Eaton which said in part, "It appears you have forgotten your job is to condition bodies – not to control minds." Fullback Sam Scarber said he played with one of the Fourteen at Northeast Junior College in Sterling, Colo. "I played with their split-end Ron Hill, and I know he wouldn't do anything he did not think was right," Scarber said.[310]

Just before the game itself, numerous black and white students walked onto the field. Following the game, and apparently having the view that the purpose of the demonstrations was to fire up the football team, UNM coach Rudy Feldman said the demonstrations "in no way assisted us to play well" and had "contributed to a lack of poise among our players who made needless mistakes and had continuous penalties."

This provoked black students to release a statement through the UNM Afro-cultural Center charging that Feldman "and other coaches like him are so self-centered with a football game that they forgot about black people's human rights and dignities." The statement from the black students pointed out that all of UNM's touchdowns in the game were scored by black players, and said the reason for the protests was that "the team we were playing was Wyoming and Coach Eaton dismissed the 14 black athletes because they were expressing freedom of speech against a racist university, BYU."

In his last UW Branding Iron sports column published Nov. 21st, David Blevins of Powell called on "all the students and citizens of Wyoming to insure that no man is deprived of an education at Wyoming because of the ideal he holds. ... The time to start planning and helping the 14 players continue their college education starts now."[311]

The 1969 season came to a horrific end at Houston the next day when the University of Houston Cougars beat Wyoming 41-14. The win sealed for UH an invitation to a major bowl for the first time in the school's history. (Not counting the 1951 Salad Bowl in which Houston defeated Dayton). Houston racked up 230 rushing yards against a UW defense that led the NCAA in rushing defense after the first five games (average of 15.2 yards per game allowed). Bob Jacobs punted 12 times in the game to set a Cowboy record which still stands, tied with Jacobs' 12 punts in 1970 against Arizona State.

---

[309] AP report in Billings Gazette 11/17/1969.

[310] Albuquerque Journal 11/15/1969 p. 25; UPI report in Wyoming Eagle, Cheyenne, Nov. 25, 1969. In a 2018 phone interview, Scarber said Houston Ross had become an attorney in Albuquerque.

[311] Blevins served in the U.S. Navy, including a tour in Vietnam, and retired as a captain. He owns an insurance agency in Powell and was elected as a State Representative in 2012. But in March, 2014, he signed on with six other Republican legislators to an opinion letter in the Casper Star opposing efforts to ban gay marriage. In the 2014 Republican primary five months later he lost his seat to Dan Laursen, who opposed gay marriage and favored guns in schools. Blevins challenged Laursen in the 2016 primary but lost again.

Split end Elmo Wright, an African American player, caught touchdown passes of 80, 45, 33 and 20 yards for Houston. His 262 receiving yards set a UH record which stood for 38 years.[312] If they had not been booted from the team, Jerome Berry, Ivie Moore and James Isaac would have been in UW's defensive backfield. Years after the 1969 Wyoming game, Wright told Berry, who had become a sports TV anchor in Houston, that it was the only game in his career where he wasn't touched the entire game.

On Nov. 25, 1969, the Cheyenne Quarterback Club held "Cowboy Night" at Little America and a large crowd was on hand to honor Lloyd Eaton, his staff and his seniors. One of the "special guests", according to a Cheyenne newspaper article, was U.S. District Judge Ewing T. Kerr, who at that moment was the presiding judge over the Black 14 case pending in his court. Four months later he dismissed the case without a trial in an opinion that ignored the most important applicable precedent from the U.S. Supreme Court, *Tinker v. Des Moines School Dist.*

Eaton told the Quarterbackers and Kerr: "It was a tremendous year in some respects but it was a long, hard year. However, in all my coaching years I've never been happier at seeing a season come to an end than I did in 1969. Let's forget 1969 and look ahead to 1970. I hope we'll be able to give you, the Wyoming fans, the kind of program you like and are used to."

Eaton said the staff would do an extensive recruiting job among the junior colleges because "we're looking for players with lots of experience, about 15 to 20 games." He said the Wyoming freshman team had some outstanding players who could be counted on the next year.

But as the state on December 10th observed the 100th anniversary of the Territorial Legislature's act granting women the right to vote, Wyoming's claim to be the "Equality State" had taken a beating by articles appearing throughout the nation that autumn about the Black 14 incident.[313]

Even Eaton seemed to be awakening to the scope of the problem he had created. Perhaps he more than anyone could sense the difficult time ahead on the football field. As a new decade approached, Wyoming's broadcasters and news writers elected Eaton as "UPI's Man of the Year". But instead of gloating like he had done after the BYU game, Eaton responded this way: "It's a

---

[312] In July 1971, Elmo Wright and Black 14 member Anthony McGee played together at Soldier Field for the College All-Stars in the 38th annual pre-season Chicago Tribune Charities Game against the NFL champions from the previous year. McGee had transferred to the historically-black Bishop College in Texas (no longer in existence) after his dismissal at UW. Also in that all-star game McGee was reunited with his 1969 Wyoming teammate, kicker Bob Jacobs, who booted a 49-year field goal for the All-Stars. In his rookie year with the Kansas City Chiefs in 1971, Elmo Wright celebrated a touchdown reception with what is generally considered to be the first end zone touchdown dance in NFL history. Another graduate of Bishop College who went on to pro football stardom is Emmitt Earl Thomas, a Kansas City Chiefs' pass defender who is in the NFL Hall of Fame.

[313] One of the reasons advanced by Wyoming historians as to why the legislators granted women the right to vote was a feeling that if African American men were being given full voting rights by the post-Civil War amendments to the U.S. Constitution, then white women should be allowed to vote also. See Rea, Tom, "Right Choice, Wrong Reasons: Wyoming Women Win the Right to Vote" at wyohistory.org. Only two months after Wyoming granted full rights to women, the Utah Territory also passed a law allowing women to vote (but not the right to hold office). Mormon leader Brigham Young supported the move, thinking that it could change the predominant national image of Utah women as downtrodden and oppressed and might help stop antipolygamy legislation by Congress. In 1887, Congress passed the Edmunds-Tucker anti-polygamy act which retracted the right of women to vote in Utah and soon led to the LDS Church's abandonment of its belief in polygamy. The right to vote and hold office was written into the new Utah Constitution in 1895.
http://ilovehistory.utah.gov/time/stories/suffrage.html

high honor, and I appreciate it very much, but I am sick at heart at what happened to those young fellows."[314] Too little, too late.

NCAA NEWS December 1969

Following the 1968 football season, the sports editor of the Provo, Utah *Herald*, Joe Watts, published a column praising San Jose State for not "giving in" to a boycott of the game by that school's black football players arising from the LDS tenet, and instead proceeding with its home game against BYU, even though both teams had 2-7 records and the game meant little on the surface. [315] The "main source of trouble were militant non-campus Negro groups who were pressuring these Negro athletes into the boycott," Watts wrote. San Jose's surprising victory, Watts wrote, "showed the Negro athletes that things can go on without them, and will, and that if they want to be a part of society they are going to have to play by the rules."

Following the Black 14's dismissal at Laramie, Joe Richmond, the sports editor of the Idaho State Journal in Pocatello – also Mormon country – expressed worry in an October 30, 1969 column concerning "all this talk about breaking up the league, or asking BYU to get out." This "hints more of an admission by other schools that they're willing to surrender when it comes to confrontation with minority groups," he wrote. Conference officials "make themselves sound pretty inept when it comes to solving what shouldn't even be a major crisis".

Richmond noted that Oregon State coach Dee Andros "didn't kick Fred Milton off the team last spring because he was a Negro – he did it because there was an open defiance of a team regulation about growing a beard."[316] Richmond suggested that BYU would not have joined the WAC in the first place "if it was so prejudiced against the blacks." He said he doubted "that any of [the Fourteen] had, or has now, the slightest interest in how the Mormon Church runs its own house. ... Unfortunately, those athletes in a moment of very bad judgment, sold themselves to a militant group ... that seems bent on causing unrest and disruption of the traditional high plane of intercollegiate athletics." Expelling BYU, he said, "will never solve any problem or prevent blacks from defying authority over some different reason."

Following the 1969 season, the National Collegiate Athletic Association itself issued a broadside which seemed to come right out of Watts' and Richmond's columns.

In his sports column appearing in Cheyenne and Laramie on December 18, 1969, the "Voice of the Cowboys" Larry Birleffi, recommended that a report in the December NCAA News "deserves careful reading by every fair-minded person in the country" and by all "meaningful students on the campuses." He then quoted a paragraph in which the NCAA News said the rebellion of black athletes was arising from "a hard-core revolutionary force designed to destroy the present governmental and educational system of the United States." These groups, Birleffi's quote of the News says, "have direct communication with communist oriented, revolutionary groups in other nations."

The NCAA News report argued that "intercollegiate athletics is a prime target" of these groups "because of the publicity value inherent in sports and the fact that the Negro or black athlete involved in a mild disorder will be a subject for newsprint from coast to coast...."

---

[314] UPI report in Lead S.D. Daily Call, Jan. 3, 1970, p. 3.

[315] Provo Herald Dec. 2, 1968.

[316] UWyo football player Henry Powell left the team just before the 1969 season began, partly because Eaton was imposing similar restrictions on facial hair. See Powell's story at pg. 164.

Without attribution to anyone, the NCAA News then declared:

> In the recent University of Wyoming situation, reliable information indicates plans were laid last summer to create an incident in the Rocky Mountain area. A Western Athletic Conference member with a stereotype football coach was to be selected as the target. The candidate colleges were narrowed to two, and the University of Wyoming was finally picked. Brigham Young U. would be the trigger. The outside leader in this case was the head of the Denver BPP, Willie Dawkins, who came to that city from Oakland.

Never in any interview or news report about the Black 14 has the author seen or heard that any of the players knew any Black Panthers or had ever encountered a Willie Dawkins from Denver. During the week after the BYU game, rumors were circulating that busloads of Black Panthers were going to descend on Laramie for the Homecoming game the next weekend. Gov. Hathaway had the National Guard at the ready under the stands to handle any trouble. Nothing of this sort ever materialized.

The Associated Press asked BSA Chancellor Willie Black to respond and he called the NCAA's report "an affront to every intelligent black athlete in this country."[317] He noted that the NCAA was wrong in saying he was "neither athlete nor student," pointing out he was a doctoral student in mathematics.[318] As to the NCAA's claim that the Wyoming football confrontation was planned and implemented by black power groups, Black responded: "They never seem to think that if a black man stands up to protest something it's because he's smart enough to do it himself. It's always a plot." Black also blasted the NCAA's failure to give the sources of their article. "They say they have overwhelming evidence. Well, if it's so evident, why don't they identify who said it?"

In Verne Boatner's regular sports column in the Arizona Republic on Dec. 21, 1969, the veteran sportswriter also recognized the shortcomings of the NCAA's two-page report on black athlete protests:

> As if the National Collegiate Athletic Association doesn't have enough problems, it has stirred up a hornet's nest of its own. ...
> The story is called "A Special NEWS Feature." It could more correctly be labeled an editorial – and a rather biased one at that.

Boatner noted that half of the article was devoted to "backgrounding such radical elements as Students for a Democratic Society, Black Panthers, etc., and to an FBI official's report on

---

[317] AP, Riverton Ranger, 12/18/1969.

[318] Black earned a Ph.D. in math from UW in 1973. His thesis was titled "An Initial Value Theory for the Integral Equations of Certain Interface Boundary Value Problems" (available in UW Coe Library). The thesis was dedicated to his adviser, his wife and four children "and to 14 young Black men." He went on to a career as a math teacher at Olive Harvey College, one of the City Colleges of Chicago. In 2017 he was retired and living in a suburb of Chicago, but later moved to the Dallas area. Black was born in Monroe, La. in 1933. The 1940 census record for Monroe shows his father as a laborer at a "heading mill". Willie grew up in Detroit and Chicago. He earned his bachelor's degree at Illinois Institute of Technology and a master's at Chicago Teachers College, now Chicago State. He taught briefly at Grambling State in Louisiana before deciding to obtain a Ph.D. In a 1993 interview he said UW's offer was $800 more than the second-best offer from the schools which had accepted his application.

radical groups on campus. From there on," he said, "facts are hard to find, but sweeping statements are plentiful."

Boatner then quoted the NCAA's paragraph about the UW Black 14 situation being plotted by the Denver Black Panther Party and responded: "I have been hearing this since the Wyoming incident first erupted. But I have yet to find any concrete evidence to substantiate a plot. ... I am inclined to agree with Willie Black's response," he said, "why don't they identify who said it?"

Sandy Padwe, columnist for the Philadelphia Inquirer, also criticized the report.[319] "One had hoped, finally, for an authoritative, documented, objective study," Padwe wrote. "Instead, the report is a waste of time and space, which, knowing the narrow-minded, crew-cut view of most college athletic officials, it figured to be. It is a report filled with generalities, banalities and almost no information.... At no point does the report mention who conducted the interviews. Nor does it mention exactly who was interviewed."

Padwe also noted that, without naming them, the NCAA News claimed that several black athletes did not compete in the 1968 Olympics "as a result of persuasion, coercion and threats of bodily harm..." But the columnist said that none of the prominent black basketball players who declined to participate in Mexico City, such as Lew Alcindor, Wes Unseld and Elvin Hayes, "have mentioned threats or coercion." In fact, he said, every black track and field athlete expected to compete had done so.

"The NCAA has not produced any answers, and through its unsatisfying report only will incite the redneck element in the coaching, athletic administration, and sporting media professionals. By simply blaming 'outside agitators', the NCAA only angers the young, aware black athletes more, because it casts all dissenters, all those who question established values, as mindless followers. The NCAA will not accept that much of this outrage is real. But then, it's always easier to blame outside elements and not yourself."

At the other extreme of the commentators was the sports editor of the Jefferson City, Mo., News, Bob Baysinger. He said that the NCAA's research "points out that the boycott of the 1968 Olympics by black athletes as well as the rebellion on the University of Wyoming football team this past fall are clearly connected with Communist-inspired organizations."

In January, 1970, a private letter from the LDS church's first presidency was made public in San Francisco. The letter said "the Negro ... should have his full constitutional privileges as a member of society" but that no change was planned with the exclusion of blacks from the LDS priesthood. "Matters of faith, conscience and theology are not within the purview of civil law," the letter said. "If we were the leaders of an enterprise created by ourselves and operated only according to our own earthly wisdom, it would be a simple thing to act according to popular will, but we believe this work is directed by God."[320]

The next month the Casper Star published a front page article about the theft of 50 handguns from two Casper firms and other thefts in Billings, plus the recent local thefts of "shaped explosives, primer cord and blasting caps" from a Casper oil well servicing company and dynamite from a powder company. Asst. Police Chief Joe McCarthy said his department had no leads, but he took the opportunity to blast the same target as the NCAA News: "McCarthy said

---

[319] Dec. 26, 1969, pp. 38, 40. After reporting on sports for the Inquirer, both wire services, Sports Illustrated and the New York Times, Sanford Padwe became a professor of professional practice in the Columbia University Graduate School of Journalism in 1992 and served for a time as Dean in 1997.

[320] Lincoln (Nebr.) Evening Journal, Jan. 12, 1970, p. 12.

that thefts of guns in other areas of the nation usually end with the weapons getting to militant groups such as the Black Panthers. He did not have any idea if the same destination would await the Casper guns"

This prompted a letter to the editor from Mrs. Robert E. Moore, a Casper African American, calling McCarthy's assertion a mere rumor. "Please do not let racist propaganda obscure the real crimes," she wrote, asking "the good people of Casper" to reject such "race polarizing statements."[321]

1970: End of the Eaton era

Lloyd Eaton attended the American Football Coaches Association meeting in D.C. in January and was present when a group of coaches from traditional black colleges, led by Tom Caldwell, head coach at Elizabeth City State University in North Carolina, complained that the major college coaches chosen to coach in the post-season all-star games "always ask black coaches to recommend their athletes, but they never ask a black coach to take part [as assistant coach] in the games." Head coaches from Grambling and Morgan State were also present. The legendary head coach of Texas, Darrell Royal, rejected their complaint, saying that "the black coach has not reached the point where his coaching is as scientific as it is in the major colleges." Caldwell disagreed, saying "we might be doing a better job than anyone else" as he reminded the group that a number of the black coaches' players were competing in professional football.[322] Royal's 1969 national championship team was the last all-white team to win that honor.

In mid-August 1970, line coach Leonard "Fritz" Shurmur substituted for Lloyd Eaton at the Western Athletic Conference's pre-season coaches and media meeting held at Aspen, Colo. According to an article by Bob Ingram in the El Paso Herald-Post on August 18th, "The young Wyoming aide appeared quite optimistic of the chances of Wyoming making a run at the championship this fall. 'We are not buying time. We are not rebuilding,' he [Shurmur] said. It looks like the Wyoming team was restructured pretty quickly. Eaton was pleased with spring practices." Yes, the Cowboy coaches were optimistic. After all, UW had not had a losing season since 1948, but this optimism was about to change dramatically.

In the statistics section of the 1970 UW football media guide, released in August, the total offense, rushing, receiving, interception returns and kickoff return statistics each showed a group called "Others" at the bottom of the lists. These "Others" were most of the Black 14.

A week before the season was to begin in the fall, the UW program suffered another severe blow. Their starting quarterback and total offense leader in 1969, Ed Synakowski of Whitesboro, N.Y., drowned while attempting to swim to shore in the chilly water after his boat overturned on Lake Hattie west of Laramie. His replacement, Gary Fox of Billings, then suffered what was described at the time as a career-ending concussion in a loss to Arizona State early in

---

[321] Casper Star-Tribune 2/19/1970 (McCarthy article), 3/8/1970 (Moore response). As to Mrs. Moore's allegation, UPI had reported on Oct. 7, 1969 that Chicago police officials testified before a Congressional committee that a retired Army major general had been given 397 guns from their department after signing a document saying the guns were being given to the U.S. Army for training purposes. Major General Carl Turner denied the guns were transferred to him for Army use but admitted that he had sold many of them.

[322] Colorado Springs Gazette, Jan. 13, 1970. Royal's insulting opinion of the black coaches' intelligence was still showing itself in subtle ways many years down the road. On November 7, 2008, for example, AP reported that only four of the 119 Division I football teams had African American head coaches. On the other hand, AP reported, 55% of all student athletes were minorities.

the season. (Fox returned the next year and led the Cowboys in passing, setting a Wyoming record with 305 passing yards in a 14-3 win over Arizona at Laramie).

Wyoming, which had not lost a home game since 1964, lost all five of its home games in 1970: by 24 points to Air Force, by 13 points to Utah State, by 49 points to Arizona State, by four points to Utah and by 10 points to New Mexico. It was the first time Wyoming lost all its home games since 1931. With the exception of the 5-win 5-loss season in 1962, Eaton's first year as head coach, the Cowboys had finished with a winning record every year from 1949 through 1969.

The Cowboys lost their last four games on the road by 20 points at BYU, 40 at UTEP, 28 at Houston and 26 at Arizona.

The Cowboys' only win came on October 10 at Fort Collins when flanker-turned-quarterback Scott Freeman of Laramie led UW over CSU 16-6. Ironically, two key plays by African American players contributed to the win. John Griffin, one of the three members of the Black 14 who returned to the team in 1970, caught a pass and took it 42 yards for a touchdown. And according to the AP article about the game: "Cowboy defenseman Steve Washington [a sophomore from Memphis who played on the freshman team in 1969] iced the victory by intercepting Smith's pass on the Wyoming one."

The next week against Utah in Laramie the Cowboys led late in the game when the Utes blocked a punt and carried the ball in for a touchdown and a 20-16 win. Lack of depth at the running back position was still a problem. "We had to keep hammering away at them with our running game and our kids aren't big enough to stand that without some relief," Eaton told Boomerang sports editor Harold Sohn after the game.

On Nov. 7, the UTEP Miners scored their first win ever against Wyoming and evened their WAC record at 3-3. Miners' halfback Phil Hatch rushed for 184 yards and three touchdowns in the 47-7 win. UW's leading rusher, Frosty Franklin, was lost for the season with a shoulder separation.

The depleted Cowboys then headed to the Astrodome for the second year in a row to face Houston. The Cowboys played gamely for most of the first half but still lost 28-0, their first shutout loss since a 13-0 defeat at West Point in 1965. Tailback Larry Garcia of Laramie rushed for 89 yards in 35 carries.

A 38-12 loss the next Saturday to Arizona at Tucson concluded the 1-win, 9-loss season, Wyoming's worst record since 1939 (no wins, seven losses and one tie) and its first season ever with nine losses. The offense failed to make a first down in the first half. Sophomore Greg Gagne took over for Freeman at quarterback in the second half and completed passes of 29, 33, and nine yards to set up a 9-yard touchdown pass to tight end Ken Hustad. A fumble recovery by Conrad Dobler set up the Cowboys' other touchdown. It was Eaton's first losing season in 27 years as a coach. Jacobs set a school record still unsurpassed with 84 punts during the season.

As the 1970 season ended, UW fans' hopes were at a low ebb not only because of the 1-9 record but also because the freshman team suffered through the first winless season by a freshman team since World War II. They lost to Air Force at the Academy 41-0 and on Nov. 7 lost to CSU in Laramie, 28-19. At CU the next weekend, the freshman team lost 49-0.

UW even lost its first Shetland pony mascot that season. The beloved Cowboy Joe the First died on October 12th at the age of 21 at the UW Stock Farm. He had appeared at Cowboy football games for 15 years before his retirement in 1965 and had traveled an estimated 50,000 miles, including two appearances at bowl games.

In September, 1970, the UW Student Senate adopted a proposal endorsed in June by all WAC student body presidents which declared that no disciplinary action should be taken against any student who finds participation in activities with BYU to be in conflict with their moral

239

principles. The resolution also recommended that BYU and other conference schools make efforts to recruit minority students, implement black studies programs and provide for minority scholarships.

1970: The post-season fallout

The six-column bold headline on the Laramie Boomerang's sports page on Tuesday, Nov. 17th, asked: **"Where Do We Go From Here?"** The long report by Sports Editor Harold Sohn noted that Wyoming had lost 13 of its last 14 games, "one of the most sudden and complete reversals of form ever", considering that UW had only lost five of 38 games before the skid began. As he had a year earlier at the Cheyenne Quarterback Club, Eaton was talking about his recruiting plans.

The article said Eaton's assistant coaches would be headed for all parts of the country looking for junior college talent initially, while Eaton would head for the East Coast "to contact high school players in New York, New Jersey and possibly the Carolinas."

Eaton said that the 1969 season was still the most disappointing ever for him. A reader who knew nothing about the events of October 1969 prior to perusing this article would have gotten the impression from Eaton's comments that the Black 14 had quit the team. "It really hurt to have those 14 kids think our program wasn't good enough and wasn't fair enough for them," he said.

In his column "Pokin' Around" on November 25, 1970, Sohn said the coaches would be spending Thanksgiving at home and then hitting the recruiting trail. "I enjoy recruiting," Eaton was quoted as saying, "but it can be very frustrating. ... We've got to get help from the freshman team or from J.C. recruiting. This, with the knowledge our young team learned through the past hard year might be able to turn the tide the other way." Asked what he would choose if given the chance to select one player from a list of top prospects Eaton said, "a big, strong, fast running back can be more devastating than any other one person." (Three of the Black 14 were running backs).

The Boomerang sports page also included Cheyenne broadcaster/sportswriter Larry Birleffi's column describing the "tired, battered Wyoming football team that headed home from Tucson Sunday." Coach Eaton told Birleffi: "We want to get the air cleared away on some things and we're ready to start our long climb back." Birleffi must have sensed that changes were in the offing, but he made an attempt to urge restraint by the fans: "Eaton deserves and must get full support in the challenge ahead, from immediate superiors through the president's office and the board of trustees."

Birleffi argued that a large factor in the Cowboys' "dismal" season was that the other teams in the league "have made a determined effort to catch up with the Cowboys. Wyoming set the pace and the pursuers have now gone by. They've learned to play the Cowboy system more effectively...." Birleffi had to admit the obvious, however: that the Black 14 incident "did hasten the tailspin this year. But it is by no means the entire cause of [what appear to be] Wyoming's sudden woes. The signs were coming on long before the episode." What these mysterious signs were Birleffi did not say.

But he declared that "athletics must be run by the department of athletics" and that "men like Red Jacoby and Lloyd Eaton can build it back. ... It's doubly important that the sport receives 100 per cent support and then some."

1970: Eaton "retires"

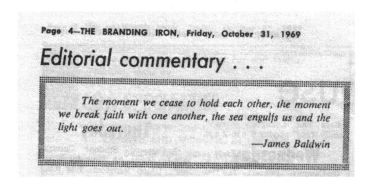

Page 4—THE BRANDING IRON, Friday, October 31, 1969

Editorial commentary . . .

The moment we cease to hold each other, the moment we break faith with one another, the sea engulfs us and the light goes out.

—*James Baldwin*

On Saturday December 5, 1970, however, Lloyd Eaton was no longer talking about recruiting. His coaching career had come to an abrupt end (and a permanent one, it turned out). In a press conference at the Fieldhouse after an all-day executive session Friday, the UW Board of Trustees announced that Eaton was retiring from active coaching and would become assistant athletic director. Defensive line coach Leonard F. (Fritz) Shurmur, 38, was appointed to replace Eaton. "I have no stars in my eyes," Shurmur said, "but I'll give it everything I have." [323]

Although only a few days earlier Eaton had been talking about his plans for the 1971 season and for stepped-up recruiting efforts, he said at the press conference that "The decision to retire is never an easy one, but I made it two years ago after completing a quarter century in the profession". Even if the team had gone 9-and-1 instead of the other way around, Eaton claimed, it would not have changed his decision to retire. He said the duties of his new job had not been defined, but said he would "work any way and in any capacity."

UW President William Carlson followed the "party line": "We deeply regret that Lloyd Eaton is leaving the active coaching field, but we feel we must honor his decision made two years ago to do this."[324]

Shurmur acknowledged at the news conference that he had found it difficult to recruit black players since the Black 14 incident. No contract had yet been signed with Shurmur, and Eaton's salary had not been determined, the UW press release said.

In "person-on-the-street" interviews with UW students and faculty by the Casper Star the next week, only two of the 13 students interviewed accepted the official university story about the coaching shuffle. "It looks a little suspicious," Mike McCall of Casper said. "My gut reaction is that the Black 14 and this season's record led up to Eaton's retirement."

English instructor Keith Hull said, "I think it's terrible to set apart funds pro sinecure for retired football coaches. I think they plan to keep Eaton around without really giving him anything to do."

Ron Rogers, a sophomore from Burns, was quoted as saying "I'm not too sure what happened but anything that gets rid of Eaton is fine with me. ... I don't know whether or not he's been fired or promoted. If we are ever to become a football power again, firing Eaton is the first step." Freshman Robert Tyler of Cheyenne, brother of James Tyler, the Black Students Alliance Chancellor in 1970-71, said the change was good. "It will take Eaton out of his capacity as a coach, although his thoughts and influence may still be felt as assistant athletic director."

---

[323] Casper Star Dec. 6, 1970, p. 1.

[324] Branding Iron article by Ben Pacheco, 12/11/1970.

Two law students, Al Young of Provo, Utah, and Robert Connor of Sheridan, were not happy with the move. "I think that if Eaton wanted to retire, then great. However, if they fired him, it's a shame," one of the two said (the article failed to identify which).

An article in the Dec. 12, 1970, Casper Star, reported that the UW student newspaper, the Branding Iron, had printed an editorial blasting UW for not informing the student newspaper about the Saturday press conference and for "leaving an entire region wondering if a guy got fired, was forced to resign, got promoted, or requested a change in duties." The editorial by editor L. Mark Bowman said the coaching shakeup was a "cloak and dagger" maneuver and "another public relations tragedy."

1971: Years of frustration follow

Nine months after his "retirement" as coach, Eaton's tenure at Wyoming came to an end altogether. In an El Paso Herald column by sports editor Bob Ingram appearing Sept. 9, 1971, the author noted that Eaton was not around when the WAC Skywriters tour visited Laramie before the 1971 season began. Later in the tour they learned that Eaton had accepted a job as a scout for four professional teams. Ingram claimed that "when Eaton handed over the coaching reins to Shurmur,...it was with the understanding that he would succeed [Glenn "Red"] Jacoby as athletic director when Red retired, which is not supposed to be too far in the future. But his failure to show up at the Jacoby dinner [a testimonial dinner during the 71-72 winter] and his acceptance of the pro scouting job can only mean that he either took himself out of the running for the A.D. job or was written off by Wyoming officials."[325]

UW Athletic Director Jacoby and President William Carlson expressed regret at the departure "of this singular individual. He has done so much for this institution and for Cowboy football," Carlson said. "He will be sorely missed and his contributions will be long remembered."[326]

In May 1972, Eaton was hired by Green Bay Packers' coach Bart Starr as director of player personnel, a position he held until 1976. Eaton died in Idaho in 2007 and his record of 57 wins as Wyoming's head coach still today is far ahead of Bowden Wyatt and Joe Tiller, tied for second with 39.

The negative publicity affected the football program for years. Following the dismissal of the 14, the Cowboys lost 26 of their next 38 games through 1972. They had only one winning season during the 1970s. Gradually, with Eaton gone, the numbers of African Americans on the football team grew, reaching 14 again in 1973 and 22 the next year. In 2017 the team had more than 35 black players.

In May, 1971, Black Hills State College honored Eaton with an Honorary Doctorate of Humane Letters.

The Spearfish Queen City Mail on June 13, 1987, carried a photo of Lloyd Eaton casting a fly on Spearfish Creek during a visit with his sister and brother-in-law, Doris and Herman Shipley, of Spearfish.

The players Move On

One of the remarkable aspects of the Black 14's visit to the coach on that October morning in 1969 was that young men of that age who were not in college, particularly young blacks or

[325] Jacoby retired July 1, 1973.

[326] Rapid City Journal 9/8/1971; Casper Star-Tribune, 9/4/1971.

Hispanics, faced an almost certain order to report for induction from draft boards that were supplying the conveyor belt of troops for slaughter in Vietnam. Fortunately, so far as we know, none of the Fourteen was forced down that road.

Several of the Black 14 managed to obtain college degrees. **Anthony Eugene McGee** of Battle Creek, Mich. transferred to Bishop College in Dallas, was drafted in the third round by the Chicago Bears in 1971 and became a dominant player in the NFL, playing in two Super Bowls for the Redskins. During his 14-season career he missed playing in only one of 204 games, a remarkable endurance record. Considering length of NFL career as the measure of pure football ability, McGee is probably the greatest player ever to don a Wyoming uniform (Tight end Jay Novacek played 11 years in the NFL). For many years since his pro career ended, McGee has hosted a sports television talk show in Washington D.C.

In an interview in 2009, Anthony McGee said, "When it was over, I had more hurt feelings from how the Wyoming people reacted and the way I was treated than the whole thing with BYU."

Joe Williams also earned a Super Bowl ring -- with the Dallas Cowboys -- and then developed his own investment consulting business in that area.

Guillermo Hysaw was taken under the wing of the Michigan attorney whom the NAACP hired to represent the Black 14 in their lawsuit. While living at William Waterman's house, Hysaw earned a degree from Oakland College and eventually became an employment diversity executive with GM and then Toyota.   **Lionel Grimes** played baseball for and graduated from Findlay College in his native Ohio. Grimes worked in the marketing department for Ford Motor Co. for 16 years and then had his own dealership in Delaware, Ohio.

Jerome Berry became a sports anchor for television stations in Tulsa, Houston, Chicago and Detroit and interviewed many of the biggest stars in the sports world. Early in his broadcasting career when he was with KPRC in Houston he was selected as the outstanding sports broadcaster in Texas by the Associated Press.

In the records section of the 2018 University of Wyoming Cowboys' Football Media Guide (available on-line), the name Jerry Berry appears with two other players who are tied for most interceptions returned for touchdowns in a season, and with three others for most "pick sixes" in a career.

Jerome Berry's entire career at UW consisted of only the first four games of the 1969 season. After his 88-yard return against Arizona he carried another interception 24 yards for a touchdown in the CSU game two weeks later.

Jerome Berry leaps high to intercept an Arizona pass on his own 12-yard-line in his first game
as a varsity player for the Cowboys on September 20, 1969. He returned it for a touchdown. Brent Engleright (45)
and Steve Adamson (63) are coming up to help. John Henberg Collection Wyoming Archives.

Neither Berry nor any of the other 14 ever played another down for a Division I team
(except for the three who returned to the UW team the next season). Many of them never played
again at any level.

Tony Gibson retired in 2011 after nearly 38 years as a lineman for a Massachusetts power
company and **Ted Williams** has worked that long as a foreman at a specialized paint
manufacturing company in Illinois. Ted played football and ran track at Adams State in Alamosa,
Colo., after leaving Laramie.

Ron Hill earned a degree from Howard University in Washington D.C. and was a PE
teacher in Colorado public schools for many years. In 2019 he was back in his home area of
Birmingham, Ala., working full time for a plant converting plastics into fibers.

After earning a degree at UW, **John Griffin** had a long career in supervisory positions for
the YMCA in Denver, for a hazardous waste abatement firm in California and as a manager for
United Airlines (ten years) and Sports Authority in Denver.

In 1990, while working in California for Thermo Process, a subsidiary of Brand Companies of Chicago, Griffin had an opportunity to meet and pose for a photo with Los Angeles Mayor Tom Bradley, the only African American mayor of Los Angeles and the longest-serving mayor.

Ivie Moore has worked as a floor subcontractor in his native Arkansas.

In addition to **Isaac** (1976), **Don Meadows** (2009) and **Earl Lee** (2013) are deceased.

Lee stayed at Wyoming for his bachelor's degree. In the fall of 1970, Earl joined other minority students on a tour of Wyoming high schools where they met minority students and parents to discuss financial aids and their personal experiences at UW. The group also included African American students Dwight James, Annie Cooper and Pat Paced, Chicano students Tony Hernandez, Leo Romero, Billy Gonzales, Mary Jane Harare and Pauline Esquire and Native Americans Iva St. Clair and Elizabeth Hainworth.[327]

Lee went on to earn a master's degree from Morgan State and had a distinguished career as a teacher, coach and principal in the Baltimore area. The Baltimore Sun carried a nice obituary and photo of Earl Lee which may still be available on the paper's web site.

Don Meadows worked in the restaurant business in Denver and Seattle.

Mel Hamilton and his Boys Town Friend Kenn Gilchrist

Mel Hamilton and his family moved from South Carolina to Wilmington, N.C. early on in his life. At about age nine, Hamilton was in Wilmington's main public building and found himself alone in the hall in front of the "White" and "Colored" drinking fountains. His curiosity got the best of him. He snuck a sip from the white fountain and was surprised and confused when he discovered that "the water tasted just as bad as the white fountain."

At some point his mother feared he was coming under the influence of a bad crowd and enlisted the help of her Catholic priest to get him into Boys Town at Omaha, Nebr. So at age 14 he boarded a bus and rode by himself to Omaha where suddenly he found himself in a high school with 500 boys from all over the world. In his senior year he was elected by his peers as mayor of

---

[327] Casper Star 11/29/1970.

Boys Town and was also selected as a Nebraska Shrine football All-Star. During the Shrine Bowl festivities, he and the other players visited the Shrine Hospital for Crippled Children in Minneapolis, as part of the theme "Strong legs run that weak legs may walk." An article in the Lincoln newspaper on August 14, 1965, reported: "'It isn't everybody that gets a picture from me,' Boys Town's Mel Hamilton said to his teammates after he had given a photo" to one of the children.[328]

Mayor Mel Hamilton, front row 3rd from left, with Council

Also elected to the All-State Class A football team after the 1964 season was Mel's best friend and teammate, center Kenn Gilchrist, an orphan from Cleveland. Gilchrist accepted a football scholarship to the University of Wyoming, and because of their friendship Mel followed him to Laramie. "Kenny didn't have anybody but me, so I chose to stay with him."

After one year, however, Gilchrist left. "He did not stay in Laramie because of the atmosphere on campus… towards blacks," Hamilton said in his 2013 wyohistory.org interview. "And then he saw also that everybody was against blacks dating whites, and he didn't like that. And I think he just — his mentality wouldn't allow him to fight those kind of discriminations without striking back, so he left."

---

[328] Thirty years before his mother sent Mel Hamilton from North Carolina to Boys Town, the grandparents rearing another African American boy in Cheyenne did the same thing for the same reason. Vernon Joseph Baker had been born in Cheyenne in 1919 and became an orphan at age 4 when his parents were killed in an auto accident. He was at Boys Town from age 11 to 14. In early 1941, he joined the U.S. Army at Cheyenne, and in April, 1945, near Viareggio, Italy, Lt. Baker showed extraordinary valor and leadership of his all-black company under fire from German machine gun nests. Although 1.2 million black Americans served during WWII, none of them had been among the 433 recipients of Medals of Honor for heroism in that war until Pres. Bill Clinton awarded the medal to seven of them in January, 1997. Baker, the only recipient still alive by then, wiped away tears as Clinton described their valor during the White House ceremony. Baker died in 2010 at St. Maries, Idaho. AP, Sitka Sentinel, 1/13/1997 and Arizona Republic, 1/14/1997. Hamilton returned to Omaha in 2015 for a ceremony inducting him into the Boys Town Hall of History, joining WWII hero Vernon Baker.

Gilchrist joined the Marine Corps and served two terms in Vietnam, suffering a shrapnel injury to a leg. He became a policeman in California and then a bass singer with the San Jose Opera. Eventually, however, he moved to Casper to be near Hamilton, earned a degree in social work through UW-Casper and became a parole officer for about 20 years, sometimes testifying by phone at a hearing of the state Board of Parole. For many years, Hamilton was an appointed member of that board.

In a February, 2003 article in the Casper Star-Tribune, Gilchrist mentioned suffering post traumatic stress from Vietnam and seeking comfort through other veterans.

In 2014 Mel and his wife Carey Holwell Hamilton from Osage, Wyoming, moved to South Carolina where Mel was born and where some of his relatives still lived. Kenn and his wife had previously moved back to his home area, landing in Akron.

But 11 days after the 2016 presidential election, Gilchrist visited a café at Highland Square in Akron wearing military garb and told organizers of a Trump protest march he wanted to speak out against hate. He walked down the street, handed his phone to a passerby and told him to make a video recording with it. Kenn doused himself with gasoline and set himself on fire. The passerby threw his coat over Kenn and others rushed out with fire extinguishers, but he suffered serious burns over 60% of his body. He died on March 9, 2017.

Hamilton came to UW in the fall of 1965 and played on the varsity of the 1966 team that beat Florida State in the Sun Bowl. In spring, 1967, he asked Eaton to give his approval for Mel and Katherine Kinne, a white student whom he planned to marry, to secure an apartment in married student housing. According to Hamilton, Eaton told him: "I can't let you marry this girl on Wyoming's money. The people of Wyoming's money."[329] At the Black 14 trial Eaton admitted asking Hamilton to wait on getting married until his football eligibility was over because Eaton feared the reaction from others could impact Hamilton's performance:

Mel Hamilton in Casper in 2013

[329] Oral history interview for www.wyohistory.org in 2013.

I said in the sparse black population of the campus, of Laramie, and of the state this could be possible, some derogatory statement could be made that she could hear or he might hear. ... [I]f it affects him as an athlete, it now would affect our program.

Eaton was asked whether it would affect the program "because you would likely get complaints from fans and alumni?" He answered: "That, and now having his thoughts divided more than on education and athletics, it is now going to be a family situation." (Tr. 321:23-322:14).

On July 23, 1967, Don and Ann Kinne, Katherine's parents, left their Elephant Head Lodge at Wapiti, Wyo., and drowned while attempting to cross the Shoshone River on horseback.

These events led Hamilton to join the U.S. Army instead of marrying, and he advanced from private to sergeant in 18 months. Fortunately, he was not deployed to Vietnam. "They went right down the alphabet ... and the guy before me was David Ham and he was the last person in the alphabet that went to Vietnam," Mel said in a 2013 interview. "Hamilton was next and I went to Turkey."

Nearly two years later, knowing of his abilities, Eaton invited him to return to the team. Not having anywhere else to go and knowing he would lose credits if he transferred, "I swallowed my pride" and returned, he said. Hamilton graduated from UW, earned a master's degree in 1992 and had a long career as a public school teacher, coach and administrator in Casper.

In the 1990s, Hamilton became the only black administrator in the Casper school district when he was named vice-principal of Roosevelt High School, and in 1996 he was selected as principal of East Junior High School. Not long into his tenure, a group of teachers told him that some other teachers and administrators were engaged in "a concerted effort to get me out of there." The district conducted an investigation and issued a report which substantiated claims that some of his staff had ridiculed Hamilton's speech, called him racist names and circulated a "Eubonics" version of the Lord's Prayer. The Casper Star-Tribune filed a public records suit and obtained a copy of the report, with names redacted. In January 2001, Jimmy Simmons, a black member of the NAACP in Casper, stood in front of the junior high building on a snowy Saturday with a poster setting forth the names of six employees he said were disciplined.[330]

ANTHONY MCGEE'S FATHER, HERMAN MCGEE

The coach, the university officials, the governor and the people of Wyoming could not understand why the 14 African American players went to the coach to discuss the Black Student Alliance's call for a protest at the BYU game. "They are just young men whose entire lives have been dedicated to mastering the game of football," many people were thinking. "What do they know about civil rights?" Tony McGee's background in Battle Creek, Mich., illustrates that many of them had more than a passing interest in the struggle of their people.

On Nov. 12, 1961, six years before McGee came to UW to play football, the McGee family was pictured in the Battle Creek Enquirer and News. During those years the McGee family had traveled to Chicago and visited the Liberian Embassy to learn about their heritage. In the article, Tony's father Herman said he first experienced racial prejudice after he enlisted in the U.S. Navy in 1943, serving with the Seabees on the Admiralty Islands. "Before the Island was

---

[330] Casper Star-Tribune, 1/14/2001 and 3/5/2015.

secured," he said, "the Negroes and the whites shared the same foxholes; we drank from the same lister bags." But as soon as the island was safe, he said, "one lister bag was marked 'White', the other 'Negroes'. We helped build a movie theater, but we weren't allowed inside. We helped build a mess hall, but we were segregated to sit at one table in the rear...."

He also noted that at the rate schools were being integrated in the south following the Brown v. Board of Education decision, "it will take a hundred years to complete the job. My wife and I and our children will never live to see the day when a Negro has true equal rights in this country."

In October, 1962, Tony McGee's parents were again in the Battle Creek Enquirer, protesting that their son, age 13, and daughter, 16, had been taken into police custody after an incident at a local movie theater, charged with interfering with two policemen who had been called to the scene. The McGees alleged that their son had been struck by one of the officers, causing his face to become swollen and putting him in the hospital overnight. They also protested that their children had been made temporary wards of the juvenile court and were taken to the juvenile home at Marshall before the parents had an opportunity to see them at the police station.

Tony McGee at the unveiling of the Black 14 plaque at the University of Wyoming September 13, 2019. Photo courtesy of former UW and Cheyenne High basketball player Robert Fred Gish.

According to the parents, their daughter Gwendolyn told them that when she objected to an officer's "manhandling" of one of her friends, the officer put a "headlock" on her and "twisted her arm." At that point, her brother yelled at the policeman to "take your hands off my sister", resulting in both of them being arrested. "I jumped between them and he hit me in the jaw," Tony McGee recounted in a 2020 interview with wyofile.com's Angus M. Thuermer Jr.[331] "I've always been a target," he said, stopped without reason many times by the police. "Any of those times it could have been something serious."

Herman McGee, who worked at Kellogg's cereal company before starting various small businesses, was a founding chairman of the local chapter of the Congress on Racial Equality, served as a vice president of the Battle Creek NAACP chapter and was vice chairman of the Calhoun County's Community Action Division. He was involved in CORE's attempt to force a grocery store to hire more African American workers because 80 percent of their customers were black.

Herman died in 1966 at the age of 40 while Tony was still in high school. In his memory the Herman McGee Scholarship Fund was created to provide higher education support to needy students.

---

[331] Laramie Boomerang, 7/5/2020 p. C5. In the article McGee and fellow Black 14 member John Griffin of Denver recounted their early experiences with racial prejudice, in light of the killing of George Floyd by Minneapolis police on May 25, 2020.

MORE TRAGEDIES FOR THE FOURTEEN

1970: Ron Hill's brother Roosevelt

When John Griffin came from California to play for Wyoming in late-summer 1969 he met fellow pass receiver Ron Hill, and on a couple of occasions went with Hill to Denver to visit Hill's brother Roosevelt, who had raised Ron during his teen years through Manual High School after Ron moved to Denver from Bessemer, Ala.

Roosevelt Hill, age 32 when Griffin met him, was the Director of the Black Studies Program at the University of Colorado Denver Center and was active in the civil rights movement in Denver.

On July 14, 1970, nine months after Ron and John were dismissed from the UW football team,
Roosevelt drove himself, his wife and some CU students in a state vehicle to the state penitentiary in Canon City where he spoke to inmates on the topic "Awareness of the Black Man." On the way back Roosevelt stopped at a Mobil gas station in Colorado Springs where an attendant filled the gas tank and was handed a state-issued credit card for payment.

The attendant was a soldier stationed at Ft. Carson who had returned from a tour in Vietnam and was working part-time at the station. He apparently suspected the credit card was stolen and went into a back room to make a phone call to verify the card. Roosevelt followed him and a dispute arose which led to the attendant pulling out a .38 caliber revolver and shooting Hill in the heart. He died on the way to the hospital.[332]

A few days later a grand jury heard testimony from several witnesses, including Hill's wife Martes Hill and another occupant of Roosevelt's vehicle. The grand jury decided not to issue an indictment against the attendant, which provoked two African American state senators and civil rights groups to call for the county attorney to charge the attendant with murder so all the facts could be heard at a public trial. Black students marched in Colorado Springs and members of the Black Students Association at UC-Boulder denounced the prosecutor. A district judge eventually refused to order the prosecutor to file charges. At the end of the year the Associated Press named the furor over the slaying as the sixth most important news story of the year in Colorado.

Six months' later, Ron Hill's mother died. These losses on the heels of the crushing of his football career had a profound effect on him. But he participated in the Sept. 25, 1993 "reunion" at the University of Wyoming. Wearing a dashiki, he and Ivie Moore were pictured in the Cheyenne Tribune the next day, talking by phone to 1969 UW President Carlson.

The author interviewed Ron Hill by phone in 2010 when he was living in Beaumont, Texas. He returned to UW for the 50th Anniversary commemoration in 2019.

1976: Don Meadows' brother Melvin

Middle guard Don Meadows, a Denver Manual High product who transferred to UW from Mesa Jr. College, was one of the three black players who returned to the UW team in 1970. In high school, Meadows was selected to play for the North team in the Colorado All-State football game in August 1967 and probably encountered Freddie Jo Steinmark of Wheat Ridge High, running back for the South team in that game. (Steinmark became a national hero when he became afflicted with cancer while playing for the Texas Longhorns).

---

[332] Colorado Springs Gazette 7/15, 7/16, 7/18, 7/26, 7/29, 8/4, 8/7, 8/8, 8/15, 12/29/1970. Missoula Missoulian 8/11.

During the 1970 season Don Meadows had a 59-yard interception return in one game but missed several other games because of ankle injuries. As a senior the next season, under new coach Fritz Shurmur, Don Meadows was selected to the All-Western Athletic Conference first team. He had 15 tackles and forced three fumbles in Wyoming's 14-3 win over Arizona.

Don's brother Mel Meadows also joined the Wyoming team in 1970 and the brothers both graduated. In 1972 Mel was a starting cornerback. His interception and 24-yard return was a key play in Wyoming's 45-43 upset over Arizona State in Laramie on Sept. 30, 1972.

Don Meadows
52

Mel Meadows
83

In September four years later, Mel and his white girlfriend went to a theater in Denver. During the movie a 33-year-old white man pulled out a .44 magnum and shot him in the back of the head. The shooter then killed himself outside the theater. Police found racist and American Nazi party literature at his apartment. A police detective was quoted as saying that the slayer "had an obsession with blacks dating whites."

Don came from Seattle to console his mother, Pauline Meadows, and his siblings. "I knew whoever shot him had to be someone who didn't know him," Don said. "A sick, obscene mind." Pauline, who worked as a housekeeper to support her large family, said she "tried to teach my kids that we all are equal because we're human -- makes no difference what color you are. There's not much more I can say. Right now my mind isn't free and my heart is full of sorrow and tears."[333]

WHITE PLAYERS AFFECTED ALSO

Forrest "Frosty" Franklin of Powell

Because senior tri-captain Joe Williams missed most of the CSU game to injury, the leading rusher heading into the BYU game was sophomore Frosty Franklin of Powell, a tailback who had gained 5.3 yards per carry on 36 runs. Frosty had become a favorite of the students. He also returned kicks and had caught 11 passes.

According to an article in the Billings Gazette on October 1, 2004, Frosty went on to become a horse veterinarian in Spokane before relocating to northern California. The article was about his nephew, a running back for Rocky Mountain College in Montana. In a 2017 phone interview from his home in Rancho Marieta, Calif., Forrest said he was supervisor of the vets who examine and test race horses at Golden Gate Fields in Berkeley.

After UW, Franklin went to CSU for veterinary school and one of the first classmates he met was Earl Carlson, son of UW President William Carlson. Pres. Carlson was present for their graduation and congratulated Forrest.

Franklin said that during WWII his grandfather Russell Franklin was one of the local dairy farmers who quickly expanded their operation to provide milk and butter to the nearby Heart Mountain internment camp, where more than 10,000 internees of Japanese descent were being

---

[333] AP report in Greeley Tribune 9/29/1976.

held. His grandfather later owned a livestock sale yard, and as a young man Frosty loved to follow the yard's veterinarian as he did his testing. He decided at a young age to become a vet also.

Reflecting from 49 years post-event, Franklin summed up the Black 14 incident this way: "What Lloyd did by dismissing the Black 14 was reactive. I feel he did not think his decision through. He depleted our team and ruined recruiting to Wyoming football for the next few years. Football at Wyoming, after the Black 14, was not much fun for me. The administration of Wyoming Athletics and the University of Wyoming should have been included regarding the decisions concerning the demands of the Black 14.

"A coach spends a lifetime building a reputation and with one decision, made in anger, ruined a career, a program, and derailed the lives of many of his players."

After his senior year, Franklin said, he declined an invitation to be drafted by the Dallas Cowboys because he wanted to pursue his childhood dream of becoming a vet.

Of the Fourteen, Franklin said he missed Jerome Berry the most. "He may have been the best athlete of all of us. He was not only fast but he could jump. I saw him deflect passes that seemed impossible to reach. He was a great person to be around. I always enjoyed him, so quiet." Franklin also liked Tony Gibson, Don Meadows and John Griffin. He admired Mel Hamilton's finesse as a pulling blocker and Joe Williams' rushing ability.

During his freshman year Franklin met senior star Gene Huey. "He was the nicest, politest guy," Franklin said, "He remembered me and gave me a hug when we ran into each other many years later."

Larry "Bo" Nels of North Syracuse, N.Y.

Nels told Ryan Thorburn that his name was removed from the roster of the Senior Bowl and the Hula Bowl after the 1969 season. "The scuttlebutt was they didn't want anyone from Wyoming because they thought there would be protests or controversy," Nels related. He also believes he would have been drafted higher than the 12th round if not for what he calls Eaton's "hard-headed" decision to remove the black players.[334]

Ramifications at BYU and LDS

A Salt Lake Tribune retrospective[335] by Jay Drew, published Nov. 6, 2009, concurrent with the 40th anniversary, related that the Black 14 incident quickly provoked changes at BYU, including the recruitment of Ronnie Knight, a black defensive back from Sand Springs, Okla. The Tribune's article pointed out the overarching irony of the Black 14 incident. Although UW's and the state's leaders justified the coach's action by raising the freedom of religion banner, the article says everyone involved would have been better off if Eaton had not acted so precipitously, without even checking with the UW athletic director. "...Eaton's actions probably led to more national scrutiny and scorn for the LDS Church and BYU than if he had allowed the protests....," the article said.

Drew's article also noted that "many believe what happened on that snowy day on the high plains of Wyoming provided an impetus for the church to change its policy."

In January, 1970, death ended the19-year reign as LDS President of 96-year-old David McKay. Many of the obituaries mentioned the widespread attacks on the church's exclusion of blacks from becoming ministers and some observers suggested that McKay's death presented an

---

[334] Thorburn, *Black 14 -- The Rise, Fall and Rebirth of Wyoming Football*, p. 65.

[335] Available on-line at archive.sltrib.com.

opportunity. An editorial in the Tucson Citizen on January 21st, for example, said "it is obvious that today's church crisis can be eased if the new Mormon leader would seek new answers to the Negro questions now being asked in and out of the church."

Nevertheless, that new answer took eight more years. On June 9, 1978, the First Presidency of the LDS Church, composed of President and Prophet Spencer Kimball, along with counselors N. Eldon Tanner and Marion G. Romney, announced that a divine revelation had been received to open the Mormon priesthood to African American men, ending the 148-year history of the tenet. An Associated Press article datelined Salt Lake City said the change came after many hours of "supplicating the Lord for divine guidance." The AP article said it was the most significant change in church doctrine since polygamy was discontinued in 1890.

Church spokesman Jerry Cahill was quoted in the article as saying, "It's a momentous day, a great day we've lived through today."

The Denver Post's 1982 Retrospective

On May 9, 1982, the Denver Post published an extended review of the Black 14 incident by Post sportswriter Rick Reilly, including what may be the only interview Eaton gave about the incident after he left UW. "Divorced, Lloyd Eaton now lives a bachelor's life in a small home in Kuna, Idaho, where he refuses to have a phone," the article said. Eaton declared that he had never regretted what happened and that he would do the same thing again if given a second chance.

U.S. District Judge turns a blind eye

Within a week of the dismissals, the NAACP sent a Detroit-area attorney named William Waterman to Wyoming to investigate the situation and represent the players. He filed a federal lawsuit seeking an injunction ordering the reinstatement of the players and asking for damages for violation of their civil rights.

In the state's brief opposing the injunction, Wyoming Attorney General James Barrett made this questionable argument at p. 6: "the said fourteen Plaintiffs had long acquiesced in said coaching rule and had, by reason thereof, waived any right to challenge, protest or contest said rule and further that said Plaintiffs had violated the terms of their contractual agreement with the University of Wyoming represented by athletic scholarships awarded to each of the Plaintiffs by acceptance of the benefits of said contract ...." In other words, Barrett contended, if a citizen does not immediately challenge an unconstitutional rule then the citizen must "forever hold his peace", so to speak. These young men were football players barely out of high school, not constitutional law experts. This argument was also suspect because for those among the 14 who had just arrived in Laramie for the first time a couple months earlier, it could hardly be said that they had "long acquiesced". And furthermore, several of the players were minors under the statutes in effect at that time, and any contract they signed could not be enforced against them.[336]

But more importantly, this argument is a direct contradiction of a fundamental principle of American constitutional law: "[The government] may not deny a benefit to a person on a basis that infringes his constitutionally protected interests – especially, his interest in freedom of speech. ... We have applied this general principle ... most often ... to denials of public employment." *Speiser v. Randall*, 357 U.S. 513, 526 (1958). This is all the more true because the

---

[336] The State never produced any contracts, probably because if they existed most of them would have been signed by the parents of the players, who were still legally minors. In its 86-page Motion to Dismiss the State said the contractual obligation it was asking the court to enforce was "inherently implied" in the athletic scholarship. (Motion, pg. 67).

scholarships received by the players were not a gratuitous government "benefit". The university was receiving a huge return on its investment from the players' football talents and effort.

Chuck Graves at the 2009 Black 14 40-year recognition in the Union.

Cheyenne attorneys Charles Graves and his associate Weston Reeves, a 1969 graduate of the UW College of Law, agreed to serve as local counsel for Waterman.[337] Their senior partner, future U.S. Rep. Teno Roncalio, told the Boomerang in November, 1969, that he had contacted Athletic Director Red Jacoby just before the BYU game. "I wanted to help mediate this terrible thing that had happened. We wanted to find some accommodation with which everyone could live," Roncalio said. "It then became apparent that there was to be no arbitration--at least until these 14 athletes had missed a few ball games." [338]

On Nov. 10, 1969, with only two games remaining on the schedule, the players' motion for a temporary restraining order reinstating the players until the case was decided, came to a hearing before U.S. District Judge Ewing T. Kerr in Cheyenne. Four of the players and UW President Carlson testified.

Joe Williams testified: "[W]e went over that morning at 9:30 a.m. to talk to Coach Eaton about some form of protest, as I have stated before, to talk to him, not to put any demands or

---

[337] During his last semester in law school, Reeves, a moderate political conservative, had authored a regular column for the Branding Iron titled "Best Weston". In his March 14, 1969, column (seven months before the Black 14 incident) he had blasted former Alabama governor and segregationist George Wallace and the ten million who had voted for him in the 1968 presidential election. "Mere support for Wallace is support for reprisal against all blacks. ... In this year more than ever before we need conciliation if twenty million Negroes are ever to escape the vise of second-class citizenship and enter the American community," Reeves wrote.

[338] Laramie Boomerang, November 12, 1969.

anything to him, but to talk to him that there was a problem. And we didn't get a chance to say anything."[339]

Kerr denied the TRO a week later, when only one game remained. If Kerr had immediately granted a temporary restraining order, restoring the players to the team, much of the harm that fell upon both the players and even upon coach Eaton himself, along with the harm to the reputation of the state and the university, could have been avoided. In legal terms, this situation was a perfect model for a restraining order because of the severe, immediate injury being perpetrated upon the 14 players with each passing Saturday. Such an intervention was appropriate also because the UW press release stated on its face that the players were dismissed for participating in a demonstration in violation of a coach's rule, a rule which even right-wing attorneys and political scientists had agreed was unconstitutional and which was revoked by UW a few days after the 14 were dismissed.[340]

Weston Reeves

But Kerr denied the injunction on Nov. 17, when the Cowboys had only one game remaining in their season. Kerr stated that "I seriously doubt if this court has supervisory jurisdiction over a verbal directive issued by a football coach when issued undoubtedly for the best interests and welfare of the team. Any coach has certain inherent powers to discipline, regulate training, and other matters incidental to the general conduct of a team."

To paraphrase: football first, Constitution irrelevant.

Twenty-four years later, in an interview with the UW TV Department for a documentary on the Black 14, Barrett remembered having a premonition during the TRO hearing:

Incidentally, the 14 players were placed in the jury box so that they could have a good view of the proceedings. ... I can recall many times during that hearing looking over to that box and I'd see these beautiful physical specimens there and I could just imagine what was going to happen to the Wyoming football team without those 14.

---

[339] Transcript, Binder 7:91.

[340] For example, in the spring of 1969 a 16-year-old student in Encinitas, Calif., was suspended for sporting a barely-visible beard. He sued and the state court judge issued a restraining order allowing him to continue in school pending the outcome. The judge eventually ruled in favor of the student, saying "tolerance for difference is one of the basic educational policies of any school district." Casper Star-Tribune 6/10/1969. See also *Burnside v. Byars*, 363 F.2d 744, a 1966 federal appeals court case in which the trial court refused to enter a preliminary injunction ordering reinstatement to students at an all-black high school who were dismissed in 1964 for wearing voting rights buttons after being warned of a school regulation prohibiting such activity. The appeals court directed the trial court to enter the injunction.

In the State's Answer and Counterclaim filed Nov. 7th, Attorney General James Barrett sought an injunction against the players to again restrict their freedom of speech, prohibiting them from claiming that race played any role in what happened to them. The State alleged the players had subjected the state, the university and its officials "to ridicule, abuse and scorn" in their media appearances, "all designed and intended to inflame the public" to the effect that the state defendants had violated their constitutional rights "as a race class, thereby imputing racial discrimination and bias unto these Defendants."[341]

Five months later Kerr threw the players' case out of court without a trial. The judge's decision placed greater emphasis on Eaton's rule than on the free speech provision of the Constitution. The opinion recites that Eaton "advised Joe Harold Williams of the coaching rule prohibiting members of the University of Wyoming football team from participating in demonstrations and protests...." [342] Kerr's opinion said the rule "was made well known to each of the fourteen plaintiffs during the Spring football practice of 1969, again during the Fall football practice of 1969...."[343]

The 10th Circuit Court of Appeals reversed that decision on May 14, 1971, but Kerr again ruled for the state on October 18th (two years to the day after the BYU game), and this time the appeals court affirmed him in an opinion that ignores the undeniable violation of free speech rights by Eaton on the morning of October 17th and looks only at what some of the players said during the meetings at Old Main that night when they were furious about the lecture they had been subjected to by Eaton that morning, and when they had had no chance to obtain legal representation to give them a "level playing field" against all the attorneys representing the university at that meeting.

During the final argument at the trial on Sept. 28, 1971, Kerr pounced on an assertion by Weston Reeves, the Cheyenne attorney representing the Black 14, who suggested that "the issue of race is inextricably woven into this whole situation." Kerr interrupted and proclaimed:

---

[341] Some 26 years later, Attorney General Barrett wrote a memoir saying he had attempted to arrange a mediation of sorts between the players and the UW officials, including the coach, on the day of the TRO hearing. Judge Kerr agreed to sit in on a meeting between the players and coaches. He said Eaton had told him that the coach was ready to come to Cheyenne on a moment's notice (as if the coach could have rejected the Attorney General's request). Barrett said he believed a satisfactory resolution could have been achieved, but the Black 14's attorney Waterman rejected the idea without running it by the players. If true, it is probably because Waterman, a practicing attorney in the Detroit area, felt he had an "open-and-shut" case that the coach's rule violated the Constitution. If he had been in most any other federal court in the country, except the Deep South perhaps, he would have been right. Or he knew that most of the players were still incensed about the verbal abuse the coach delivered to them on Oct. 17th and then his refusal to meet with them later that day, before they had missed any games. In the lawsuit, Barrett's defense was that the state could not allow the players to wear arm bands on their state-provided uniforms in a state-provided stadium because this would violate the separation of church and state clause in the First Amendment. But the issue of whether the players would wear armbands on the field against BYU was moot as soon as that game ended. Their expulsion for the entire season could only have arisen from the players' "defiance" of the coach's no-demonstrations-anywhere-anytime rule by wearing arm bands the previous day.

[342] The citations to the four federal court decisions in the case of Williams v. Eaton are as follows: 310 F.Supp. 1342 (D.Wyo. March 1970), reversed in part by the 10th Circuit in 443 F.2d 422 (May 1971). Decision after remand to the federal district court in Cheyenne: 333 F.Supp. 107 (October 1971), affirmed by the 10th Circuit 468 F.2d 1079 (October 1972).

[343] Some players, both black and white, at the time disputed that they had been advised of the rule against demonstrations. Albuquerque Journal 10/20/1969 (compiled from wire service articles). Several of the Fourteen were not yet enrolled at UW during spring practices.

From my observation of almost half a century in Wyoming I have never known of any prejudice against any race in the state of Wyoming and I think the fact that the coach went out and solicited and gave scholarships to a large number of colored people is strong evidence that he was not prejudiced against any race.

This prompted Alberta Johnson, president of the NAACP chapter in Cheyenne, to point out that Wyoming newspapers just a short time earlier had printed an article reporting that the Wyoming Fair Employment Commission had concluded that a black teacher had been illegally discriminated against by the Rock River School Board on the basis of his race. Mrs. Johnson said Kerr showed "an unbelievable naivete" about racial prejudice.[344]

ALBERTA JOHNSON
Cheyenne Democrat

Jim Flinchum, editor of the right-wing Republican Wyoming State Tribune, Cheyenne's afternoon paper, immediately jumped to Kerr's defense in an editorial on Oct. 1, 1971, asserting that throughout the case there had been no evidence of racial discrimination and that Kerr's reputation as a fair and impartial judge was "too widely known ... for him to suffer such indignities, and for such specious purposes."

The incident to which Alberta Johnson referred was a ruling by the Wyoming Fair Employment Commission described in a page one article and photo in Cheyenne's Democratic newspaper, the *Wyoming Eagle*, on July 20, 1971.[345] The Commission concluded the Rock River School District (30 miles north of Laramie) had illegally discriminated against an African American teacher named Henry Fitzpatrick, a 1971 University of Wyoming graduate in education, on the basis of his race and ordered the district to pay him $3,000 in back pay. They also ordered the district to hire him if he reapplied.

At a hearing before the Commission on June 1, Ted Nelson, the president of the Rock River School Board, testified he told the high school principal Richard Preston that Nelson would "rather hire a white man if one were available." He testified he made the statement without

---

[344] Alberta Johnson and her husband William hosted a meeting of several UW African Americans in Laramie during Christmas break in late 1968, where plans were laid to form the UW Black Students Alliance. William Johnson, an eight-year veteran of the U.S. Air Force and a UW accounting graduate, became an IRS agent and the family moved to Cheyenne, where Alberta was elected to the city council for the 1973-74 term. UPI declared that she was the first member of her race to win elective office since W. J. Hardin served in the territorial legislature in the 1880s. (Casper Star Tribune 11/12/1972). The leaders of women's organizations in the state selected Alberta as the Wyoming's Outstanding Young Woman of the Year in November, 1974. (Casper Star Tribune 11/27/1974). In 1976 she ran unsuccessfully for the State House as a Democrat. William also sought office, running unsuccessfully for the school board in Cheyenne. In a release published in the *Eagle* on June 17, 1971, William said the problems of student unrest required more understanding and intelligence than the usual clamor for more administrators and for stricter discipline. He suggested that "making education more relevant and more interesting to the students themselves" was also important. After the Johnsons moved to Houston, Alberta obtained a law degree and worked for the city attorney's office.

[345] Because the two Cheyenne newspapers were owned by the McCracken family, and because many Cheyenne residents subscribed to only one of the papers, the news staff of the Tribune would almost always rewrite every news story appearing first in the Eagle, and vice versa. In Fitzpatrick's case, however, the Tribune carried no mention of the Eagle's page one article on the Commission's ruling. Perhaps Judge Kerr only read his close friend Flinchum's censored paper.

knowledge of Fitzpatrick's credentials and that he believed at the time that hiring a black teacher "might disrupt" the school because "we never had (a black teacher) before."

The Commission stated that Fitzpatrick's college transcript "evidences outstanding grades in the work he has undertaken." A former professor in the UW Education College testified he was "not just a good teacher; he's an excellent teacher."

At the time of the decision, Fitzpatrick was working as education director for Community Action of Laramie County in Cheyenne. When contacted by the *Eagle* reporter, he said he would not be reapplying because "the job has been eliminated." According to Alberta Johnson, who attended Fitzpatrick's wedding at the home of Cheyenne attorney Charles Graves, Fitzpatrick and his wife moved to the southeast part of the U.S. not too long after the Commission's ruling.

Sophistry in the federal courts

On the evening of October 17-18, 1969, the University of Wyoming Trustees and Gov. Hathaway met separately with the Black 14 and the coaches. The special meeting lasted from 8 p.m. Friday night to 3:15 a.m., at which time UW issued a press release saying the trustees had confirmed the dismissal of the 14 players. The release said the players "will not play in today's game or any during the balance of the season" and **"The dismissals result from a violation of a football coaching rule Friday morning."**

The release quoted Athletic Director Jacoby as saying: "Ample notice was given to all members of the football team regarding **rules and regulations of the squad, some of which cover a ban on participation in student demonstrations of any kind**. ... It is unfortunate this happened, but an open defiance of a coaching staff regulation cannot be tolerated."

In a Denver Post article by Irv Moss published on Monday, Oct. 20th, Eaton claimed that some white players had requested they be allowed to participate in the Vietnam Moratorium demonstration on Wednesday before the BYU game. "We reminded them of our team rule and told them to stay clear of it," Eaton was quoted as saying. "We reminded the whole squad last Tuesday that we didn't want any of them taking part in the Vietnam demonstration and they all adhered to the rule and request. If you get open defiance on a team, how do you expect to have team morale and discipline if you ignore it." An Arizona Republic article on Oct. 22nd said Gov. Hathaway "supports [Eaton] who, according to the governor, would have booted any white athlete who had similarly broken a rule."

UW's press release contained no mention of maintaining separation of church and state or protecting religious freedom as a cause of the purge of the black players. Even as late as Tuesday of the next week, the Associated Press report in the Arizona Star said "The 14 football players were booted off the team for violating Eaton's rule of no participation in any kind of demonstration, in or out of uniform." That same report, however, quoted Wyoming basketball coach Bill Strannigan as saying his players could join any campus demonstration as long as they "don't take their demonstrations onto the basketball court."

In wire service reports published on Wednesday, Gov. Hathaway said that during the long trustees meeting some of the players said they would not play without armbands or under coach Eaton. But Guillermo Hysaw was quoted as saying that the players had not adopted this position until later in the day, after Eaton had already dismissed them from the team, lectured them and then refused UW President's Carlson's request to meet the players at Old Main. "Because Eaton refused to see us or talk with us we changed our minds about wearing the armbands on the field," Hysaw said.

UW's and the state's lawyers soon realized that UW would be in constitutional quicksand if they stuck to the position that the coach's "ban on participation in student demonstrations of any kind" was a higher authority than the U.S. Constitution and the recent decision of the U.S. Supreme Court in the *Tinker v. Des Moines School District* case. So they began recasting the dismissals as representing the protection of rights of religion. U.S. District Judge Ewing T. Kerr was more than happy to accommodate the state, ignoring the press release to rule against the players.

His first dismissal was handed down in March 1970, but was partially reversed by the U.S. 10th Circuit Court of Appeals because the court found Judge Kerr was in error in dismissing the case without considering the Tinker case and without holding a trial on the conflicting facts.[346] The circuit court upheld the dismissal of the players' claim for monetary damages, meaning that even if the coach was found to have violated their civil rights by punishing them for the exercise of their right of free speech, the ruling would have had no practical effect on the players and their football careers.

Nearly two years after Eaton dismissed the players, the trial occurred in the U.S. District Court in Cheyenne. The only player able to attend was Mel Hamilton. A report in the Wyoming State Tribune on September 28, 1971, described Eaton's testimony. While on the stand, Eaton confirmed what the Black 14 had claimed all along: that during his tirade one of the statements he made to the players was "that if the program at Wyoming was not satisfactory then perhaps they had better think about going to Morgan State or Grambling" (both traditional black colleges). Eaton also clarified the terms of an offer of reinstatement saying the players would not only have to talk to Eaton individually, but also seek approval from the white players. Because none of the white players had supported them, the 14 black players understandably were not receptive to this idea.

In his second dismissal order, Kerr adopted Barrett's argument that directly contradicted the press release approved by the Trustees at the end of their late-night meeting. Kerr ruled:

> [T]he Board of Trustees sustained the action of Coach Lloyd Eaton dismissing the Plaintiffs from the University of Wyoming football team on the ground that should the University of Wyoming or its governing officials permit or allow the Plaintiffs, as representatives of the University of Wyoming ... to appear on the playing field during the scheduled game on the afternoon of October 18, 1969, wearing black armbands in protest-demonstration to certain claimed religious beliefs of the Mormon Church and Brigham Young University, that the State of Wyoming ... would be in violation of the mandate requiring complete neutrality relating to religion and non-religion and in violation of the principle of separation of Church and State....**The action and order of dismissal by the Board of Trustees of the University of Wyoming was not predicated upon the existence or non-existence of any football coaching rule** ...."[347]

In 1972, the same three circuit court judges who had reversed Judge Kerr in the first appeal decided to affirm him in the second.[348] The court's opinion is internally contradictory and

---

[346] William Johnson, one of the founders of the BSA, posted the bond for the appeal. He became an IRS agent posted in Cheyenne and Houston.

[347] *Williams v. Eaton*, 333 F.Supp. 107 (D.Wyo. October 18, 1971).

[348] 468 F.2d 1084.

its reasoning is mystifying, in light of the Supreme Court's ruling in the *Tinker* case, where the court held that "[A] student['s] rights ... do not embrace merely classroom hours. When he is ... on the playing field, or on the campus during the authorized hours, he may express his opinions, even on controversial subjects like the conflict in Vietnam." 393 U.S. 503 at 512. The high court in *Tinker* reversed the dismissals of students from junior and senior high school for wearing armbands in a Vietnam War protest. The court said the dismissals in the Tinker case were "based upon an urgent wish to avoid the controversy which might result from the expression" and held this was not a sufficient justification to punish them for the exercise of their right of free speech.[349]

In the final appeals court decision, the Tenth Circuit's nebulous reasoning revolved around a finding that wearing armbands during the game would have been a "hostile expression" to the BYU players. In the context of a college football game, this is almost laughable. At practically every stadium across the country, visiting football players, coaches and fans were routinely subjected to demeaning, hostile and even obscene mocking by home team fans, particularly against arch-rivals such as when BYU came to Laramie .[350] Black arm bands on the uniforms of some of the players in 1969 might not have even been noticed.

This was the final word from the federal appeals court:

We do not treat certain additional propositions forcefully argued for the athletes on this appeal. Arguments are made that the football coaching rule against participation generally by the athletes in demonstrations was invalid. However, we feel that questions concerning the rule need not be decided. The original dismissal of the athletes by Coach Eaton for violation of the rule was not the end of the matter. Later the controversy was considered by the Trustees and President Carlson at a conference with the athletes and the athletic officials. It was found by the trial court that the decision of the Trustees to sustain the dismissal of the athletes was made after this conference during which the athletes insisted on the right to wear the armbands during the game. And it was further found that the Trustees' decision was made on the ground that permitting the wearing of the armbands would be in violation of the constitutional mandate requiring complete neutrality on religion.
...
The plaintiffs vigorously deny that there would have been state action or a violation of the First Amendment principles on religion by permitting the armband display. **Without deciding whether approval of the armband display would have involved state action or a violation of the religion clauses, we are persuaded that the Trustees' decision was lawful within the limitations of the Tinker case itself. Their decision protected against invasion of the rights of others by avoiding a hostile expression to them by some members of the**

---

[349]393 U.S. at 510.

[350] A Casper Star-Tribune report on April 6, 1987, said two legislators who attended the game against BYU earlier that year had written to the UW president to complain about "unconscionably rude behavior ... and an almost constant stream of obscenities" from UW students. "I was embarrassed that my family had to listen to this profanity and observe the obscene gestures," the letter said. During the following days in the letters-to-the-editor, the two legislators were vilified for daring to complain about the "Sixth Man's" antics." Dave Lindsey of Laramie wrote: "To all the real Wyoming fans and especially the students, don't let a little bad publicity get you down; manners were never our strong suit anyway."

University team. It was in furtherance of the policy of religious neutrality by the State. It denied only the request for the armband display by some members of the team, on the field and during the game. In these limited circumstances we conclude that the Trustees' decision was in conformity with the Tinker case and did not violate the First Amendment right of expression of the plaintiffs.

During a panel discussion organized by the UW American Heritage Center in 2010, former UW College of Law Dean Jerry Parkinson said "the most disappointing thing for me was the reaction of the federal courts. The trial court flatly ignored the rights set forth just months before in the *Tinker* case."

In the only legal source which has analyzed the 10th Circuit decision in some depth, the authors, a Duke University law professor and an Atlanta attorney, concluded that the case "appears to have been improperly decided. As noted, the basis for the court's decision was that barring the armband demonstration would avoid a 'hostile expression' to others, which 'hostile expression' would invade their rights. The natural desire to seek to avoid offending others is, however, not a constitutionally valid reason to regulate speech-related activity."[351]

In the first place the circuit court's assertion that "the athletes insisted on the right to wear the armbands during the game" was just simply not true. The testimony at trial from Hathaway and Carlson was that one or more, but not all, of them responded "no" to the hypothetical question of whether they would play without arm bands. The rest said nothing. The governor and the trustees never gave those others the option of being reinstated and playing without arm bands.

Ultimately, however, the federal courts' reaction to this case was a perfect example of avoiding the central issue. Kerr, and eventually the Circuit Court, ignored the fact that the players had not showed up on the sidelines of the BYU game wearing black arm bands on their uniforms. Instead they took the responsible course of going to the coach to discuss the issue the day before the game. Even if, for argument's sake, the circuit court decision is deemed to be correct -- that allowing the players to wear arm bands during the game would have violated state religious neutrality -- that isn't what got the Black 14 dismissed for the season in the first place. That all happened the day before the game. The governor and the trustees, particularly the lawyers among them, should have told the coach that his rule was unconstitutional, his severe punishment for the exercise of their right to wear arm bands violated the federal Civil Rights Act and the players were being reinstated. If any refused to play without arm bands the next day at the game, the issue of religious freedom might have then become involved.[352] Another undeniable fact was also ignored by the courts: the religious issue became a non-justiciable moot question the minute the BYU game ended.

---

[351] Weistart, John and Cym Lowell, *The Law of Sports*, Bobbs-Merrill Co., 1979 at 29-30.

[352] In *Hysaw v. Washburn Univ. of Topeka*, 690 F.Supp. 940 (D. Kan. 1987) (not involving Guillermo Hysaw of the Black 14), U.S. District Judge Dale Saffels denied some parts of the state defendants' motion for summary judgment in a free speech case brought by five black players dismissed from the Washburn Univ. football team after they boycotted practices. They claimed the university and the coaching staff had not responded to their allegations of racially discriminatory treatment. The judge looked to the Tinker case and issued a ruling that seems much more aligned with the intentions of that decision than the tortuous reasoning of the 10th Circuit in the Black 14 case. Judge Saffels ruled: "The court will not place the interests of participants in a university extracurricular activity above the rights of any citizen to speak out against alleged racial injustice without fear of government retribution."

This Black 14 mural was created by Adrienne Vetter in the alley behind 213 E. Grand Ave. in Laramie. The players (with their home states in 1969) are, back row L-R: Tony Gibson, MA; Joe Williams, TX; Lionel Grimes, OH; Mel Hamilton, NC and Boy's Town NE; James Isaac, WY; Ivie Moore, AR. Front row: Ron Hill, AL and CO; Guillermo Hysaw, CA; Anthony McGee, MI; Jerome Berry, OK; Ted Williams, CA; John Griffin, CA; Earl Lee, TN; Don Meadows, CO.

1955-1992: JUDGE KERR AND THE U.S. DISTRICT COURT OF WYOMING

Ewing T. Kerr was born in January, 1900, in Bowie, Texas and came to Cheyenne as a teacher in 1925. No one could have imagined that 44 years later as a federal judge he would preside over a case such as the one the Black 14 incident presented to him. But it was no surprise that once the case was filed, Kerr would delight the state's power structure and football fans by ruling against the 14 young black football players.

After becoming an attorney by "reading law" in an Oklahoma attorney's office, Kerr was appointed as U.S. Attorney for Wyoming from 1930-33 and as state attorney general from 1939 to 1943. He was an officer during WWII, serving in military government and the Judge Advocate General corps in North Africa and Europe.

Before Democratic U.S. Sen. Lester C. Hunt killed himself in his Washington D.C. office in June, 1954, Cheyenne attorney Kerr had resigned as state Republican chairman and had entered the race for the Republican nomination to oppose the heavily-favored Hunt that fall. After Hunt's death, Wyoming's U.S. Rep. William Henry Harrison, a direct descendant of two U.S. presidents, dropped out of his race for re-election to the House and entered the Senate race.

In an ad in the Cheyenne Tribune on August 10th, Kerr said he had been unanimously elected as Republican state chairman five times. But within the next week, "a relatively quiet person-to-person campaign exploded into bitter verbal blasts" between Kerr and Harrison.[353] Kerr claimed that Harrison's absence from Washington to campaign in Wyoming allowed a House

---

[353] Report by Bob Leeright from the Cheyenne AP bureau, Wyoming State Tribune, Aug. 16, 1954.

262

committee to delete a $2 million appropriation for construction of the Glendo dam. Kerr also claimed that some party leaders felt that Harrison's switch from the House to the Senate race was "an act of cowardice."

Harrison countered that he had persuaded the committee to restore $1 million for the project. "I vigorously denounce [Kerr's] irresponsible allegations as borne of desperation and desire for selfish gain--no more and no less."

In a statement issued from Harrison's office, Rep. Miller (R-Neb.), chair of the House interior committee, said "the personal attack" leveled against Harrison "is one of the most unfair and unsportsmanlike actions ever to come to my attention."[354]

Harrison easily won the nomination. Kerr came in third, more than 6,000 votes behind Harrison and 600 votes behind Sam C. Hyatt (1894-1978), a Hyattville cattleman and the son of S.W. Hyatt, founder of the town. Kerr promptly congratulated Harrison and promised his full support.[355] Harrison lost to Joseph C. O'Mahoney by three points in the general election.

Just over a year later, on October 22, 1955, President Eisenhower appointed Kerr as Wyoming's sole U.S. district judge.

In an oral history interview on November 29, 1982, Kerr was asked about the Black 14 case. He summed it up this way: "There was a fellow by the name of [Willie] Black, who was in school getting his Masters or Ph.D. in mathematics and the state was financing him, $300 a month, he was the one who was behind all that. If he'd left it up to the players, they would have never insisted. Stan Hathaway and the president and coach, Eaton, it ruined Eaton. ... It was a good team. We'd won too. If we hadn't been at the top, you'd never heard of the Black 14. You see, that's the way they attack."[356]

Just over a year later, on October 22, 1955, President Eisenhower appointed Kerr as Wyoming's sole U.S. district judge.

Toward the end of the contentious 1982 election campaign between Republican incumbent U.S. Sen. Malcolm Wallop and Cheyenne attorney and legislator Rodger McDaniel, Wallop ran an advertisement in Wyoming newspapers showing numerous "individual Wyoming contributors" to the Republican's re-election drive. The ad listed "Ewing and Irene Kerr" as contributors.

The Code of Judicial Conduct for U.S. judges stated at that time that "a judge should refrain from political activity" and clarified that statement by saying, "A judge should not ... make a contribution to a political organization or candidate...." It also said, "a judicial officer has a duty to try to dissuade his spouse from participating in a political campaign."

When contacted by a news reporter about the contribution, Kerr said his name was used "in error," that he had not made a contribution but that his wife may have made a contribution using a check form that bore both names. Even if she did, he insisted, she "hasn't participated in a campaign in any way."

---

[354] Tribune, Aug. 13, 1954.

[355] Also in its election results issue in 1954, the Cheyenne Tribune carried a syndicated column by Lee Mortimer on its opinion page. This column alerted readers to a "new fad among the hope of the future, 'choclajuana' made by mixing liquid marijuana in a chocolate soda. Especially prevalent in California where the kids go on 'choc' sprees at movie drive-ins. What has the junk squads more than worried is the source of the liquid hemp, otherwise known as hasheesh (from which comes our word 'assassin'). Until now hemp has been seen here only in the less potent smoking form of 'reefers.'"

[356] Transcript of interview, Wyoming State Archives, Cheyenne.

After the interview, Kerr phoned the publisher and editor at the Casper Star-Tribune in an unsuccessful effort to prevent publication of any article about the contribution.

In an oral history interview just after that 1982 election, Kerr was asked about the Black 14 case. He summed it up this way: "There was a fellow by the name of [Willie] Black, who was in school getting his Masters or Ph.D. in mathematics and the state was financing him, $300 a month, he was the one who was behind all that. If he'd left it up to the players, they would have never insisted. Stan Hathaway and the president and coach, Eaton, it ruined Eaton. ... It was a good team. We'd won too. If we hadn't been at the top, you'd never heard of the Black 14. You see, that's the way they attack."[357]

In the early 1990s, Judge Kerr posed for a photograph beneath a portrait of his predecessor, Judge T. Blake Kennedy (see chapter on the prosecution of the internment camp draft resisters in 1944 pg. 150). The photo appears in a book titled *The Wind Is My Witness* by Mark Junge. Beside the photo is Kerr's description of his pride in the fact that he had played a major role in preventing any Democrat from being appointed as a federal court judge in Wyoming during the first 100 years of the state's existence. In that interview Kerr said:

> I'm proud of this. We have a record in Wyoming. The first eighty-five years of statehood we've had three judges. ... Every federal judge since 1890 has been state chairman of the Republican Party. ... Judge Kennedy ... retired after he was eighty. He was waiting for Eisenhower to be elected. He didn't want to be succeeded by a Democrat. ...
>
> I've enjoyed being a judge all the time I've been on. That's the reason I'm still on the job. If I'm still able to hold court at ninety-one, I'll still be down there.

Kerr, who went on senior status in 1974 but maintained a caseload at the court, was "still down there" at the age of 91. He retired shortly before his death on July 1, 1992. Three months earlier Congress named the reconstructed U.S. courthouse and federal building in Casper after him. The act said Kerr "has embodied the spirit of public service and has been dedicated to upholding the law of the land."

In an interview with Hathaway for her Casper Star-Tribune column shortly after Kerr's passing and 23 years after the Black 14 incident, Joan Barron found the former governor and attorney still clinging to the erroneous concept that the Constitution's free speech protection did not extend to criticizing a religion. Speaking of Kerr's decision, Hathaway declared: "In a legal sense, it was a great case. If you're going to demonstrate, don't demonstrate against another freedom."

EARLY 1970S: CIVIL RIGHTS SPEAKERS AT UW

Two months after the Black 14 incident, the UW Black Students Alliance brought their first speaker to campus in the person of James Farmer, the Asst. Secretary in the Department of Health, Education and Welfare, an African American who was one of the founders of the Congress on Racial Equality (CORE). The statement by Texas coach Darrell Royal a month later tended to prove one of Farmer's comments in Laramie: he said the doctrine of white superiority and black inferiority had been programmed into both white and black children. Farmer said the decade of struggle from 1954-64 had helped middle class blacks but not "the young black person

[357] Transcript of interview, Wyoming State Archives, Cheyenne.

who is poor--who is living in the ghetto...." The Dec. 18, 1969 Laramie Boomerang report on his speech did not include any comments he may have made about the Black 14.

The year before, Farmer had lost his bid for a seat in Congress from Brooklyn to Shirley Chisholm, the first black woman to serve as a U.S. Representative. In March, 1969, in her first speech on the floor of that body, Chisholm declared her opposition to the Vietnam War and called for the support of "every mother, wife and widow in this land who ever asked herself why the generals can play with billions while families crumble under the weight of sickness, hunger and unemployment."[358] Rep. Chisholm ran for President in the 1972 Democratic primary but lost to Sen. George McGovern (D-S.D.). On October 30, 1970, the BSA brought black Congressman Julian Bond of Georgia to campus. He spoke before a standing-room-only audience in the A&S Auditorium. "Blacks are first in war, last in peace and seldom in the hearts of their countrymen," he said.

On May 15, 1972, black comedian and civil rights activist Dick Gregory spoke to a capacity crowd in the UW Arts & Sciences auditorium, several hours after Alabama Gov. George Wallace was shot four times in Laurel, Md. while campaigning for president -- this time as a Democrat. In his UW speech, Gregory condemned the shooting, which left Wallace a paraplegic. Gregory said anyone who felt good about it was no different than those who felt good about the assassination of Martin Luther King. (UPI/Greeley Tribune 5/16/1972). He told the audience: "You youngsters have to erase this madness. You haven't got much time." (Boomerang, 5/16/1972). He said the young people of the day were "the most honest, moral and committed generation in history." But they should address the local issues first, he said, such as the problems of Native Americans and other minorities in Wyoming. Gregory appeared frail due to his solid food fast as a Vietnam War protest, reducing his weight from more than 200 pounds to just under 100.[359]

Gregory also talked about the ease with which former German soldiers could find jobs in the U.S. after World War II while African Americans who fought against them were facing discrimination at every turn.

Don Riddle[360], an advertising salesman in Casper who was Gov. Wallace's Rocky Mountain campaign coordinator, told UPI that day: "I presume [the shooting] has something to do with the Communist conspiracy trying to take this country over." (Boomerang, 5/16/1972). Authorities later concluded that the shooter, a 21-year-old white man from Milwaukee, was a loner without friends and with mental problems. (AP, Winona (Minn.) News, 5/17/1972).

On January 6, 1971, the Casper Star reported that Charles Sanchez, acting president of the UW Student Hispano Organization, had announced that United Farm Workers' leader Cesar Chavez would be unable to appear as scheduled at UW that week. Sanchez said Chavez's health had been poor since his 1968 fast during the grape boycott and he had been taken ill while imprisoned in a "damp cell" in Salinas, Calif. for 19 days in December after he refused to abide by a court order to terminate a later boycott aimed at a large lettuce grower. But Sanchez said 23-year-old Jessica Govea, who directed the boycott during Chavez's time in jail, would speak in his stead.

---

[358] Arizona Republic, March 27, 1969, p. 67.

[359] Gregory died on August 19, 2017.

[360] Three years earlier, after the Black 14 were dismissed from the UW football team, bumper stickers saying "We Support Coach Lloyd Eaton" were distributed around the state. The stickers said "ORDER FROM: Don Riddle Adv." giving a PO box address in Casper. "Pkgs. 100 – $26.00 Post Paid."

Govea, the daughter of farm workers, told a large UW audience of the tragedies that farm workers in her family had suffered and of the inhumane conditions at some of the farms. She said the UFW's new lettuce boycott was progressing "beautifully".[361] She said the UFW had filed suit against the U.S. Defense Department, saying the DOD was attempting to break the strike by buying large quantities of lettuce from the grower being targeted. According to a Branding Iron article by Ben Pacheco, she urged Wyomingites to force retailers to obtain union lettuce identified by the black Aztec eagle on the box (which is also on the flag she is holding in a BI photo accompanying the article). The article said student senator Sue Crist would introduce a resolution to support the strike.

Jessica Govea Thorbourne went on to become a "labor educator" at Rutgers and Cornell. She died in New Jersey at age 58 in 2005 believing that her illness was connected to the pesticides used in the farm fields of her youth.[362]

An article about a claim of job discrimination being brought against UW by Manuel Sisneros appears on the same BI page one. Sisneros alleged that his applications had been passed over for 14 years before he was hired as a journeyman electrician.

1973: NUKES BELOW PINEDALE

The April 17, 1973 issue of the Cheyenne Eagle carried articles about a proposed underground nuclear explosion southeast of Pinedale in 1977 to release natural gas, and about Vietnam bombing.

A UPI story datelined Rock Springs said that city's council had approved a resolution opposing the Wagon Wheel Project, a plan put forward by El Paso Natural Gas Co. and the U.S. Atomic Energy Commission to detonate a series of nuclear blasts far underground near Pinedale. Sally Mackey of Pinedale, a member of the Corthell family of Laramie, was chairwoman of the Wagon Wheel Information Committee, composed of some ranchers and other residents, which opposed the project. It was to be the fourth such explosion. On January 8, 1973, AP reported that the committee had sent a telegram to Colorado Gov. John Love urging him to veto the Rio Blanco Project in his state, calling it a dangerous and uneconomical program of "the atomic industrial establishment."

The first device had been detonated in late 1967 near Farmington, N.M. Then a 40-kiloton device, more than twice as powerful as the Hiroshima bomb, was detonated near Rifle, Colorado in 1969 as part of Project Rulison, followed by the simultaneous detonation of three 30-kiloton devices more than a mile deep in May, 1973, also near Rifle.

In February, 1973, representatives of the Wagon Wheel Information Committee met with officials of the Atomic Energy Commission and El Paso Gas in D.C. Sen. Cliff Hansen (R-Wyo.) read a letter from the mayor of Rock Springs expressing concerns that the test could cause movement in already unstable coal mine land nearby. The ranchers argued the test could contaminate the air, cause earthquakes and break dams and irrigation canals.[363]

---

[361] Casper Star Jan. 9, 1971; Branding Iron Jan. 8, 1971.

[362] Cornell University Chronicle Feb. 1, 2005.

[363] AP article Greenwood S.C. Index-Journal Feb. 8, 1973. The article also said the Town of Pinedale had gone on record against Wagon Wheel.

Sally Mackey and her associates eventually carried the day and the Wagon Wheel idea was dropped. The draft Environmental Impact Statement for the project released in early 1972 called for the sequential detonation of five 100-kiloton devices more than a mile and a half below the surface in 1977. (They couldn't detonate them at once because it would have violated JFK's nuclear test ban treaty). U.S. Rep. Teno Roncalio said geologists had told him that the project "is like going after a fly with a howitzer."[364]

The Eagle also reported that only hours after President Nixon ordered a halt to the bombing of North Vietnam as peace talks progressed, U.S. warplanes stepped up bombing raids against the Ho Chi Minh trail complex in Laos and against North Vietnamese and Viet Cong positions in South Vietnam. Aircraft losses and American casualties continued to mount in the south, the article said.

CHEYENNE CENTRAL 1972: COMFORTS AND ADVANTAGES

In 1942, while World War II was raging, the U.S. Supreme Court issued a ruling in a case where public school students had been dismissed for refusing to salute the flag and say the pledge of allegiance:

> We think the action of the local authorities in compelling the flag salute and pledge transcends constitutional limitations on their power and invades the sphere of intellect and spirit which it is the purpose of the First Amendment to our Constitution to reserve from all official control. ...
>
> To enforce those rights today ... is only to adhere as a means of strength to individual freedom of mind in preference to officially disciplined uniformity for which history indicates a disappointing and disastrous end. ... That [Boards of Education] are educating the young for citizenship is reason for scrupulous protection of Constitutional freedoms of the individual, if we are not to strangle the free mind at its source and teach youth to discount important principles of our government as mere platitudes. ...
>
> Those who begin coercive elimination of dissent soon find themselves exterminating dissenters. Compulsory unification of opinion achieves only the unanimity of the graveyard.
>
> Justice Robert H. Jackson, U.S. Supreme Court, *West Virginia State Board of Education v. Barnette*, 319 U.S. 624 (1942).[365]

Thirty years later, during a dispute about the flag salute at Cheyenne Central High, the editor of the State Tribune in Cheyenne took a different view:

---

[364] Lander Wyo. State Journal, 6/12/1972.

[365] After the NFL owners ruled on May 23, 2018, that players who do not stand for the national anthem would be fined, President Trump praised the decision, along with a majority of NFL fans. "You have to stand proudly for the national anthem," Trump said. "Or you shouldn't be playing, you shouldn't be there. Maybe you shouldn't be in the country." It would be interesting to know whether Trump had the same view of the Vietnam War protesters when he was securing his medical deferment during the war. If so, he would have been joining with Nixon's "silent majority" in shouting: "America -- Love It or Leave It."

What is lost sight of in our country especially is that we must of necessity live in an authoritarian society, and particularly so when the people themselves run that society, individual discipline being one of the basic factors in the smooth operation of such a social organization.

James M. Flinchum, Wyoming State Tribune (Cheyenne) editorial April 25, 1972.

Hair and dress codes

The Casper school district, where a 9th grader had been expelled in 1967 for two years because of his long hair, was not the only Wyoming district experiencing conflicts at that time between the World War II generation and its children. The students were beginning to recognize the hypocrisy involved in how young people -- particularly young males -- were being treated. They were being severely punished for hair and dress code violations or for expressing dissent, and at the same time the draft and the Vietnam War loomed just ahead for many of them. "Why should the authorities be so concerned about hair length when in just a few months we could be facing death in Vietnam", many of them wondered.

The October 23, 1969 edition of the Gillette News-Record carried a short item with the headline, "Two Suspended For Long Hair," reporting that Gerry Egland and Jesse Lubkin had been suspended for violating the Gillette School Board's hair policy which prohibited "extreme hair styles ... such as Beatle cuts, duck tails, Mohawks" or those long enough to cover the collar.

Principal James Brisson at Cheyenne Central High had a running battle with students and some teachers from 1969 until at least 1973, when his CCHS tenure ended. As with the expulsion of the Black 14 at UW in 1969, the authorities involved in the conflict at Central ignored or disregarded the U.S. Constitution -- and its interpretations by the Supreme Court -- by pointing to the overriding need for discipline.

Shortly after the school year began in September, 1969, an unidentified student representing an organization called the Cheyenne Student Union protested the dress and hair code at a school board meeting. He said the rules were "unnecessary and repressive" and that "no student can work to his fullest if he is in a situation where he has to be more concerned with discipline than education." The student claimed that when anything unconventional was proposed, the authorities quickly repressed it.

A UPI article transmitted on November 12, 1969, quoted Brisson, age 40, as saying that 26 Central students had been suspended for violating the dress and grooming code he had imposed. But then, Brisson said, 40 other students "decided to get into the act and therefore also received suspensions."

An AP article on November 20th, reported that five Central students had been expelled "following their suspensions for violating dress codes and for demonstrating." Brisson stated that all but five of the students originally suspended had come in for conferences with their parents and were reinstated. The other five, four boys and a girl, would have to seek reinstatement from the school board, Brisson said. (A longtime teacher at Central said in a 2013 interview that one of the students was the son of Wyoming's Secretary of State and was reinstated. He said that at least one of the others, a Latino boy, never returned to high school).

The article reported that the demonstrations against the dress code occurred after 26 students had been told by Brisson to go home and "shave, cut their hair, or put on a longer skirt." He said 37 students then began picketing.

The code required that a boy's hair could not cover the ear or "push the shirt collar" and sideburns could not be longer than the bottom of the ear, according to a UPI article transmitted

268

November 11th. "For the girls," the article reported, "extreme dress would be considered where the undergarments are visible when a girl stands at the student counter or sits at a school desk."[366]

In November of 1970, 123 of the 900 Laramie High School students submitted a petition to the school board calling for modification of the hair and dress code there. The code had been adopted in 1956 and banned moustaches, beards and long sideburns and provided that hair "must not touch the ears and must be tapered in back." The code provided that girls could wear pants to school but must change into a skirt or dress before classes began.

School administration officials argued that hair rules were necessary to maintain discipline and enhance the school's image. Mike McNamee, board chairman, said "radical departures from what the community considers normal are distractive in the school system."

Two mothers challenged these assumptions at a school board meeting that month. One of them was Estella Black, wife of Willie Black, the chancellor of the UW Black Students Alliance when the Black 14 event happened a year earlier. She told the board that "you have made hair a problem. School is supposed to make students intelligent, not rubber stamps." Mrs. Carl Dierks asserted that "long hair and new styles in clothes do not disrupt anything."[367]

The students and parents also protested the athletic department regulations which apparently applied only to boys. Coach Bill Bernatow said his department required athletes' hair to be no longer than a quarter of an inch and any student not complying with the requirement was docked points from their grades. One reason for the rule, he said, was the expense incurred to clean the school swimming pool of hair (which would seem to be a problem caused in large part by girls' hair).

1962: NAACP Youth Council

To most of the white students at Cheyenne high schools in the early Sixties, the civil rights struggles in the South seemed to be a distant problem which didn't concern them. But of course this was not the case with the few African American students.

On January 9, 1962, the Cheyenne newspapers carried an article about a Central High student named Kim Robinson who was organizing "an NAACP youth council in Cheyenne" with its first meeting slated for the African Methodist Episcopal Church at 18th and Thomes. Miss Robinson was quoted as saying the council "will give teenagers a chance to work for noble ideas such as brotherhood, democracy and equality. President Kennedy is sending young people out in the Peace Corps to help certain foreign nations make progress, but I think we need to make some progress in certain areas right here in the United States."

The council, she said, "will be part of the NAACP's national effort to fight racial discrimination and prejudice of all kinds and to secure equal justice for everyone under law – which is the American dream." She said young people of all races were invited to participate in the council's activities, including study groups "in Negro history and reports on contributions of Negroes to American literature, poetry, music and art."

Clifford Jeffrey, a classmate of Miss Robinson's, said in a 2014 interview from his home in Oakland that the powers-that-be put a stop to Miss Robinson's initiative almost immediately.

---

[366] At some point prior to the flag salute events of April, 1972, the school board rescinded the hair and dress code.

[367] Casper Star 11/29/1970 p.2.

1972: Brisson and Urbigkit vs. the Constitution in Cheyenne

According to a letter he wrote to the parents of some Central High students on April 21, 1972, Principal Brisson on April 6, 1972, warned students -- during the daily announcements over the Central High intercom -- "that assemblies were for their benefit and that proper respect to the flag, participating in the pledge ... was expected and any violation could possibly lead to suspension. Students were reminded that standing was one of the courtesies expected."

On that day a young staff attorney at Legal Services of Laramie County, a federally-funded law firm representing low income people, answered the phone when a Central student called, explained what Brisson had said that morning and asked if it was legal for a student to be punished for refusing to salute the flag. He said an assembly was planned for late morning the next day. The attorney's legal research quickly turned up the 1942 Barnette case from the Supreme Court, quoted above.

To avoid possible problems both for students and the school district the attorney decided to type up two pages of quotations from that opinion and take them to Brisson. The attorney was shown into his office and the quotations were handed to him. Brisson set the letter on his desk and then used both hands to raise a foot-high stack of papers next to it which he firmly set on top of the letter, saying he would address it in due course.

A week later, according to a front-page article in the Wyoming State Tribune, the Republican afternoon newspaper, Superintendent Joe Lutjeharms "said as far as he was concerned, the school administration would not retreat from the policy of requiring students to stand [for the flag] or else face the possibility of suspension." School board chairman Walter Urbigkit, a future Democratic legislator and a future Wyoming Supreme Court justice, took the position that even sitting silently during the presentation of the flag and recitation of the pledge was "disruptive behavior directed at the organization and conduct of the schools to a degree that their severance from the system will be required because of the necessity of maintenance of reasonable order in view of the facilities and overcrowding problems."

At a student election assembly on April 13, seven students (most of them African American) disobeyed Brisson's directive. According to Brisson's April 21st letter, they "were sent home [the next day] to get their parents for a conference prior to being allowed to re-enter Central High School." Brisson related that "most conferences were satisfactory." The Cheyenne NAACP charged that some white students had also refused to salute the flag but were not suspended.

Apparently conceding that they could not expel students for refusing to say the pledge, Brisson and Lutjeharms, after consultation with Urbigkit, devised another way to essentially inflict punishment on these non-compliant students without expelling them. According to his April 21st letter to parents, Brisson informed the students on April 18th, prior to a concert by the U.S. Army Field Band in the adjacent Storey Gym, as follows:

> Any student whose convictions, moral, religious or otherwise, will not permit him to stand and show proper respect to the flag of our country when the pledge of allegiance is given or the National Anthem is played will be excused from the first part of the assembly. However, since all students present in school this morning must be accountable during the assembly period, students who feel they cannot participate in the opening of the assembly will report to the auditorium at 10 o'clock where roll will be taken. The auditorium group will be permitted to view the remainder of the assembly.

Brisson and the superintendent had a surprise coming. Yes, the seven black students as expected chose the option of waiting in the auditorium in the main building before walking across to Storey Gym. But around 115 other students -- mostly whites and a few Hispanics -- joined their classmates in the auditorium. This group amounted to nearly 10% of the student population.

Nevertheless, Brisson proceeded to write and send his April 21st letter to the parents of all 121 students, informing them of what their child had done, and he made sure to place a copy in each of their official student files. On April 18th he had told the Wyoming Eagle that "the protesting students will not be reprimanded."

The procedure Brisson and Lutjeharm adopted was probably also unconstitutional because it did not recognize that the students had a right to sit in the assembly and exercise their right of free speech as to the flag and the pledge, without being ostracized in this way. Justice Brennan of the U.S. Supreme Court recognized this in his 1963 concurring opinion in *School Dist. of Abington Township v. Schempp*, 374 U.S. 203 (1963), where the high court by an 8-1 vote ruled that a statute requiring school authorities to conduct a Bible-reading session at the opening of school each day was unconstitutional. The opportunity to be excused from that exercise "does not mitigate the obligatory nature of the ceremony," Brennan wrote. He also recognized that choosing to be excused from the ceremony could lead to the students being "stigmatized as atheists or nonconformists." Brennan quoted from a Wisconsin Supreme Court decision in 1893 which said, "...the excluded pupil loses caste with his fellows, and is liable to be regarded with aversion and subjected to reproach and insult."

In a letter on Laramie County School District Number One stationery dated April 13, 1972, Urbigkit told the staff attorney for Legal Services: "...the fruit of the dragon's teeth may be bitter indeed to eat. ... It is my unqualified view that it is stupid, absurd and self-defeating not to recognize the benefits bestowed by American citizenship by actions of respect such as standing for our Nation's flag. ... Enlightened citizenship in my opinion requires recognition of the efforts of those in the past who have made possible the comforts and advantages now enjoyed plus the knowledge of our responsibility for the future to even more fully afford such rights and benefits to those who will follow."[368] Urbigkit also sent a letter to the director of Legal Services for Laramie County dated April 25th in which he suggested that the students' school files now contained information that might prevent them from being selected for Boys' State or Girls' State, for a military academy or for some employment opportunities in the future.

Urbigkit indicated that Legal Services should not have informed the students as to the unconstitutionality of Brisson's original edict. In neither letter did Urbigkit mention the Barnette decision. Despite the specific reference to "flag salute" in the excerpt from that case quoted above, Brisson persisted in an argument that requiring students to stand for the flag was permissible if they were not required to say the pledge.

And nowhere – in any of the editorials or letters – was there any interest or concern as to why 121 Central High students chose to refuse to salute the flag. Editor Flinchum in an April 17th editorial claimed he had no idea why the students would do this and he raised the old "outside agitators" claim used by segregationists in the South and by supporters of coach Eaton at UW. "[I]t seems reasonable to conclude that these young people were the recipients of some very bad advice. It would further seem probable that they are the unwitting victims of individuals and perhaps organizations of very questionable purpose and motive, and certainly lacking the best

---

[368] Quoted in a page one story in the State Tribune 4/14/1972. How punishing students for exercising their clear constitutional rights in 1972 would "more fully afford such rights" to those who follow remains a mystery.

interests of the students involved...." But this belief did not slow the authorities in their effort to poison the students' school records.

The flag salute issue was next addressed at a school board meeting on April 24. A UPI article appeared in the afternoon State Tribune that day describing anti-war protests in five states spurred by the stepped-up U.S. bombing. It also described an unusual one-man protest by a 24-year-old Vietnam veteran named Robert Pigsley in Atlantic, Iowa, during Sunday mass at the local Catholic church. The man walked down the aisle during the sermon -- dressed in camo helmet, boots and Army fatigues and with mud on his face -- threw his two Purple Hearts, his Bronze Star and four other medals toward the altar and then lifted a WWII M1 rifle -- the type used by University of Wyoming Army R.O.T.C. cadets in the early '60s -- and fired a shot into the wall above the altar. As he was being subdued by several parishioners he shouted, "Make love not war: That's what he died for." Another witness reported him saying "the people weren't going to do anything about the war so it was up to the younger generation." Later the veteran told a reporter for the Des Moines Register that he was showing "the hypocrisy of religion in teaching thou shalt not kill and then acting contrarily by not making any moves to stop the war." His grandfather, with whom the unemployed vet lived, was quoted as saying: "You couldn't find a better boy until he went to the service, but, when he came back, well, that was it."

Ten months later he was sentenced to probation for two years for malicious injury to a building. He died in 2011 at his home in Des Moines and military graveside rites were conducted in Atlantic.

Could it be that the males among the student dissenters at Central High, like this veteran, did not regard being forced across the Pacific to fight and die in a doomed war to be a "comfort and advantage"?

NAACP seeks "sensitivity training" for Brisson

The president of the Cheyenne NAACP chapter, Alberta Johnson, appeared at the school board meeting on April 24th and read off a long list of alleged grievances against the Central principal. Mrs. Johnson, who was soon to be elected to the Cheyenne City Council, called for Brisson's suspension so that he could undergo "sensitivity training." She also called for two counselors for minority students, saying "blacks are put in the general courses, lower level courses." Chairman Urbigkit responded by saying "we do not meet demands or threats."

On June 2, the State Tribune carried an article revealing that the Cheyenne chapter of the NAACP filed a federal civil rights complaint against Brisson as a result of the suspension of the seven black students on April 13th. The Civil Rights office in Denver asked Lutjeharms to respond to the allegation that some white students had also refused to salute the flag that day and the superintendent responded with "a strict denial that any discrimination took place."

More suspensions and expulsions in 1973

On January 13, 1973, Cheyenne's Wyoming Eagle carried a front page headline saying "Equal Rights Clause Gets Initial Backing" after the Wyoming House voted 29-14 on first reading to add Wyoming to the list of states approving the proposed equal rights amendment to the U.S. Constitution (which never did receive the endorsement of enough states to be adopted into the Constitution). "It was here in Wyoming 102 years ago that a government made up entirely of men bestowed full citizenship on women," Rep. Edness Kimball Wilkins, D-Natrona, said during the debate.

At the bottom of the front page a headline read: "10 Students at CHS Suspended." The article said Principal Brisson sent the students home after they "circulated leaflets prior to class yesterday morning which urged attendance at a voluntary assembly on Monday to honor the late Dr. Martin Luther King Jr." The leaflets, signed "Black Student Alliance," said, "If you are Black and proud, Brown and smart, White and concerned, urge your home room teacher to allow your class to attend the Martin Luther King Day assembly."[369]

One of those suspended was honor roll student Michael Tyler, brother of James and Robert who are mentioned elsewhere in this work in connection with the Black 14.[370]

As with the coach's rule which led to the purge of the Black 14 at UW in 1969, the authorities again took the position that 1) if the rule is on the books you must follow it -- end of discussion, and 2) the punishment was justified because the students' actions were "a direct challenge" to the person in charge.

Brisson was quoted as saying, "The ones who instigated it knew it was contrary to school rules. It is clearly stated in the student handbook" that all posters and printed materials for distribution must be cleared by the faculty sponsor or the administration.

Three days later the Eagle reported that the Wyoming House had approved the ERA by a 40-21 vote. A front page photo showed Coretta Scott King and others honoring Dr. King on his birthday by visiting his grave in Atlanta. At the bottom of the page was an article saying Brisson had recommended that two students be expelled for distributing the leaflets.

The MLK assembly was well attended, the article stated. The program consisted of three readings and a film giving a historical view of blacks in the military and problems faced after service.

The Eagle on January 23, 1973, reported that the school board had voted to expel three Central students for the remainder of the school year for "continued willful disobedience or open and persistent defiance of the authority of school personnel." The rule "is clearly stated in the handbook," Brisson told the board. One of the students was a senior honor student who had been suspended for distributing the MLK leaflets. She read the rule, which stated that all posters, campaign notices and other information "to be posted" must receive approval of school authorities. Another student said he was told that "the tone of my voice was the reason for my suspension."

In that issue of the paper, the lead story was the death of former president Lyndon Johnson, 64, at his ranch on the Pedernales in Texas. He was a man, the article said, "whose dreams of a 'Great Society' to end poverty and social injustice were shattered by the Vietnam War." His death came within a month of the death of Harry Truman, leaving the country with no living former presidents. (Fortunately Nixon resigned in disgrace a few months later, filling that "void").

In the February 13th Eagle, two Central High students with the last name Spiegel appeared before the school board to express concerns about that school being made a "closed campus" after the MLK leaflets episode. One of them asked whether a student would be expelled for passing out leaflets for the March of Dimes. She suggested that if the administration and faculty had

---

[369] Wyoming Eagle of Jan. 12, 1973.

[370] Michael overcame the defiance of the Constitution by the school board and administrators and went on to graduate with honors from Morehouse College in Atlanta, earn a law degree from Harvard and become a successful attorney in Atlanta. He was the featured speaker at the 36th annual Martin Luther King Jr. Day March in Cheyenne in January 2018. "We have made tremendous progress since Dr. King's passing," Tyler told the marchers. "But we now find ourselves in the Trump swamp, the bloodhounds nipping our heels, the KKK, Nazis and other white supremacists are emboldened and resurgent in Virginia and elsewhere." Wyoming Tribune Eagle, 1/16/2018 updated 1/19/2018,

considered the students' feelings and consulted with them, racial problems would have been limited. She questioned whether students could learn and be creative under the "tense atmosphere" at Central. She asked why only 10 were suspended when many more students passed out leaflets.

Board chairman Urbigkit responded by saying that the students who were expelled knew beforehand that they would be suspended for passing out leaflets. (This point was also emphasized by Judge Kerr in his Black 14 decisions. The essence of this dangerous argument is that it is permissible for the government to deny its citizens the right of free speech as long as the citizens are warned in advance).

Another Central student at the same meeting named Stark, said, "But what I believe separates this nation from communist nations is the freedom of dissent. When this is taken away, we come down to their level."

Soon after this meeting the school authorities set about trying to silence the head of the Spiegel family for good.

THE SPIRIT OF LIBERTY: SYDNEY SPIEGEL

Even WWII veterans had better toe the line

After years of battling with students who would not walk the strict patriotic and obedient path that they expected, the administrators in the Cheyenne school district turned their attention to one of the district's most experienced teachers, a brilliant thinker and scholar named Sydney Spiegel. School district superintendent Joe Lutjeharms and the school board, including attorney Urbigkit, decided to silence and punish the teacher and remove his influence from the halls of the high schools.

When the Class of '63 entered Cheyenne Central High School in the fall of 1960, they soon became curious about this Mr. Spiegel, a 37-year-old history teacher. He had been teaching about nine years then, but he was youthful looking, small in stature with dark curly hair. He had earned his master's degree from UW in 1961 and he exuded the aura of an intellectual. Looking back more than 50 years later, several of his former students recalled him as being a stimulating mentor.

A longtime attorney for Wyoming's Legislative Service Office, John Rivera, was effusive in praise: "Sydney Spiegel was very influential in developing students' critical thinking skills. And he was not afraid to stand up for what he believed was right, even in the face of criticism or threat of sanctions from the administration. I consider him one of the best teachers I had the good fortune of learning from in K-12." Another member of the class reflected that view: "He was a hard teacher but he was an individual who was at least 40 years ahead of his time, as was Rod Crowlie [another Central teacher]. Our school was fortunate to have those two great teachers," said Tom Dougherty, who became the regional leader for the National Wildlife Federation.

"Excellent instructor, a little bit liberal. Taught me a lot," said Morris Gardner, who headed the Wyoming Board of Charities and Reform before his retirement. Vietnam combat veteran and career airline employee John Pacheco said, "He was a very interesting teacher....He taught well and I enjoyed his class. I can still see him putting his whole being into demonstrating how to pronounce 'Avignon.'" A member of the Class of 1964 had a different slant: "I did not have Mr Spiegel--- but I do remember walking down the hall to Miss Beck's class and hearing the pop song 'The Lion Sleeps Tonight' blaring out of Spiegel's classroom from the record player. That seemed like so much better of a deal than going in to my tame history class," said Aduard Kaufholz, who had a long career as a pilot weather briefer for the Federal Aviation Administration in Texas. Chuck Nash of Laramie recalled in 2018 that "you wanted to give him your full attention because he was absolutely exceptional."

Allen Gardzelewski, an attorney with Wyoming's oldest law firm, Corthell & King in Laramie who served in Vietnam, said of Spiegel: "He came across as being very caring about what we learned. He would probably be my favorite teacher of all my years in Cheyenne schools." Gardzelewski also had Crowlie as a teacher at Central. He was in Crowlie's class when word came over the public address speakers that Pres. Kennedy had been killed in Dallas. Crowlie, the county Democratic chairman, had greeted JFK at the Cheyenne airport two months earlier. "He broke down in tears and dismissed the class," Gardzelewski recalled.

But in Wyoming in the Sixties, standing up for what one believed eventually led to trouble -- if it wasn't what the power structure wanted to hear, and trouble would come even to Spiegel, a World War II European theater veteran.

His leanings were evident early in the '60s. On March 13, 1963, the president of the Cheyenne NAACP chapter announced that the featured speaker for the next meeting would be Central history teacher Sydney Spiegel who would give a book review of Langston Hughes' history of that organization.

Throughout his teaching career he was a leader of a Cheyenne teachers' union and was involved in efforts to improve education, protect civil rights and end the Vietnam War. Even though these activities occurred away from the classroom, they did not sit well with some of the administrators and trustees.

Parade Magazine profiles Spiegel

Mr. Spiegel taught at different times at both Central and East high schools and he had attracted some national attention to his innovative courses of study.

In a UPI article appearing on March 28, 1968, Spiegel was identified as the president of the Cheyenne Federation of Teachers, a branch of the AFL-CIO. He said the CFT would conduct a six-week period of debates on the Vietnam War and would then take a poll as to whether the branch should adhere to the parent organization's "no position" stance on the war.

In November, 1969, Spiegel was a white member of the NAACP's Cheyenne chapter and spearheaded an effort to raise funds to defray legal expenses being incurred by the fourteen black football players kicked off the UW team. Spiegel was quoted in an AP article as saying that several ministers had been unwilling – without the prior approval of their congregations -- to offer their facilities for the Black 14 banquet. He said the group had also asked to use the cafeteria at East High School but had received no response.

A column in Parade Magazine distributed with numerous Sunday newspapers across the country on August 22, 1971, recited that Spiegel had taught a black studies course at East High in Cheyenne during the previous year and would be teaching an elective course on the history of women during the upcoming school year. "The women's revolution has even filtered down to the high school level," the magazine stated.

On July 21, 1972, an Associated Press article about Spiegel's women's history class was published nationally. The class was taught during the previous school year, nearly two years after it met "some resistance" when he proposed it. He said he proposed the class because "what we've been teaching for the last millennium has been white male history--and that has to be a slightly distorted viewpoint of the world." He said the course looked at the lifestyles and challenges of women from ancient times through the Salem witch trials, suffragettes and abolitionists and up to contemporary New York Congresswoman Bella Abzug's equal rights amendment.

Spiegel said some 30 male students had taken the class and some felt threatened by discussions of changing the status quo. "Perhaps I at least succeeded in lifting some of the old stereotypes. But it's really not my job to convince them of the rightness of women's liberation. My job is to teach more of history than has been taught before and to recognize contributions that have been forgotten."

1972: Another teacher challenges the power structure and pays the price

About this time, Spiegel's career became entwined with a new music teacher in the Cheyenne schools who was among those protesting a campaign appearance by Nixon's Vice President Spiro Agnew. That such a protest could occur even in arch-conservative Wyoming was an indication of the breadth and depth of disaffection in the land.

A UPI article published November 3, 1972, said about 20 persons in a crowd of 4,000 at Storey Gym "began shouting and blowing whistles during his speech at Cheyenne." An AP article said "a group of 60 demonstrators in the upper reaches of the bleachers" engaged in "a constant din of whistle-blowing." This article noted that "Agnew had introduced the whistle into the campaign two weeks ago to heckle his hecklers." Agnew ridiculed the protesters in Cheyenne: "I see we have the kids from the Romper Room and Captain Kangaroo again. You'll have to forgive them--the drug store ran out of Pampers in their size." He then criticized Democratic presidential candidate George McGovern's record on income tax reform (less than a year later, Agnew would be convicted and sentenced for federal income tax evasion).

Agnew had become Nixon's point man for denigrating Vietnam War protesters and promoting the president's law and order agenda. He had called the war protesters "nattering nabobs of negativism" and "effete snobs." In a November, 1970 speech, for example, he called his hecklers "fringe specimens of our society" and urged his audience to vote for candidates who favored a tough stance on law and order so as to "get them out of our hair where they do not obstruct progress."

On December 15, 1972, an AP article reported that the Cheyenne school board had discussed the dismissal of Patricia Pedretti, the non-tenured music teacher who allegedly participated in the demonstration. Spiegel, as president of the American Federation of Teachers Cheyenne chapter, said AFT would defend her if she was dismissed. "This is an infringement of constitutional rights and we will take it to court."

In a UPI article published March 10, 1973, Spiegel announced that a conference on racism would take place on April 14th in Cheyenne under the sponsorship of the Cheyenne AFT and several other organizations and churches. Spiegel said "the purpose of the conference is to try to use the humanities to help us gain deeper insights into the causes of racial prejudice."

Three days after that article appeared, the Cheyenne school board determined that 50-year-old Spiegel, who had taught in the district for 19 years, and Patricia Pedretti would not be rehired for the next school year.

After being turned out by the Cheyenne school district for demonstrating against Agnew, Patricia Pedretti left Cheyenne. She went on to a long career as a classroom music teacher and then as a school library media specialist in southwest Wisconsin. She was organist for St. Mary's Church in Viroqua for more than 30 years. She died in a car accident while visiting family in Texas in November of 2011.

Agnew's and Nixon's law and order agenda eventually came calling at their own doors. On October 10, 1973, Agnew resigned his office and pled no contest to a charge of income tax evasion, as part of a plea agreement that resolved several criminal charges that he had accepted bribes while serving in Maryland state offices, including as governor. He was disbarred as a lawyer and in 1983 he paid the state of Maryland more than $250,000 to settle a suit by citizens and the state of Maryland seeking return of the bribes -- plus interest -- paid to him and state highway officials by private sector engineers and contractors. Soon, too, Agnew's champion, President Richard M. Nixon, would resign in disgrace to avoid possible removal from office because of his obstruction of justice during Watergate. Thus, the U.S. was left with two unelected Republicans as president and vice-president for 2 ½ years (Gerald Ford and Nelson Rockefeller).

The Cheyenne school board's action also came only four days after Spiegel's wife had suffered severe frostbite to her feet when she and Sydney were lost in the snow-covered mountains for 24 hours. While recovering in the hospital she read about Sydney's firing. According to a UPI report of March 19, 1973, she said, "What hurts me is the terrible injustice to the man. The students like him very much and everybody likes him. And there he is on the front page like he's dirt. So I'm not worried about my feet. I'm worried about Syd."

AFL-CIO Executive Secretary Keith Henning in Cheyenne was quoted in the article as saying the termination of the contracts "smells strongly of a witch hunt and completely disregards" their constitutional rights. The UPI report said students at East High had circulated petitions in support of Spiegel and were raising funds for his defense. An AP article printed March 23, 1973, said 125 Cheyenne East students had attended a meeting to voice their support for Spiegel.

The board claimed Spiegel's philosophies were in conflict with the board, that students did not want to take his classes and that he did not have the ability to work harmoniously with the board and the administration. Spiegel said in reply that his classes were always full and that "The board never indicated before that we had a difference in philosophy."

The AP reported on March 26 that the CFT was collecting donations to pay Spiegel's legal fees.

The appeal hearing -- before the same Board which had terminated his contract -- was held in April (the board having denied Spiegel's motion to have an independent panel consider his case). Arguments of counsel occurred at the end of May and the dismissal was then upheld. Spiegel, who was reelected as CFT president in May, challenged the board's decision in state district court.

1974: Spiegel calls for recognition of Hispanic culture
Forced to look elsewhere to make a living, Spiegel took a teaching job at Adams County School District 12 in the Denver area, headed by former Cheyenne school superintendent George Bailey. In the summer and fall of 1974 Spiegel won a primary race against the Worland school superintendent and became the Democratic nominee to challenge incumbent state superintendent of public instruction Robert Schrader.

During the campaign, Spiegel argued that Wyoming's schools failed to recognize the contributions of minority students, including the state's largest ethnic group the Mexican-American. "There are neglected treasures of Spanish and Latin American culture which

277

our schools, because of their inherited British background, have ignored much too long. Why shouldn't every school in the state demonstrate dramatically to our racial minorities that our schools belong to them as well as to the majority? Why couldn't there be pictures on the walls of Mexican heroes," he asked, according to an AP article of June 2nd.[371]

Spiegel urged support for a proposed 12 mill statewide school tax levy. He said such a measure would comply with the equal protection clause of the constitution and allow the state "to provide all the kids in the state with a decent education." (Years later, the Wyoming Supreme Court would adopt Spiegel's view, ruling that it could no longer ignore the disparity in quality of education between the rich counties and the poor counties). Spiegel also advocated doubling the severance tax on minerals to provide substantially more state support for education.

On August 7, 1974, Spiegel questioned the use of drugs to deal with hyperactive children. "A repressive school environment is more often the source of misbehavior than individual psychological disturbance among the students," he said.

On September 11, 1974, Spiegel said the factory assembly line philosophy for education is "psychologically disastrous, resulting often in sabotage and absenteeism." He carried his campaign statewide, but incumbent Robert Schrader easily won reelection in early November with 75,277 votes to Spiegel's 46,428.

1974: Judge Kenneth Hamm affirmed by Wyoming Supreme Court

Three days later, however, came news that softened the election results for Spiegel to some extent.

District Court Judge Kenneth Hamm of Green River issued an order finding for Spiegel in his lawsuit and directing the district to reinstate him. The district court ruled the school board did not act impartially, that its actions and decisions were arbitrary and an abuse of discretion, that the board's findings of fact were contrary to the evidence and that the hearing procedures violated his constitutional rights.

After filing an appeal, School District Superintendent Lutjeharms announced that Spiegel would be rehired on a temporary basis pending the outcome of the appeal. "This is good news," Mrs. Spiegel was quoted as saying. "It means I will have my husband back."

Apparently he did not accept the school district's offer. A newspaper article in October of 1975 identified him as the state Department of Health and Social Services' coordinator of alcohol and drug abuse programs.

The appeal was argued before the Wyoming Supreme Court on November 15, 1975. On April 22, 1976, the high court issued its decision, unanimously siding with Spiegel on almost all of his claims of unlawful actions by the school board. (*Board of Trustees, Laramie County Sch. Dist. No. 1 v. Spiegel*, 549 P.2d 1161 (Wyo. 1976).

The opinion by Judge Robert R. Rose began this way: "[This case] is a contest about liberty. There is involved in this appeal the question of 'Liberty' as conceived by the free speech provisions of the First Amendment to the Federal Constitution and ... as it is contemplated by the fair-hearing provisions of the Fourteenth Amendment of the Federal Constitution."

Judge Rose then quoted a titan of American law, Judge Learned Hand, from a speech he delivered to a group of newly-naturalized citizens in New York's Central Park in 1944:

The spirit of liberty is the spirit which is not too sure that it is right; the spirit of liberty is the spirit which seeks to understand the minds of other men and women;

---

[371] The Spring 2001 edition of Annals of Wyoming is devoted entirely to the history of Latinos in Wyoming.

278

the spirit of liberty is the spirit which weighs their interests alongside its own without bias; the spirit of liberty remembers that not even a sparrow falls to earth unheeded ....

The opinion began by noting that on March 12, 1973, the school board, upon motion of Willits Brewster, had passed a resolution terminating Spiegel at the close of the school year. The high court quoted the notice sent to Spiegel which set forth the vague charges made against him in the resolution.

But then Judge Rose looked to what may have been a major factor in Spiegel's removal, a factor that arose from Principal James Brisson's ongoing war with outspoken Central students, some of them African-Americans who were students in Spiegel's Black History class. (See Cheyenne Central Chapter at pg. 274). The opinion stated that "in 1972-1973 a race-relations problem existed at Central High School in Cheyenne." Two African-American students were told by Central officials not to distribute leaflets concerning an assembly to honor Martin Luther King which had been authorized by school officials, "but they did it anyway. The school says that Mr. Spiegel knew of the boys' plan but did not report this to the officials, all in violation of his duty to the school. One of the boys was expelled and another suspended and the Board found -- after a hearing on their suspensions -- that their testimony was 'willfully incorrect and untrue in significant detail.' The Board found Spiegel's 'attitude' deficient in that he did not help the administration before the incident and in that he attended a protest meeting afterwards."

The Supreme Court rejected these reasons. The court ruled that the board should have granted Spiegel's motion to require a more specific statement of the charges against him. "For [Spiegel] to have to defend against these vague and indefinite charges was a denial of not only his rights under the statute, but also a constitutional denial of due process," the court ruled. The high court characterized the evidence relied upon by the board as "remote and picayune" and said the board's decision "describes, sadly, an atmosphere and attitude of bias and prejudice which permeates this entire relationship." The Court also ruled that the board should have granted Spiegel's motion for an extension of time to prepare for the hearing.

The court asserted that simply because teachers are on the public payroll does not make them second-class citizens in regard to their constitutional rights. The court concluded that Spiegel's dismissal was illegal because his criticism of education policies generally and of the administration of the school in which he taught occurred outside the school as part of his union activities and were constitutionally-protected expression. And unlike Judge Kerr in his first dismissal of the Black 14 case, the Wyoming Supreme Court cited and quoted from the U.S. Supreme Court's February, 1969, decision in the *Tinker v. Des Moines School Dist.* case: "It can hardly be argued that either students or teachers shed their constitutional rights to freedom of speech or expression at the schoolhouse gate." [372]

Spiegel said the decision in his case "can only result in a net improvement of Wyoming education. It strengthens the right of teachers to speak freely and publicly about education policies." He said teachers have the most intimate knowledge of school problems and that school boards should seek their advice and counsel.

In 1983, the Air Force faced growing grass roots and political opposition to basing the MX missiles in Nevada. The Pentagon turned to Wyoming, where political and business interests in Cheyenne were slavering over the prospect of another missile boom. Spiegel emerged as a leader of a group called "Wyoming Against MX." He told the Casper Star that the MX would not add to U.S. deterrence strength because the hundreds of nuclear weapons on submarines "could devastate the Soviet Union with a tenfold overkill." The MX, he claimed, was an attempt to develop a first-strike capability against Soviet missiles and that an arms race of that sort "can only end in nuclear war." [373]

In 2000, Spiegel published a fascinating book titled "All Empires Die" in which he created imaginary conversations between the world's great historical figures. He brought together a "Congress of Resurrected Rebels" including Sun Yat-Sen, Thomas Jefferson, Gandhi and Frederick Douglas. He had his own colloquy with Nietzsche. In a chapter titled "Lessons from a Worker's Life" he gave insights into his own pre-teaching life history and discussed his dismissal by the school board.

In June, 2013, Spiegel turned 90 and was living near one of his children in Colorado. He died in January, 2016. A photo of him with some of his students is included in the book *The Wind Is My Witness* by Mark Junge.

Rodger McDaniel, a Central High grad and former Democratic State Senator, published a memoir praising Spiegel in the Wyoming Tribune-Eagle on Feb. 6, 2016. "If Wyoming ever builds monuments to those who committed their lives to working people and their families, there will be a statue of Sydney Spiegel," McDaniel said.

Brisson and Lutjeharms move to Nebraska

At some point during the events of 1972-73, Brisson issued an edict that Central's female teachers could not wear pantsuits. The next day, at least three of them came to school wearing the banned outfits.

---

[372] U.S. District Judge William Downes also quoted from the Tinker case in a ruling in April, 2010, ordering the University of Wyoming to permit 1960s radical anti-war protester William Ayres to speak on campus. Bowing to super-patriot donors, UW President Tom Buchanan cited safety concerns for denying Ayres a forum on the UW campus. In marked contrast to the federal courts' decisions in the Black 14 case, Downes ruled in favor of Ayres and a UW student who was sponsoring the Ayres appearance. Downes cited the First Amendment right of free speech, ruling that "[O]ur history says that it is this sort of hazardous freedom – this kind of openness – that is the basis of our national strength and of the independence and vigor of Americans who grow up and live in this relatively permissive, often disputatious society." The ruling meant that UW had to pay about $50,000 in attorneys fees to a Denver firm representing the student and Ayres. UW sociology professor David Ashley was quoted as saying that "the university should [not] have ever got itself into this situation. I just wish we had had more involvement and protests from the faculty, instead of having to rely on a ruling from a federal judge. Most of the faculty were hiding under their desks." wyofile.com, April 27, 2010. With a few notable exceptions, that was what the UW faculty did in 1969 also.

[373] Casper Star-Tribune, 2/10/1983.

Brisson had met his match. After the 1972 flag salute uproar and the firing of Cheyenne teacher Sydney Spiegel in 1973, Brisson went off to Nebraska. In 1984 the U.S. Air Force produced a 200-page analysis of human services, health, education, arts and law enforcement in western Nebraska as part of the MX missile project. One of the appendices indicates that "James Brisson", superintendent of Scottsbluff Public Schools, had responded to a survey. In 1991 a person named "Jim Brisson" was one of three persons given an award by the Nebraska Council of School Administrators for demonstrating "exceptional, distinguished leadership in public education."

Lutjeharms too went east, eventually becoming the Commissioner of Education in Nebraska.

1970: ANOTHER RULE, ANOTHER DEBACLE

On November 6, 1970, the UW student newspaper, The Branding Iron, reported that an Hispanic woman named Nelda Lara, a lifetime Laramie resident, had accompanied her friends, a white couple, to a Laramie Moose Lodge club for a drink the previous weekend. Although her friends had been members for 18 years, the gatekeeper told Mrs. Lara she could not enter "because you are a Mexican." The BI contacted the club, and a representative confirmed that "we do not allow Mexicans in the club."

According to Ms. Lara, her friends were shocked and embarrassed. When told that she was an American citizen, the bouncer reprised what most of Wyoming was saying after the Black 14: "I'm sorry, but it's one of the rules." The bouncer then reminded the three that two past Moose members had forfeited their memberships by marrying Mexican-American girls.

The BI also printed the club's "Official Membership Application and Health Statement" which stated right at the top that membership was only open to Caucasians, so long as the applicant is "not married to one of another race."

The town's newspaper, the Boomerang, carried an article on the incident the next week. The Lodge's secretary was quoted as saying that the BI had violated copyright laws by printing the club's application form.

As a result of the Moose's action, the Bartenders' Local Union 857 changed its annual banquet and dance from the Moose Lodge to the Connor Hotel, according to Tom Parnell, president of the union.

Two years prior to this incident a University of Wyoming Fulbright Scholar graduate student named Joseph Gomez began a petition drive urging the local school board to end what he called "the racial separation of the Mexican American children in the Lincoln School." (Lincoln School was located just west of the UPRR yard on the "West Side" and was abandoned as a school years ago. However, Laramie citizens converted it to a community center and it is still in use today). His petition, which appeared in the Laramie Boomerang on May 8, 1968, said "the racial imbalance in the Lincoln School ... denies the right to equal opportunity for learning" and caused "stereotyped, exaggerated and false impressions between majority and minority groups in the community." Gomez presented the petition with 125 signatures to the Board at its meeting on May 22, alleging that students from Lincoln did not perform as well as other students in junior and senior high, and dropped out more often. But according to an AP report, "many attending the meeting, mostly Mexican-Americans who either went to Lincoln School or have children there," opposed the petition.

"It was the age of selfishness. It was the age of self-indulgence. It was the age of anti-authority. It was an age in which people did all kinds of wrong things."[374]

President Reagan's attorney general Edwin Meese in the PBS documentary "The Sixties".

When instructed to behave in a certain fashion, they [students] are expected to respond. In short, it is not their role to run the school. ... For our part, we believe [the student dissent] stems more largely from today's middle-aged parents, a Depression-reared generation, lavishing material goods on their ungrateful offspring in most cases, including a blank check to do as they jolly well please anywhere under any circumstances.

James M. Flinchum, editorial 4-25-1972, Wyoming State Tribune (Cheyenne)

And I dreamed I saw the bombers
Turning into butterflies above our nation.
We are stardust, billion-year-old carbon.
We are golden
And we've got to get ourselves back to the garden.
Joni Mitchell, "Woodstock" 1969

1970: Let Freedom Ring

In late December 1969, Wyoming newspapers carried an article reporting that a "tri-state Vietnam Moratorium gathering" was being planned for the tiny town of Freedom, Wyo., located right on the Idaho border in western Wyoming, on Feb. 15. This idea provoked a strong negative reaction from Freedom. A petition signed by 98 people said "We are not in sympathy with you in this action. We do not want it in our town."[375] The petition said the event "will only give aid and comfort to the enemy." The committee responded by condemning the war as a "shameful and racist episode."

At the state press convention in late January, 1970, UW journalism professor Erne Linford declared that the "Mary Jane Kesey" named as spokesperson in the original press release was obviously a fictitious name formed by combining a synonym for marijuana with Ken Kesey, subject of the book *The Electric Kool-Aid Acid Test*, raising questions as to whether the whole thing was a hoax. David Hansard of Cheyenne, head of a student peace group at UW, responded by saying it was not a hoax and Linford then clarified that he did not mean to imply the whole

---

[374] Presumably he wasn't referring to the Vietnam War.

[375] UPI, Billings Gazette, 12/23/1969; 1/27,1970.

thing was a hoax. "In fact, I am philosophically in favor of the peace movement and have supported it from the start," he said.[376]

On Feb. 12, the Star Valley Independent ran a long letter from Henry E. Croft of Freedom, warning "Mr. 22-year-old philosophy major" [Hansard] and his followers against trying to do a "Red Square" event in Freedom. "This may be the damndest football game you ever attended," he said. "Many of us were kicking around when men were men and so were most of the women in these parts. ... You may find you are in a hot skillet."

In late January the moratorium was postponed until May. The committee spokesperson said they "would like a Freedom meeting to be a microcosmic demonstration that all men can live together in happiness." The Independent ran an editorial in late April saying the rally organizer's "propaganda might well be taken from a communist handbook." The editor charged that the war protesters ignored the atrocities of "our cold, calculating and ruthless enemy bent on world domination, whose leaders place no value on human life."[377]

At the end of April the Freedom Rally was canceled. Hansard said "our purpose is to promote peace, not to invoke violence. In a couple of cases [the reaction from residents] went beyond simple hostility to blatant threats." He said he did not want anyone to get hurt for no reason "the way the boys in Vietnam are killed for no reason." He said organizers instead would be taking their "freedom bus" to the Institute for the Study of Non-Violence in Golden, Colo.[378]

1971: "Wyoming Green"

In early August, 1971, a 17-year-old youth was arrested in Billings, Mont., on charges of selling marijuana. The suspect said he had obtained the substance being sold in a meadow on Casper Mountain south of Casper, Wyo. A Billings newspaper reporter interviewed some marijuana users who had tried what was now being called "Wyoming Green." Some of them reported, perhaps as a prank, that they did get a "high."[379]

This prompted law enforcement officers from Montana and Casper to travel to Casper Mountain where they located what they called a 5-acre "patch" of the plant. They performed a chemical field test, which was considered infallible and was accepted by courts as reason for probable cause, which "showed a strong marijuana reaction." The officers burned the "patch".

"We found it easily," one agent said, "but then we saw it growing everywhere. There's a whole damn mountain of it."

Within a day, Wyoming Attorney General Clarence Brimmer reported that samples of the plant had been analyzed by University of Wyoming botanist Dr. John Reed and identified as "Potentilla gracilis", also known as silver weed. The test showed the plant lacked an alkaloid and was therefore not hallucinogenic.

Brimmer said that if Wyoming Green was found to have a potential for abuse and risk to public health and the potential to produce physical or mental dependence, "as commissioner of

---

[376] Star Valley Independent, 2/5/1970.

[377] Casper Star 1/27/1970; Independent 4/30/1970. The Institute was an offshoot of the one founded by anti-war activist Joan Baez in Carmel Valley, Calif. Listen to her "Saigon Bride" (lyrics by Nina Duschek).

[378] Casper Star-Tribune 4/28/1970. The reference to "bus" was probably an emanation from Tom Wolfe's book *The Electric Kool-Aid Acid Test* about Ken Kesey and his Merry Pranksters' U.S. tour in a modified school bus.

[379] AP report in Great Falls (Mont.) Tribune, 8/13/1971).

drugs I will certainly add it to the controlled substances list so possession, use and sale will become a criminal offense." Right now, Brimmer said, persons selling the plant claiming it had drug-like qualities could be convicted of fraud.[154]

Wyoming law enforcement officials immediately confirmed that the plant, which grows "in any high mountain meadow in the state," according to Natrona County Attorney John Burk[155], was not marijuana. "If it was we would have all of California here," Burk said.[156]

The assistant police chief in Billings was worried about enforcing the law if the plant had hallucinogenic properties. "The problems are unbelievable," Norm Patterson said. "How do you police the Rocky Mountains?"

Newspapers' headline writers had great fun with this pseudo-drug situation:

Inside Dope by High Sources: 'Green' Is 'Grassier' Up North (Salt Lake Tribune)

Pot Theory Goes to Pot (Great Falls Tribune)

Flower Loses 'High' Favor with Youth (Los Angeles Times)

Casper Mountain had been in the national news only two weeks earlier after a mentally-handicapped and epileptic 9-year-old boy had followed some other children from a church camp into the woods. The others returned, but Kevin Dye did not. His parents soon realized he was missing and began to search and call out for him, without success. Eventually, thousands of volunteer searchers, including helicopter crews, tracking dogs and the best rescue teams in the region participated in the search.

Kevin was located nearly 10 days later by "bearded Mike Murphy, 25, who had put on his mackinaw and flown to the search area only the night before from his home in Boulder, Colo."[157] Kevin had lost 20 of his original 80 pounds and was too weak to have lasted another 48 hours in the woods, his doctor said.

---

[155] In a 2017 interview, one of Burk's former assistant county attorneys said Burk was an accomplished jazz trumpeter who had performed in New Orleans and other cities and was probably quite familiar with marijuana. In Casper he played with county coroner Jim Thorpen in a jazz band called Salt Creek on weekends at Dick Sedar's Colonial Lounge. Earlier that summer he had filed 114 charges against five defendants following an investigation by federal authorities into the killing of bald and golden eagles in the state. In 1973, Burk also prosecuted two Casper men in their 20s for one of the most heinous crimes in state history. Ronald Kennedy and Jerry Jenkins of Casper were convicted of murder for abducting and later throwing an 11-year old girl and her 18-year-old sister off a bridge high above the North Platte River 35 miles southwest of Casper. The older girl was raped by the men. Despite a broken hip and other injuries, she hid until morning and then managed to climb out of the canyon using only her arms and was found by a passing motorist. The perpetrators were convicted of first-degree murder and sentenced to death, but part of the statute was held to be unconstitutional by the Wyoming Supreme Court in 1977, resulting in life sentences. The Wyoming Dept. of Corrections search page showed Kennedy to still be an inmate as of January, 2017. Jenkins died in 1998. The surviving girl never recovered from the emotional scars of that night. In 1992 she returned to the bridge and died after she either fell or jumped. See *Fall: The Rape and Murder of Innocence* by Ron Franscell, New Horizon Press 2007, and a Sept. 22, 2013 article in the Casper Star-Tribune.

[156] Report by the author in *Rolling Stone*, Oct. 28, 1971.

[157] UPI report in San Mateo (Calif.) Times.

Within hours of Kevin's discovery, Mrs. Dye went to Casper's airport to personally shake the hands of bearded, long-haired youths who helped look for Kevin through the wilderness of 6,945-foot Casper Mountain.[158] (Its highest point is 8,130 feet).

Milestones for the war, the draft and Nixon

The compulsory selective service draft effectively ended on January 27, 1973, when Secretary of Defense Melvin R. Laird moved the armed forces to an all-volunteer status. The requirement for all young men to register for the draft was repealed in 1975 (but five years later it was reinstated).

The treaty ending the Vietnam War was signed on January 27, 1973, five days after LBJ died at his ranch on the Pedernales. The treaty brought rejoicing from almost everyone, including former state House member Ed Whitehead of Cheyenne, who had supported McGovern in the 1972 election. "I don't believe the settlement is any different than we could have gotten 10 years ago," he said. The reunification of Vietnam would follow, Whitehead said, "which is what they had in Geneva when we screwed them up. Peace with honor [Nixon's favorite phrase during the previous two elections] is for home consumption. It doesn't mean a damn thing." All the American people wanted was "out", Whitehead said.[159]

Mrs. Ted Gostas of Sheridan said she had "high hopes" that her husband would be among the prisoners released. "Everybody should be really happy tonight. At least we have the peace now and that is the most important thing," she said. "The long wait is over." Rep. Rodger McDaniel of Cheyenne said the nation should turn its attention to guaranteeing jobs for returning veterans and helping POWs adjust.

Nixon resigned on August 9, 1974.

The last American personnel and embassy staff, along with hundreds of friendly South Vietnamese refugees, left Saigon on April 29, 1975.

During the war, the U.S. had 58,119 killed (including eight women), 153,303 wounded and 1,948 missing in action.

The Wyoming football team went 8-3 in the 1976 regular season and then lost big to Oklahoma in the Fiesta Bowl. It was the only winning season of the 1970s.

1990-POSTSCRIPT: POLITICS ON THE FOOTBALL FIELD

One of the two assistant coaches whose career was endangered by Lloyd Eaton's purge of the Black 14 in the Fieldhouse that October day in 1969 was offense backfield coach Paul Roach, a native of Spring Green, Wis. who graduated from Rapid City High School and starred in football at Black Hills Teacher's College in Spearfish, S.D., graduating in 1952. (Roach played alongside future Casper Natrona head coach Art Hill. Lloyd Eaton was also a BHTC alum). Shortly after the late-season collapse in 1969, Roach left UW to become the offensive coordinator at another UW, the University of Wisconsin. In a UPI report of January 4, 1970, Roach was asked whether the dismissal of the players entered into his decision to leave. "Absolutely not," he replied.

---

[158] AP report in the Sheboygan (Wisc.) Press, 7/29/1971.

[159] Casper Star, 1/24/1973.

Paul Roach went on to a career as an NFL assistant coach with Denver, Green Bay and Oakland. In February, 1975, he was named offensive coordinator by new Packer head coach Bart Starr.[160]

Ten years later, Roach returned to Laramie to head the Cowboy Joe Club, the athletics' booster organization, under Athletic Director Gary Cunningham. Toward the end of the 1985 football season, coach Al Kincaid was fired and University of Idaho coach Dennis Erickson was hired on a four-year contract. Erickson's 1986 team managed a 6-win, 6-loss season, but early in 1987 Erickson bolted for Washington State in Pullman, Wash., 10 miles from UI in Moscow, Idaho. Shortly thereafter the 59-year-old Roach, who had by then become UW Athletic Director, called a meeting of the football team and told them he had decided upon their next coach. "You're looking at him," he said.

Roach's teams responded with a 10-3 season in 1987 and an 11-2 showing the next year, losing in the Holiday Bowl both years. In 1990 the team went 9-4 and became indirectly embroiled in another racial controversy when they were invited to the Copper Bowl to be played New Year's Eve at Tucson.

1990: Sen. Harriet Elizabeth Byrd's MLK Holiday

By action of the Legislature in early 1990, Wyoming became one of the last of the 50 states to adopt the Martin Luther King Jr. federal holiday as a state holiday. As a State Representative and then Senator, Elizabeth Byrd of Cheyenne had fought for the bill for nine years. It would only pass, however, after the Legislature amended the bill to call the holiday "Equality Day"

Mel Hamilton, one of the Black14 who was a teacher in Casper, told the Star-Tribune on March 13th that, although he was happy it passed, changing the name showed "a covert kind of racism" on the part of some citizens. "I'm a little bit personally disturbed that they ... diluted it the way they did," he said. The Rev. Aaron Phillips, pastor of Christ First Baptist Church in Casper, said the 8-year delay may have encouraged white supremacists to believe that Wyoming was ripe for their ideology. "We need to be mindful that this is not over," he said.

According to a biography of Byrd by Evelyn Haskell in *Annals of Wyoming* (Winter 2006), Mrs. Byrd achieved several milestones: the first fully certified and full-time African American teacher (1960) in Wyoming, the first African American legislator since statehood in 1890 and the first African American woman state legislator (1981).

Harriet Elizabeth Rhone, daughter of Robert "Buck" and Sudie Smith Rhone, was born at 2300 O'Neill Street in Cheyenne in 1926, becoming a member of the third generation of her family to be born in Wyoming.

Growing up in Laramie, her father's name had made several appearances in the Boomerang or the Republican. An item on August 8, 1915, reported that Robert Rhone, "his face wreathed in smiles, burst into the Boomerang office proudly carrying a fish 16 inches long and weighing four pounds." Two years later, Robert was one of the soldiers in the cast of "Pixie Show" presented at the Empress Theater by the UW training grade school. The article says the presentation "drew what

---

[160] In February, 1971, defensive backfield coach Burt Gustafson left UW to become the Packers' linebacker coach. Fritz Shurmur also had a long coaching career in the NFL. He was the defensive coordinator for the 1996 Green Bay Packers who won Super Bowl XXXI.

Manager King declared was the largest sale ever made in the house."[161] His name also appeared in two articles for growing and canning vegetables on vacant lots during the summer of 1917 while WWI was raging in Europe.

When Elizabeth graduated from Cheyenne High with a dream of becoming a teacher she was admitted to UW and to what is now the University of Northern Colorado, but both institutions informed her that she would not be allowed to live in campus housing because of the color of her skin.

So, since her father worked for the railroad, she traveled by herself on a pass to West Virginia to attend the predominately-black West Virginia State College at Institute, W.V.[162] In 1949, with her degree and teaching certificate in hand, she returned to her family home in Cheyenne and applied for a teaching position in the public schools. Again, her efforts were unsuccessful because she was black, even though white teachers without degrees were being hired. She was able to obtain a position at the Warren Air Force Base, teaching servicemen, until finally, after informing Democratic Gov. Joe Hickey of her discriminatory treatment, she was hired to teach in the Cheyenne schools, which she did until her retirement.

Liz Byrd with her class in 1960

[161] March 24, 1917, Laramie Republican. The manager was J. S. King, one of the builders of the Empress (later Fox) Theater. He was the husband of the author's great aunt, Mary Alice Graham King, sister of the author's grandmother Fourthy Ann Graham White (born on the 4th of July). The Kings moved to Laramie after all three of their young children died of diseases within a three-week period at their Kings Canon ranch in North Park, Colo., in 1902, despite the efforts of a doctor and nurses who had traveled from Laramie to the ranch.

[162] Katherine Johnson, an honor graduate of WVSC in 1937, became a mathematician for NASA Langley from 1953-1962, calculating trajectories by hand during early space flights. Her story is told in the movie "Hidden Figures". She turned 100 in August, 2018.

Mrs. Byrd met her husband, James Byrd, when he was stationed as a U.S. Army soldier at Fort Warren during the war. He became the first black police chief in Wyoming and also served an appointment as U.S. Marshal for Wyoming. Their son James W. Byrd followed his mother to the State Capitol, first elected as a State Representative from Cheyenne in 2008. His mother died in January, 2015.

1990: Copper Bowl

Arizona's gyrations over the Martin Luther King Jr. state holiday became entwined with college bowl games in the fall of 1990 and even with the previous selection of Phoenix as the site for the 1993 NFL Super Bowl.

In 1986, following rejection of the state holiday by one vote in the legislature in the spring, Arizona's Democratic Gov. Bruce Babbitt created the MLK holiday by executive order as he began a campaign for U.S. President. Republican Gov.-elect Evan Mecham vowed to rescind the order on the basis that it was illegal (which he did after his inauguration). Mecham also said neither King nor any other American deserved a holiday except for Washington and Lincoln.[163] In 1989, the Arizona legislature passed a bill recognizing the MLK holiday, but "de-recognizing" Columbus Day, so as to avoid creation of another paid holiday. This upset Arizona's Italian-Americans. On Dec. 21st, they and groups opposed to the King holiday itself, filed petitions that prevented the act from going into effect and placing the issue on the 1990 general election ballot.

On Sept. 14, 1990, former UW and NFL football star Vic Washington, a resident of Scottsdale, spoke at a press conference supporting the MLK holiday.[164] "We are going to ask everyone to come together because it is the right thing to do," Washington said.

Arizona voters rejected the holiday, despite the fact the NFL commissioner had reminded voters that selection of Phoenix as the site for the 1993 Super Bowl had been conditional on the holiday being recognized. (In 1991 the NFL moved the game to Pasadena, Calif.)

So when Wyoming was invited to play California in the Copper Bowl, Arizona was one of only three states which did not recognize the holiday. New Hampshire and Montana were the others. Calls were issued for teams to boycott both the Fiesta Bowl in Phoenix and the Copper Bowl.

A Nov. 12th UPI release said the NAACP had condemned the University of California for accepting a bowl bid to a post-season game in Arizona. "We do not look kindly on this action," said James Williams, head of public relations at the organization's headquarters in D.C. "The University has always been a campus that has fostered humanitarian ideals." After the team had voted to participate, Cal's quarterback said, "Football is not a place for politics. I just play to play."

News reports on Nov. 13th said coach Roach had met with his Wyoming team. "We got the squad together and the players voted to accept," he said, "but if a tremendous wave of opposition develops, whether it be our legislature, the state, administration, faculty, whatever, we probably won't go."[165] Roach said he had been informed "that the opposition to the holiday was due primarily to economic reasons."

---

[163] Mecham served only 15 months before he was removed from office following his conviction on charges of obstruction of justice and misuse of public funds.

[164] Photo p. A2 and article on B4, Arizona Republic, 9/15/1990.

[165] Casper Star-Tribune 11/13 and 14/1990

Roach was then quoted as saying: "The players requested that due to the situation with the Martin Luther King Jr. state holiday that they wear an emblem somewhere on the uniform as a tribute to Dr. King."

2015-2018: DEJA VU AT OL' MIZZOU AND THE NFL

With funding from the Associated Students of UW, a statue commemorating the Black 14 was sculpted in bronze by Guadalupe Barajas of Cheyenne and was placed on display in the Wyoming Union in 2002. The statue depicts a shoulder, a black arm band over a football jersey and a raised arm and clenched fist. In reality, of course, the Black 14 never placed arm bands on their uniforms. John Griffin and Mel Hamilton posed with the statue during a 40th anniversary recognition at the Wyoming Union in November, 2009.

John Griffin, left, and Mel Hamilton with the Black 14 statue in 2009.

The Black 14 incident came back into national prominence in November, 2015, when the African American players at the University of Missouri threatened to boycott an upcoming football game[166] to show sympathy to campus protests about the administration's lack of response to charges of racism on campus. The entire team and the coaches supported the players, causing the two highest administrators in the University of Missouri system to resign.

The Washington Post contacted Mel Hamilton of the Black 14 and ran an article on Nov. 10, 2015, contrasting the two incidents. "Missouri's players received widespread support and sparked instant results, a reaction diametrically opposite from what Hamilton and his 13 teammates endured," the article said.

Hamilton said the incident affected him for years during his working life in Casper, his first wife's hometown. "I couldn't go to have a drink without somebody in a drunken stupor pointing at me and saying 'you are the reason Wyoming is not winning today,'" he said. "It never went away for me." He said he was proud of the Missouri players and to see that "the kids were still aware that institutional racism is well and alive in America."

The Missouri events, as well as the controversy over NFL players kneeling for the national anthem in 2016-17, led to a CBS Sports Network hour-long documentary on the Black 14 incident which aired in February, 2017.

---

[166] Coincidentally, BYU was to be Mizzou's opponent in the game.

In October, 2017, six members of the Black 14 were present in Orlando to receive the "Barrier Breakers" award at the National Consortium for Academics and Sports "Giant Steps Awards Banquet." (L-R below) Lionel "Dowdy" Grimes of Ohio, Ivie Moore of Arkansas, Tony Gibson of Massachusetts, Jay Berry of Detroit, John Griffin of Denver and Anthony McGee of Atlanta were present to receive plaques with the inscription, "Your selfless sacrifice helped further expose the need for change in society throughout the nation."

Photo courtesy of Jerome Berry.

Six of the Black 14 members highlighted Black History Month events at UW in February 2019. Pictured here are Mel Hamilton, Anthony McGee, current UW football quarterback Sean Chambers, Guillermo Hysaw, John Griffin, Tony Gibson and Ivy Moore. Photo by Laura Pollard.

Acknowledgments

The author spoke to more than 100 people during the five years working on this manuscript. Almost all of them were helpful and supportive, but they are too numerous to mention here for fear of unintentionally omitting someone. Their contributions are sincerely appreciated. My wife Kathleen D. White deserves special recognition for her inspiration, and also Wyoming's "Historian Laureate" Phil Roberts who corrected errors and encouraged the author during the process.

Among those many who should be accorded mention, the author recognizes Mel Hamilton, Jay Berry, John Griffin (who scanned the record of the Black 14 case at the National Archives in Denver), Tony Gibson, Lionel Grimes, Anthony McGee, Ted Williams, Ivie Moore, Ron Hill and Joe Williams of the Black 14, Clinton Isaac, Gene Huey, Vikki Washington Nicholson, Kim Viner, David Roberts, Vince Crolla of the Western History Center at Casper College, John Waggener and the UW American Heritage Center staff, Suzi Taylor at Wyoming Archives, Ed Pollard, Kathy Karpan, Fred Gish, Mark Junge, Dakota Russell at Heart Mountain Interpretive Center, Dan Nelson, Ken Calkins, Roger Daniels, Dave Markum at LCCC, Katherine Kasckow, Allen and Majel Gardzelewski, Lisa Kinney and Rod Lang, Barbara and Terry Deshler, Frank and Jane Nelson, Pembroke Woodhink and all of those who encouraged the author to keep going.

"Afro-American" Lecture Series 1969. 175
Abernathy, Rev. Ralph. 82
Agent Orange. 11, 42
Agnew, Spiro. 16, 217, 276
Aguilar, Nancy. 130
Ahoskie N.C. 3
Alexandria, Va.. 42
Alumni Association. 212
Amend, Donald. 229
Amer. Assn. Univ. Professors. 226
Amer. Football Coaches Assn. 236, 238
    Black college coaches protest. 238
American Friends Service Committee. 34
Anderson, Marian. 4
Anderson, Robert. 210
Ando, Curtis. 127
Appeal to Cheyenne-1958. 33
Archuleta, Bob. 210
Arlington Street Church, Boston. 84
Armstrong, Larry. 169
Arnold, Joe. 133, 198
Arnold, Thurman. 197
Atlas nuclear missile.. . . . . 12, 31, 42
Aycock, Ike. 171
Ayres, William. 279
Baez, Joan. 283
Bagley, Bill. 46
Baker, Bill. 63
Baker, Vernon. 246
Baldwin, Melvin. 217
Bannister, Barbara. 53, 111
Bannister, Gaurdie. 25, 212
Bannister, Mike. 207
Bannister, Mrs. Gaurdie. 85
Barajas, Guadalupe. 289
Barker, Elver. 137
Barrett, Dr. Francis.. 4
Barrett, Frank. 32, 75, 116, 134, 174, 196
Barrett, James. 170, 174, 253, 256
    1995 Memoir. 256
Barron, Joan. 155, 199, 264
Bartels, Clay. 127
Bartels, Don. 125, 127
Bass, Betty Rider. 229
Baston, Karla. 46
Baux, Phil.. 52
Baxter, George. 206
Beat Generation. 40
Beatles. 73
Beck, Michael. 125
Befus, Ev. 13
Bell, Ollie. 9
Bell, Rick. 207
Bentley, George. 159
Bentley, Vernon. 159

Bergera, Gary. 71
Berry, Jerome. . . 14, 164, 178, 180, 192, 193, 243, 252,
                                    290
Bever, Bernie. 225, 226
Birleffi, Larry. 63, 144, 179, 219, 235, 240
Birmingham, Ala.. 7, 48
Bishop, Jay. 210
Black 14. . . . . 14, 16
Black 14 lawsuit citations.. 256
Black 14-Assembling the cast. 170
Black 14-Nat'l Urban League. 21
BLACK 14-Prelude. 58
Black 14-Previous BYU game. 71
Black Panthers. 236
Black Students Alliance. 14, 170, 257
Black trackmen.. 207
Black, Estella. 269
Black, Willie S.. . . . . 171, 183, 209, 236
Blackner, Craig. 123
Blanchard, Okie. 42
Blevins, David. 233
Block, Herb. 84
Bloody Sunday. 79
Bloomenthal, Harold. 227
Boal, Steven. 124
Boatner, Verne. 236
Bolshevism.. 95
Bond, Julian. 176, 265
Bonner, Dave. 9, 30, 108, 178, 216
Borino, Bob. 179
Bostick, Robyne. 27
Bostick, Ron. 26
Bostwick, Richard. 158
Bowen, Clotilde Dent. 57
Bowker, Stan. 31
Bowl game segregation. 214
Bowman, L. Mark. 242
Bowron, Frank. 83
Bradlee, Ben. 52
Brady, Jon. 91
Breonna Taylor.. 110
Brewster, Willits.. 279
Brigham Young University: A House of Faith. 71
Brimmer, Clarence. 170, 283
Briscoe, Marlin.. 70
Brisson, James. 141, 268
    1972 Flag salute. 270
Brockmann, Thomas. 176
Brodrick, Gordon. 188
Brown eyes, blue eyes documentary.. 218
Brown, Shannon. 220
Brubaker, Terry. 208
Bruner, James. 230
Bryan, Gene. 13, 42, 93
Bryan, Gene and Mike. 114

Bryan, Mike. 103
Bugas, Jack. 24
Bullock, Clifford. 96
Bunn, Don. 49
Burgess, Robert. 99
Burke, Dan. 192
Burnstad, Sheriff Ted. 63
Burton, Carrie. 18
Burwell, Peggy. 136
Bush, Gilbert. 114, 123
Byrd, Elizabeth Rhone. 9, 286
Byrd, James W. 111, 288
Cabre, Hank. 30
Caldwell, Tom. 238
Calkins, Ellanor. 34
Calkins, Kenneth. 32, 33, 39, 42
Calkins, Rev. Charles. 35
Carbon County, Wyo., jail. 102
Carey, Joseph M. 87
Carlos, John. 71
Carlson, Bob. 226
Carlson, Earl. 97
Carlson, Pres. William. 177, 189
Carlson, William D. 15, 96, 163
Carnegie Library Cheyenne. 105
Carpenter, Garrett. 137
Carroll, Candy. 206
Carson, Rachel. 12
Casper Baby Contest. 1
Casper Interracial Council. 111
Catterall, John. 89, 103
Catterall, Lee. 96
Cheney, Dick. 11, 58, 146
Cheney, Elizabeth. 146
Cheney, Lynne. 11
Cheyenne Central High School. 11, 17
Cheyenne Quarterback Club
    Cowboy Night 1969. 234
Chisholm, Shirley. 265
Christopulous, Mike. 140
Church, Frank. 117
Clark, Leon. 30, 207
Clissold, Harry. 52
Clough, Wilson. 57
Coad, Arden. 136
Coed dress code. 92
Colorado State College. 9
Confederate flag. 84
Congress of Racial Equality. 149, 264
Connor Hotel Laramie. 5
Connor, Eugene "Bull". 84
Connor, Robert. 242
conscientious objector. 37
Cook, Pete. 9
Cook, Quentin. 119
Cooke, Brec. 136
Cooke, Helen. 136

Cooper, Annie. 245
Cooper, Ken. 111
Copper Bowl
    MLK holiday. 286
Corgan, Mike. 59
Corthell & King. 142
Corthell, N. E. 19
Cottle, Eugene. 5
Cottle, Stephanie. 5
Cowboy Joe Shetland pony. 43, 239
Craven, Kassis Ken. 121, 225
Craven, Prof. R. Kenton. 120
    Confusion with Kassis Ken. 225
    Moving expenses offer. 206, 226
    Vietnam Protest. 135, 157
Cressey, Dennis. 118
Cresswell, Barbara. 122
Crews, Jack. 160
Crist, Sue. 100, 266
Crowley, Ellen. 160
Crowlie, Rod. 48, 275
Cuban Missile Crisis. 13
Curfew hours for coeds. 89
Da Nang, Vietnam. 12
Daley, Mrs. P.E. 10
Daniel, Glenn Bud. 116
Daniels, Roger. 150, 176, 190
Daughters of the American Revolution. 5
Davey, Jerry. 141
Davis Jr., Sammy. 32
Davis, Billy. 13
Davis, Cliff. 211
Davis, John W. 168
Davis, Wm. Bud. 97
Dawkins, Willie. 236
Day Jr., Samuel. 35
Dearinger, Hilton. 24
Dearinger, Sanford. 24
Deike, Karen. 199
Dekanek, Paul. 49
Dell'Osso, Louis. 89
Demas, Lane. 23, 183, 215
Denver Post
    1982 Rick Reilly article. 253
Denver Post editorial. 212
DePoyster, Jerry. 66
Deshler, Terry. 122
Devaney, Bob. 58
Devereaux, Fred. 83, 110, 111, 168, 197
Devereaux, Mike. 83
Dickens, Phil. 9
Dickinson, Laverne. 70
Dieterich, Herbert. 206
Dirks, Mike. 66
Dobler, Conrad. 181, 239
domino theory. 116
Dougherty, Tom. 274

Douglas, Wm. O.. . . . . 98, 143
Dowdell, John. 30
Dowler, Boyd. 22
Dowler, Lloyd. 22
Dowler, Walter. 22, 24
Draft. 139, 147
       Ends in 1973. 285
       Moral Objection. 158
Draft-Selective Service.. 12
Dress codes in schools. 97
Driscoll, Don. 226
Drury, Allen. 43
Dunder, Clarine. 92
Durgain, Michael. 122
Durling, Jerry. 66
Eaton. 195
Eaton, El'Louise Dickey. 60
Eaton, Lloyd.. 14, 15, 58-60, 66, 68, 72, 164, 178, 182,
              186, 189, 191, 192, 194, 200, 203,
                         204, 207, 210
       "Man of the Year". 174
       100th career win. 181
       1968 blizzard. 106
       1971 trial. 193
       1971-Leaves UW. 242
       1982 Denver Post 253
       Death in 2007. 242
       Disproportionate punishment. 194
       Early years. 60
       Eaton "retires" as coach. 241
       In Kuna, Idaho 1982. 253
       Man of the Year. 234
       Memorial proposed. 210, 211
       Most satisfying victory. 203
       On discipline. 177
       Other opportunities. 68, 178, 182
       Trial testimony. 259
Eaton, Rosa Hall.. 60
Eaton, Thomas.. 61
Eaton's rule modified. 204
Edwards, Harry. 221
Einstein, Albert. 5
Ellsberg, Daniel. 147
Empire Wyo.. 25
Engstrom, William. 24
Enzer, Erica. 36
Equal Rights Amendment.. 272
Erickson, Ramona. 36
Erickson, Swede. 27
Esquibel, Pauline. 245
Esslinger, Wm.. 123
Evers, Medgar. 13
Ezell, Earland. 66
Faculty responses. 191, 206
Fair Housing Act of 1968. 4
Farmer, James.. . . . . 176, 264
Farthing Ranch. 43

Faubus, Gov. Orval. 43
Fearno, Joseph. 123
Feeney, Peter. 208
Fellowship of Reconciliation. 34, 137
Fermon, Bonnie Mae. 6
Fetsco, Pete. 132
Fey, John T.. . . . . 88, 90
Fillerup, Melvin. 9
Findley, Sally Harris. 24
Fintus, Bob. 140
First Person Coffeehouse. 82
First women jurors 1870.. 157
Fitzpatrick, Henry.. 257
Flag salute at Central High. 267
Flinchum, James. 155, 206, 282
       Attacks Sister Frances. 35
       MX foes aid the devil.. 41
       Praises authoritarian society. 268
       Reaction to MLK killing. 109
       Vietnam war foes disgusting. 139
Flippin, George. 23
Floy Tonkin. 109
Ford, Don. 131
Ford, Marcie. 49
Foreman, Al. 83
Foreman, Jim. 120
Fowler, Corbin. 15, 100, 191
Fowler, Dr. Robert. 111
Fowler, N. E.. 98
Fox, Ellen. 199
Fox, Gary. 238
Francis, Tom. 73
Franklin, Forrest. 203, 210, 232, 239, 251
Franscell. Ron. 284
Frazier, Mike. 207
Free Lunch. 226
Freedom of religion. 218, 229-231, 252, 259, 260
       Polygamy in 1869. 230
Freedom Riders. 7
Freedom Summer 1964. 74
Freedom Wyoming.. 282
Freeman, Scott. 239
Frisby, Bob.. 49
Frost, Robert.. 11
Frye, Marquette. 154, 166
       Watts Riot. 167
Frye, Ronnie. 167
Gadlin, Jerry. 171
Gage, Herbert. 24
Gage, Jack. 142
Gagne, Greg. 239
Garcia, Larry. 239
Gardiner, Pete.. 204
Gardner, Morris. 274
Gardzelewski, Allen. 205, 275
Gaskill, Ronald. 226
Gator Bowl 1951. 75

Generation gap. 17
George Floyd. 110
George, Mary. 27
Geraud, Joe. 190
Gerdom, Dode. 206
Gibson, Tony. 180, 192, 244, 252, 290
Gilchrist, Kenn. 246
Giles, Mrs. Jettie. 8
Girault, Thomas. 9
Gish, Dick. 13, 31
Gish, Robert Fred. 31, 42
Gish, Ron. 31
Goins Elementary School. 10
Gonzales, Billy. 245
Gonzales, Corky. 104
Gostas, Ted. 54
        Meeting with Nixon. 57
Govea, Jessica. 266
Grambling University. 238
Grand Teton Nat'l Monument. 134
Graves, Chuck. 37, 150, 199, 254
Graves, William Boyd. 168
Gray, Doc. 25
Gray, Effie Mae. 1
Gray, Mable. 7
Gray, Norman "Tiny". 174
Gray, Ronnie. 1, 72
Green Book. 73
Greensboro, N.C. 43
Gregory, Dick. 265
Griffin, John. 181, 187, 239, 244, 249, 252, 290
Grimes, Lionel. 164, 290
Grove, Robert. 118
Guenther, Todd. 219
Gustafson, Burt. 286
Guy, George. 197
Guzzo, Anthony. 206
Haag, Jeff. 76, 169
Haines, Ken. 92
Hainworth, Elizabeth. 245
Hair and Dress Codes. 268
        1969 Cheyenne Central. 268
        1969 Gillette Wyo. 268
        1970 Laramie. 269
        Casper School Board. 97
        Finot case-Teacher's beard. 99
Haldeman, H. R. 39
Hall, Harry. 30, 207
Hallock, Wiles. 208
Ham the Astrochimp. 43
Hamilton, Carey Holwell. 247
Hamilton, Mel. 15, 85, 180, 192, 252, 286
        1967 Eaton encounter. 247
        Mayor of Boys Town. 245
Hamm, Kenneth. 278
Hammond, Bob. 21, 26, 69
Hammond, Oscar. 197

Hampton, Dave. 70
Hand, Jerry. 212
Hanna, Wyo. 163
Hansard, David. 282
Hanscum, Art. 191
Hanscum, Bob. 45
Hansen, Clifford. 49, 84, 96, 134, 161
Hansen, Matilda. 38
Hardin, William Jefferson. 86
Hardy, Deborah. 18
Harkins, Chuck. 201
Harlem Globe Trotters. 25
Harris, Taft. 9, 21
Harris, Taft Jr. 24
Harrod, Lawrence. 138
Hart, Alabama. 22
Hart, William. 22
Harvey, Ill. 30
Hathaway, Gov. Stanley. 14, 15, 93, 102, 170, 187, 208
Haverford College. 37, 148
Hayden, Tom. 11
Heart Mountain Camp. 128
        Draft resisters trial. 150
Hefkin, Don. 45
Hemenway, Robert. 176
Henderson, Julie. 210
Hendricks, Al. 136
Henning, Keith. 277
Hernandez, Tony. 245
Herrera, Mary Jane. 245
Hershey, Louis. 141, 143
Hewgley, C. W. 62
Hickey, J. J. 58, 142, 287
Higby, Alison. 133
Hill, Kathi. 46
Hill, Mignon. 38
Hill, Ron. 178, 180, 244, 250
Hill, Roosevelt. 250
Hinckley, Gordon. 14
Hinckley, John. 74
Hippie Ordinance. 101
Hoffman, Abbie. 179
Holland, Carlton Jake. 117
Hollon, C. E. "Jerry". 190, 200
Holycross, Col. Tom. 38
Hoover, J. Edgar. 39
Hopkinson, Mark. 163
Horton, Bernard. 49
        On the Black 14. 219
House Un-American Activities Committee. 89
House, Jim. 66
Howard University. 20
Howard, Emily. 103
Howard, Mrs. Roscoe. 1
Howe, Jon and Roger. 49
Howlett, Rev. Duncan. 78, 82

295

Hudspeth, Tom. 67
Huey, Gene. 66, 68, 70, 107, 252
Hull, Keith. 241
Humphrey, George Duke. 5, 9, 88
Humphrey, Oscar & Reathy. 162
Hunsucker, Suzanne. 224
Hunt, Lester. 43, 51, 140, 151, 262
Hunt, Stanley. 106
Huntley-Brinkley Report. 229
Hustad, Ken. 239
Hysaw, Guillermo. 65, 178, 190, 192, 243
Ibach, Kim. 4
ICBM. 13
Illingworth, Don. 140
In loco parentis. 91
Ingram, Bob
    Eaton passed over for AD?. 242
Inter-racial dating. 76, 203, 214
Isaac, Clinton. 131, 162
Isaac, James. 130, 161, 180
    Dakota Weslyan. 165
    Killed in San Bernardino. 165
Isaac, Jeanie. 164
Ivinson, Edward. 18
Jackson State in Mississippi. 40
Jackson, Britney. 166
Jackson, Robbie. 166
Jackson, Wendell. 164
Jacobs, Bob. 66
Jacobson, Skip. 70, 205
Jacoby, Glenn. 8, 9, 59, 190, 240, 242
    UW press release. 190
James Earl Ray. 108
James Griffith Jr. 109
James, Dwight. 112, 171, 192, 245
Jefferson, Bob. 170
Jefferson, Ted. 5, 6, 8
Jeffrey, Clifford. 269
Jeffrey, Ronn. 171
Jeffryes, Paul. 103
Jehovah's Witnesses. 152
Jimerson, Curt. 21, 26, 62
John Muir High School. 99
Johnson County Invasion. 168
Johnson, Alberta. 171, 257, 258, 272
Johnson, Cheryl. 55
Johnson, Eph. 188
Johnson, Huey. 207
Johnson, John "J. J.". 31
Johnson, Percy. 171
Johnson, Pres. Lyndon. 44, 74, 75, 118
    Reference to Reeb. 83
Johnson, William. 171, 257, 259
Jones, Araby. 112
Jones, Bill. 94
Jones, Harvey. 3
Jones, Jack. 95
Jones, Marshall. 206
Junge, Mark. 264, 280
Kahler, Dean. 39
Karpan, Kathy. 44, 50, 54, 88, 136
Kaufholz, Aduard. 274
Kaul, Mike. 114
Kehler, Randall. 37
    1970 Trial. 154
    Influence on Ellsberg. 147
    Nuclear Freeze. 157
Kelly, Pete. 144
Kennedy clan. 46
Kennedy, Jackie. 46
Kennedy, Judge T. Blake. 152
Kennedy, Mary. 199
Kennedy, Pres. John F. 11, 38, 43-45
    1963 Wyoming visit. 47
    PT-109. 46
Kennedy, Robert F. 46
Kennedy, Ted. 44, 46, 142, 197
Kennedy, Thomas. 119
Kent State. 16
Kent State University. 15, 39, 40
Kerouac, Jack in Cheyenne. 206
Kerr, Ewing T. 142, 170, 188
    1954 run for Senate. 262
    Denies TRO. 254
    Guest at Eaton dinner. 234
    Kehler trial 1970. 150
    Pre-bench life. 262
    Recollection on Black 14. 263
Kesey, Ken. 282, 283
Kettunen-Schubert, Irene. 227
Khrushchev, Nikita. 43
Kiick, Jim. 66, 107
Killing of eagles. 284
Kimball, Spencer. 253
King, John E.& Glennie. 90, 95
King, Martin Luther. 79, 82, 108, 113
    Opposition to war. 141
King, Rev. Dr. Martin Luther. 5, 9, 80, 107
Kingham, Herb. 105
Kingston Trio at UW. 103
Kinne, Katherine. 247
Kirkbride, Alan. 191
Kirkbride, Mae. 13
Kiwanis Club. 3
Kleager, Jerry. 13
Knisely, Jay. 106
Knudsen, Wm. 100, 121
Kobelin, John. 129
Kogan, Rick. 122
Korhonen, Rose. 208
Krogh, Egil "Bud"
    UW Law School 2011. 148
Ku Klux Klan. 11, 74, 152
Kuczewski, Len. 59

Kush, Frank. 178
KUWR. 93
Lamb, Linda. 210
Lange, Bob. 226
Lara, Nelda. 281
Laramie County Jail. 37
Laramie County Library. 105
Laramie landlords. 89
Laramie Unitarian Fellowship. 82
Larson, Dr. Leonard. 9
Larson, T. A. Al. 206, 224, 228
Laybourn, Margaret. 32, 38
Laybourn, Robert. 38
LDS Church. 10
LDS tenet. 184, 214, 218
    1970-No change planned. 237
    1978 revelation. 253
    BYU students protest. 205
Lederberg, Joshua. 6
Lee, Earl. 181, 193, 245
Lent, John. 225
Lester, Ken. 49
Lindsey, Hub. 66, 68
Linford, Ernest. 3, 116, 206, 282
Little Rock, Ark. 43
Liuzzo, Viola Gregg. 84
Long hair in schools. 97
Long hair rules. 14, 97
Look Magazine 1963. 184
Lorenz, Paul. 152
Lost Cowboys, The Story of Bud Daniel. 116
Louis, Andrew D. 112, 135, 230
Loving v. Virginia. 88
Loyola of Chicago. 29
Lucom, Graham. 102
Lummis, Cynthia. 135, 147
lunch counter sit-ins. 43
Lyman, Sharon. 199
Lynching. 25, 219
Mackey, Sally. 266
MacMillan, Hoke. 179, 191, 205
Maddox, Gov. Lester. 112
Mahoney, Barry. 24
Mahoney, Jerry. 16
Manatos, Mike. 51
Mankus, Lou. 34, 41
Manning, Grady. 207
Marijuana. 169, 179, 263, 283
    Wyoming Green. 283
Marion, Dave. 61
    Tragedy in dorm 1963. 62
Marion, Jerry. 65, 68
Martin, Ben. 68
Martinez, Patty. 55
Mathison, John. 206
Matthei, Charles. 102
Maxfield, Peter. 100

McAtee, Bill. 130
McAtee, Edward R. 130, 141, 162
McAuley, Phil. 16
McCall, Donn. 15
McCall, Mike. 241
McCarthy, Joe of Casper Police. 237
McClellan, Michael. 49
McConnell, Dewey. 71
McConnell, Rev. John. 8
McCracken, Robert. 199
McCracken, Tracy. 44, 116, 142
McDaniel, Rodger. 51, 280
McEwan, Leonard. 174
McGee, Anthony. . . . 70, 178, 180, 234, 243, 248, 290
McGee, Gale. 13, 42, 50, 74, 115, 117, 136
    Civil Rights record. 196
    Defending LBJ's deceit. 148
McGee, Gwendolyn. 249
McGee, Tony. 234, 290
McGee, Tony's father Herman. 248
McGill, Bill "The Hill". 31
McGinty, Ed. 24
McIntyre, John. 174
McKay, David O. 252
McKinney, John "Junior". 144
McKinney, Johnnie. 14, 110
McKinney, Kevin
    Gen. Hershey. 143
McMullen, John. 93
McNamara, Robert. 52
McNichols, Gov. Steve. 9
Meadows, Don. 187, 245, 250, 252
Meadows, Mel. 251
Mealey, Catherine. 100
Meenan, Patrick. 83
Meeuwsen, Terry. 54
Melinkovich, Mary. 192
Melinkovich, Paul. 192
Menin, Samuel D. 2, 152
Meyer, E. G. 90, 226
Meyer, Karl of Catholic Workers. 38
Meyer, Rep. William of Vermont. 38
Miller, Jerry. 207
Miller, Mayne. 122
Miller, Monica. 206
Miller, Rev. Orloff W. 81, 111
Miller, Sammie. 211
Milton, Fred of Oregon State. 235
Minick, Robert. 158
Minuteman missile. 40, 58
Miscegenation law. 85
Miss America Pageant. 55
Missett, William. 96
Mississippi State. 29, 88
Mitchell, Joni. 282
Mitchell, Minnie. 196
MLK Holiday. 286

Modernism 1931. 95
Monroe, Marilyn. 44
Mooney, John. 21
Moore, Ivie. 178, 192, 250, 290
Moore, Johnetta. 83
Moore, Mrs. Robert. 238
Moore, Robert. 25
Moore, William Howard. 4
Moose Lodge
        Laramie 1970. 281
Moose lodge of Casper. 1, 2
Moose lodge of Laramie. 3
Moose, Loyal Order of. 3
Morgan State. 238
Morgan, Ken. 221
Moyers, Bill. 198
Mullan, Ken. 15, 183
Muller, Burt. 121, 206
Muller, Eric. 151
Munoz, Pablo. 129
Murdock, Steve. 220, 222
        The Nation article. 222
        Wesley Robert Wells. 223
Murie, Mardy. 75
Murie, Olaus. 134
Murphy, Dr. Joseph. 83
Murphy, Jim. 38
Muste, A. J.. 38
MX missile. 13, 32, 38, 41, 280
My Lai. 134
Myers, J. W.. 87, 172
NAACP
        -National. 21
        Casper. 7
        Cheyenne Central 1962. 269
        Utah 1963. 184
Nagasaki, Japan. 38
napalm. 11
Nash, Chuck. 275
Nash, Gary B. 11
Nation, Bill. 48
National Endowment for the Humanities. 11
National Urban League. 21
Native Americans. 10
NCAA News Dec. 1969. 235
        Prominent writers respond. 236
        Willie Black response. 236
NCAA tournament 1963. 29
Nels, Larry. 66, 211, 252
Nelson, Aven. 21
Nelson, Dan. 44, 49, 161
Nelson, Doug. 228
Nelson, Frank. 227
Newell, Rev. Hubert. 123
Newton, Harold. 30, 88
Newton, L. L.. 150
Nickeson, Steve. 202, 208

Nixon, Richard M.. . . . . 39, 113
Norris, William. 49
Northern Colorado University. 9
Northwest Junior College in Powell. 30
Nuclear Freeze Campaign. 157
Nunley, John.. 107
Nye, Jeff. 184
O'Mahoney, Joseph C.. 49
Oestereich, James. 140
Ogburn, C. W.. 101
Ogburn, Sheriff C. W.. 101
Olson, Theodore.. 33
Osborne, Cliff.. 26
Pacheco, Ben. 241, 266
Pacheco, Henry. 32, 122
Pacheco, John.. 274
Padwe, Sanford "Sandy". 237
panty raid 1961. 54
Parham, Bart.. 211
Parker, Glenn. 174
Parker, Jenny. 202
Parker, Ronald. 206
Parkinson, Jerry. 261
Parnell, Tom.. . . . . 211, 281
Patterson, Gov. John. 7
Peace Corps. 122
Peace Pilgrim. 38
Pearson, Drew
        Friendship Train 1947. 197
Peck, Bob.. . . . . 108, 217
Pedretti, Patricia. 276
Perry, Ken. 225
Person, H. T.. 93
Peter, Paul & Mary at UW. 104
Peterson, Douglas. 127
Peterson, Owen.. 1
Petranovich, Mada. 90
Petsch, Jack. 13
Petting controversy 1931. 94
Petzoldt, Paul. 133
Phelan, Walter. 37, 49, 160
Phillips, Aaron. 286
Pigsley, Robert. 272
Pilch, John. 9, 272
Pillsbury, Jane. 133
Pinchot, Gifford. 48
Pine Bluffs, Wyo. 161
Plains Hotel Cheyenne. 4
Poindexter, Reuben. 30
Pollard, Ed. 107, 170
Polygamy protests 1869. 231
        Republican Party platform. 231
        Utah statehood. 231
Porter, Frederic.. 106
Pouttu, John. 122
Powell Ministerial Association.. 31
Powell Wyo.. . . . . 15, 30, 183

Powell, Henry.. 164
Power, Francis Gary. 43
Pownall, Quita. 58
President's Commission on Campus Unrest. 39
Presley, Elvis the Pelvis. 43, 148
Price, Blaine. 13
Price, Marquette. 154
Price, Rena. 154, 166
Prosser, Dean. 147, 174
Public Accommodations. 4
public displays of affection. 92
Puckett, Pat. 245
Putney, Rev. Richard. 102
Pyenson, Lew. 208
Quarterman, George. 137
Rames, John. 5
Rawlings, Richelle. 213
Ray, Rick. 29
Rayko, Paul. 13
Ready, Karen. 41
Reeb, James. 1, 76, 82
        Ashes scattered in Shirley Basin. 82
        Eulogy by MLK. 82
        Murdered at Selma. 79
Reeb, James-Casper years. 76
Reeb, James-Ordination. 77
Reeb, James-Selma. 79
Reeb, Marie Deason. 77, 81, 82, 85
Reeb, Steven. 85
Reed, C. E. 203
Reeves, Doug. 75, 199
Reeves, Weston. 150, 254
        Best Weston column. 254
Renneisen, Arthur. 42
Resor, Stanley.. 132
        My Lai massacre. 134
Revelations publication. 208
Reynolds, Mrs. Stillman. 212
Rhodes, Gov. James. 39
Rhodes, John. 23
Rhone, Mrs. Robert. 9
Rhone, Robert. 18, 286
Rhone, Tom. 9
Richardson, Randy. 29
Richey, Glen. 22
Riddle, Don. 203, 265
Rikard, Cathi. 46
Riles, Wilson. 27
Riske, Don. 104
Ritchie, Mark. 12
Rivera, John. 274
Roach, Paul. 72, 285
Robert F. Kennedy. 108
Roberts, Phil. 44, 151
Robinson, Flynn. 26, 27
Robinson, Kim. 269
Robinson, Phil. 123

Rogers, Ron. 241
Romero, Joe. 15
Romero, Leo. 245
Romney, Marion.. 253
Roncalio, Teno. 4, 46, 51, 84, 197, 203
        Attempt to mediate. 254
Roosevelt, Eleanor. 5, 152
Roosevelt, Franklin. 5
Rose, Robert R. Jr.. 278
Rosenthal, Jack.. 213
Ross, Ed. 24
Ross, Nellie Tayloe. 24
Ross, William Bradford. 24
ROTC. 140
Royal, Darrell. 238
Rubin, Jerry. 178
Rucker, Myrtle. 83
Rudolph, Ernie. 42
Russell, Sister Frances. 35
Russin, Robert. 206
San Jose State. 186, 210, 235
San Jose State game. 208, 221
Sanchez brothers of Laramie. 115
Sanchez, Daniel. 167
Sanders, M. E.. 2
Sanders, Sen. Bernie.. 39
Santos, Greg. 207
Scheer, Dennis. 13
Scholl, Sophie. 204
Schrader, Robert.. 106
Schrage, William. 62
Schubert, Frank "Mick". 228
Schubert, Irene. 209
Schuster, Bob. 192
Schwartz, Mary Ann.. 210
Scott, Nellie. 10
Seahorn, Tony. 130
Sedar, Dan. 25
Sedar, Dick. 25
Selective Service 139
Selma Ala.. 76
Seltenrich, Charles. 64, 73
Shaw, Cecil.. 47
Shaw, Doug. 205
Shelton, Vern. 116
Shepard, Matthew.. 104
Sherman, Dick. 140
Shirley Basin, Wyo.. 82
Shriver, Sergeant. 46
Shurmur, Fritz. 65, 72, 238, 241, 286
Silver Spur Ranch.. 149
Simons, Lynn. 199
Simpson, Alan. 64, 142, 199, 213
Simpson, Charlie. 119
Simpson, Milward. 4, 32, 73, 119, 134, 142
Small, Cynthia. 74, 75
Smith, Nels.. 150

Smith, Prof. John. 226
Smith, Tommie. 71
Snyder, Gary. 40
Sohn, Harold. 61, 239, 240
Sounding Sides, Diana. 166
Sounding Sides, John. 166
Spangler, Dan. 46, 121
Speece, Margaret. 25
Speese, Charles and Howard. 25
Speights, Dick. 66, 68
Spiegel, Sydney. 274
    1969 raises funds for Black 14. 275
    Hispanic culture. 277
    Profiled in Parade Mag. 275
Spiegelberg, James. 125
Springer, Arthur. 33
St. Clair, Iva. 245
St. Stephen's Mission. 220
Stanford University. 214
Star Valley Independent. 217
Steadman, Jack. 121
Steadman, Jim. 12, 125
Steadman, Karin. 127
Steckel, William. 49
Steffenson, Dave. 2, 120
Sternberg, Robert. 88, 93
Stevens, Alice Hardie. 21
Stevens, Pat. 49
Stogsdill, Byron. 106
Stolts, Bob. 49
Stoval, Bill. 104
Student Bill of Rights. 177
Student Non-Violent Coor. Comm.. 89
Student Peace Union. 39
Student Senate resolution. 191, 239
Students for Democratic Society. 11, 120
Stump, Gene. 119
Sugar Bowl. 69, 107
Sullivan, Dan. 22
Sullivan, Joseph. 188
Sullivan, Mike. 142
Suyematsu, Ben. 160
Suyematsu, Kiyo. 159
Suyematsu, Ronnie. 161
Suyematsu, Taro. 161
Suyematsu, Tosh. 34, 140, 150, 158-160, 199
Swain, Vern. 49
Synakowski, Ed. 238
Takaki, Marguerite. 127
Talboom, Eddie. 75
Tangeman, Dennis. 104
TCE. 42
Tet Offensive. 56
Texas Western track. 184
Textbook Inquiry of 1947. 115
Thomas, Pamela. 74
Thomson, Keith. 142

Thomson, Thyra. 142, 197
Thorburn, Ryan. 192
Thornton High in Harvey, Ill. 30
Thuermer, Angus. 249
Till, Emmett. 112
Tinker v. Des Moines Dist.. . . . . . . 194, 204, 234, 259
Tobin, Margaret. 76, 90
Toelle, Steve.. 12
Tonkin Gulf Resolution. 74
Toscano, Paul. 66, 107
track athletes protest. 207
Treagle Train. 196
    Protest by women. 198
Trelease, Frank. 94, 174
Trump, Donald. 118, 147
    2018 NFL anthem. 267
Tuck, Sheriff N. E. 34
Tucker, Randy. 166
Twyford, Wavis. 156
Tyler, James. 10
Tyler, Michael. 273
Tyler, Robert. 241
Unitarian Church. 78
University of New Mexico. 233
Upton, Stu. 232
Urbigkit, Walter. 270
UW Press release. 190, 258
UW Vietnam Memorial. 123
Varineau, Jane. 227
Vehar, Vincent. 163
Vietnam Moratorium. 136, 138, 191
    Boomerang blast. 137
    Freedom Wyo. 282
Vietnam War. 12
    1963. 48
    Assurances of progress.. 138
    Congressmen's sons. 118
    Wyoming's first casualty. 117
Viner, Kim. 21
Vinich, Mike. 44
Volz, Jacqueline. 135
Voting age. 171
    Congress acts 1970. 175
    Wyo. Supreme Court. 173
Voting Rights Act. 82
Wadsworth, Lex. 15
Wagon Wheel Project. 266
Walker, John. 112
Walker, Mike. 21, 62, 65
Wallace, George. 48, 80
Wallop, Malcolm. 199
Walsh, Dave. 144
Walsh, S. Kelly. 97
Walthall, Annie Marie. 187
Walthall, Wilson. 206
Wapiti, Wyo. 248
War Memorial Stadium expansion. 182

War Resisters League.......................... 148
Warburton, Willatta........................... 130
Warner, Robert............................... 50, 65
Warren Air Force Base........................ 12, 40
     WWII Army Quartermaster Corps........ 31
Washington, Steve............................ 239
Washington, Vic....... 66-68, 107, 169, 170, 200, 288
Wasson, Gary................................ 45
Watergate.................................... 39
Waterman, Wm................... 14, 232, 253
Watson, Loren............................... 104
Watt, Joe................................... 94
Watts, Joe of Provo Herald................... 235
Webb, Sheyann.............................. 81
Weinberg, Ron.............................. 191
West Point Class of 1967..................... 12
West, Barry................................. 171
Western Athletic Conference................. 213
     Response to Black 14................ 208
Weston, Meredith "Skeet".................... 141
Wexall, William............................. 10
Wharton, Clifton........................ 136, 195
Wheeler, Duane............................. 154
Whelan, Toni............................... 124
White, Dan.............................. 92, 191
White, John................................ 36
White, Peggy Jo............................ 92
White, Philip Sr............................ 159
Whitehead, Ed.............................. 285
Wiederspahn, Al........................ 135, 191
Wiley, Virginia............................. 76
Wilkerson, Ernest.......................... 135
Wilkins, Roy............................... 83
Wilkinson, Tom............................. 66
Williams, Joe........ 67, 68, 70, 180, 201, 243, 252
Williams, Ted.............................. 181
Williams, Tom.............................. 170
Wilson, Charles............................ 25
Wirin, A. L................................ 153
Wittler, Shirley............................ 199
Women's right to vote...................... 234
Women's suffrage.......................... 234
Wounded Knee............................. 161
Wright, Elmo............................... 234
Wyatt, Bowden............................ 9, 75
Wyo. Civil Rights Adv. Comm................ 8
Wyoming Alumni Association................ 107
Wyoming Green............................. 283
Wyoming's last casualty.................... 118
XIX Olympiad.............................. 71
York, Jim.................................. 149
Young, Al.................................. 242
Young, Bill................................ 144
Young, Whitney......................... 21, 213
Youth movement 1931...................... 95
Yuthas, Tony.............................. 93
Zimmerman, Paul...................... 125, 141